W9-AGP-935

The Cognitive Brain

The Cognitive Brain

Arnold Trehub

A Bradford Book
The MIT Press
Cambridge, Massachusetts
London, England

This book was set in Palatino by Achorn Graphic Services, Worcester, MA and was printed and bound in the United States of America.

Library of Congress Cataloging-in-Publication Data

Trehub, Arnold.
The cognitive brain / Arnold Trehub.
p. cm.
"A Bradford book."
Includes bibliographical references and index.
ISBN 0-262-20085-6
1. Brain. 2. Brain—Computer simulation. 3. Cognition.
4. Cognitive science. 5. Cognitive psychology. I. Title.
[DNLM: 1. Cognition. 2. Models, Psychological.
3. Psycholinguistics. 4. Visual Perception. BF 311 T786c]
QP376.T72 1991
153—dc20
DNLM/DLC
for Library of Congress

91-8800
CIP

To Elaine

Contents

Acknowledgments

I am indebted to colleagues who read selected chapters of the manuscript and provided valuable criticism and comment, particularly Charles Clifton, David Rosenbaum, James Chumbley, Neil Stillings, Gordon Wyse, Alexander Pollatsek, Judith Kroll, and Keith Rayner. I also thank the many anonymous reviewers who made helpful comments. My greatest debt is to my wife, Elaine, whose unflagging support and assistance over many challenging years made this book possible.

The Cognitive Brain

Mind, n. A mysterious form of matter secreted by the brain. Its chief activity consists in the endeavor to ascertain its own nature, the futility of the attempt being due to the fact that it has nothing but itself to know itself with.

Ambrose Bierce, *The Devil's Dictionary*

The Brain is wider than the Sky
For put them side by side
The one the other will contain
With ease and You beside

Emily Dickinson

Chapter 1
Introduction

We cannot know exactly when it happened, but some time after the dawn of humankind our hominoid ancestors must have wondered—as we do—about the mystery of their inner world. The idea of a body-inhabiting spirit that animates a lifeless form with feeling and cunning, that reveals the myriad elements of the world around, is a strong and recurring theme in myth. Throughout human history there has been an abiding need to comprehend this primal mystery. Plato proposed a rational soul located in the head as the source of all our mental functions. However inadequate Plato's view might be as an explanation of mind, who can doubt that however it happens, it happens in secret places behind the eyes and between the ears in that quirky-shaped lump of tissue.

Since the late 1800s, the principal effort to understand the human mind has shifted from the domain of the philosopher to that of the psychologist, who carries on this exploration as a scientific task (Boring, 1929). More recently, groups within disciplines ranging from linguistics to computer science have focused on the problem of cognition (mindlike activity) and call their joint endeavor "cognitive science." Among cognitive scientists, however, the study of human cognition is chiefly the concern of the cognitive psychologist.

The cognitive science community at large commonly asserts that neuroscience has little to contribute to cognitive theory because it has not yet produced a substantial body of knowledge relevant to cognitive processes. Yet to the extent that cognitive science can provide a valid explanation of how human cognition is accomplished, it must conform to the limiting as well as the enabling properties of the human brain. No account can be a serious explanatory model of human cognition if it cannot pass this test. My central thesis here is that we now have sufficient knowledge of the physiology of nerve cells and the structure of the brain to advance the theoretical formulation of putative brain mechanisms that can account for the basic competencies of human cognition and, at the same time, satisfy a reasonable demand for plausibility within the constraints of neurophysiology and neuroanatomy. This is not to say that the models we construct will necessarily allow direct verification or disconfirmation by the current tools of neuroscience but that they can be assessed as being consistent with known biological processes, as opposed to contradicting established findings or demanding new physiological properties that strain current understanding.

Of course, it might be argued that if no model can be found to account for the important facts of human cognition without straining the credulity of neuroscientists, then perhaps neuroscience is not keen enough, has misinterpreted its own evidence, or just needs to look further. In any event, should there be a fit between the demands of a cognitive model and the constraints of neuroscience, then our confidence in at least the cognitive science side of the endeavor will grow, and such a model might suggest new foci for direct exploration in the vast physical search space confronting neuroscientists.

Discourse and debate often founder on unacknowledged differences in belief about (or sense of) the meaning of terms common among the discussants. This is particularly true in consideration of "cognitive processes" because of their relatively cryptic and complex nature. I must, therefore, acknowledge at the outset that the models I present do not aim to explain directly such ineffable matters as the felt qualities of a breathtaking sunset or why I *believe* my *intention* to open the door causes me to do so. They do, however, attempt to explain how a range of cognitive tasks that are of fundamental importance can be accomplished by the biological machinery of the human brain, and it is not unreasonable to assume that they might well offer useful clues to the more subtle aspects of human experience.

The theoretical strategy that guides this work is constructionist in flavor. The belief that neuroscience has not provided enough of the right kind of facts about the brain to be of much help to the cognitive scientist is true in a limited sense. That is, to the extent that the cognitive scientist frames proposed models only in terms of interactions among functional stages or "black box" computational modules, one finds that neuroscience is as yet unable to elucidate the micropatterns of intercellular connectivity or the dynamics of information processing in the brain with sufficient scope and precision to provide evidence either for or against proposals at this level of explanation.

My approach is to start with first principles. Beginning with the principal cognitive tasks that are unquestionably solved by humans and those properties of nerve cells that are relevant to their role as primitive components in a variety of possible information-processing mechanisms, the problem is to construct model neuronal mechanisms and systems with the minimal properties required to perform the selected tasks (Trehub 1975a, 1977, 1978, 1983, 1987). In the neuronal-constructionist approach, the initial constraints of neurophysiology and neuroanatomy are not merely suggestive in guiding model development, they are crucial, and their application distinguishes a neuronal model from other kinds of connectionist models that are said to have a neural "flavor" and are often called neural models (Anderson et al. 1977, Feldman 1985, Feldman and Ballard 1982, Grossberg 1988, Hopfield and Tank 1986, Kohonen 1977, Rosenblatt 1962, Rumelhart and McClelland 1986; see also Smolensky 1988).

Widespread adoption of a computational information-processing paradigm since the mid-1970s has resulted in a surge of experimentation and theory in cognitive psychology. But while the new computational enthusiasm sparked a wealth of empirical studies and algorithmic models, it failed to stimulate a comparable intellectual probing into the kinds of biological mechanisms required to carry out the cognitive computations. In short, although it was suggested how abstract computations could account for some natural observations and various experimental results, it was not explained how the biological person could carry out the necessary cognitive computations. I take the latter explanatory burden to be at least as much the responsibility of the cognitive psychologist as it is of the neuroscientist. Other cognitive scientists whose primary interests might relate to the properties of abstract automata or machine instantiations of algorithms in the cognitive domain do not share this burden.

Levels of Explanation

David Marr (1982) proposed and laid great stress on the independence of three levels of explanation at which any information-processing machine must be understood: (1) the level of computational theory at which the computational goal and its logic are formulated, (2) the level of representation and algorithm at which the representations for input and output and the algorithm for transformation are formulated, and (3) the level of hardware (or biological) implementation at which the physical means for realizing the representations and algorithms are formulated. Marr has had a notably strong influence on the field of cognitive psychology, and the psychologist might say in response to a charge of neglecting the brain that the computational theories and algorithmic models should be all worked out before worrying about biological implementation. Indeed, Rumelhart and McClelland (1985) write, "However, Marr certainly does not propose that a theory at the computational level of description is an adequate psychological theory. As psychologists, we are committed to an elucidation of the algorithmic level." Yet they also assert, "We believe that psychology is properly concerned with all three of these levels." And in a later publication McClelland, Rumelhart, and Hinton (1986) state that one reason for the appeal of parallel distributed processing (PDP) models is their "'physiological' flavor."

It appears that while cognitive psychology is not prepared to dismiss the physiology of the brain as irrelevant, it is committed to what it perceives as an orderly development of theory in the spirit of Marr's independence of explanatory levels: first develop models that provide understanding at the levels of computational and algorithmic theory and then (perhaps) address the issue of their implementation in the human brain. I believe, however, that a less hierarchically ordered strategy of theory development can be more productive in achieving the goal of understanding human cognition, and I believe that the failure of psychology to acknowledge explicitly the critical role of biological constraints on human information processing is in part responsible for the frustratingly slow incremental development of a coherent body of theory and knowledge (Newell 1973). Adoption of the independent-levels paradigm provides a principled basis for many more candidate models (and the empirical studies they suggest) than would otherwise be justified and tends to obscure the distinction between those proposals that are consonant with biology and those that are not. An optimal search strategy for explanatory models of human cognition calls for the virtual parallel application of multiple-level constraints instead of a search for "sufficient" models within the bounds of each assumed "independent" level of explanation.

Figure 1.1 illustrates the difference between an independent-levels search (top) and an interdependent-levels search (bottom). The first circle at the top of the illustration represents the domain of logically possible computational objectives that might lead to a solution for the problem. The right circle is the domain of possible and distinct algorithmic operations, subroutines, and full routines that can satisfy each adequate set of computational objectives. The third circle is the domain of plausible computational mechanisms in the human brain. In this scheme, the algorithmic level is the most troublesome because it is essentially unbounded. Since algorithms are wholly symbolic systems, governed only by formal rules, any specified set of algorithms can be emulated by a different set with equivalent computational effect. If we try to reduce the size of the domain of possible algorithms by simply applying a selection rule that accepts only algo-

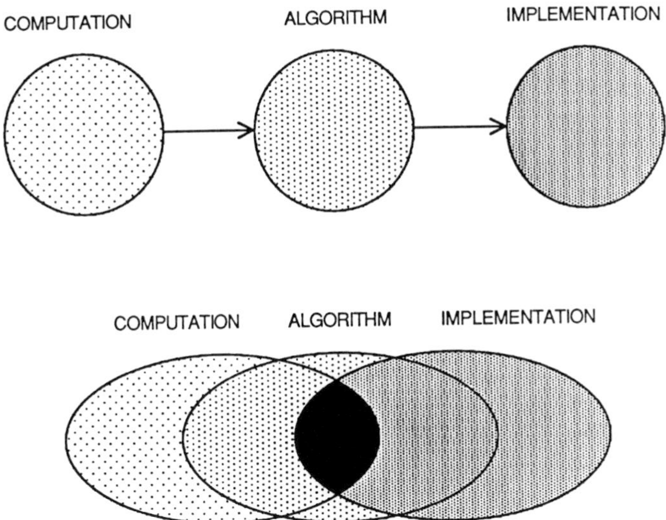

Figure 1.1
Top: An independent-levels search in theory development. *Bottom:* An interdependent-levels search.

rithms with the fewest number of computational steps, we face two problems; the number of steps required for a given algorithm may be quite different depending on its biological implementation, and, more important, any chosen algorithm may be composed of elementary operations or subroutines that the brain does not compute.

A better way to reduce the size of the domain is to prune, during the course of composing an algorithm, each assumption that is not credible on the evidence of neurophysiology and neuroanatomy. This violates the neat separation of explanatory levels and is, in fact, the strategy for theory development represented by the interdependent-levels search shown at the bottom of figure 1.1. In this paradigm, search is always confined to the much smaller domain established by the parallel constraints of all three levels. For expository or didactic purposes, any adequate model resulting from this approach can be analytically decomposed into the three independent levels of description even though their logical independence was not honored during the construction of the model.

Competence and Style

Few psychologists would disagree that the central theoretical goal of cognitive psychology is to explain how humans are able to know and understand their physical-social environment and act productively and creatively. But instead of attempting to provide an explanation for cognitive competence, psychologists simply assume that competent cognitive mechanisms exist and model them in terms of abstract nodes, modules, and processing stages with appropriate functional labels (canonical feature detector, window of attention) attached (see for example Biederman 1987, Kosslyn 1980, Kosslyn et al. 1990). At the same time, their principal theoretical effort is directed at determining the combination of properties (e.g., serial operations, parallel operations) in an unexplicated (nominally empowered) central cognitive apparatus that might force its output to conform with the curves of performance obtained in experimental studies. This prevailing approach cannot explain basic competence, but it can explain cognitive style and provide empirical evidence useful in assessing explicit models of competent brain mechanisms.

A proper model of a competent mechanism has four important characteristics: (1) it is described in sufficient detail to establish its biological plausibility; (2) logical analysis and computer simulation demonstrate that it does perform the task(s) required of it; (3) its biological instantiation can reasonably be expected to accomplish the task(s) within a time period commensurate with the normal ecological demands on the organism modeled (Feldman 1981, Trehub 1987); and (4) its interface with other mechanisms in its system is biologically plausible. Among models that have already demonstrated basic explanatory competence, secondary aspects, such as parsimony and style of performance, are also considered. For example, if two competing models of associative learning are judged equally competent and parsimonious but display different acquisition curves, the model with performance that better matches the data of relevant laboratory experiments should be preferred. In addition, the ability of a model to explain cognitive epiphenomena should be considered in choosing among models equally competent on primary tasks. If the explanation of a known visual illusion, for example, were to "fall out" of a model formulated to account for other phenomena, we would take this as additional evidence in its favor.

On these grounds, then, I have chosen initially to explore models that might provide solutions to some of the fundamental tasks for the human cognitive brain. If, after basic competence can be demonstrated, it should turn out that the behavior of a given putative mechanism or system of mechanisms also conforms to experimental findings in the domain of behavioral style and cognitive epiphenomena, then we will have increased confidence that our theory building is on the right track.

Issues in the Design of a Cognitive Model

Any investigator attempting to formulate a model of human cognition must make initial design choices about scope and process. As he or she confronts the demand for competence over an increasing variety and complexity of tasks, these basic choices will necessarily be augmented. An evolving model architecture will include modular components that were developed initially and at the same time will be constrained by the physical principles instantiated in these earlier modules. Thus, the generality, competence, and operating characteristics of an articulated model will be strongly influenced by basic design choices (in practice, often implicit and unexamined) made at the earliest stages of model building. Some of these issues are particularly important in planning and analyzing the design of a cognitive system.

System Input-Output

Is the input to the model system to be the low-level output of a selected sensory modality (visual, auditory, somasthetic) or composed of the preprocessed categories that are assumed to have been extracted from a modality in some unexplicated fashion? Existing semantic models, for example, typically assume a high-level network of abstract nodes or else vectors of activation levels over an assembly of units, where each node or vector represents a word or concept in an established lexicon (Anderson and Bower 1973, Fahlman 1979, Hinton 1981). It is highly unlikely that any single model of human cognition can be comprehensive, and simplifications of this kind are inevitable. But where tactical simplification evades a fundamental cognitive problem, the fact of the problem should be acknowledged and some indication of its possible solution given.

The neuronal models that I propose, in addition to addressing issues of high-level cognition, attempt to deal with the important computations required to interpret the first level of information extracted by the sensory transducers from complex external and internal environments. A fundamental problem common to all modalities centers on the critical process of pattern classification (Harnad 1987, Margolis 1987). In the models presented in the following chapters, patterns are defined as the distribution of cell discharge over physically indexed arrays of neurons. The signaling of a particular distribution of activity in an array by the discharge of a single physically indexed cell in a detection set (or by N equivalent cells) constitutes pattern classification. All of the axonal branches of any given detection cell, taken together, may be thought of as a single discrete information channel or line. Thus, pattern classification is an array-to-line mapping.

If each possible sensory pattern were mapped to a distinct line, the number of lines required would grow in a combinatorial explosion as the number of cells in the sensory array increased. Such a scheme would quickly exceed the capacity of even the human brain despite its many billions of neurons. On the other hand, if the system could not map patterns having very small arbitrary differences onto different lines, important environmental distinctions might escape detection. For some tasks, it might be advantageous or simply innocuous to lump many physically different inputs into a single category (generalization); for others, a failure to make a fine distinction (discrimination) might carry a serious penalty. Thus, a fundamental design issue for any model of human cognition centers on the capacity of the system to adjust the delicacy of its sensory classifications according to the ecological requirements of its host.

A number of connectionist models are designed to map input vectors onto output vectors by processes of iterative relaxation involving widespread positive and negative feedback among cells or by direct feed-forward algorithms, which do not depend on relaxation (Rumelhart and McClelland 1986). These models are among a class of computational schemes that transform a set of input patterns into a smaller set of patterns represented by differing activity distributions over a fixed population of cells constituting the output of the system. Models of this kind, commonly called parallel distributed processing (PDP) models, are said to have distributed representation as opposed to local representation, as is the case when an input pattern is identified by activity on an indexed line.

From a strictly computational point of view, it might appear that there is an advantage to mapping from array to pattern instead of from array to line. For any fixed number N of output units (or lines), there will be many more possible discrete output states for the patterns composed by the activity levels of all N units than for the activity of only one of N units. In the case of a whole pattern, the potential number of distinct outputs increases as a combinatorial function of N; in the case of a single line, the potential number of distinct outputs increases only as a linear function of N. Thus, it might seem that an array-to-pattern model would enjoy the economy of fewer units required to make any given number of classifications when compared to an array-to-line model. But there are other factors to take into account.

First, can the algorithms that map input patterns onto output patterns utilize the full potential range of output states? Simulation studies have shown that the proportion of N possible output vectors that can be used in the array-to-pattern paradigm without severe degradation of system performance is only a small fraction of the full range (Hopfield 1982, 1984; Ratcliff 1990). Second, if the system is one that must select an action conditional on the environmental input, then each output of an array-to-line model represents a distinct physical channel that can be directly connected to the subsystem that generates the action required. Thus, a simple action potential from the axon (line) representing the class of the input pattern can trigger or modulate the appropriate response. In contrast, the output of an array-to-pattern model represents a complex signal that must be decoded and then selectively routed before the appropriate action can be triggered (figure 1.2). The requirement of a separate decoding stage for pattern classification and signal routing makes the array-to-pattern model a weaker computational candidate than the array-to-line model unless there is an overriding advantage on other grounds.

Relaxation and Feed-Forward PDP versus Comb-Filter Processing of Input

Another important design issue concerns the nature of the computations required to map input to output. One common approach in connectionist models is to generate each output state by the computational process of iterative relaxation (Rumelhart and McClelland 1986). In such models, each processing unit U_j is directly connected to all other processing units through a pattern of activation-transfer weights W_{ij} typically ranging from -1 to $+1$. The activity level of any given unit U_j at a given time t is some specified function of its activity level at $t - 1$ and the sum of all the outputs from other units after each is multiplied by its transfer weight W_{ij} on U_j. If there is an appropriate pattern of transfer weights, then after an indeterminate number of time steps, the profile of activity over the population of output units (output vector) will settle into a state desired by a predetermined criterion of goodness. When a stimulus is applied to the system (for example, an input vector of features), we can think of the activity over all units as undergoing a process of dynamic reorganization, finally converging (relaxing) on a stable output pattern (a *local* energy minimum).

An alternative approach utilizes a direct feed-forward filter design and can be characterized as a one-pass processing mechanism. In a system of this kind, each unit α_i of the input vector connects directly to each output unit U_j through a transfer weight W_{ij}. In one version of this approach, at the start of processing (t_0), all output units are either at zero activity or have uniform low-level activity, and all trans-

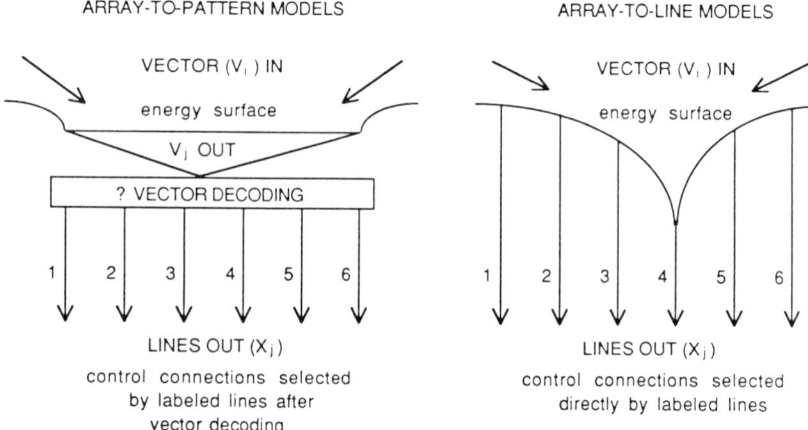

Figure 1.2
Illustration of the differences between array-to-pattern (A/P) and array-to-line (A/L) models. In A/P, input vectors are mapped to output vectors (patterns of unit activity over a population of cells). The output patterns must then be remapped to labeled lines (decoded) for selective control. In A/L, input vectors are directly mapped to the labeled line (discrete filter within a comb filter system) having the highest correlation with the input vector (line 4 in the figure on the right). If the pattern of activity represented by the input vector changes sufficiently, the energy minimum will shift from line 4 to a different line with a higher correlation with the new vector. This will be the newly activated labeled line.

fer weights range from near zero to some higher positive value. At $t + 1$, the activity level of each output unit is a function of the sum of the products of the activity in each unit of the input array and its particular transfer weight W_{ij} on the unit of the output array. If there is an appropriate pattern of transfer weights at any time during the presentation of a stimulus, the output unit desired by a predetermined criterion of goodness will have a higher level of activity than any other output unit. This model can be thought of as a parallel-access comb filter (analogous to an array of independent narrow pass-band filters in electronic signal processing) in which the distribution of transfer weights on each output unit determines its selective tuning for particular input patterns (Trehub 1967, 1975a, 1987).

After considering the relative merits of relaxation, feedforward PDP, and comb filtering for cognitive systems, I decided that comb filtering should be the preferred approach. It does not require additional decoding; it seeks the absolute energy minimum, which is, in fact, the output unit having the highest correlation with the current input vector (figure 1.2); it does not exhibit the limitations in memory efficiency and discrimination that characterize PDP models (Ratcliff 1990, Hopfield 1982). The level of activity in each unit of a comb-filter scheme is independent of any of its neighbors, so the number of arbitrary input-output memories that can exist simultaneously in storage is exactly the number of processing units—filters/output lines—in the system (because of the independence of processing units, subtle distinctions between mappings will not be confounded or distorted in memory, a clear advantage from the standpoint of system competence); it generates a useful output within a single synaptic delay plus the time required for integration to threshold (typically, 1–5 milliseconds); and it makes the minimal assumption that all activation-transfer weights in the filtering cells have a positive sign (excitatory) and that each processing cell in the extended model maintains its activity as either an excitatory or an inhibitory neuron, thus conforming with the constraints of real mammalian synapses and neurons. These considerations, together with additional factors related to efficient learning, imagery, the recall of specific events, and symbol manipulation, convinced me to develop cognitive models based on comb-filter mechanisms.

Representation

At any given moment, a cognitive computational system can be characterized by the internal state that maps an input onto an output. This state can be thought of as the memory of the system. In connectionist models, memory resides in their complex distribution of transfer weights. These complex distributions define an internal set of standards against which arbitrary input stimuli are matched for appropriate routing or classification. The internal standards can be taken as representations of particular kinds of external events that are significant for the system and require a selective response. We may think of such representations as the concepts held by an individual. Since the kinds of events to which the system must respond may vary in a number of particulars yet still maintain their general significance, the question arises of how best to structure the internal representations for adaptive response despite individual variation within significant classes of stimuli.

What kind of computational process should we adopt to provide an appropriate repertoire of concepts? One approach opts for the construction and storage of generalized prototypes where each prototype is a unitary representation of a stimulus class, consisting of some average pattern of features obtained by weighting each feature of a stimulus according to the frequency of its occurrence among the exemplars of its class (Rosch and Mervis 1975, Stillings et al. 1987).

There is a serious problem with this kind of model, however. If the brain were to store its concepts in memory only as unitary averaged prototypes, it would be unable to recognize individuality among particular exemplars of a concept. We recognize a face not only as a face but also as a young face, an old face, a face that is happy or sad. These distinctions are not trivial and could not occur by matching sensory input against an averaged prototypical standard. On the other hand, if we were to maintain in memory a representation for each sensory entity experienced, then the notion of concept would have little meaning, and the storage capacity of the brain would soon be exceeded.

There is a solution to this dilemma, however: store exemplars and establish new classification standards only when the existing conceptual structure fails a real or imagined test of its current utility or when a stimulus is experienced as a novel one in a significant context. In this scheme, the number of representations that one maintains grows as needed by the individual or demanded by the physical and social environment. Clearly, if representations are built in such a fashion, then there must be critical interactions among conceptual structure, motivation, attention, imagination, and learning. The behavior of the cognitive brain model that I propose depends on just such interactions.

Figure 1.3 illustrates the distinction between representation by averaged prototypes and representation by significant exemplars. Imagine the stippled and black regions in the top box as enclosing the point locations, in a multidimensional space, of all experienced variations of two different classes of stimuli. An exhaustive representation within the brain of all instances of each class is neither physically possible nor desirable, so some procedure must be employed before storage to reduce the vast number of stimulus instances depicted at the top. The box at the bottom left shows all exemplars of the two kinds of entities collapsed into two distinct multidimensional points (prototypes) by a process of weighted averaging. Let us call the stippled point A and the black point B. Given an input stimulus, the system will classify the stimulus as either A or B by determining its multidimensional distance from A and B and selecting the class having the lesser distance. The box at the bottom right shows significant exemplars of each kind as subsets of multidimensional points with individual characteristics. In this case, the multidimensional distance of a stimulus from each of the points in the representational space will not only determine its class membership but will also categorize it as having the properties of its closest exemplar.

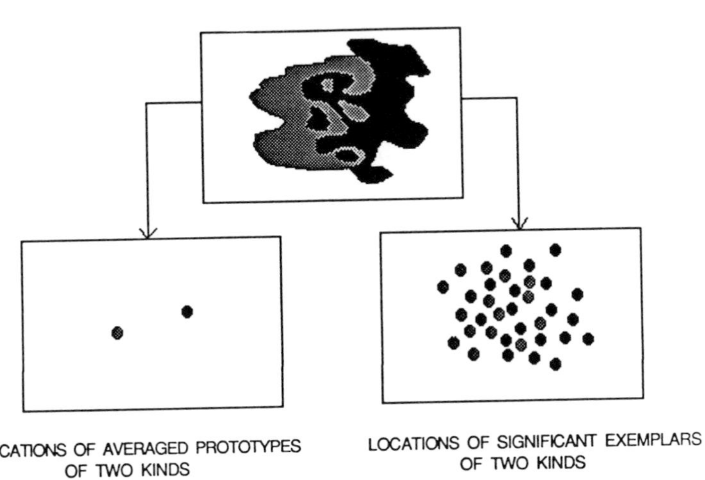

Figure 1.3
Illustration of the difference between the averaged-prototypes paradigm and the significant-exemplars paradigm for the representation of concepts.

Learning
In connectionist models, the distribution of activation-transfer weights determines the memories the system has, its concepts, and the input-output mappings it will make. Thus, the issue of how transfer weights are set, organized, and modified must have a high priority in any effort to provide a full physical explanation for cognitive processes. In other words, a satisfactory model of learning is of fundamental importance.

Among the many problems that arise in attempting to formulate a neuronal model of human learning, particularly significant are those related to the biological basis for normalization of transfer weights, the number of stimulus repetitions required to reach a satisfactory criterion of performance, and the mechanism for representing the temporal context of a learned event.

The problem of normalization arises because all stimulus patterns that must be learned may vary over a wide range in terms of the number of active units in their input vectors. Moreover, while equal levels of performance may be demanded in response to a variety of stimuli, the number of opportunities for learning may be markedly different for each stimulus. Since the magnitude and distribution of change in transfer weights during learning can be influenced by the number of active input units evoked by a stimulus and the number of times the same stimulus is experienced, as well as its characteristic pattern, some mechanism is required to prevent system degradation by an excessive bias in favor of stimuli that are relatively large (discharge many units) or that occur relatively frequently. Normalization is important and must be accounted for within the operation of any proposed learning model (Trehub 1975a).

For some problems, many stimulus-response trials are needed before learning can reach an acceptable level of performance, and for others only a single trial is necessary. Most computational models of learning depend on processes that require many trials to reach an acceptable criterion of performance (Rumelhart and McClelland 1986). Typically, a stochastic convergence operation is assumed or incremental weight adjustments are made in an iterative search for a distribution of transfer weights that will lead to an appropriate separation of input patterns. Such models are unable to account for one-trial learning. Ideally, we seek a plausible biological system capable of one-trial learning but that also can manifest the characteristics of progressive improvement over trials.

Another important aspect of any model of learning is whether it allows for self-initiated and self-organized learning. A prevailing paradigm for learning in PDP models is the so-called generalized delta rule (Rumelhart and McClelland 1986; see also Minsky and Papert 1988), which requires the prior specification of a desired output vector. The object is to adjust connection weights throughout the network so that a desired mapping from input vector to output vector is obtained. When the network is stimulated, the activity of every output unit is compared to its desired (target) activity. If there is a discrepancy, its magnitude and sign are measured and used as criteria for adjusting all connection weights to the examined unit in a direction that reduces the observed discrepancy. Typically the magnitude of weight adjustment is proportional to the measured discrepancy. In multilayer networks, the procedure is repeated for corresponding units, working backward to the input layer. For this reason, the error correction scheme is often called back propagation.

Learning of this kind requires an external agent (teacher) to set a standard. It cannot be self-initiated and self-organized unless one assumes that there is an innate store of desired output vectors (targets) appropriate to each stimulus situation; however, in this case, learning would be quite irrelevant. The model I propose is able to learn without the intervention of an external agent but can profit by outside guidance.

A substantial part of human learning and memory is episodic in character (Tulving 1972). Sequences of experience are interrelated and rendered meaningful by contiguity within particular time frames. Episodic representations are also essential for chaining inferences and for planning future action. Models should be able to learn and conserve, in proper temporal order, sequences of stimuli, as well as nontemporal representations of input patterns.

One final point should be emphasized: any ecologically relevant model of learning must have a mechanism that can selectively retrieve learned representations as a function of an individual's current motivation and environmental contingencies. This introduces the collateral problem of structuring effective and plausible interfaces among the learning mechanism, the various sense modalities, and the motivational system that guides human behavior.

Selecting the First Modality

The choice of which modality to model first will play a role in shaping the subsequent development of the cognitive model.

I have chosen to start with the visual system, for both objective considerations and intuitive preferences. If we assume that the number of neurons in each of the functional/anatomical areas of the human brain gives an indication of the relative ecological importance of that function, then vision must be taken as the most important of our sensory processes. The primary and secondary sensory areas of the human visual cortex contain more than 1.2 billion nerve cells. In contrast, the closest competing cortical areas, devoted to processing bodily sensations, contain roughly 160 million cells (Blinkov and Glezer 1968). Thus, in terms of sheer biological resources, evolution seems to have invested the human brain with at least seven and a half times as many cells for its visual computations as for its somesthetic computations. Another anatomical indication of the importance of vision is revealed when we examine the ratio of the number of cells in the primary visual area of the cortex (area 17) to the number of cells in the lateral geniculate nucleus (a lower visual center) over a variety of mammalian species: in the rabbit, the ratio is 20:1; in the macaque monkey, 145:1; in humans, 900:1 (Blinkov and Glezer 1968). And if secondary visual areas of the cortex were counted in computing these ratios, the divergence among the species would be even greater. This evolutionary progression underscores the central role of vision in human adaptation.

In explaining why people need to have so much more of their brain resources devoted to visual processing than other creatures have, it can be argued that, say, a monkey, as it swings and leaps from tree to tree, must make exquisite discriminations, judgments of distance, clearance, and the weight-bearing properties of branches, all of which require greater visual acuity and processing speed than do normal human activities. Humans, however, must not only respond to the affordances of the visual environment but must know and understand the world revealed to them through the medium of sight. Vision is the modality that provides the richest direct source of information about the nature of our physical world. Beyond purely sensory considerations, visual experience and imagery give us the most important extensional anchors for the semantics of language (Johnson-Laird, Herrmann, and Chaffin 1984; Miller and Johnson-Laird 1976). One of the key problems in the development of a biologically plausible model for human cognition is to elucidate the relationship between vision and language and to detail the physical interactions between visual and linguistic mechanisms.

Tasks to Be Performed

A list of basic tasks that a cognitive model must be capable of performing tends to focus the design of the system and helps sharpen the test criteria for objective assessment of the model's competence. It is highly unlikely that any such list will cover all cognitive tasks, but whatever is explicitly described will aid the theorist and provide common points of reference for proponents and critics of the model.

Following are a number of general tasks that I have taken as reasonable tests of a human cognitive system. The list starts with tasks specific to the visual domain and broadens to include those related to semantic processing, reasoning, and planning. The model must be able to:

1. Parse an object or a part of an object as a stimulus entity when presented with any arbitrary object or an arrangement of objects (a scene).
2. Represent the relative location of any parsed object in a three-dimensional viewer-centered space.
3. See an object or a scene on at least one occasion and recognize it later despite substantial changes in object size, angular orientation, or position in space.
4. Search for and locate an object that has been learned if it is present in a complex scene.
5. Reconstruct an approximate image of an object or image that has been learned when it is absent.
6. Construct and learn new images by combining parts of objects and scenes recalled from its learned repertoire (memory).

7. Recognize learned patterns despite inputs that are substantially incomplete or degraded by noise.
8. Disambiguate the stimulus and sequentially recognize the constituent patterns if the model is presented with a complex pattern composed by the superposition of previously learned patterns.
9. Detect, learn, and recall spatial relationships among objects in a scene.
10. Respond, given any arbitrary input pattern, with a series of recognition indicants and their associated images recalled from its learned repertoire, which are ordered in output according to some measure of pattern similarity with the arbitrary stimulus.
11. Learn substantial sequences of visual input and later accurately recall at least parts of the image content of selected sequences in correct temporal order.
12. Learn and recall a name for each entity it has learned.
13. Organize and relate its internal representations as equivalents to subject and predicate in a propositional structure.
14. Generate sequences of related inferences, a substantial proportion of which are logically true within the terms of a complex propositional structure.
15. Image, or otherwise recall, if the model is presented with a name, its representation of the object, entity, characteristic, or relationship that the name stands for.
16. Control its behavior in accordance with its motivational needs.
17. Attach some indicant of value to any current or imaged environment (scene) or episode according to the degree to which it meets its motivational needs.
18. Plan, execute, and learn sequences of its own behavior that lead to environments or episodes that meet its motivational needs.

These requirements motivated the mechanisms and the system architecture of the brain model that I propose. They represent a basic core of processes that must be explained as we progress toward a full account. The following chapters address these requirements and present the details of a brain model that I believe provides a credible biophysical and structural foundation for understanding human cognitive competence.

Chapter 2
Neuronal Properties

The structure and dynamic characteristics that account for the competence of any articulated physical system are critically dependent on the properties of its primitive components. In the development of a neuronal model, we must first specify the minimal relevant properties of the nerve cells that are to compose it. Then the theoretical problem is to formulate a competent computational structure that is biologically plausible with respect to the postulated characteristics of the individual neurons and to their patterns of connectivity.

Any living neuron is an enormously complex biophysical system. For the purposes of what is to be a system-theoretical account of the human cognitive brain, I need to explicate only those properties and assumptions that are essential for the operational integrity of the proposed models. We will take for granted all of the biochemical, electrical, and structural processes and characteristics that contribute to the singular viability of a functioning nerve cell (Cotman and McGaugh 1980; Horridge 1968; Kandel 1976; Kuffler, Nicholls, and Martin 1984; Shepherd 1983) and focus initially on those aspects specifically required in the mechanisms and networks to follow.

Basic Properties of Neurons

In terms of shape (figure 2.1), mammalian neurons exhibit great diversity. The cell body of a neuron can range from 5 to 100 microns on its longest axis. Projection neurons such as pyramidal cells may have dendrites that are several millimeters in length and axons that extend many centimeters. Local circuit neurons may have no axon and only very short dendritic processes that extend no more than a few microns. Modern estimates of the number of neurons that occupy the cortical mantle of the human brain range from 10 billion to somewhat more than 16 billion (Blinkov and Glezer 1968). Despite their striking variability in size and shape, neurons are all alike in one respect: their principal function is to receive and integrate electrochemical pulses from sensory transducers or other neurons and, con-

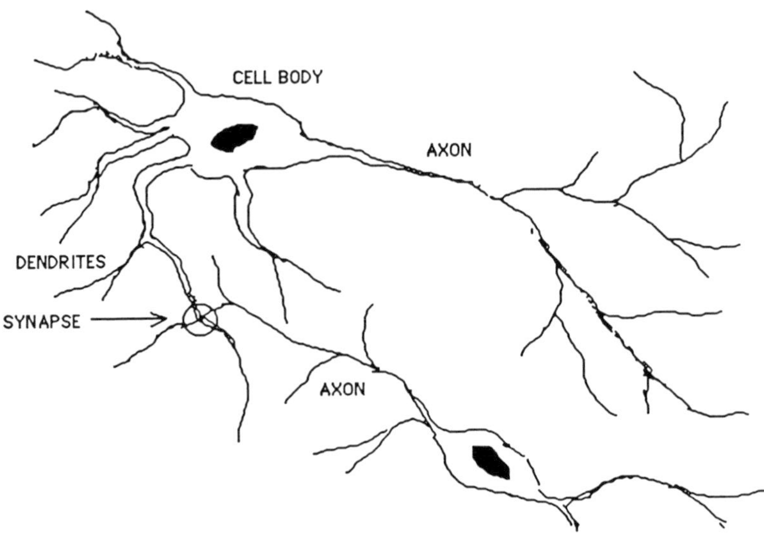

Figure 2.1
Two neurons with a synaptic junction between the axon of one and a dendrite of the other.

tingent on the characteristics of the received pulses, output their own characteristic pulses to other neurons or muscle fibers.

The fact that there are contingencies between the input activity on a neuron and the output it sends to its targets means that it is not simply a biological device for relaying signals. It performs a computation on its input. The combined computations of many neurons in specialized connective architectures account for cognition.

Figure 2.2 illustrates some fundamental properties of neurons. At the top of the figure is a schematic drawing of a generalized nerve cell. Stimulation to the cell is provided at discrete junctions (synapses) by quanta of neurotransmitters released into the gap (synaptic cleft) between an active axon terminal (S_i) of a presynaptic cell and a specialized receptor patch on the postsynaptic cell membrane. The neurotransmitters released by the donor cell may either excite or inhibit a target cell. An excitatory input induces an inward flow of sodium and other cations that drives the resting membrane potential of the target cell (typically, near -70 millivolts at equilibrium) in a positive direction (depolarization) toward discharge threshold. A change in membrane potential of this kind is called an excitatory postsynaptic potential (EPSP) (see the bottom illustration in figure 2.2). If discharge threshold is reached, an action potential (a positive-

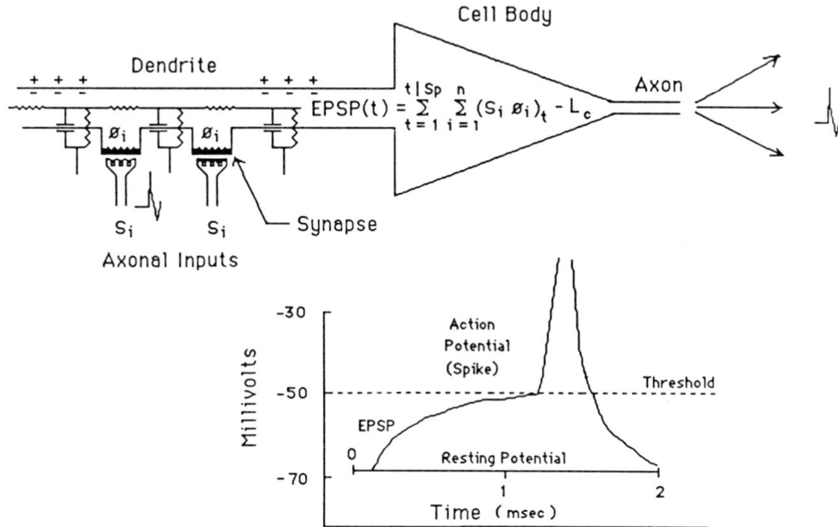

Figure 2.2
Top: Schematic showing the bioelectrical properties of a typical neuron. A single dendritic shaft represents the available surface of all the dendritic branches of the cell. *Bottom:* Dynamic characteristics of a typical neuron showing relationship of resting potential, EPSP, discharge threshold, and action potential.

going spike of voltage that is measured inside the cell against an outside reference) is initiated near the junction of the axon and the cell body. This voltage spike is the result of an abrupt regenerative local increase in the membrane's permeability to sodium cations. The action potential propagates down the length of the axon and its branches, where it induces the release of neurotransmitter at each of the cell's synaptic terminals. After each action potential, the neuron will exhibit a brief period of absolute and then relative refractoriness in its response to stimulation. In contrast, an inhibitory input increases the membrane's permeability to potassium cations and/or chloride anions and drives the membrane potential in the direction of greater negativity (hyperpolarization), away from the threshold potential required for spike discharge and toward the lower equilibrium potential for these ion species (increased within-cell negativity). A change in membrane potential of this kind is called an inhibitory postsynaptic potential (IPSP). The specialized postsynaptic receptors at the dendritic membrane (the darkened areas beneath the synaptic cleft in the top schematic) can be characterized in terms of their efficacy in mediating changes in EPSP and IPSP in response to presynaptic neurotransmitter release. This property is termed the synaptic transfer weight and is designated by the symbol ϕ (Trehub 1975a).

The dendritic membrane in figure 2.2 presents a parallel circuit of capacitance and resistance to any potential gradient across the membrane, causing the neuron to behave as a leaky spatial-temporal integrator of its synaptic inputs (see the summation expression within the cell body shown at the top of figure 2.2). The expression

$$MP(t) = RP + \left(\sum_{t=1}^{t/S_p} \sum_{i=1}^{n} (S_i \phi_i)_t - L_c \right) \tag{2.1}$$

gives a rough linear approximation for the relative value of the membrane potential (*MP*) in a cell at time t after the initiation of synaptic input. In this formula, *RP* represents the resting potential of the neuron, S_i represents the activity level of the ith axonal input terminal where each excitatory input has a positive sign and each inhibitory input a negative sign; ϕ_i is a coefficient representing the synaptic transfer weight at the ith axon-dendrite junction; $(S_i\phi_i)_t$ is the product of S_i and ϕ_i at time t; t/S_p is the time following stimulus onset at which threshold is reached and a spike discharge is generated; and L_c represents the reduction of EPSP by leakage of the membrane charge. As we shall see later, the simple fact that neurons are time-sensitive leaky integrators is a useful property in the behavior of certain kinds of neuronal mechanisms.

Equation 2.1 implies that with transfer weights (ϕ_i) held constant, the slope of time-integrated EPSP will increase as the net excitatory input to a cell is increased, either by having a greater number of active excitatory inputs, an increase in the activity level in one or more of a fixed set of excitatory inputs, or a decrease in the total inhibitory input (IPSP) to the cell. A rise in the rate of EPSP integration means that the latency to discharge threshold will decrease during the stimulation epoch. If the stimulus is sustained, the neuron will exhibit a frequency of discharge that is monotonically related to the slope of EPSP integration. Thus

$$F \propto \frac{d(EPSP)}{d(t)} \tag{2.2}$$

where F represents the frequency of cell discharge. The relationship between the rate of EPSP integration and the frequency of spike output is illustrated in figure 2.3. The higher the frequency of discharge is in any given cell, the stronger is its stimulation to its target cells and, if the output is excitatory, the shorter is the latency to discharge

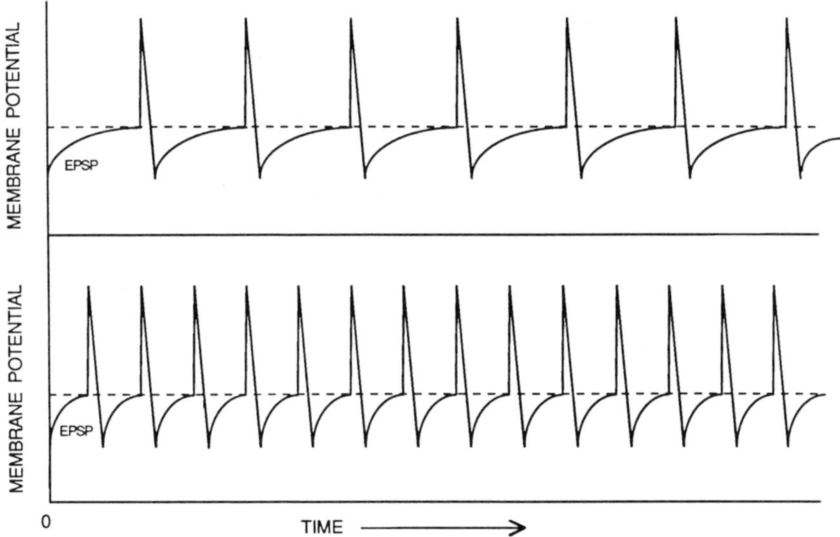

Figure 2.3
Relationship between rate of EPSP integration and frequency of spike discharge.

in the target cells. Discharge frequencies as high as 800 spikes per second have been recorded in large myelinated neurons.

Suppose that there are two general sources of input to a cell: a source of excitatory information to which the cell must respond and a subthreshold source of biasing input that shifts the membrane potential closer to or farther away from its discharge potential. The closer to threshold that a neuron is biased, the fewer the number of stimulus spikes that will be required to fire the cell, the shorter its response latency will be, and the higher its output frequency will be in response to a given sustained excitatory input. Conversely, the farther from threshold a neuron is biased (by inhibitory input), the longer its response latency will be and the lower will be its output frequency (figure 2.4). In a neuronal system of many cells that receive parallel input from a common stimulus source but control a variety of competing response options, the selective biasing of the cells can profoundly shape the stimulus-response behavior of the system.

So far, I have mentioned only synaptic junctions between axons and dendrites (axodendritic synapse), but there are a variety of other kinds of synaptic contacts among neurons: contacts between an axon and a cell body (axosomatic), between two axons (axoaxonic), and between dendrites (dendrodendritic). Presynaptic activity at any of

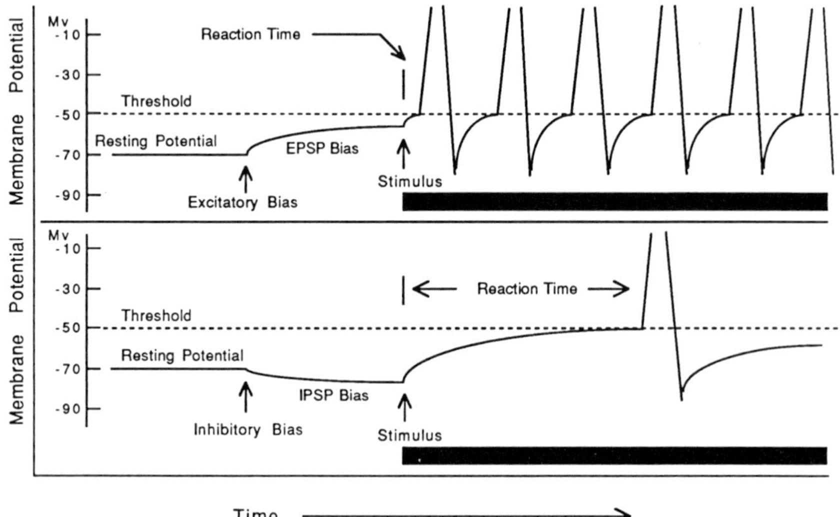

Figure 2.4
Relationship of cell bias, reaction time (latency), and discharge frequency given a standard stimulus. Dark bar represents onset and continuation of stimulus.

the various kinds of synaptic arrangements will affect the nature and degree of ionic flows across the membrane of the target cell and, thus, the membrane potential. In the case of dendrodendritic synapses, cell-to-cell influences are typically mediated by graded ionic processes without the requirement of a spike discharge at the presynaptic terminal. As we shall see, the dendrodendritic structure is well suited for establishing gradients of membrane bias over large neuronal arrays.

Autaptic Neurons

Autaptic neurons, which are characterized by having one or more of their axon collaterals in feedback synapse with their own dendrites or cell body (Shepherd 1979, van der Loos and Glaser 1972), have a simple structural property that allows them to serve as short-term memory processors in cognitive mechanisms (top, figure 2.5). In cells of this kind, it is assumed that if there is sufficient sustained positive bias (for example, by subthreshold excitatory input from the reticular activating system), a transient stimulus will cause the autaptic cell to continue firing even after input from the initiating stimulus has stopped. If the subthreshold bias is removed, excitation from its own recurrent axon collateral is insufficient to sustain spike discharge, and the autaptic neuron stops firing (figure 2.5, bottom).

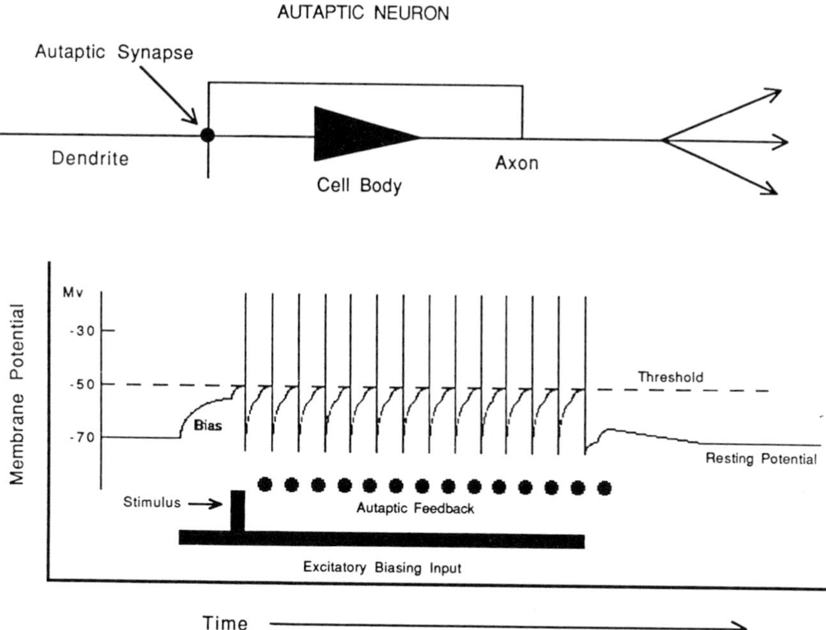

Figure 2.5
Top: Schematic of autaptic neuron. *Bottom:* Dynamic characteristics of an autaptic neuron. Cell continues to discharge after a single suprathreshold stimulus pulse as long as subthreshold excitatory bias is sustained.

Autaptic cells can serve as bistable elements in more complex neuronal circuits and mechanisms. For example, large arrays of autaptic cells can "capture" a transient afferent pattern and hold it as a short-term memory representation for any additional processing required, or a fleeting categorical event on a single axonal line can be represented by continuing activity in an autaptic target so that it can be effectively related to other brain events that may require more time to evolve. Since autaptic output can also be used as a subthreshold biasing (priming) input to other processing modules, autaptic cells can play a useful role as gating or strobing mechanisms in networks that perform delicate timing operations.

Adaptive Neurons

How can the human brain establish new internal representations and input-output mappings that are adaptive to the changing physical and social environment and the motivational needs unique to each individual? When we raise this question, we confront the challenge of explaining how complex learning can be effectively accomplished within the biological constraints of a neuronal system. For the reasons given in chapter 1, I believe that a comb-filter model is the preferred approach to cognitive representation and mapping. In models of this kind (and in PDP systems as well), the pattern of activation-transfer weights among similar processing units determines the content of the system's memory, its concepts, and its input-output mappings. Selective modification of synaptic transfer weights (ϕ) is generally assumed to be the principal physical process underlying learning and memory in the neuronal networks of the brain. But what specific processes might provide a reasonable biological basis for these adaptive synaptic changes?

Before I describe the proposed mechanism for selective synaptic modification, it will be helpful to consider a number of basic problems that must be solved in a biological system that is to learn useful representations and stimulus-response mappings. At the level of a single adaptive neuron, we should ask the following questions:

1. Under what conditions will an adaptive synapse change its transfer weight (ϕ)?
2. How are transfer weights (ϕ) on the adaptive cell normalized to prevent significant system errors that can occur because the complete segment of unit activity representing one stimulus may be included within the pattern of a different stimulus, because of variation in the sheer number of active input units associated with particular stimuli, or because some stimuli are experienced more frequently than others?
3. How is a particular learned pattern of ϕ on a cell protected from "overwriting" by subsequent inputs?
4. How quickly do appropriate changes in ϕ take place, and how long are particular changes in ϕ maintained?

Initiating Change in Transfer Weights

Each of us builds and elaborates an expanding base of world knowledge by establishing internal representations (memories) of our cumulative sensory experiences. Because we cannot maintain representations of all sensory input, even over relatively short periods of time, we are obliged to specify those principles by which a constant stream of sensory input is to be sampled and registered by discrete and enduring physical changes in the brain. In terms of adaptive cells within a neuronal model, this means that we must propose biologically plausible mechanisms for initiating change in their synaptic transfer weights on principles that can account for an appropriate sampling of afferent activity.

Normalization of Transfer Weights
Recall that a fundamental computational problem in processing information from complex external and internal environments is that of pattern categorization. In a comb filter system, we want a physically indexed cell that has been tuned to a particular pattern of activation over the array of input lines to signal reliably that pattern's presence by producing an output greater than that of any other cell, which may be tuned to a different input pattern. To illustrate the kind of difficulty that can arise in relation to the settings of transfer weights, let us imagine a simple comb filter consisting of only two adaptive cells (table 2.1). Suppose that when a stimulus vector V1 was presented, a learning mechanism simply changed the values of ϕ on cell A from 0 to 1 at each synaptic junction corresponding to the axonal contact from an active cell in the input array and that the values of ϕ on cell B were changed in a similar fashion when stimulus V2 was presented. Now, suppose that V1 corresponds to the stimulus vector 000111000 and V2 to the vector 110111011, where 1 represents an active unit and 0 an inactive unit in the input array. In this case, if V2 were presented later, cell B would correctly respond with a spike output frequency greater than cell A because its sum of the products between active axonal inputs and their corresponding activation transfer weights would be greater than that for cell A. If V1 were presented, however, the sum of products for cells A and B would be equal, and there would be no difference in the spike output frequencies of the cells. Given these circumstances, the system is unable to classify the input properly.

Suppose, on the other hand, the weights given by this procedure were strictly normalized by dividing each by the number of active units in the input vector at the time of learning. In this case, if V1 were later presented, cell A would respond appropriately, but if V2 were presented, the sum of products for cells A and B would be equal, and again the system would be unable to classify the input. What seems to be required is a mechanism that combines the respective advantages of unnormalized and normalized synaptic weightings. This problem in categorization, related to the inclusion of a given pattern within another, is one that must be solved in a biologically credible fashion.

Another consideration in pattern recognition concerns the relative effects of noise on performance in response to stimuli that evoke a

Table 2.1
Sum of products for each cell of a two-cell filter

Input (S_i)	ϕ_i Cell A[a]	ϕ_i Cell B[a]
0	0 (0)	1 (.14)
0	0 (0)	1 (.14)
0	0 (0)	0 (0)
1	1 (.33)	1 (.14)
1	1 (.33)	1 (.14)
1	1 (.33)	1 (.14)
0	0 (0)	0 (0)
0	0 (0)	1 (.14)
0	0 (0)	1 (.14)
	3 (.99)	3 (.42)

a. Nonnormalized weights are in the left part of the columns; normalized weights appear in parentheses.

small number of active input units compared to those evoking a large number of active units. We would expect small stimuli to be more vulnerable to noise than large stimuli, but since small stimuli can be just as important in an ecological sense as large stimuli, it would be advantageous for adaptive neurons to compensate, at least partially, for such differences in vulnerability to noise. Problems of this kind, related to differences in stimulus size, can be reduced to the extent that synaptic transfer weights approach true normalization over a wide range in the number of coactive input units.

An analogous difficulty must be addressed with respect to the number of times a particular stimulus might be experienced. Since an appropriate response to a stimulus that is infrequently encountered can be more critical in some circumstances than a response to a more commonly experienced stimulus, the selective tuning of adaptive cells should occur after as few stimulus repetitions as possible.

Overwriting Weight Distributions

After the distribution of synaptic transfer weights on an adaptive cell has been changed so that the cell is tuned to respond maximally to a particular stimulus, how is its established ϕ pattern protected from further change or overwriting by subsequent stimuli? If such overwriting could occur fortuitously, then memory would be volatile and short-lived. Thus, the mechanism for adaptive weight change must be able to ensure the stability of desired ϕ distributions.

Duration of Established Weights

Related to the problem of overwriting is the question of the length of time a particular memory is to be maintained. Certainly forgetting is a significant phenomenon in cognitive behavior. Must the ϕ changes that represent each learned stimulus remain intact throughout the life of the neuron that undergoes such changes? If so, then forgetting must occur because of some failure to process the output of adapted cells properly. Alternatively, synaptic weights, once established after learning, might decay to their original base values. Might there be several classes of adaptive cells so that some exhibit little, if any, decay while others decay at varying rates?

The implications of all of these issues should be taken into account in the formulation of hypothesized mechanisms for adaptive neurons and in the design of the processing modules in which they serve as component parts.

A Model for Synaptic Plasticity

Figure 2.6 represents the synaptic junctions of several axons on the dendrite of an adaptive neuron. The following assumptions govern the dynamics of plastic changes in such synapses and constitute a provisional physiological model for learning and memory that can satisfy the basic computational requirements of an adaptive array-to-line filter.

1. Two kinds of biochemical species are essential for the long-term modification (increase) of synaptic transfer weight (ϕ): axon transfer factor (ATF) and dendrite transfer factor (DTF).
2. A long-term increase in ϕ can occur if and only if ATF and DTF are locally coactive within the postsynaptic dendritic matter.
3. Effective interaction of ATF and DTF can occur if and only if the presynaptic cell(s) discharges when activity in the postsynaptic target cell(s) is above some threshold level (θ).
4. During ATF-DTF coactivity, ϕ elevation occurs only at active synapses and is mediated by specific macromolecular changes induced by ATF-DTF interaction.
5. The magnitude of ϕ at each synapse is limited by saturation, determined by the maximum amount of DTF that can be utilized in the macromolecular change at the local receptor region (figure 2.7).
6. In all ATF-DTF interactions, ATF makes a fixed contribution to the transfer weight (ϕ) of its local synapse, whereas DTF is

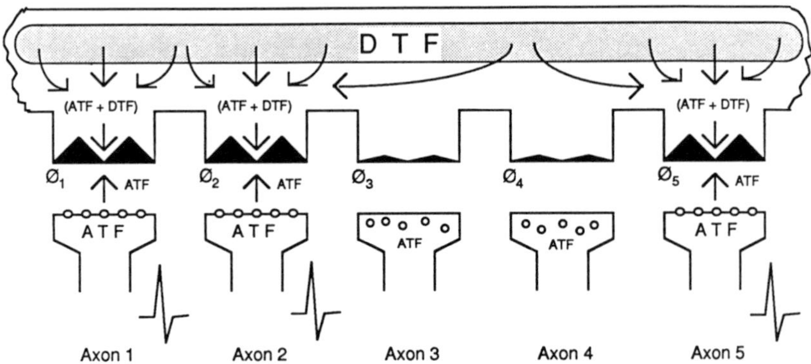

Figure 2.6
Schematic of synaptic junctions among the axons of five cells and the dendrite of an adaptive neuron. Input cells 1, 2, and 5 have fired, resulting in an ATF-DTF reaction at receptors in the corresponding synapses of the postsynaptic membrane. Volume of darkened area represents magnitude of transfer weight following synaptic modification. No change has occurred at the synapses of inactive axons 3 and 4.

distributed over all active synapses and makes a ϕ contribution to each that is, up to the local saturation limit, inversely proportional to the number of concurrently active axonal inputs on the postsynaptic cell (figure 2.7).

7. ATF is constantly generated and rapidly renewed and available for release in axon terminals.

8. DTF is renewed relatively slowly and at different rates in different populations of adaptive cells.

9. The threshold (θ) for ATF-DTF interaction is an inverse function of the concentration of free DTF in the postsynaptic dendrite (figure 2.8).

10. Synaptic transfer weights (ϕ) decay at different rates in different populations of adaptive cells.

11. There is a positive correlation between the rate of ϕ decay and the rate of DTF renewal in any given adaptive cell.

Expression 2.3 gives the general formula for determining the transfer weight of any plastic synapse that has been modified in the course of learning.

$$\underset{b \to Lim}{\phi_{im}} = b + S_{im}(c + kN^{-1}) \tag{2.3}$$

where $\underset{b \to Lim}{\phi_{im}}$ is the transfer weight of ϕ_{im}, from the basal value (b) to the saturation limit (Lim), on an adaptive cell m; b is the initial transfer

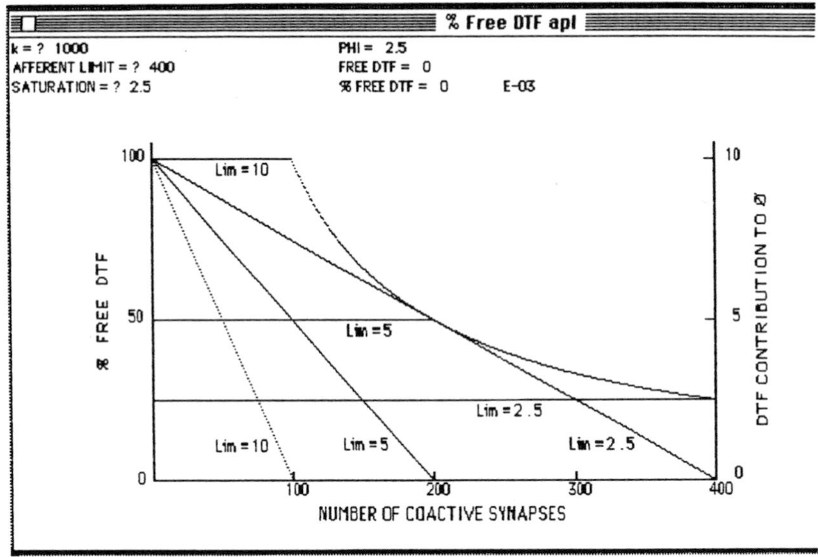

Figure 2.7
Graph showing the change in percentage free DTF and DTF contribution to the transfer weight (ϕ) as a function of the number of coactive synapses. Examples are given for three different saturation limits (*Lim* = 10, 5, 2.5) and an arbitrary initial store of DTF (k = 1000). Linear, negatively sloping plots at left represent change in percentage free DTF. Plots starting with flat horizontal segments represent change in DTF contribution to ϕ.

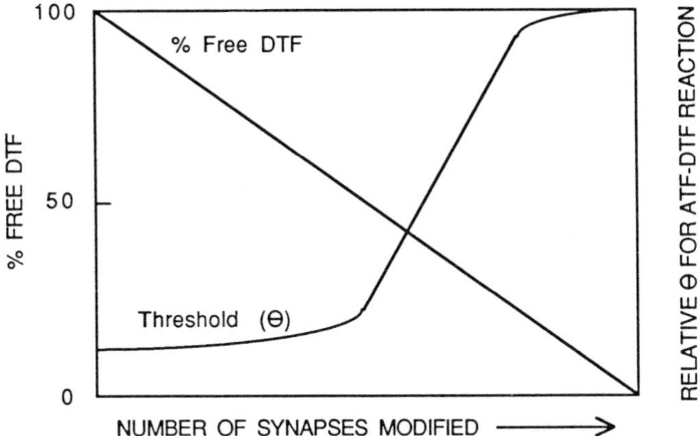

Figure 2.8
Threshold (θ) for ATF-DTF interaction as a function of the concentration of free DTF.

weight of the unmodified synapse; c is the ATF contribution from the active axonal contact; kN^{-1} is the proportional contribution of DTF in the postsynaptic cell, taking account of N coactive axons on the cell m and the total store of free DTF in the postsynaptic cell, which is represented by the coefficient k; and S_{im} is the activity level of axonal input at ϕ_{im}. It is assumed that $b < c \ll k$. These formulations constitute the basic learning rule for the systems described later.

There is no direct physiological confirmation of the specific details of this model for synaptic plasticity; however, the model is broadly consistent with a number of relatively recent empirical findings at the neurophysiological level. The discovery of a long-term increase in the efficacy of synaptic transmission in the hippocampus following brief high-frequency stimulation of the perforant pathway (Bliss and Gardner-Medwin 1973, Bliss and Lømo 1973) provided direct evidence of synaptic plasticity in vertebrates and has prompted investigators to search vigorously for the underlying mechanisms for this effect. Since the initial observations by Bliss and his colleagues of long-term potentiation (LTP) of the hippocampal response, other studies have demonstrated LTP in a number of different brain structures at the cortical and subcortical levels (Gerren and Weinberger 1983; Ito 1983; Komatsu et al. 1981; Lee 1982; Racine, Milgram, and Hafner 1983; Racine et al. 1986; Voronin 1985).

There appears to be general agreement about some of the events in the cellular processes involved in LTP. Figure 2.9 summarizes the details that have been revealed by various neurochemical probes and together seem to represent a broadly accepted basic description of neuronal processes underlying LTP (Akers et al. 1986; Bank, LoTurco, and Alkon 1987; Brown et al. 1988; Browning et al. 1979; Larson and Lynch 1987; Linden, Sheu, and Routtenberg 1987; LoTurco et al. 1987; Lynch and Baudry 1984; Murakami, Whitely, and Routtenberg 1987; Routtenberg 1984). Brief high-frequency stimulation (typically 100 pulses per second for 1 second) results in a sharp influx of calcium cations and translocation of protein kinase C (PKC) from the cytosol of the postsynaptic neuron to its membrane, where it induces a stable phosphorylation of membrane-bound protein. This phosphorylation is thought to be associated with an increase in the activity of a particular subclass of postsynaptic receptors, which occurs only beyond some high threshold of stimulation. These specialized postsynaptic receptors are called NMDA receptors because they are specifically responsive to the compound N-methyl-D-aspartate, a synthetic analog of aspartate that is a putative neurotransmitter. Significantly, low-frequency stimulation (1 pulse per second for 100 seconds) does not result in long-term potentiation. Moreover, specific chemical

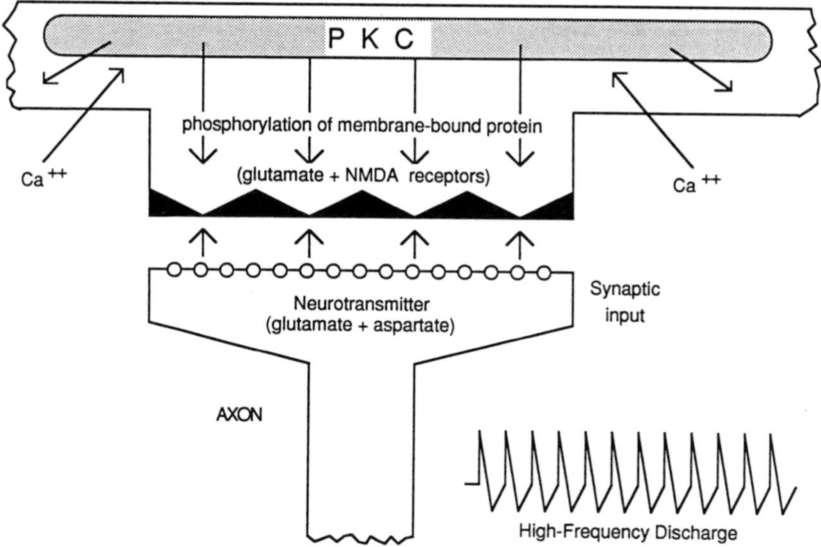

Figure 2.9
Neuronal processes underlying long-term potentiation.

blockade of NMDA receptors prevents the initiation of LTP without eliminating normal synaptic transmission. If LTP has already been induced, then blockade of NMDA receptors does not reduce the established increase in synaptic efficacy (Larson and Lynch 1987; Linden, Sheu, and Routtenberg 1987).

These recent empirical findings are consistent with the main features of the earlier proposed model for synaptic plasticity (Trehub 1975a):

1. Synaptic modification can occur on a single brief input if the axonal spike frequency is high enough to reach the threshold for protein phosphorylation.
2. The increase in synaptic weight (potentiation), once established, is relatively stable over time.
3. Aspartate (or an analog of it) provides a plausible candidate for the substance represented by ATF (the axon transfer factor in the earlier model).
4. PKC provides a plausible candidate for the substance represented by DTF (the dendrite transfer factor in the earlier model).
5. When LTP is induced, PKC translocates from the cytosol of

the dendrite to bind at the dendritic membrane. This corresponds to the reduction in free DTF after synaptic modification, as I hypothesized in my model.

The assumption of an inverse relationship between the number of coactive axonal inputs and the magnitude of the DTF contribution to each active synapse expressed in the basic learning formula (equation 2.3) is consistent with the experimental findings of Hillman and Chen (1979), who demonstrated in the cerebellum that when the number of parallel fiber inputs is experimentally reduced (fewer coactive axons), the area of postsynaptic density (transfer weight) at the lesser number of synapses on the target Purkinje cells increases proportionally. Thus, the inverse relationship between the contribution of DTF at synaptic sites and the number of coactive axons predicted in equation 2.3 conforms with a physiological process actually found to occur in a part of the brain that is accessible to the appropriate experimental procedures. The inverse relationship between transfer weight (ϕ) caused by local DTF effects and the number of coactive axons on an adaptive cell provides an intrinsic mechanism for quasi-normalization of synaptic transfer weights that is critical in pattern learning.

Summary of Neuronal Properties

The following key properties that I assume to be true characteristics of real neurons are relevant to the models in the following chapters:

- There are two major classes of neurons: excitatory and inhibitory. Spike discharge along the axon of an excitatory neuron causes an EPSP in its contiguous target neuron(s); similar discharge of an inhibitory neuron causes an inhibitory postsynaptic potential in its contiguous target neuron(s).
- When EPSPs and IPSPs occur concurrently on a common neuron, total EPSP is reduced as some monotonic function of total IPSP.
- Spatially and temporally distributed postsynaptic potentials (PSPs) are integrated in leaky fashion within the neuron.
- Whenever the integrated EPSP reaches a threshold level, the neuron discharges a spike output.
- The membrane potential of a neuron that has shifted in a positive direction, reflecting EPSP integration, can be reset to its initial resting level by sufficiently strong IPSP input to the cell.
- Some neurons (autaptic cells) receive excitatory synaptic input from recurrent collaterals of their own axons and will continue

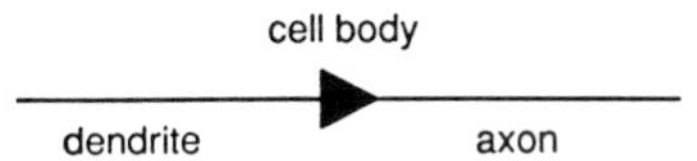

excitatory synapses

inhibitory synapses

adaptive (plastic) excitatory synapses

autaptic cells

or

autaptic cell with one excitatory output, two excitatory inputs, and two inhibitory inputs

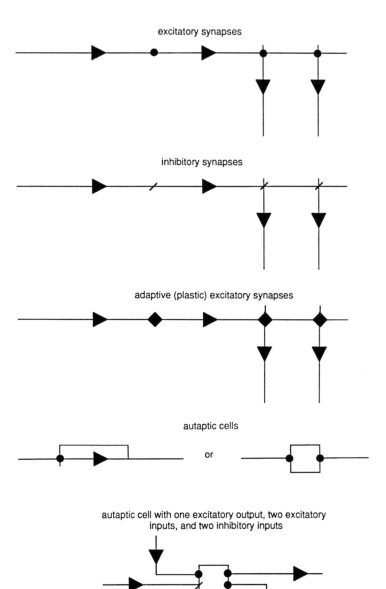

Figure 2.10
Standard symbols used for the neurons and synapses illustrated in this book.

discharging after a transient suprathreshold stimulus if there is sufficient subthreshold priming input from another source.

• Some neurons have excitatory synapses that can be modified in a graded and relatively stable fashion with respect to the magnitude of their contribution to the integrated EPSP of the associated cells (synaptic plasticity) given standard presynaptic input.

• The chemical factor within the axonal terminal of the presynaptic cell (ATF) that contributes to a change in synaptic efficacy during learning is constantly regenerated and available for use at its local synapse.

• The chemical factor within the dendrite of the postsynaptic cell (DTF) that contributes to a change in synaptic efficacy during learning is limited in quantity, is distributed over all coactive synaptic junctions up to the limit of utilization at each synapse, and is regenerated relatively slowly.

• The threshold for a reaction between ATF and DTF that is required for an increase in synaptic efficacy (transfer weight) to occur is inversely related to the proportion of free DTF in the target dendrite.

Symbols Used for Circuit Diagrams

Many of the model mechanisms and networks I set forth will be illustrated by circuit diagrams. The standard symbols I will use in these drawings are shown in figure 2.10.

Chapter 3

Learning, Imagery, Tokens, and Types: The Synaptic Matrix

An underlying premise of this book is that the cognitive brain consists of many special-purpose mechanisms synergistically organized in integrated networks. The first multineuronal mechanism that we will consider is a key processing module called a synaptic matrix (Trehub 1967). It is a putative brain mechanism with the capacity to learn and classify complex input patterns, store them in long-term memory, and recall images of them in the absence of external stimulation or when only fragments of them are presented as input. It is a self-organizing neuronal implementation of a parallel, adaptive comb filter that maps large input vectors onto unitary connectively labeled output lines (axons) and selectively maps these output lines onto correlated state vectors that are homologous with learned inputs (Trehub 1975a, 1977, 1987).

In the schematic drawing of a synaptic matrix shown in figure 3.1, there are nine afferent input lines (S_{ij}) and five output lines (Ω_i). In the human brain, a single synaptic matrix may have tens of thousands of axonal inputs and hundreds of thousands of outputs. Two subscripts, i and j, are used in figure 3.1 to index the input vector S because, in this case, it is assumed that the input neurons map from a two-dimensional transducer array. Inputs S_{ij} are in discrete point-to-point synapse with a second set of afferent neurons, called mosaic cells (M). The axon of each mosaic cell is in parallel adaptive synapse with all members of a set of cells in the detection matrix, which are called filter cells (f). Each filter cell is in discrete synapse with an output neuron called a class cell (Ω). The axon of each class cell bifurcates, sending a collateral back in adaptive synapse with the dendrites of all mosaic cells (M) in the imaging matrix. Finally, an inhibitory neuron (marked $-$) receives as its input the axons of all class cells and, in turn, sends its axon in parallel synapse to the dendrites (or cell bodies) of all class cells. This inhibitory cell is called a reset neuron.

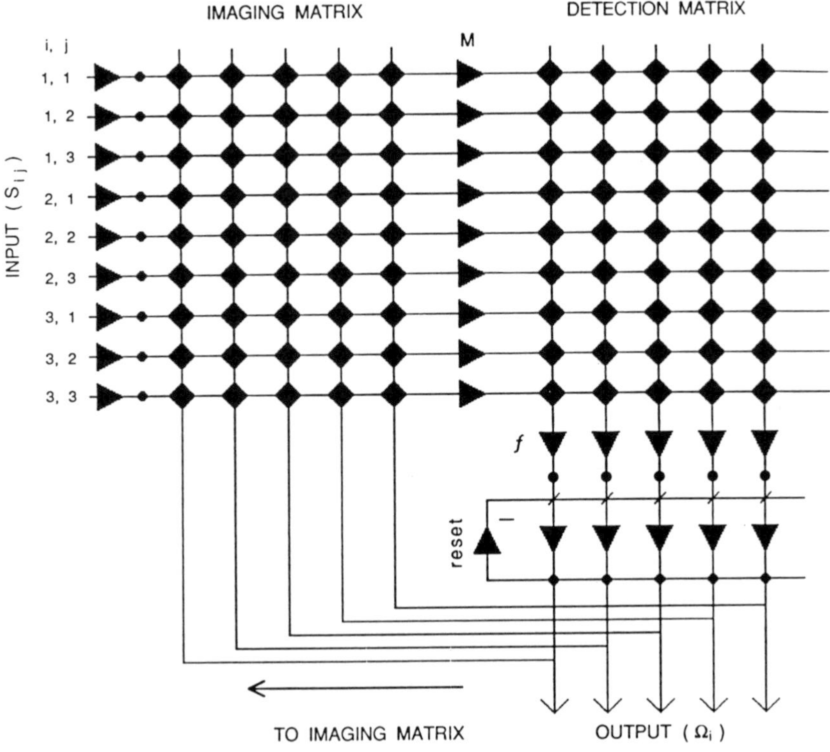

Figure 3.1
Schematic of a synaptic matrix. Afferent inputs are designated S_{ij}, and mosaic cells are designated M. Dots represent fixed excitatory synapses; short oblique slashes represent fixed inhibitory synapses; filled lozenges represent adaptive excitatory synapses. Reset neuron (−) generates an inhibitory postsynaptic potential to reset all class cells when discharged. Given any arbitrary input, the class cell coupled with the filter cell having the highest product sum of afferent axon activity and corresponding transfer weights will fire first and inhibit all competing class cells.

Learning and Pattern Recognition

For the purposes of illustration, let us assume a minimal adaptive system in the visual modality. There is a retina with nine discrete receptor cells arranged in a two-dimensional 3 × 3 array. Each receptor cell connects to an afferent neuron, which is indexed by the position of its associated receptor in the retinal array. We can represent this biological index by using retinotopic two-dimensional coordinate subscripts as index labels. Thus, each afferent neuron in figure 3.1 is designated S_{ij} where *ij* represents the retinotopic coordinate of its associated retinal cell. Let us also assume that center-surround inhibition (Kuffler 1953) and threshold properties at the retinal layer and lower visual centers result in the extraction of a binary-valued contour transform of the light intensity distribution caused by an image falling on the retina. Each afferent neuron discharges (activity = 1) if an edge is detected at its associated retinal locus; it remains silent (activity = 0) if an edge is not detected at its retinal locus. This array of edge detection signals composes the afferent excitation pattern (input vector) on the mosaic cell array (*M*). Taking the contour transform of the light-intensity distribution on the retina as input to the synaptic matrix is consistent with the recent experimental finding of Biederman and Ju (1988) showing that initial access to a mental representation of an object can be modeled as a matching of an edge-based representation.

At some early stage of maturation, the synaptic matrix becomes an effective adaptive brain mechanism. ATF and DTF are produced in its mosaic cells and filter cells, and ATF alone is produced in its class cells. With the production of the substances essential for synaptic plasticity, transfer weights (ϕ_i) can be modified by afferent excitation and sustained at their new levels. In this process of learning, the value of ϕ at each synapse will be set in accordance with equation 2.3,

$$\underset{b \rightarrow Lim}{\phi_{im}} = b + S_{im}(c + kN^{-1}),$$

where the parameters *b*, *c*, and *k* are subject to the loose constraint $b < c << k$.

Before any learning has occurred, all ϕ will be small; taking visual learning as the example, an image falling on the retina would normally produce relatively feeble, infrequent, and random firing of filter cells. If, however, cells in the synaptic matrix are positively biased by arousal (excitation from the reticular activating system), then added visual stimulation can induce a level of activity in some filter cells that exceeds the threshold Θ for ATF-DTF interaction. In this case, any filter cell (f_1) receiving sufficient excitation from a retinal input pattern (pattern A) via the mosaic cell array will undergo an effectively stable increase in ϕ at those of its synapses that intersect the afferent firing pattern (A) in the detection matrix. After this has happened, since the products of afferent stimulus units (S_{ij}) and their corresponding synaptic transfer weights (ϕ_i) are integrated in each filter cell (equation 2.1), whenever pattern A is presented, f_1 will fire at a higher frequency than other filter cells in the detection matrix because its rate of increase of EPSP, given A, will be higher than that for any other filter cell that has not been conditioned by the pattern A (expression 2.2). If uniform rates of integration and thresholds of discharge in the following class cells are assumed, the class cell connected to f_1 (Ω_1) will fire before any other Ω_i in the matrix output array because its spike input frequency will be higher than any other. In effect, this class cell (Ω_1) represents the biological name for the learned pattern A. Thus, relative spike frequency on labeled lines (class cells) is the effective code in this neuronal system.

The first class cell to fire (in this case, Ω_1) will discharge the inhibitory reset cell ($-$), which will reset the integration level of each neuron in the entire class cell array before EPSP in the other class cells can reach the firing threshold. The same process of Ω_1 discharge and cell reset will recycle continuously as long as the same stimulus (in this case, A) is present (or until the more active cells fatigue). In this fashion, any given visual pattern is identified at the neuronal level by the particular class cell it discharges. If there were no reset mechanism, all class cells in the detection matrix would continuously integrate EPSP and would reach their individual firing thresholds at random moments independently of the input pattern present at the time.

Imagery

Notice in figure 3.1 the bundle of axon collaterals from the set of class cells (Ω_i) that courses back to form adaptive synapses with the dendrites of all mosaic cells in the imaging matrix. When the visual stimulus A is presented, mosaic cells responding to the afferent input of A will discharge, thus firing the appropriate filter cell (f_1) at the highest frequency in the detection matrix and causing its paired class cell (Ω_1) to fire. The transfer weights (ϕ_i) of the adaptive synaptic junctions between the active Ω_1 collateral and mosaic cells (M) that are not discharging in the presence of stimulus A will remain unchanged, but those adaptive synaptic junctions on the mosaic cells that are firing (as afferents responding to the input pattern A) will be modified in accordance with equation 2.3. Synaptic transfer weights between the class cell Ω_1, and the mosaic cells will therefore be selectively increased for the *M* pattern A in the imaging matrix. After this synaptic change has occurred, if Ω_1 is fired (addressed), by either its associated filter cell (f_1) or any other input, it will evoke the afferent firing pattern on the mosaic cell array that is normally evoked by A, even when the stimulus A is not present. In this way, by means of automatic, selective synaptic weighting in the imaging matrix, the neuronal condition is established for retrieving, in the absence of retinal stimulation, an entire afferent pattern previously coded by a particular class cell. The capacity to recreate a specific discharge pattern on the mosaic cell array in the absence of a corresponding retinal stimulus provides one of the neuronal mechanisms for human imagination (Kosslyn 1980, Sheikh 1983, Shepard 1978, Trehub 1977).

Since only a single class cell collateral is normally active at any given time during the discharge of mosaic cells in the array, the reduction of free DTF in each active mosaic cell is minimal when an image is learned. Thus, a single mosaic cell can participate in the adaptive construction of many different visual representations in the imaging matrix.

An Example of Performance

Following is a simple example of how the synaptic matrix with input from a 3 × 3 cell retina performs the task of learning, recognizing, and imaging four different stimuli. In this simulation, the saturation limit (*Lim*) was set at a value of 6 for filter cells in the detection matrix and at a value of 3 for mosaic cells in the imaging matrix. It was assumed that all active afferent lines (S_{ij}) carried uniform excitation. Inputs were designated 1 for an active input line or 0 for an inactive line. Parameters in the learning equation (equation 2.3) were arbitrarily set as follows: $b = 1$, $c = 2$, $k = 10$. For simplicity of illustration, stimuli are designated by numbers corresponding to the order in which they were presented and learned, and each filter cell–class cell couplet is indexed by the pattern that modified it. Figure 3.2 shows the distribution of synaptic transfer weights on each adaptive neuron in the detection matrix and the imaging matrix (rounded to the nearest integer) after each stimulus was presented one time. Filter cell 5 has not been modified and is available for learning another pattern because its store of free DTF has not been depleted and remains at its maximum level.

After the four stimuli (vertical bar, square, horizontal bar, and cross) were learned, the synaptic matrix was tested for recognition of each of the stimuli. Figure 3.3 shows the relative frequency of

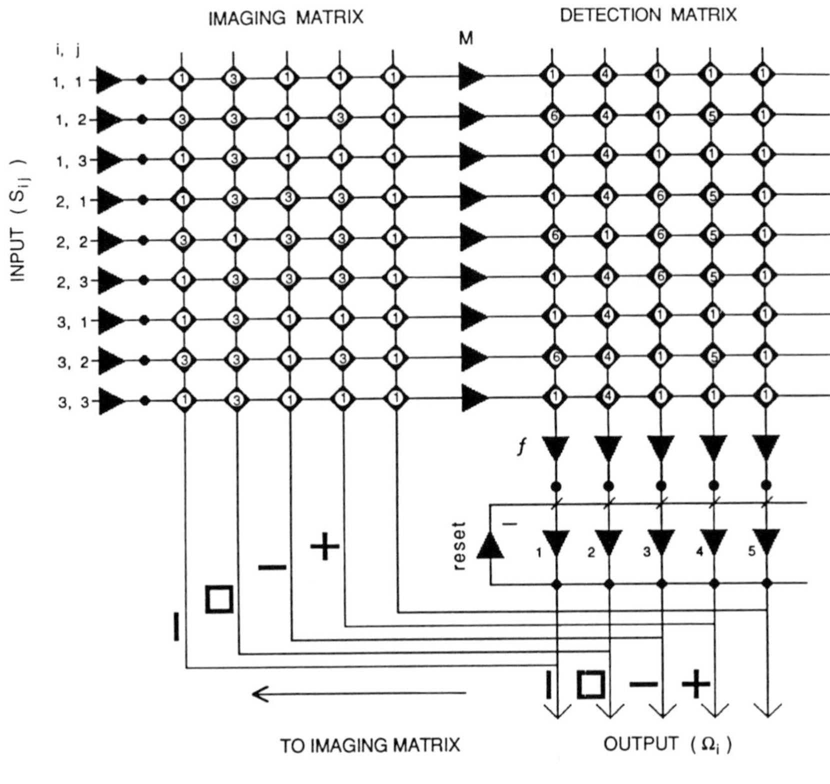

Figure 3.2
Synaptic matrix showing synaptic transfer weights after four different stimuli have been learned. The distribution of transfer weights in the detection matrix reflects a peak tuning of each filter cell to one of the input patterns. If any class cell is discharged, the distribution of transfer weights in the imaging matrix can evoke a pattern of excitation on the mosaic cell array that corresponds to the stimulus originally mapped to that class cell.

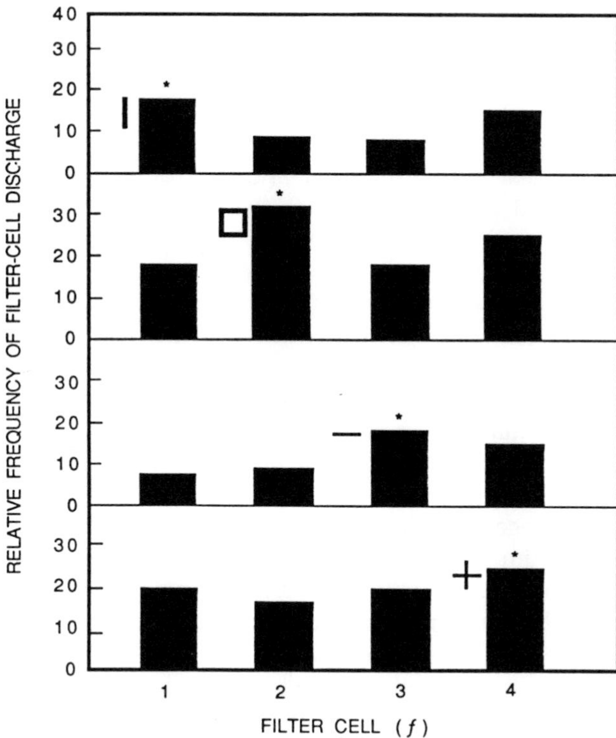

Figure 3.3
Bar graph of relative discharge frequency for each filter cell in the synaptic matrix shown in figure 3.2 when each of the four stimuli is presented after all have been learned. The cell showing maximum output in response to the stimulus presented has an asterisk above it. Shapes next to bars in graph identify both the stimulus presented on the trial and the filter cell that originally learned the stimulus.

discharge in all filter cells (constituting input to each of their coupled class cells) for each of the stimuli. Activity is maximum for the appropriate filter cell in all presentations, resulting in the discharge of the correct class cells (figure 3.2).

Notice that stimulus 4 (the cross) completely includes two other stimuli that had been learned (vertical bar and horizontal bar), yet the system discriminated the cross and gave the proper recognition response. And the vertical and the horizontal bars, both fully included in the cross stimulus, were also correctly recognized. The problems of normalization discussed in chapter 2 are remedied by the learning mechanism implicit in equation 2.3. The quasi-normalized DTF contribution and the small, fixed ATF contribution have a joint effect on synaptic transfer weights that gives the detection matrix the ability to make appropriate discriminations even when a learned stimulus is a substantial integral part of another learned stimulus.

Turning to figure 3.2 again, examination of the pattern of modified transfer weights in the imaging matrix reveals that discharge of any arbitrarily chosen class cell will evoke a distribution of excitation over the array of mosaic cells that corresponds to the afferent pattern signalled by that class cell. Since each mosaic-cell dendrite receives an active input from only one excited class-cell collateral at any given time, depletion of DTF will be minimal. Thus, each mosaic cell can adaptively change its synaptic weights to accommodate many subsequent image representations (memories).

Operating Characteristics of the Synaptic Matrix

In addition to its primary processing capabilities, other properties of the synaptic matrix deserve particular attention. An early simulation test of the model (Trehub 1975a) presented nine different visual patterns through a 5 × 5-cell retina. To satisfy the constraint $b < c << k$, the following values were arbitrarily assigned: $b = 1$, $c = 5$, $k = 100$. After all the patterns had been presented once during the learning phase, each was used in repeated stimulus-response trials to test recognition. Each stimulus was either an intact figure, as originally learned, or a degraded version of the original figure formed by randomly eliminating approximately 40 percent of the pixels forming the pattern (figure 3.4).

The upper half of figure 3.4 shows that when the learned patterns were presented intact in the test phase, response was 100 percent correct. The robustness of performance of the synaptic matrix is illustrated in the bottom half of figure 3.4, which shows what happens

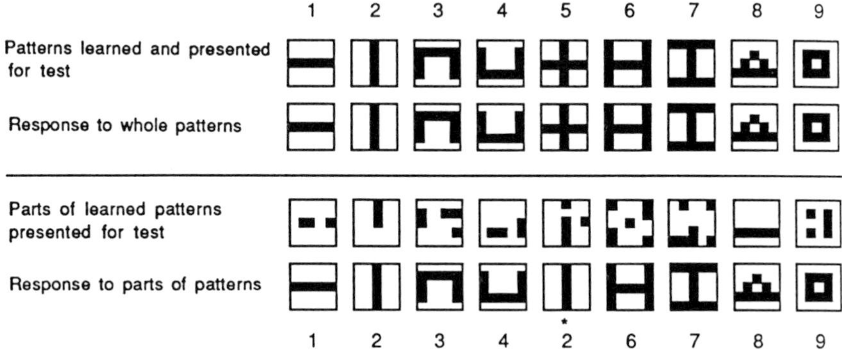

Figure 3.4
Results of simulation test. Numbers at top identify the nine stimuli that were learned. Notice the error (indicated by asterisk at bottom) made in response to the randomly degraded cross.

when the matrix must recognize pattern fragments having approximately 40 percent of the originally learned pattern randomly omitted. In this highly degraded condition, only one error of classification is committed—mistaking the fragment of a cross for a vertical bar. Inspection of those fragments of the cross presented as a stimulus reveals how intuitively appropriate the erroneous response was. Repeated tests with randomly generated fragments of the original stimuli (approximately 60 percent of each learned prototype) yielded correct responses in 92 percent of the tests. This early simulation demonstrated that the synaptic matrix performs well in the presence of subtractive noise. (Other simulations to be presented demonstrate robust recognition performance in the presence of both additive and subtractive noise, as well as when stimuli are confounded by the superposition of learned patterns.)

The synaptic matrix operates on the basis of ordinal logic rather than point logic. When a stimulus is presented, the sum of the products for mosaic cells and their corresponding synaptic transfer weights on the filter cells (f_m) does not have to be any particular value (a point criterion) for the mechanism to respond appropriately. All that is required is that the sum of these products for a correct filter cell be greater than the sum for each of the other competing filter cells (an ordinal criterion).

The model has direct implications for our understanding of what a concept might be in terms of brain function. The detection matrix does not compute a single prototypical distribution of synaptic transfer weights for a given class of objects. Thus, there is no representation of an "average" pattern that might be taken as a person's concept of an object. Rather, in the course of human learning, filter cells may be tuned to different exemplars of a single object class. Since the decision about class (category) membership is made on the basis of competitive, first-order pickoff among the possible class cell outputs, the system exhibits robust intrinsic generalization and can, in principle, assign proper category membership to many objects that it has never learned as exemplars of their class. This is true because the mechanism operates on the principle of ordinal logic, which ensures that even in the absence of a good match between an input pattern and its appropriate filter cell, if there is no better match with an inappropriate filter cell, the correct recognition response will be given. The effect of this operating principle is to make the system appear as if it is responding on the basis of the fit of each stimulus against a set of averaged internal standards (Estes 1986) when, in fact, there are no averaged standards. It will be seen later that when the bare synaptic matrix is augmented by other putative brain mechanisms, the occurrence of a poor match against all filter cells in the detection matrix results in a signal that the current stimulus is novel, and if the ecological and motivational context warrants it, the level of arousal will increase and the stimulus will be automatically learned (Trehub 1977).

With respect to the distinction between concept and category, one might say (from the biophysical standpoint) that a concept consists of that subset of exemplar-tuned filter cells together with their coupled class cells that has at least one common output effect distinct from the output effects of any other subset in the detection matrix. For example, the presentation of the stimulus object A will maximally stimulate one of the cells in the subset of filter cells that defines the concept of A-ness. The discharge of its coupled class cell will cause the output signal (A), which then defines the category of the stimulus instance. A proper category signal can be any arbitrary but distinct and stable correlate of the class cells that evoke the signal.

The synaptic matrix does not employ feature extraction or feature list checkoff in the learning and subsequent recognition process. For instance, in the examples presented, learning the cross did not require that its constituent features of a vertical and horizontal bar be isolated and learned as separate representations. Nor did the recognition of the cross require that there be discrete representations of the bar features in the detection matrix. The excitation pattern of a stimulus on the mosaic cell array was learned holistically and represented holistically in the distribution of synaptic transfer weights on the filter cells.

The competence of this theoretical model suggests that natural pattern recognition can proceed very well without prior feature extraction, as an example at the level of insect behavior shows. In a carefully controlled study that explored how bees remember the shape of flowers, it was found that bees apparently store flower patterns as "low-resolution eidetic images" (Gould 1985). But this does not imply that organisms are necessarily incapable of feature extraction. The issue of what constitutes a feature and how it might be extracted from a complex visual stimulus is still quite murky (Pinker 1984). For example, study of the visual system in lower vertebrates suggests that they respond best to simple stimuli, such as small, horizontally elongated blobs in motion (Ingle 1968). In such cases, however, it seems more appropriate to ascribe the feature selectivity to an absolute constraint on the visuo-motor system imposed by primitive, relatively simple, pretuned filtering mechanisms that are suited only to the basic survival needs (prey catching, avoidance of predators). It is assumed that in the higher mammals or at least in humans, mosaic cell excitation can be limited to salient parts of a complex object, and these pattern parts can then be learned separately as constituent features of the larger object. In this way, filter cells can be constructed that detect and classify not only whole objects and scenes but their salient components as well.

In perceptual situations where immediate discrimination of a particular object on the basis of holistic filters is difficult, analytic detection of the previously learned parts of that object can assist the recognition process—for example, recognizing a semirigid object, such as the human body. In this case, isolation of a relatively rigid part, such as the head, enables the viewer to infer the whole figure from a recognized component.

To the extent that features may be regarded as important aspects of shapes that deserve special weighting, this approach provides intrinsic weighting of especially significant object parts on the following bases:

1. Parts that are invariant aspects of objects over a variety of perturbations will, on average, be represented in the transfer weight distributions of more filter cells than will noninvariant parts.
2. Parts of objects that have particular ecological relevance or utility (the handle of a cup) will naturally tend to be the focus of perceptual orientation, and more exemplars of such parts (features) will tend to be represented in the detection matrix.
3. If experience teaches that an ambiguous stimulus can be re-

> solved by determining the presence or absence of a particular part, the part that solves the problem will tend to be isolated and learned as a useful feature.

Thus, in this model, recognition by feature detection is a special case within the general pattern recognition process.

Another significant property of the synaptic matrix is that its reaction time depends on the relationship between the current stimulus and the learning experience of the matrix. Because class cells integrate filter cell output over time and fire when their integrated EPSP reaches threshold, the reaction time for output from the detection matrix is a monotonic function of the correlation between the current input pattern and the best-fitting ϕ representation among the filter cells that have been modified by previous learning. Thus, the more familiar a stimulus is, the faster will the system respond.

Propositional and Analogical Representation

If we examine the physical state of a synaptic matrix after a stimulus pattern has been learned, we can characterize the modified distribution of synaptic weights as a latent representation, a deep structure that determines the subsequent surface behavior of the system. In the detection matrix, this synaptic structure results in the selection of output lines (class cells) that are selectively contingent on particular stimulus properties. In effect, the discharge of a class cell that is evoked by a pattern of activity (S) in the mosaic array is the physical equivalent of a propositional representation in the simple form S (noun) *is* p (predicate) (see Jackendoff 1987). It is comparable, for example, to the assertion that a stimulus object A belongs to the specific category Ω_1 or that B belongs to the category Ω_{394}. Discharge of any particular class cell can also be considered as a physical symbol (Derthick and Plaut 1986, Newell 1980) or token of the object (more accurately, of the object's proximal neuronal analog in the imaging matrix) to which its coupled filter cell has been synaptically tuned.

On the other hand, when the imaging matrix is excited by the input of a class cell collateral, the deep distribution of synaptic weights causes a surface response on the mosaic array that is an analog of some particular stimulus object. In effect, activation of a specific physical predicate evokes an analog representation of its proper subject—somewhat like depositing a monetary token in a slot and getting back its face value in currency. The ability of the synaptic matrix to operate interactively and with facility in the domains of both analogical and propositional representation provides an efficient biological mechanism for higher-order cognitive processing.

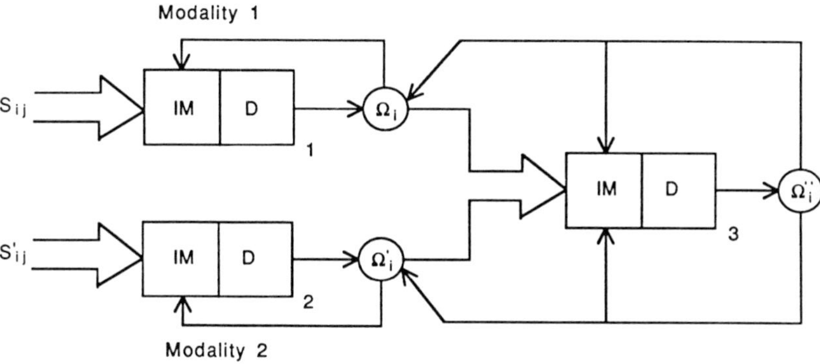

Figure 3.5
Flow diagram of three synaptic matrices in a feedforward-feedback network. Parallel inputs from two different sensory modalities. IM = imaging matrix; D = detection matrix.

Networks of Matrices

Up to this point, we have considered the basic capabilities of the synaptic matrix as a single neurocognitive module. Other important properties become evident when multiple synaptic matrices are organized in complex networks with parallel, feedforward, and feedback connections.

Figure 3.5 is a flow diagram illustrating three interconnected synaptic matrices. In this example, two separate modules (1 and 2) receive parallel volleys of stimulation from their respective sensory input modalities S_{ij} and S'_{ij} (vision and audition). The class cell outputs (Ω_i and Ω'_i) of these matrices, in turn, constitute an input vector to a third synaptic matrix that lacks direct access to the sensory arrays. After learning has occurred, each token Ω_i and Ω'_i can directly evoke an afferent image of its associated sensory pattern, but Ω''_i can directly only evoke a representation of its associated token inputs in its mosaic cell array. However, if associative excitatory collateral connections from class cells Ω''_i to Ω_i and Ω'_i are learned, output from the synaptic matrix that does not have access to sensory input (module 3) can indirectly evoke the sensory images originally associated with the class cells in sensory modules 1 and 2. In networks of this kind, the dendrites of class cells would have adaptive synapses just as mosaic cells do and would receive axon collaterals as feedback from the synaptic matrix at the next higher level (figure 3.6). Thus, a backward chain of selective excitation from higher-level class cells to lower-level class cells can elicit neuronal analogs of the appropriate

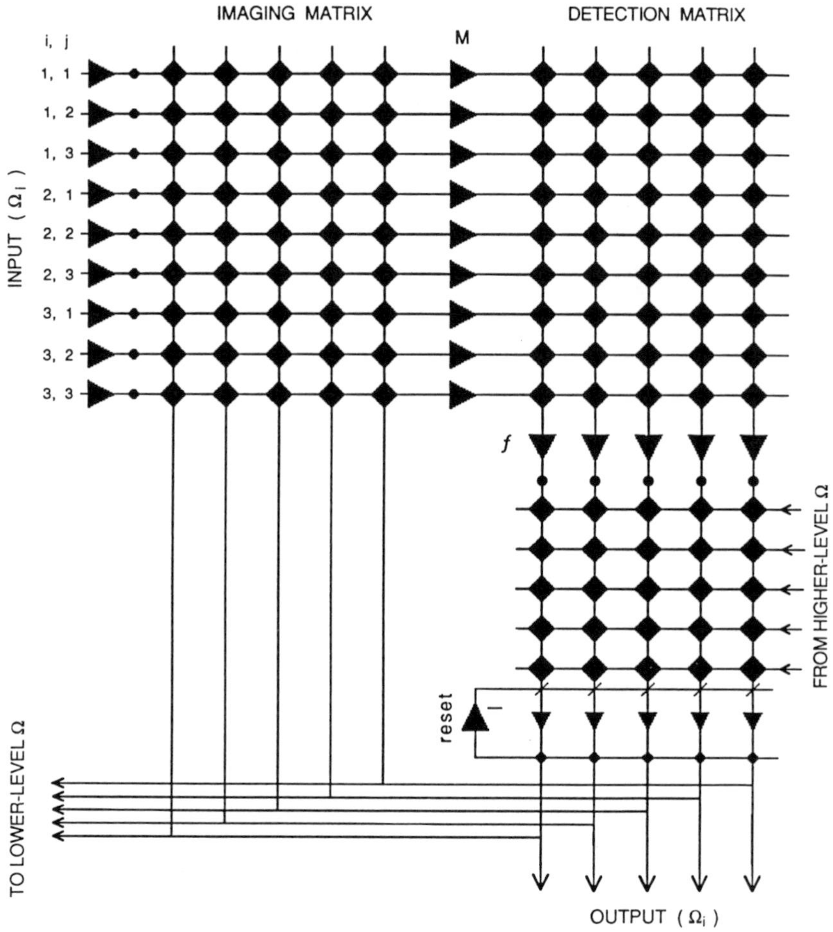

Figure 3.6
Schematic of a synaptic matrix in a network with feedback from a higher level to a lower level through adaptive class cells.

environmental stimuli. That analogs of endosomatic stimulus states (kinesthetic, somasthetic, vestibular) can also be recovered in the same fashion is implicit in this account.

The type-token distinction (Jackendoff 1985) can be roughly captured in a natural way in synaptic matrix networks of this kind. Class cells that signal particular exemplars of an object type (as in the sensory modules) can be taken as tokens of those objects, whereas class cells that fire in response to the input of any of a particular subset of class cell tokens are physical signals of the subset, and in effect, their activity announces a type name in the biological system. As synaptic matrices are cascaded, class cells can signal types of types (figure 3.7). Thus, neuronal representations at increasingly higher levels of abstraction can be instantiated in these putative brain networks. For example, in a feed-forward chain of synaptic matrices, my pet cat named Duffy can be represented by a series of distinct class cell signals as follows: Duffy (sitting on the floor in front of me) $\rightarrow \Omega_1$ (Duffy) $\rightarrow \Omega_2$ (cat) $\rightarrow \Omega_3$ (mammal) $\rightarrow \Omega_4$ (animal) $\rightarrow \Omega_5$ (animate). Moreover, given the backward-chaining mechanism illustrated in figure 3.6, excitation of any class cell in the chain can evoke appropriate subordinate representations as well as those that are superordinate.

Selective Association of Input and Output

So far, we have considered only models in which synaptic modification (learning) occurs as a result of an increase in arousal (excitatory bias) on all adaptive cells in the synaptic matrix. Since this kind of neuronal priming is diffuse, which particular filter cells will happen to fire in the presence of a stimulus and thus undergo a change in their distribution of synaptic transfer weights is a matter of chance (though the specific input-output mapping, once established, becomes a systematic property of the matrix). However, in order to achieve adaptive goals, it is necessary that particular stimuli be mapped onto just those output lines (class cells) that can evoke (either directly or indirectly) the appropriate behavioral responses.

Let us say that I already have vocalization routines in my motor repertoire that allow me to utter the words *Duffy* and *cat*. The problem is to forge privileged excitation paths from the retinal excitation pattern of Duffy (object) through its class cell token (Ω_1) to a cell that gates the utterance *Duffy* and from the first token (Ω_1) through another class cell (Ω_2, at a higher level of abstraction) to a cell that gates the utterance *cat*. The desired selection of associations will occur if, instead of initiating diffuse priming (general excitatory bias) of filter cells (f_i), only those f_i that are coupled to the appropriate class cells

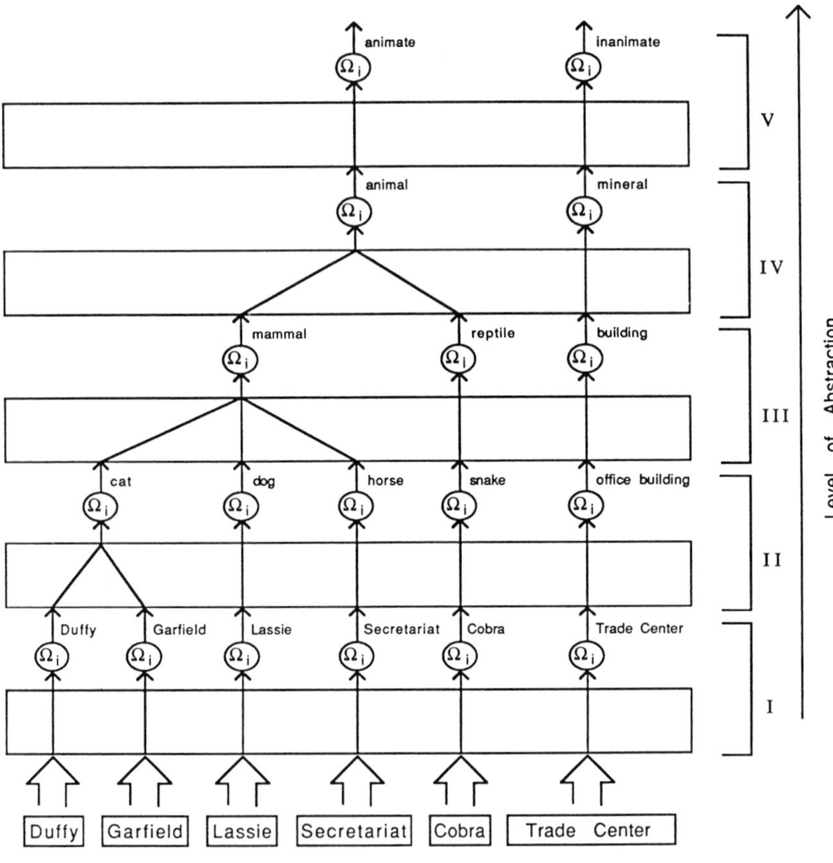

Figure 3.7
Flow diagram through five synaptic matrices. Token mappings from sensory input to progressively higher levels of abstraction.

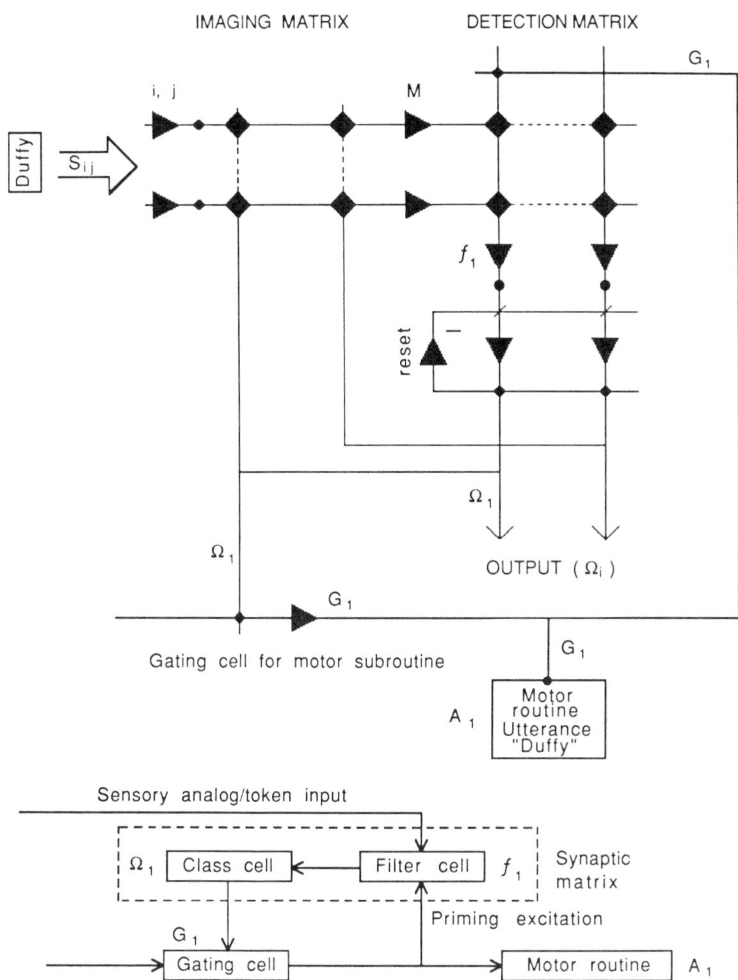

Figure 3.8
Top: Gating cell G_1 selectively primes a filter cell–class cell channel dedicated to a particular motor routine (A_1). *Bottom*: Simplified flow diagram of sensory motor loop. Analog (S_{ij}) or propositional (Ω) input learned by filter cell (f_1) becomes a potential trigger for its associated behavior.

are primed (in this case, f_1 and f_2). This can be accomplished if there is a collateral axonal-input line leading from each cell that gates a specific motor routine to a discrete filter cell in a synaptic matrix that is an adaptive processor of the retinal input. Figure 3.8 shows how the basic synaptic matrix is augmented to learn this kind of stimulus-response selectivity. In these networks, the initiation of a particular behavior in the presence of a particular stimulus (or a token of it) will induce a privileged excitation path from a class cell token of the stimulus to its coactivated behavior. Thus, if I say *Duffy* (vocally or subvocally) when I see the cat that is to be my household pet, this animal is labeled in my brain in two different ways: by a biological "name" (token Ω_1) and by a specific efferent routine that can generate the signal utterance *Duffy*. It is a specific claim of the model that all learned sensory/token-motor behaviors are mediated by action-dedicated neuronal loops of the form $G_1 \rightarrow f_1 \rightarrow \Omega_1 \rightarrow G_1$. After the filter cell in such a loop has been tuned to a particular input, any subsequent instance of this input can evoke the appropriate action.

Putting Motivation into the Network

In the previous examples, we considered two principal kinds of inputs to the synaptic matrix: exteroceptive sensory stimuli and class cell tokens of such stimuli. But motivational states produce specific interoceptive stimuli, and these can be processed in the same way as exteroceptive inputs. Thus, for example, an interoceptive vector that corresponds to the physiological state of hunger can be coded (mapped) to a class cell in a detection matrix, and activation of this cell can serve as a token in subsequent adaptive associations (Trehub 1970). For example, say that a hungry person wants to eat. Because there must be food available to eat, the joint tokens of hunger (Ω_1) and available food (Ω_2) must be activated to initiate the motor subroutines that constitute the act of eating. The double $\Omega_1\Omega_2$ tokens could constitute a pattern that is mapped to Ω_3 in a sensory motor loop that gates the action of eating. In this case, Ω_1 alone would be in a sensory motor loop that gates the look-for-food subroutines (go to the refrigerator, open the door, take an apple). After completion of the search behavior induced by Ω_1, the sensory input evoked by the apple would activate Ω_2, the condition for discharge of Ω_3 would be established, and the apple would be eaten.

This is a glimpse of how motivational and sensory tokens can be processed as joint patterns. As the structure and dynamics of the model are elaborated, we will see that high-level, goal-directed behavior can be initiated and adaptively controlled in networks of synaptic matrices.

Chapter 4

Modeling the World, Locating the Self, and Selective Attention: The Retinoid System

When we look at the world in front of us, we see a stable, coherent arrangement of objects and environmental features in a spatially extended layout. And when we recall a previously experienced scene, we visualize it in an appropriately integral fashion. Yet it is a physical fact that on any fixation, our window of sharp foveal vision allows us to register clearly only 2 to 5 degrees (at the most) of an extended frontal scene. Nevertheless, by a series of saccadic eye movements, we are able to construct in our brain a properly laid-out representation of the scene as observed from a particular viewpoint. Given that saccadic eye movements present a viewer with a series of scattered glimpses of a spatially extended visual environment, where all sharply defined visual impressions are superposed on the fovea, how can the visual system disentangle the overlaid fovea-centered images and construct an integrated veridical representation of the environment in an egocentric spatial frame?

This fundamental problem led me to hypothesize the existence and detail the neuronal structure of a dynamic postretinal buffer, which I call a retinoid, that in a layered system can register and appropriately combine disparate foveal stimuli into a proper unified representation of a larger real-world scene (Trehub 1977). In the process of modeling the retinoid, it became clear that, together with some relatively simple accessory mechanisms, it can perform many other important cognitive functions:

- Parsing objects in complex visual environments.
- Constructing visual representations of objects and scenes (veridical and/or hypothetical).
- Performing geometric and relational analysis of veridical and hypothetical objects or scenes.
- Locating a representation of oneself within a represented environment.
- Representing the paths of moving objects as well as self-excursion paths in complex environments.

- Effecting selective shifts of focal attention.
- Performing spatial translation of binocular images in stereopsis.

This module, like the retina, registers information in visual space and projects afferents to higher visual centers. It can organize successive retinocentric visual patterns into a unified egocentric or allocentric representation of object space. It serves as a visual scratch pad with spatially organized information stored as short-term memory. The mechanism of storage is assumed to be a retinotopically organized array of excitatory autaptic neurons (Shepherd 1979, van der Loos and Glaser 1972). In the retinoid, an autaptic cell that receives a transitory suprathreshold stimulus will continue to fire for some period of time if it is properly biased by another source of subthreshold excitatory input (arousal). Thus, a sheet of autaptic neurons can represent in its sustained discharge pattern any transitory organized input for as long as diffuse priming excitation is sustained (up to the limit of cell fatigue). If the priming background input is removed or sufficiently reduced, the captured pattern on the retinoid rapidly decays.

Figure 4.1 shows a retinoid composed of an array of autaptic neurons connected by a balanced grid structure of excitatory and inhibitory interneurons. Axon collaterals of shift control cells are in excitatory synapse with selected groups of these interneurons. Any momentary suprathreshold input from an afferent visual array to its homologous autaptic retinoid cells will evoke sustained firing of the retinoid targets if there is a sufficient level of diffuse tonic bias. Thus, any retinal stimulation induces a comparable retinoid pattern of spatially organized discharge. At the same time, each active autaptic neuron induces a subthreshold, priming excitatory postsynaptic potential (EPSP) in each of the eight contiguous interneurons capable of eliciting excitatory and inhibitory potentials (IPSP) in their targeted autaptic cells. A primed interneuron that receives a sufficient increment of excitation from one of the shift control cells will fire and send spike input to its target cell. The retinoid behaves according to the following implicit rules.

1. If an autaptic cell that is not discharging (off) receives sufficient EPSP from an interneuron, it will fire (turn on).
2. If an autaptic cell that is on receives IPSP from an interneuron, it will turn off unless it receives simultaneously EPSP from another interneuron, in which case it will remain on.
3. If diffuse excitatory bias to the retinoid falls below a critical level, all cells in the retinoid turn off.

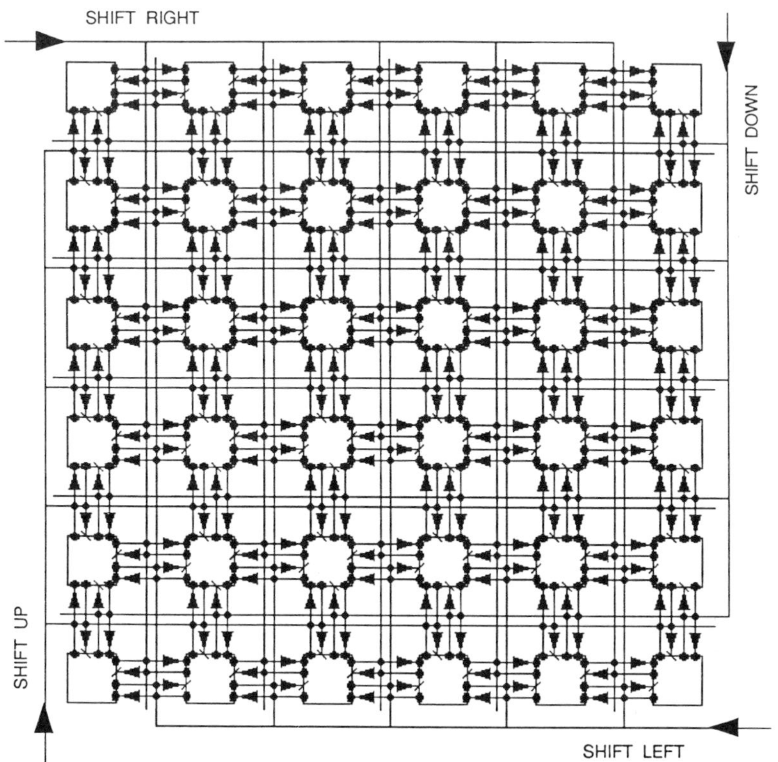

Figure 4.1
Translation retinoid. Squares represent autaptic cells serving short-term memory. Small, filled triangles between autaptic cells represent excitatory and inhibitory interneurons. Shift control cells designated by direction of effect.

Imagine that the sight of an object has evoked its pattern of retinotopic excitation on a normally biased retinoid. The visual pattern will be captured in short-term memory as a spatial analog on the retinoid; this captured pattern can be spatially translated in any direction by appropriate pulse (discharge spikes) from the shift control command cells. For example, a spike train from the shift-right line will transfer standing activity (via interneurons) from any active autaptic cell to the adjacent autaptic cell on its right and erase (via interneurons) the activity in the previously active donor (on the left) unless the donor is also receiving transfered excitation from its left-adjacent autaptic cell. Thus, sustained command discharges from the shift-right control cell will move the entire retinoid pattern to the right in successive increments of a single autaptic cell. Similarly, commands to shift left,

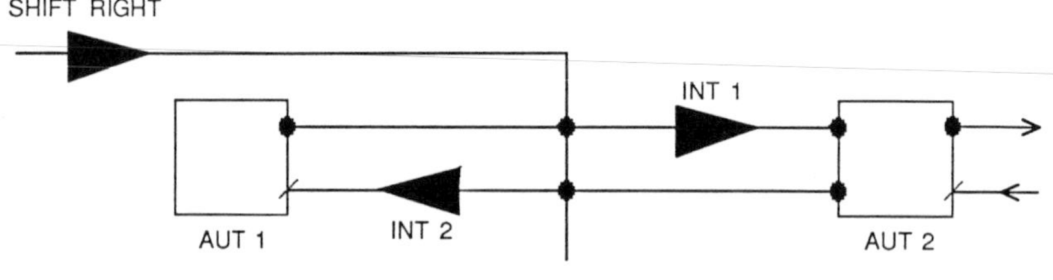

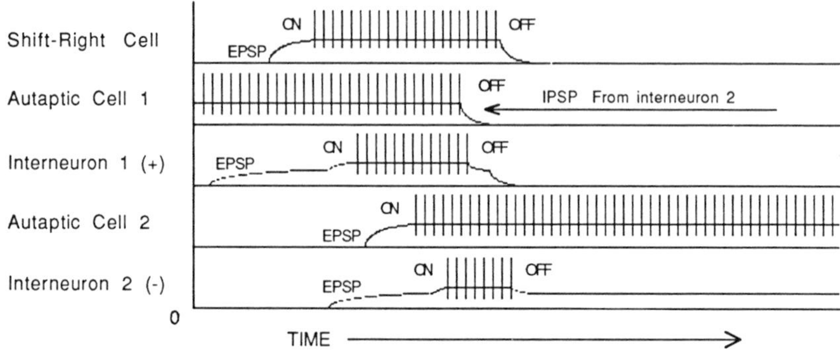

Figure 4.2
Top: Schematic showing two autaptic cells coupled by an excitatory (INT 1) and an inhibitory (INT 2) interneuron. With this arrangement, a pulse from the shift-right cell can transfer autaptic cell activity from left (AUT 1) to right (AUT 2) and inhibit the initial activity of AUT 1. *Bottom*: Illustration of the temporal course of EPSP integration, decay, and spike discharge in each of the five neurons depicted at top.

up, or down will move the captured pattern in the appropriate direction.

The schematic diagram of a local circuit within a retinoid shown at the top of figure 4.2 illustrates the synaptic connections involving a shift-right control cell at the junction between two autaptic cells and the two interneurons required to shift excitation on a retinoid from one autaptic unit to its autaptic neighbor on the right. The bottom part of the figure illustrates the sequence of EPSP and spike activity in each of the five neurons included in the circuit shown at the top as a stimulus is shifted from one autaptic cell to another. Temporally staggered directional pulses, such as right and up or left and down, will move the pattern in oblique directions, with the angle of translation depending on the relative frequencies of the component directional pulses. The higher the frequency is of the discharge spikes

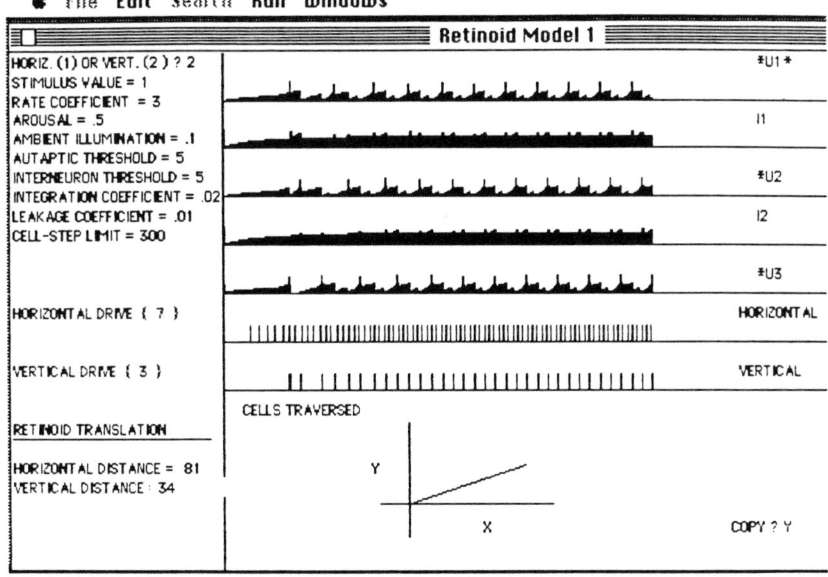

Figure 4.3
Screen printout of retinoid simulation. Lines labeled U show autaptic cell activity. Lines labeled I show interneuron activity. Relative shift-right rate = 7; relative shift-up rate = 3. Successive instances of autaptic cell transfer from left to right are shown on the line labeled HORIZONTAL. Successive instances of upward transfer are shown on the line labeled VERTICAL. In this simulation, initial retinoid activity was translated to a locus represented by a shift of 81 autaptic cells to the right and 34 cells in the vertical direction (shown on the X,Y plot at the bottom of the figure).

within the shift-control pulses, the more rapid will the retinoid representation move. The longer the pulse train is sustained, the greater will be the distance through which the representation is moved. Appropriate control pulse sequences of shift right/left and shift up/down can move a captured stimulus pattern to any position within retinoid space.

Figure 4.3 shows the results of a computer simulation in which a stimulus is translated to a position in the upper right quadrant of retinoid space by input from horizontal and vertical shift control cells. The final position (represented by the terminus of the oblique line within the X and Y axes at the bottom of the figure) is a function of the number of pulses on the shift control lines and the spike frequency within the directionally selective pulses.

Retinoid theory assumes that automatic spatial translation of retinoid patterns can occur when shift control neurons are driven by eye and/or head movements and by the discharge of cells in lower-level visual mechanisms that detect the motion of objects in the field of view. Cells of the latter type are selectively tuned to both the direction and velocity of motion in the visual field (Barlow, Hill, and Levick 1964; Benevento and Miller 1981). (It should be noted in passing that the translation of images across retinoids is probably also induced by signals from the vestibular apparatus, but detailed consideration of this topic is beyond my scope.)

In the case of pattern translation induced by eye or head motion, the direction in which a representation is shifted on a retinoid sheet is determined by the direction of gaze; the extent to which it is shifted is proportional to the visual angle between the current fixation and the egocentric reference projection, which I call the normal foveal axis. This is the retinoid's coordinate of origin for the egocentric frame. The normal foveal axis corresponds to the line of sight of the fovea when the eyes are straight ahead, the head unturned, and the shoulders square with the upright body.

The Retinoid System

A single retinoid cannot serve as a neuronal substrate for constructing and maintaining in short-term memory a coherent and reasonably accurate representation of a spatially extended scene. Suppose that looking to our right we see a tree and that this pattern is captured on the retinoid and shifted in accordance with the angle of gaze to its appropriate egocentric coordinates. Now if we look leftward and see a barn, its image would also be registered and shifted appropriately on the retinoid. However, a serious problem is encountered at this point: the very same shift-left pulses that translate the image of the barn to its proper retinoid location would also move the image of the tree from its former correct position to an incorrect one (more to the left than it should be). The solution to this problem lies in a layered system of intercommunicating retinoid registers (figure 4.4). With several retinoids in homologous projection, selectively coupled and decoupled, an extremely powerful mechanism is provided that can both assemble a coherent representation of visual space and also perform a variety of other integrative and analytic tasks (Trehub 1977).

In this chapter, we will examine the properties of a retinoid system capable of capturing and restructuring representations of object layouts in a three-dimensional visual environment. But before we deal with operations in 3-D space, it is necessary to describe how a module

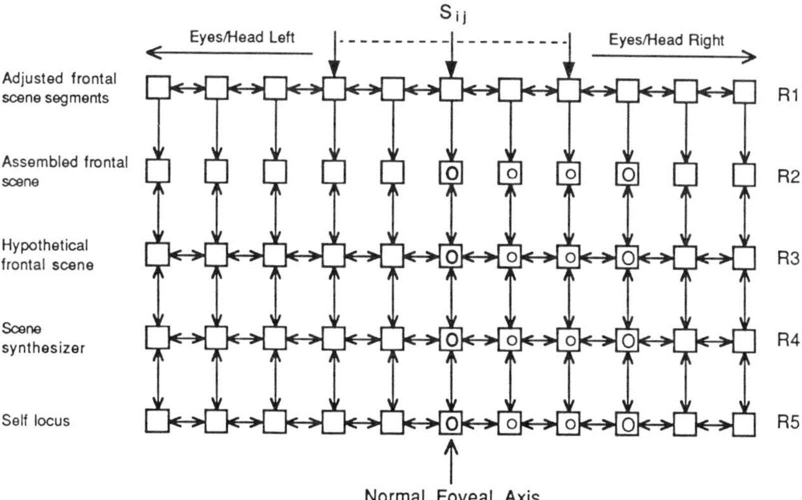

Figure 4.4
Stacked retinoid registers labeled R1–R5. Imagine a dimension of each retinoid array projecting orthogonally to the plane of the page in replicated autaptic cells. Arrows indicate the cells to which excitation can be transferred within the array. Self-locus designated by **0**. Heuristic self-locus designated 0. Excursion path designated o.

of layered retinoids processes inputs from the 2-D surface of the eye's retina.

Scene Assembly from a Two-Dimensional Projection

Let us assume a complete frontal scene to be all discriminable objects within an environment subtended by 180 degrees, with the vertex taken as the head in the normal frontal position. Since the receptive field for sharp monocular foveal vision is 2 to 5 degrees at most, it follows that the eye and/or the head must pivot (either in saccadic or smooth fashion) to scan the whole frontal scene. Thus, a sequence of excitation patterns will be evoked on the foveal region of the retina, and these must be represented in the brain in a way that conserves their real spatial relationships on the 2-D frontal plane.

Figure 4.4 shows a module consisting of a number of retinoid layers (R1–R5). The autaptic cells of each layer are in homologous and reciprocal projection (with the exception of an absence of R2 to R1 input) to the corresponding cells of the neighboring retinoids. The first layer (R1) receives retinotopic input (S_{ij}) from the foveal and near parafoveal region of the retina. Retinoid R1 is a translation retinoid in which the output of its shift control neurons is modulated by eye and/or head position. It is assumed that the direction and extent of pattern translation on this layer is directly proportional to the degree of eye and/or head shift from the normal foveal axis. As each scene segment is registered on R1 and appropriately shifted in accordance with eye and head position, it is immediately transferred in its proper relative egocentric location to a second nontranslating retinoid (R2) and then erased on R1 by reset inhibition to all cells in the first layer. With successive fixations, a complete and homologously ordered representation of the frontal scene can be assembled on R2, and this information will provide the larger scene context for particular sensory inputs. For simplicity of illustration, an example of a 180 degree frontal scene assembly has been given; however, it is clear that similar mechanisms can assemble a 360-degree scene. Notice that by transferring the retinal image from a retinoid driven by eye and head movements (R1) to another that is decoupled from eye and head movements (R2), positional errors in object representation due to inappropriate effects of shift-control signals are avoided.

Hypothetical Scenes

The retinoid layer labeled R3 in figure 4.4 can construct representations of hypothetical environmental situations (scenes). It is a translation array that receives veridical information from the assembled frontal scene (in R2) and internally fabricated patterns from the retinoid complex labeled R4, called a scene synthesizer. The scene synthesizer consists of two translation retinoids coupled as a functional unit so that either can serve as a stable storage buffer while the other may be engaged in moving excitation patterns from one place to another in its representational space. The source of these patterns can be inputs from other retinoids, memories recalled and projected from the mosaic array in the synaptic matrix, or tracings created by movements of the heuristic self-locus. The combined output of the retinoids in the scene synthesizer is projected to R3. Thus, whereas R2 in figure 4.4 represents the current veridical scene, R3, by combining and spatially rearranging veridical, remembered, and/or fabricated object representations, can create complex hypothetical frontal scenes. With neuronal mechanisms that will be described later, retinoid scenes can be tested according to individual needs. If the properties of a hypothetical scene are judged better than those of a veridical scene and if the person is able to change the environment so that the veridical scene conforms to the hypothetical, the environment may be changed or reorganized to this end.

Self-Location

In order for one to engage in effective behavior within the local environment and to assess the personal consequences of various external states, one must have some internal representation of the real and hypothetical spatial relationships between oneself and other significant objects in veridical space. The self-locus retinoid, together with the other retinoid registers shown in figure 4.4, serves this purpose.

The self-locus retinoid can be thought of as a standard translation retinoid that has no afferent input but does have the capability of point-to-point output projection to other retinoids. The self-locus register is distinctive in that it maintains a uniquely coded region of autaptic discharge with its central "point" located at the center of retinoid space. This fixed position of self-locus corresponds to the normal foveal axis. Autaptic neurons representing the central self-location (the "home" location of the self, so to speak) are constantly active, and autaptic discharge originating from this source of excitation can be spatially translated to any position on the surface of the retinoid by the usual shift control commands. Such heuristic locations and excursion paths of the self-locus can be projected to other retinoids and can be combined with real and/or hypothetical objects and scenes that may be represented on their surfaces to construct internal maps representing goal regions, obstacles, and direct and indirect paths to a goal.

Selective Attention

An important consequence arises from the ability to move replicated excitation from the source point of self-locus to selected regions of retinoid space: the autaptic cells in those regions of a retinoid that are stimulated by the added local excitation of a self-locus excursion (the heuristic self-locus) are preferentially primed and marked relative to other cells in the retinoid grid. These events provide a biological substrate for selective attention on the following bases: cells in a primed region respond more quickly and vigorously than those in other regions, and the heuristic self-locus marker can serve as a spatial reference so that the simple reverse of a self-locus excursion command can be used directly to back-translate any stimulus pattern found at the heuristic coordinate. The latter operation will shift a representation of the environmental pattern so that the region of interest will fall on the normal foveal axis, the source coordinate of the self-locus (figure 4.5). Once the stimulus is in this position, the pattern can be projected to the mosaic array, where it can be recognized with maximum acuity in the detection matrix. In a multilayered retinoid system, it is possible to have two (or more) simultaneous

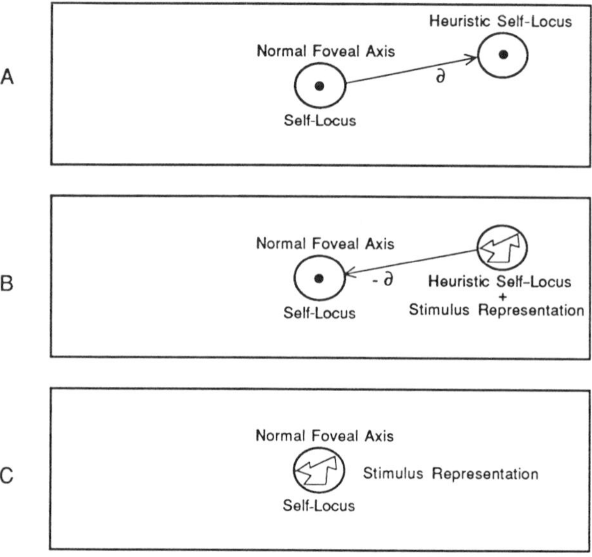

Figure 4.5
Selective attention by excursion of the self-locus. *A*: Priming a region of retinoid space by an excursion of the self-locus that is induced by shift control command ∂. *B*: Stimulus pattern appears in primed region of retinoid. Reversal of the sign of the shift control command ($-\partial$) translates both the heuristic self-locus and the stimulus back to the normal foveal axis. *C*: Stimulus pattern standardized at normal foveal axis where it can be projected to the synaptic matrix to be learned or recognized.

representations of a visual environment—for instance, one with the region of interest at its veridical coordinate with respect to the normal foveal axis and the other with the region of interest translated so that it is centered on the normal foveal axis or both of the layouts together with a representation of a hypothetical scene.

The neuronal process described makes it possible for a person to shift attention covertly over different regions of visual space without corresponding eye movements (Posner 1980; Posner, Snyder, and Davidson 1980; Shulman, Remington, and McClean 1979). Indeed, I suspect that when the tools of neuroscience are sufficiently advanced, it will be found that shifts in the heuristic self-locus normally precede saccades and play an integral role in the programming of saccadic eye movements. Recent findings about the relationship between saccades to visual and auditory targets and the discharge characteristics of single cells in the superior colliculus tend to support this view

(Mays and Sparks 1980, Sparks and Mays 1983, Sparks and Jay 1987). In a summary of their investigations, Sparks and Jay (1987) conclude that it is the difference between a current eye position and a desired position that determines the direction and extent of the subsequent saccade. The retinoid model assumes that heightened autaptic cell activity, induced by the heuristic self-locus at its resting coordinate, always marks a "desired" eye position, at least in the sense of targeting a localized region of space to be explored. It follows from this formulation that unless eye movements are inhibited, the point of foveal fixation will normally correspond to the resting coordinate of the heuristic self-locus.

Finding and Positioning Pattern Centroids

In normal viewing, the projected image of an object of interest commonly is not centered on the fovea. Saccadic fixations on regions of the visual field do not ensure that the image of an object in a circumscribed region will be centered on the normal foveal axis even if the retinoid representation of that region is translated back to this reference coordinate of the self-locus. For the purpose of efficient learning and subsequent recognition of objects, it is desirable that patterns be positioned in a standard way before they are gated to the synaptic matrix, either to be learned or to be recognized by a best match against a particular profile of synaptic weights in the detection matrix. One way of accomplishing this is to provide a mechanism that ensures that the centroid of an excitation pattern on a retinoid will be shifted automatically so that it falls on the normal foveal axis.

Figure 4.6 illustrates how the standardization of image position is achieved in a retinoid system (Trehub 1986, 1990). Imagine a retinoid structure as if it were organized quadrantally, with each quadrant of its surface receiving retinotopic afferents from its respective retinal quadrant. On a given fixation, if the excitation of a captured pattern is summed independently over each quadrant of the retinoid and if the relative magnitudes of the summed discharges are used to drive its shift control cells, we then have a postretinal neuronal mechanism that can align the centroid of any parafoveal stimulus with the central axis of retinoid space (the normal foveal axis).

In the algorithm shown at the bottom of figure 4.6, each active autaptic cell represents one unit of excitation. The value of the difference in total excitation between the left and right hemifields is compared to a threshold that represents error tolerance (ET), where error is, in effect, determined by the degree of mismatch in excitation. As long as error tolerance is exceeded, a signal is sent to the appropriate

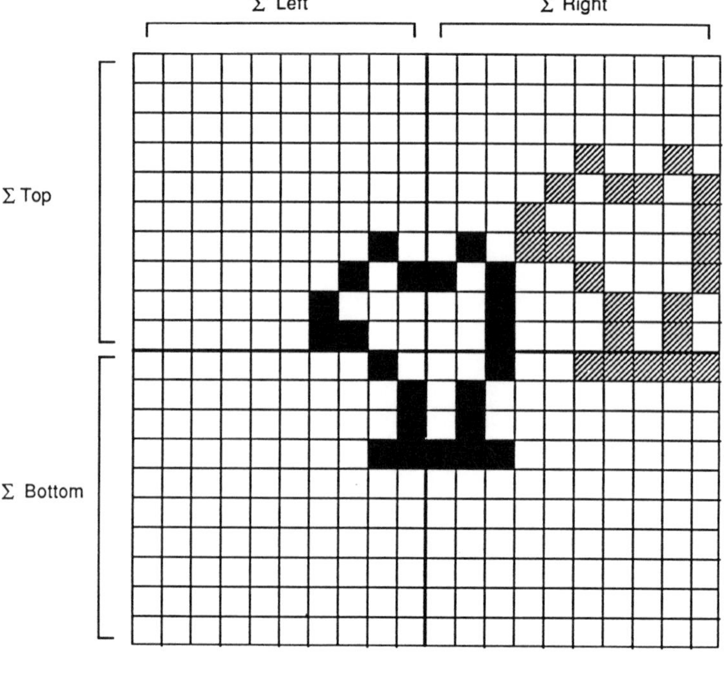

[(Σ Left - Σ Right) > ET] ====> Shift Right

[(Σ Right - Σ Left) > ET] ====> Shift Left

[(Σ Top - Σ Bottom) > ET] ====> Shift Down

[(Σ Bottom - Σ Top) > ET] ====> Shift Up

Figure 4.6
Quadrantally organized retinoid. Intersection of vertical and horizontal axes defines normal foveal axis. Each square represents an autaptic cell. Excitation evoked by a stimulus pattern is summed independently for each of the vertical and horizontal hemifields. The algorithm shown at the bottom of the figure shifts a pattern so that its centroid falls on the normal foveal axis. Diagonally hatched cells show initial retinoid position of a parafoveal stimulus. Solid cells show the stimulus with its centroid on the normal foveal axis after it has been shifted to balance mismatches in quadrantal excitation.

shift control cell to drive the retinoid pattern in a direction that reduces error (to the left if excitation in the right hemifield is greater than in the left and to the right if excitation in the left hemifield is greater). Exactly the same kind of mechanism adjusts the position of a pattern of excitation over the top and bottom fields. Thus, mismatches of excitation across the retinoid hemifields modulate the activity of shift control cells so that excitation is balanced over the retinoid quadrants (within error tolerance) and bring the centroid of an image to the normal foveal axis.

It is easy to see how an algorithm like the one presented can find a pattern centroid and position it on the desired axis. What minimal neuronal mechanism can perform the necessary computation? Figure 4.7 shows a schematic of a neuronal circuit that can do the job. Each active autaptic cell stimulates a paired interneuron (int), which provides excitatory input to a hemifield summation cell—L for summation of all left-field excitation and R for summation of all right-field excitation. Cells L and R are competitively cross-coupled by a pair of inhibitory interneurons so that the level of activity (output frequency) in the dominant summation cell increases as a function of the difference in activity between these two cells (reflecting the disparity in retinoid activity across the hemifields). Cell RC receives as its input and output of the left-field summation cell (L), and it commands the retinoid pattern to shift to the right. Cell LC receives as its input the output of the right-field summation cell (R), and it commands the retinoid pattern to shift to the left. If the activity of L is greater than R, neuron RC (having the steeper integration slope) will fire before LC, and the representation on the retinoid will be shifted a unit to the right. At the same time, the reset cell (marked −) will drive the membrane potential of both RC and LC to baseline, and the process will recycle as long as the hemifield mismatch is above error tolerance. The cell labeled "Tolerance" in figure 4.7 sets the level of inhibitory bias on the hemifield summation cells so that the higher the error tolerance is (reflecting the magnitude of inhibitory bias), the greater will be the disparity in retinoid field input to L and R that is required to initiate a pattern shift across the retinoid surface. It is assumed that error tolerance is normally proportional to the size of the retinoid pattern (small objects have low error tolerance; large objects have higher error tolerance). In this example, the mechanism for balancing left and right hemifields was described. The same kind of neuronal structure balances top and bottom hemifields in the process of finding and positioning the centroid of an image.

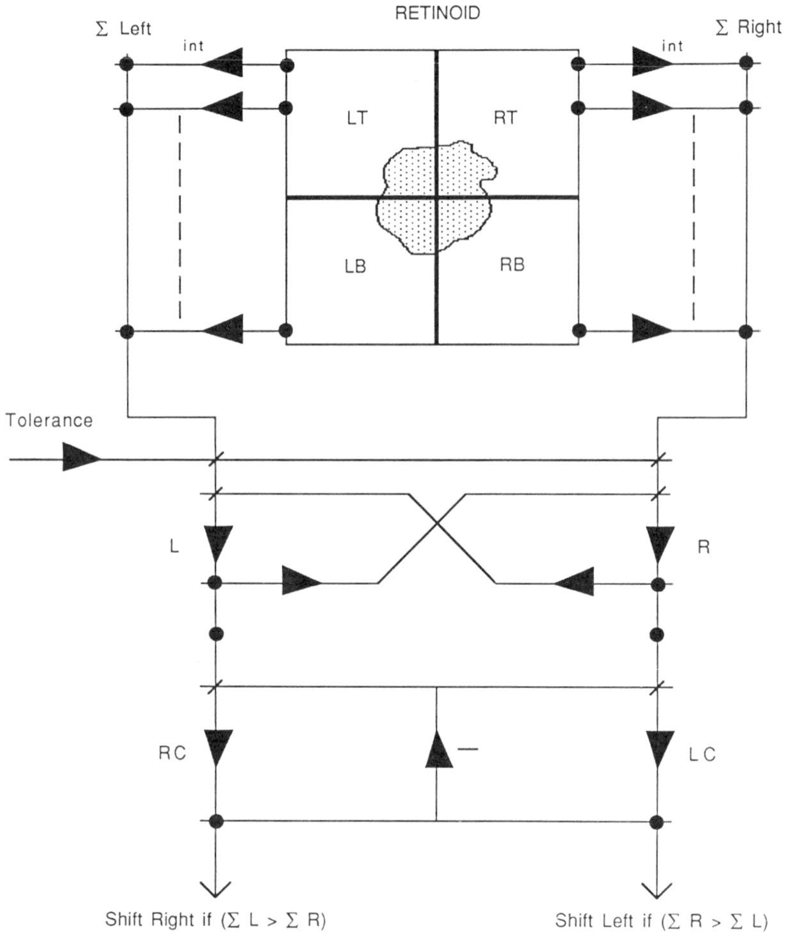

Figure 4.7
Schematic of neuronal mechanism for finding and positioning pattern centroids.

Depth Perception and Stereoscopic Vision

The mechanisms outlined can account for some essential visual-cognitive processes in a 2-D space. The network described here can integrate monocular retinoid outputs in a full binocular system to achieve depth perception and stereopsis in 3-D visual space.

A neuronal structure for stereoscopic vision is illustrated in schematic fashion in figure 4.8, which shows the arrangement of sensory and neuronal elements required for depth perception at one horizontal plane in the binocular visual field—a plane defined along the x-axis (L to R) for the horizontal dimension and along the z-axis in depth. Each small square in the strips designated "left-eye retina" and "right-eye retina" is assumed to contain a uniform 2-D array of retinal receptors and associated ganglion cells. The retinal image at each eye is transmitted retinotopically as a binary-coded edge transform to its associated retinoid, where it is mapped to the egocentric frame and shifted in accordance with the direction and degree of eye deviation from the normal foveal axis. Thus, the position of the visual pattern on each monocular retinoid corresponds to the relative angular position of objects and their features in the frontal field of each eye.

Correlation Clusters

Each diamond-shaped box in the 3-D retinoid shown at the bottom part of figure 4.8 contains a single cluster of retinotopically organized neurons corresponding to the ganglion cells that provide their sensory inputs through the two monocular retinoids. Thus, every cell in each 3-D cluster receives two afferent axons: one relayed from its corresponding ganglion cell in the left-eye retinoid and the other from its corresponding cell in the right-eye retinoid. Each diagonal string of cell clusters in the 3-D retinoid in figure 4.8 represents a line-of-sight array. The principal function of each cluster is to perform a cross-correlation between the micropatterns of inputs arriving from the left eye and the right eye. For this reason, these cell clusters are called correlation clusters (Trehub 1978).

The basic neuronal circuitry of a correlation cluster is shown in figure 4.9. Each of the nine principal cells in the cluster innervates a paired inhibitory neuron, which, in turn, synapses with all other principal cells in the cluster (note that it does not have an inhibitory synapse on its paired principal cell). It is assumed that all inhibitory neurons in this network are of the low-saturation type; they reach a constant peak output at minimal sensory input to their paired presynaptic cell. The magnitude of the correlation between the two micro-

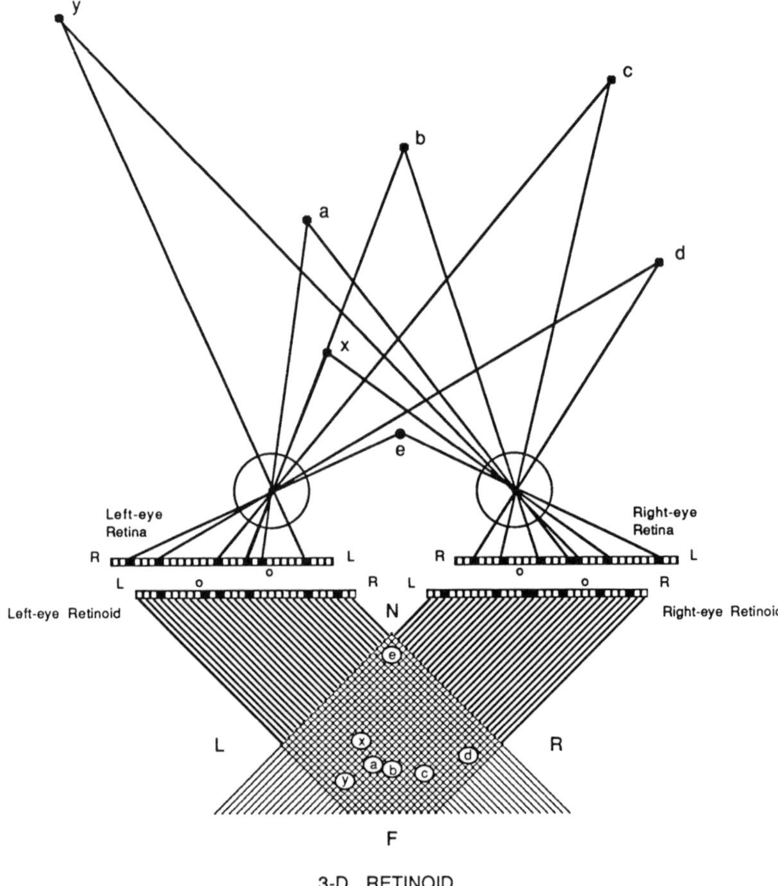

Figure 4.8
Schematic of binocular visual system. Imagine all retinoid elements stacked orthogonally to the plane of the page. Lowercase letters at top of figure represent objects in space with their projections to left-eye and right-eye retinas. Line-of-sight projections from each object terminate on filled squares representing stimulated retinal cells. Left-eye and right-eye retinoids are depicted just below their corresponding retinas. Filled retinoid squares represent stimulated autaptic cells. L and R indicate left and right visual fields. Notice that retinal representations are transformed at each retinoid to correspond with the relative egocentric positions of objects in terms of monocular visual angle. Diamond-shaped cells in the 3-D retinoid represent correlation clusters (A_j) that are innervated by intersecting retinotopic axon projections from the left-eye and right-eye retinoids. N (at top of 3-D retinoid) indicates the near visual field. F (at bottom of 3-D retinoid) indicates the far visual field. Lowercase letters within the 3-D retinoid indicate correlation clusters having maximum evoked activity in response to the corresponding objects in the visual field. The N-F dimension defines the Z-axis. Rows of correlation clusters orthogonal to the Z-axis define Z-planes (disparity planes; depth planes). Notice that relative depth discrimination decreases with object distance.

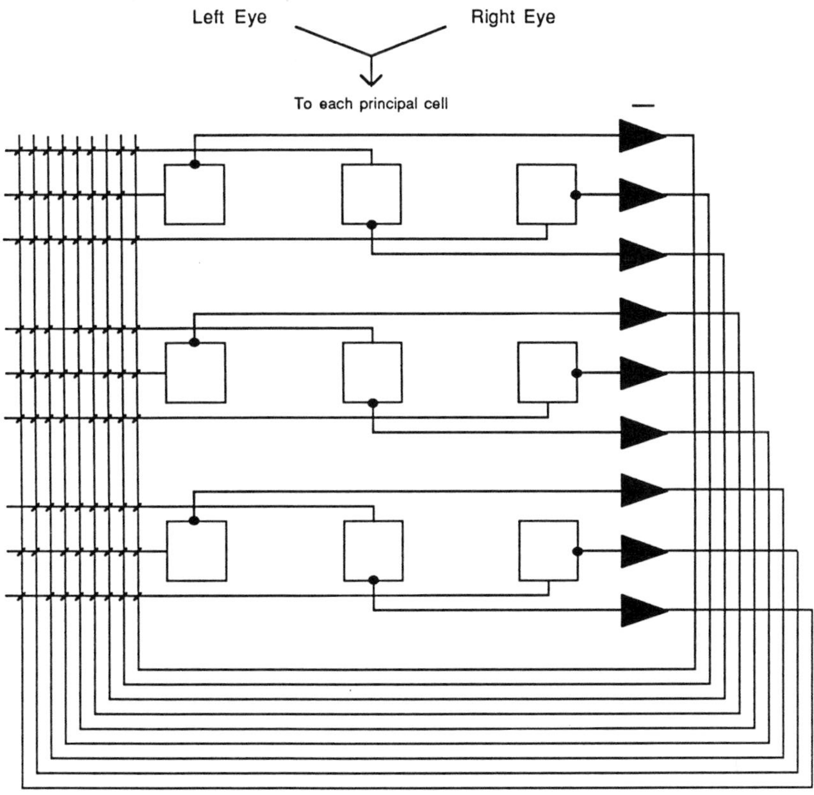

Figure 4.9
Correlation cluster (A_j). Squares represent principal cells of correlation cluster. Small, solid triangles represent inhibitory interneurons ($-$).

patterns impinging from the left and right retinas on each cluster is given by the total discharge density over all principal cells in the correlation cluster. Assuming that the output of each principal cell increases one unit for each active sensory input, we can write

$$E_j = k + \sum_{i=1}^{n} \dot{\mu}_{ij}\alpha_{ij} - \sum_{i=1}^{n} b(\dot{\mu}_{ij}\beta_{ij}) \qquad (4.1)$$

where E_j is the total output of correlation cluster j; k is the endogenous cluster activity constant; $\dot{\mu}_{ij}$ is the ith stimulated principal cell of correlation cluster j; α_{ij} is the number of active sensory inputs on $\dot{\mu}_{ij}$ (1 or 2); β_{ij} is equal to $\sum_{i=1}^{n} \dot{\mu}_{ij} - 1$, the number of active inhibitory inputs on $\dot{\mu}_{ij}$; b is the coefficient of inhibition.

Brightening Neurons

Total output (E_j) from each correlation cluster (A_j) in each line-of-sight cluster string stimulated by the dominant eye converges on an associated neuron I call a brightening cell (λ) (figure 4.10), an excitatory neuron that sends an axon collateral to every principal cell in its paired correlation cluster, provides input for an inhibitory neuron that connects to all A_j in its line-of-sight string, and sends a horizontally and vertically oriented axon collateral to all principal cells along its disparity (Z-plane) row and column in the 3-D retinoid (see figure 4.8).

Given a pattern of binocular input, each brightening cell (λ) integrates E_j from its associated correlation cluster (A_j). Assuming uniform spike thresholds for all λ, the latency of discharge for λ will be a monotonic function of the magnitude of stereoscopic correlation at its associated A_j. Within any line-of-sight string of A_j (with respect to the dominant eye), the first brightening cell to fire inhibits all activity in all correlation clusters except its associated A_j (which receives an increment of feedback excitation from the active λ that is sufficient to null-out the inhibitory input). Thus, only those principal cell groups that correspond to the highest binocular cross-correlation of pattern fragments at each dominant line-of-sight cluster string in the 3-D retinoid will be active. Unless the images of an object seen with both eyes are significantly distorted by normal visual parallax, a single veridical micropattern or a pair of identical micropatterns projecting to the same horizontal retinal plane and within the range of stereoscopic fusion will yield the highest intercorrelation. Since the latter condition (two concurrent identical micropatterns in the range

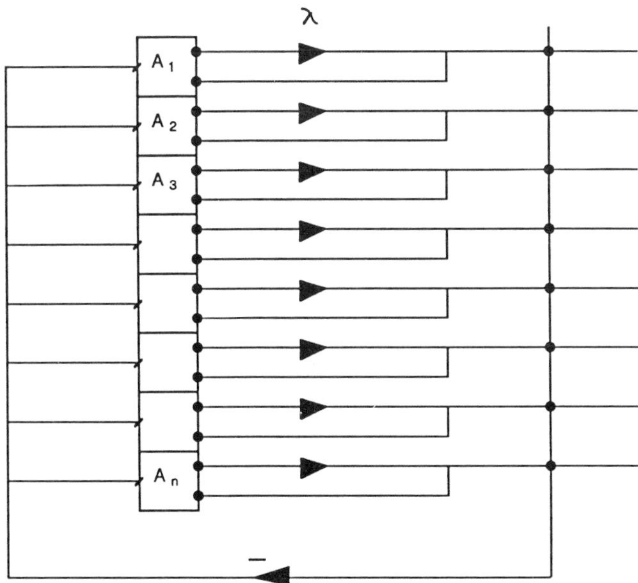

Figure 4.10
Line-of-sight string of correlation clusters (A_j; $j = 1, 2, 3, \ldots, n$) with associated brightening cells (λ) and squelching neuron (−). Each dot represents an excitatory contact with all cells in A_j, and each diagonal slash represents an inhibitory contact with all cells in A_j.

of fusion) is highly unlikely to occur in nature without deliberate contrivance, this putative neuronal mechanism should be effective in squelching false binocular targets.

Julesz (1971) has provided an interesting demonstration of how 3-D shapes can be perceived binocularly in the absence of any monocular shape information. If a 2-D random pattern of dots is presented as a stimulus to one eye and the other eye is simultaneously stimulated with the same pattern having some of its surface slightly offset horizontally, the offset regions appear as discrete shapes at different depths depending on the direction and degree of offset. Monocular viewing of either display reveals nothing but a 2-D dot pattern. The binocular disparity information in the random dot stereogram is sufficient to induce a vivid perception of bounded dot patterns at various depths (Z-planes), and the patterns are seen as belonging to coherent shaped surfaces. The neuronal mechanism for stereopsis described responds similarly. At each Z-plane, the veridical input is conserved in the pattern of stimulus-evoked excitation, which, in turn, is embedded in a flux of low-level excitation projected to all principal cells

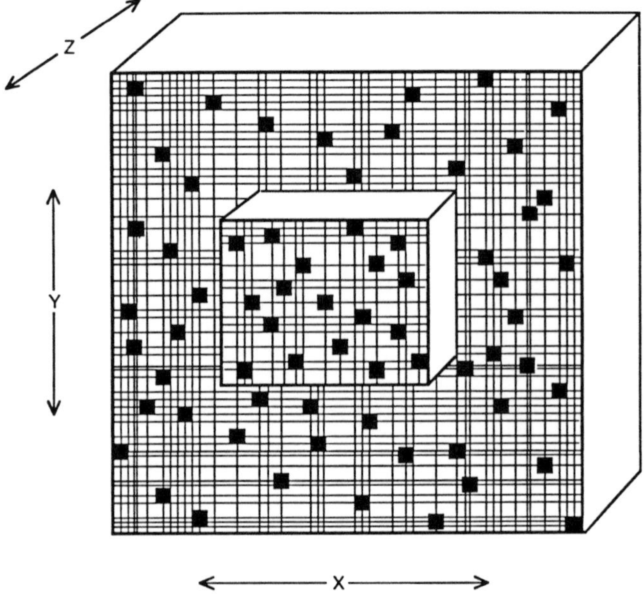

Figure 4.11
Enhancement of planar surfaces (Z-plane brightening in 3-D retinoid). Surface excitation is distributed en passant (Shepherd 1979) to principal cells in each correlation cluster (A_j) via brightening cell (λ) collaterals oriented along the x- and y-axis on Z-planes defined by the stimulus-evoked discharge of the clusters together with complementary inhibition along line-of-sight cluster strings (see figure 4.8). Nodes of excitation are densely distributed over the planar surfaces at the regions of λ-collateral intersection. Brightening cells are represented by solid squares. Lines projecting from each cell represent axon collaterals.

in the plane by λ axon collaterals (Z-plane brightening; see figure 4.11). Sharp planar boundaries are established by the abrupt inhibition of brightening in the appropriate region of one plane and the evocation of adjacent brightening on a different plane in accordance with the activity of correlation clusters and their coupled λ-cells on the Z-axis.

An Example of Performance

This stereopsis model was simulated, using random dot stereograms, to assess performance (Trehub 1978). Each correlation cluster (A_j) in the 3-D retinoid consisted of nine principal cells arranged in a square array as shown in figure 4.9. Random dot stereograms were generated by computer, with each black dot representing a point of stimulation to be registered on the retina. Dot density was arbitrarily set

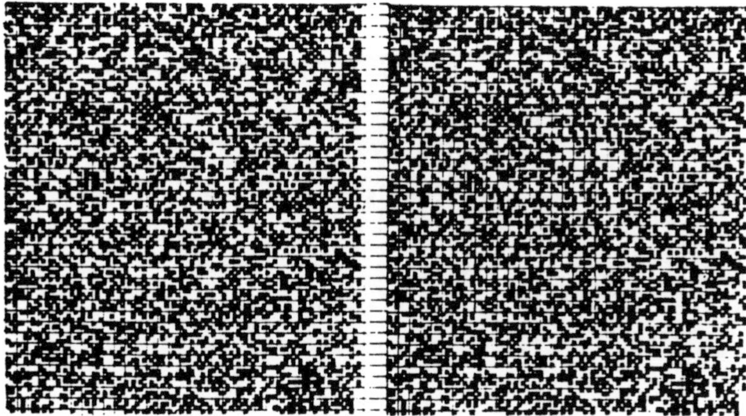

Figure 4.12
Random dot stereograms used as binocular stimuli for simulation test of 3-D retinoid model. Random dot density, 40 percent. Left, pattern A; right, pattern B, identical except for dot displacement. Each A_j cluster is indicated by grid overlay. In pattern B, a large vertically oriented rectangular area of dots has been displaced three A_j units to the left, and within this rectangular area a small square region has been displaced five A_j units to the left with respect to A. Pattern A stimulates left regina. Pattern B stimulates right retina. Source: Trehub 1978. Copyright Academic Press (London) Ltd. Reproduced by permission.

at 40 percent (figure 4.12). Retinal activity was assumed to be appropriately shifted in the left-eye and right-eye retinoids with reference to egocentric spatial coordinates and projected from each monocular retinoid as line-of-sight units of stimulation to the corresponding principal cells in the 3-D retinoid.

The initial output of each correlation cluster (A_j) was determined by equation 4.1, where the endogenous activity constant (k) was arbitrarily set at $k = 10$ and the coefficient of inhibition (b) was set at $b = 0.4$. Excitation on each principal cell from plane-brightening neurons (λ) on each plane over the Z-axis was arbitrarily set at $\lambda = 0.05$ and limited to $\lambda = 0.10$ at cross-over nodes (see figure 4.11). On the basis of the squelching principle and illustrated in figure 4.10, the correlation cluster (A_j) yielding the highest output in each line-of-sight string from the dominant eye inhibited all other cell clusters in its string.

The random dot stimuli presented to each eye are shown in figure 4.12; the result of the simulation test is shown in figure 4.13. The model discriminated the disparity planes (Z-planes) correctly, assigned the proper boundary contours to each of the patterns in depth, and conserved the original surface information.

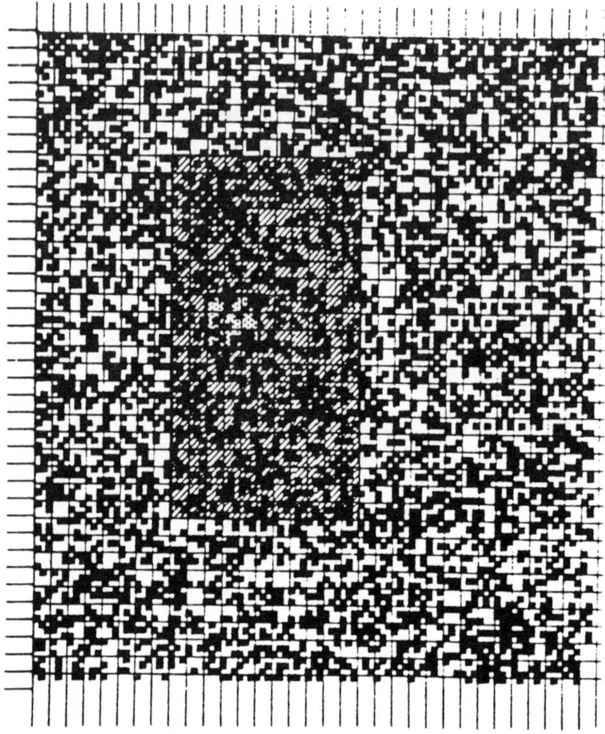

Figure 4.13
Result of simulation test. Large, diagonally hatched rectangular area is "seen" (represented) in midground of 3-D retinoid. Small, stippled square area within hatched rectangle is seen as nearest. Unmarked area is seen as background (behind the other surfaces on Z-axis). Planar coherence is established by contour-demarcated brightening on each Z-plane. Internal planar details are conserved. Source: Ibid. Copyright Academic Press (London) Ltd. Reproduced by permission.

Other Properties of the Retinoid System

The retinoid system and similar neuronal mechanisms based on the dynamic characteristics of autaptic cells can provide a variety of visual-cognitive functions in addition to those considered so far. Two of these properties are described below; other functions, some of which depend on system integration with other circuits, will be introduced in later chapters.

3-D Representation in Monocular Viewing

Beyond the capability of the 3-D retinoid to represent the depth of objects and surfaces on the basis of binocular disparity, there is the fact that depth perception is normally adequate even in the case of monocular viewing. Furthermore, a strong sense of depth can be experienced when we look at 2-D perspective drawings of 3-D objects. From a psychological standpoint, there are a number of cues that are known to contribute to depth perception (relative size, interposition, aerial perspective), but we will consider two biological processes that regulate the 3-D retinoid so that objects in depth are represented on appropriate Z-planes in monocular perception.

The sensory-motor structures that govern ocular convergence and accommodation are assumed to generate corollary signals that provide excitatory bias to the appropriate Z-planes in the 3-D retinoid. For example, in the case of convergence, an inward rotation of the eyes (even with one eye occluded) to achieve fixation of a near object in the central frontal field would selectively bias Z-planes representing near space. The greater the degree of inward rotation is, the closer is the retinoid representation of the object; the less the degree of inward rotation is, the more distant is the representation on the Z-axis. Accommodation influences the 3-D retinoid in a similar fashion. The more convex the lens of the eye is, the nearer would be the Z-planes receiving excitatory bias; the less convex, the more distant would be the representational planes that are biased. Notice that the preferential priming of a particular retinoid plane has an effect comparable to that given by a peak binocular correlation on that plane; in each case, correlation clusters that fall on other planes along a common line-of-sight string are inhibited.

3-D Imagery

Individuals are able to imagine a previously viewed object at different distances in response to an instruction to do so (Kosslyn 1978, 1980). The 3-D retinoid provides a physical explanation for this capability.

Figure 4.14 illustrates how this can be done. An image evoked on

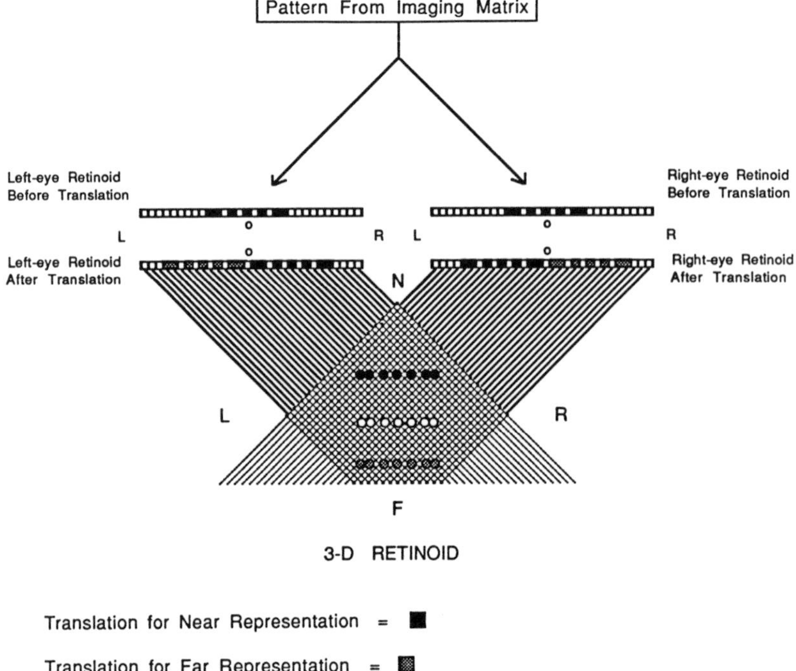

Figure 4.14
Moving imaginary patterns in depth. Input from imaging matrix is captured in the left-eye and right-eye retinoids. Initial position of the pattern within the 3-D retinoid is indicated by unfilled circles. Binocular translation in the medial direction (black squares) moves the image nearer in the 3-D retinoid (black circles). Translation in the temporal direction (stippled squares) moves the image farther away in the 3-D retinoid (stippled circles).

the mosaic cell array by a class cell collateral to the imaging matrix is sent as a retinotopic pattern to both the left-eye and right-eye retinoids. These captured patterns can then be translated in opposite lateral directions by appropriate pulses to the shift control cells governing such retinoid. The result of this operation will be to move the representation of the imagined object along the Z-axis in the 3-D retinoid. For example, if a common pattern is translated to the left on the left-eye retinoid and to the right on the right-eye retinoid, its representation on the 3-D retinoid will shift to a more distant Z-plane. Reversal of the direction of translation in the left-eye and right-eye retinoids will bring the imagined object closer in 3-D representational space (figure 4.14).

Chapter 5
Accessory Circuits

In principle, the synaptic matrix and the retinoid system can perform important cognitive operations in the networks of the brain. For these neuronal modules to function effectively, however, given the normal range of variation in stimulus properties and the constantly shifting relationships between an individual and significant objects within the immediate environment, the brain's basic modules must be augmented by appropriate accessory circuits. This chapter describes a number of such accessory mechanisms and shows how they work with the synaptic matrix and the retinoid registers.

Dendrodendritic Gradients of Excitation

The simulation tests of the synaptic matrix described in chapter 3 assumed a discrete point-to-point projection of excitation going from each active cell in the afferent bundle to its corresponding cell in the mosaic array within a retinotopic coordinate frame (see, for example, figure 3.2). The problem with this kind of strict channeling of excitation is that it results in brittle performance. An object that was learned in one retinotopic position could be abruptly mismatched against its synaptic profile on a test of recognition if its retinal location deviated even slightly from the position in which it was originally learned. Performance would be more robust if the synaptic representation on filter cells were composed of a gradient of transfer weights (ϕ) with peak values corresponding to the input coordinates of the originally learned stimulus and having progressivly decreasing ϕ values at neighboring points.

Illustrated at the top of figure 5.1 is a retinotopically organized neuronal array with dendrodendritic synapses between each of its neighboring cells. This structure is assumed to serve during learning as a local diffusion (gradient) layer between the mosaic cell array (M) and the ungraded pattern input to M from the afferent bundle.

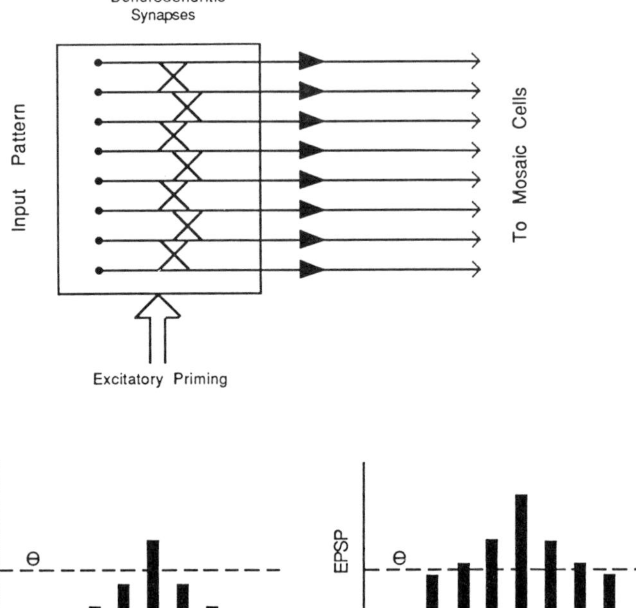

Figure 5.1
Top: Dendrodendritic diffusion layer. Retinotopically organized cells between retinal output and mosaic cells create a gradient of EPSP around primary stimulus pattern by dendrodendritic excitation to neighboring cells. *Bottom:* Cell 4 is discharged directly by retinal stimulation. Priming of cells in diffusion layer raises total EPSP in each cell so that EPSP in cells close to cell 4 exceeds threshold (θ) and evokes a gradient of discharge over these neighboring cells.

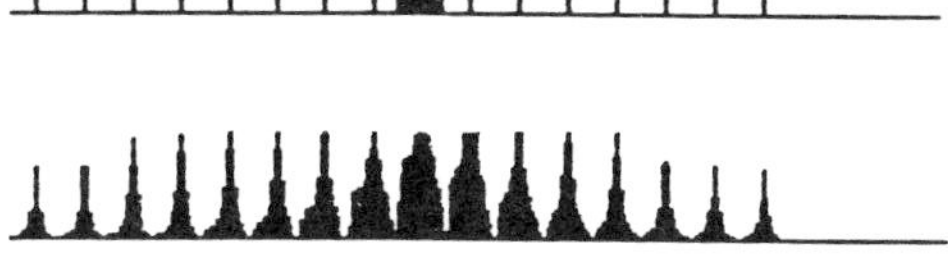

Figure 5.2
Distribution of synaptic transfer weights (ϕ) on filter cells in detection matrix. *Top:* Without dendrodendritic diffusion. *Bottom:* With diffusion. Each point on the dendritic line represents a discrete synaptic location.

Learning is assumed to occur only with a sufficient level of general activation (arousal) to the synaptic matrix. Similarly, in the gradient layer, the general activation normally associated with learning is required to raise the profile of EPSP transfer by dendrodendritic contacts so that the neighboring cells surrounding a primary afferent input target can reach discharge threshold, though their spike frequency will be less than that of the primary target cell (figure 5.1, bottom). When this occurs, mosaic cells neighboring the primary stimulus targets will discharge accordingly, and this activity will be reflected in the distribution of synaptic transfer weights on the filter cell that is modified during learning.

An example of the effect on synaptic transfer weights (ϕ) in a filter cell when a dendrodendritic gradient layer intervenes between the sensory input tract and the mosaic array is shown by the comparative simulation results in figure 5.2. In this case, a visual stimulus (a cross) was presented to a 16 × 16 cell retina to be learned in the synaptic matrix. The screen printout at the top of figure 5.2 presents the distribution profile of ϕ on the modified filter cell after learning without a dendrodendritic gradient layer. The bottom of the figure shows the distribution profile of ϕ on the filter cell when the model incorporated a dendrodendritic gradient layer. The underlying models and the stimulus for both simulations were identical except for the inclusion of a gradient layer in one. An arbitrary activation transfer coefficient of 0.6 was set for dendrodendritic excitation among neighboring cells in the gradient layer, which was incorporated in the simulation producing the profile shown at the bottom of figure 5.2. Because instances of a moderately close mismatch between stimulus coordinates and coordinates of maximum synaptic efficacy intersect elevated (though reduced) filter cell transfer weights in the latter case, it can be seen that such mismatches will be less critical for pattern recognition when there is a ϕ gradient around each primary synaptic locus.

Retinal-Afferent Organization

If the neuronal models proposed here are to operate effectively as processors of events in visual space, the retinotopic coordinates of the retinal receptor field must be conserved through the afferent channels and in the mechanisms for central processing. Although there are a number of different coordinate representations that one might choose for retinotopic indexing, I have found a ring-ray representation to be more useful and efficient than any other that I have considered. In this representational scheme, receptor cells in the retina (and their associated ganglion cell projections) are indexed with respect to the central foveal axis in terms of their locations on imaginary concentric rings (i) centering on the axis, and imaginary rays (j) projecting from the axis and intersecting all rings. Concentric rings (i) are indexed from the smallest ($i = 1$) to the largest ($i = n$). Rays (j) are indexed in clockwise sequence from the twelve o'clock position ($j = 1$) through one rotation to the last position before twelve o'clock ($j = n$).

In correspondence with the decreasing density of retinal receptors, the indexing scheme proposed here assumes that in terms of visual field coordinates, the spacing between concentric rings increases progressively as rings become larger and the distance between points of intersection of adjacent rays on the successively larger rings increases. This principle of ring-ray organization of the retina is illustrated in figure 5.3.

Afferent-Field Aperture

The ring-ray organization of the retina lends itself to central nervous system control of the effective processing aperture for input from the afferent visual field. Inhibitory neurons that synapse with selected ring groups of mosaic array cells can constrict the diameter of the visual window around the foveal axis. Conversely, termination of the activity of these inhibitory neurons can result in expansion of the effective visual window (figure 5.4). This afferent control circuit modulates the field of view and allows either aperture widening or dynamic masking and cropping of images before they are conveyed to the synaptic matrix for learning or recognition (Trehub 1977). Control of the afferent field aperture plays an integral part in the processes of focal attention and scene analysis.

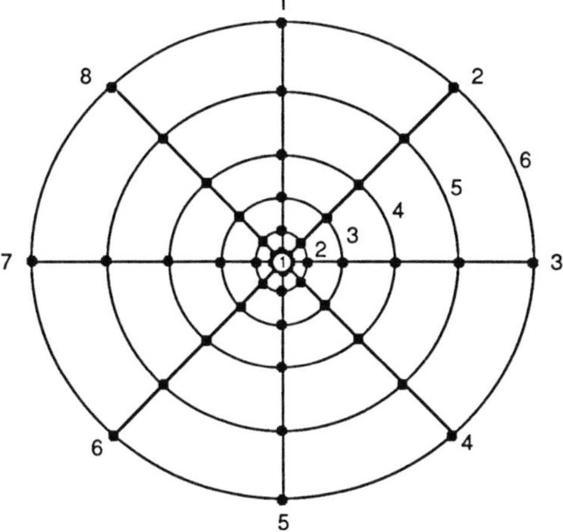

Figure 5.3
Ring-ray organization of retina. Each receptor and its afferent projection is identified by its coordinate in terms of the intersection of its *i*th ring on its *j*th ray.

Novelty Detection

During the earliest years of human maturation, learning is probably usually passive and nonselective. It is assumed that this kind of early learning depends on a high level of generalized arousal (corticipetal discharge diffusely distributed by the reticular activating system), which lowers thresholds in the synaptic matrix so that filter cells are sporadically fired and their transfer weights (ϕ) modified by whatever stimuli the alert child happens to encounter. In the more mature individual, however, it is more likely that stimuli must be salient before threshold priming and subsequent changes in ϕ occur in the synaptic matrix. It is assumed that whatever is relevant to the needs of the individual and also novel (not previously learned) should be learned. By what physical process might the novelty of the input be determined? In this model, classification time—the interval between the presentation of a stimulus and the firing of a class cell—is taken as the basis for determining the novelty of a stimulus.

Figure 5.5 shows a neuronal mechanism for detecting novelty. At the detection of an input in a context relevant to current motivation, a novelty test cell is discharged at an activity level (spike rate) sufficient to fire its target novelty cell after the elapse of a standard period of time. During this latency interval, the novelty cell integrates EPSP from the novelty test cell. An inhibitory neuron (−), which serves to reset the novelty cell, receives its input from the axons of all class

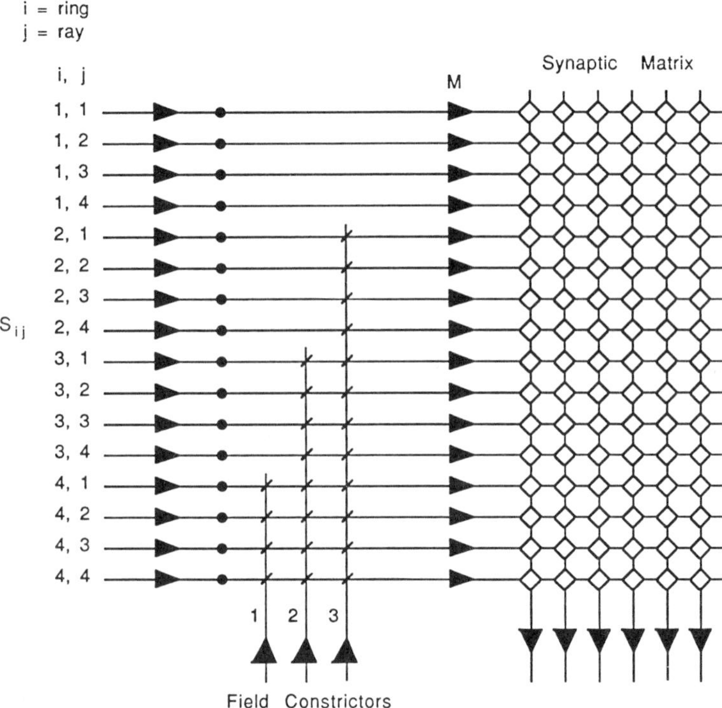

Figure 5.4
Mechanism for constricting effective visual field. Discharge of constrictor cell 1 blocks input from ring 4 (outer ring). Discharge of constrictor 3 blocks input from rings 4, 3, and 2, restricting input to ring 1, the innermost ring of receptors and afferents.

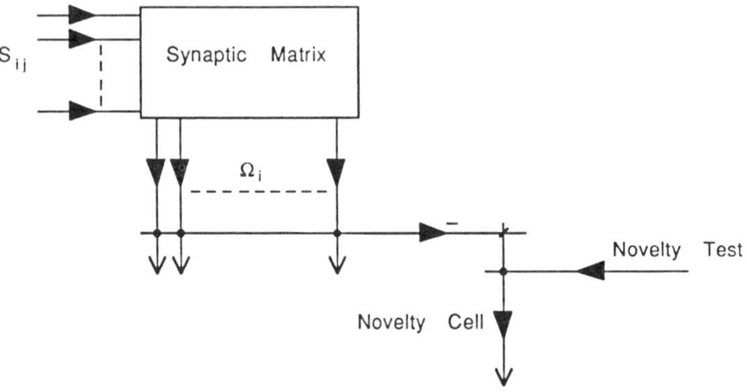

Figure 5.5
Schematic of novelty detection circuit.

cells (Ω) in the synaptic matrix. If a stimulus has been recognized (a class cell discharges) before the elapse of the criterion period, the novelty cell will be reset before it reaches spike threshold, and the stimulus will be treated as a familiar one. If an input pattern has not been learned, no class cell will fire within the criterion period, and the novelty cell (not having received a resetting pulse) will reach threshold and fire, signaling that the current stimulus is novel (Trehub 1977). In this case, it is assumed that the firing of the novelty cell commands an increment of diffuse excitation to the synaptic matrix, thus lowering the thresholds of filter cells (f) so that a previously unmodified f will fire and become tuned to the novel stimulus in accordance with the learning formula.

Transformations of Size and Angular Orientation

An object with a particular size and angular orientation at the time it is learned can usually be recognized later as the same object despite wide variations in its projected retinal size and orientation. The neuronal mechanisms described below provide a means for internally reorganizing the retinotopic projections of visual patterns that undergo such transformations.

Shown in figure 5.6 is a network in which the mosaic cells of a synaptic matrix project retinotopically through two series-connected intermatrix neuronal layers onto a second detection matrix. The dendrite of each cell in the first intermatrix layer receives an excitatory input from each of two decoupler cells, one activated by an initiate zoom command the other by an initiate rotation command. The axon of each cell in the first layer projects in excitatory synapse to its coordinate cell in the second layer and also sends off two excitatory collaterals—one that contacts its retinotopically coordinate cell in the size transformer mechanism and the other that contacts its coordinate cell in the rotation transformer. The dendrite of each cell in the second layer receives, in addition, excitatory inputs from its coordinate cells in the size transformer and the rotation transformer. Finally, the axon of each second layer cell projects to form an adaptive synapse with all filter cells in the second detection matrix.

Size Transformer

The spatial transformation mechanism located above the synaptic matrix in figure 5.6 operates to expand (or contract) an initial activation pattern represented retinotopically on the mosaic cell array. Inputs from the intermatrix cells that represent the initial pattern do not

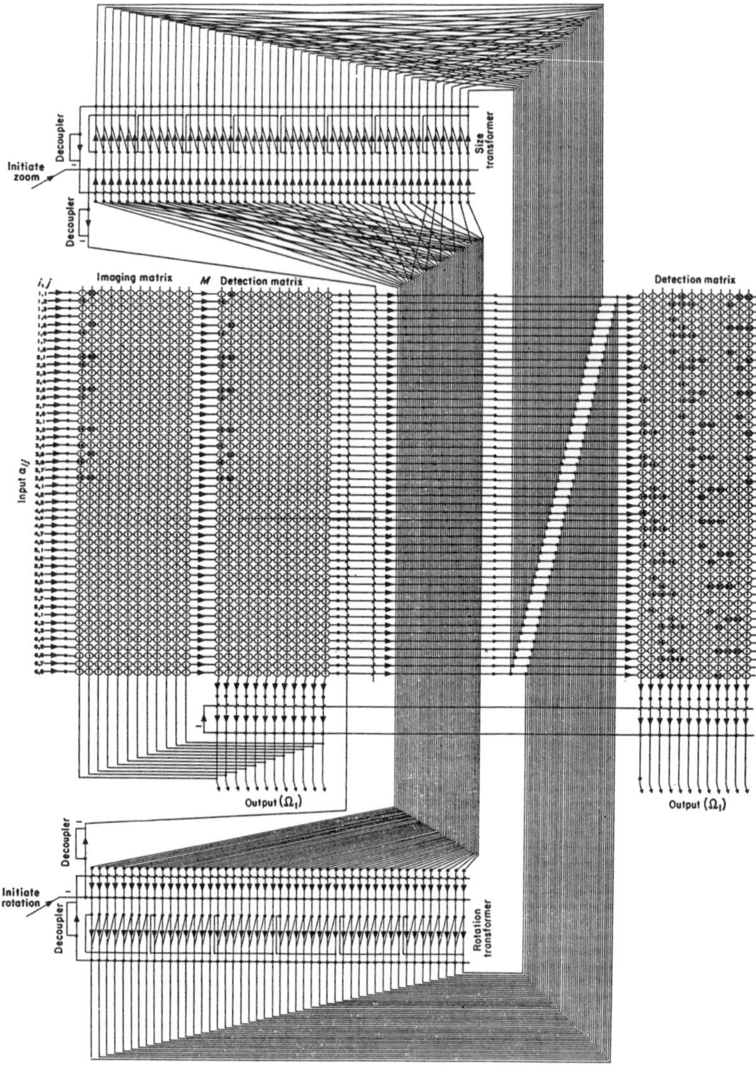

Figure 5.6
Synaptic matrices and neuronal circuits for transformation of size and angular orientation of input patterns. Values in detection matrix 1 represent synaptic transfer weights (ϕ) associated with the veridical input of two learned patterns (T and Z). Values in detection matrix 2 represent ϕ associated with all possible retinal sizes of the two patterns. Source: Trehub 1977. Copyright Academic Press (London) Ltd. Reproduced by permission.

activate the size transformer until the thresholds of neurons in the transformer are lowered by a concurrent pulse from the initiate zoom cell. When this occurs, the pattern of discharge that represents the current retinal image is evoked within the size transformer, and other input to the transformer is blocked by the inhibitory action of two decoupler cells. One decoupler line, activated immediately by input from the initiate zoom cell, inhibits the first array of intermatrix neurons. The other decoupler, activated by the output of any cell(s) in the size transformer, inhibits the array of interneurons that link the size transformer to the axons that have provided its initial pattern of excitation (the image to be transformed). This initial pattern may be considered a prototypical image, which can then be neuronally re-represented for learning or recognition at all the size variations that are within the capacity of the size transformer.

The action of the size transformer can be considered similar to that of a zoom lens. Given a retina with an output of 48 ganglion cells (as in figure 5.6) organized into six rings and eight rays, the size transformer has a corresponding functional organization. When an initial input pattern is presented and the size transformer is activated, the transformer sends this pattern to the second array of intermatrix cells and then to the second detection matrix. However, when any cell on a given transformer ring is fired, it in turn fires the cell in the next-larger ring on its own ray (see figure 5.6). Reversal of the direction of ring-to-ring excitation in an otherwise similar-size transformer produces successive contraction in the projected size of any mosaic cell pattern. Thus, the original pattern is successively enlarged or contracted by the appropriate retinotopic increment in a succession of projections to the second detection matrix, where it can be learned and subsequently recognized over a wide range of sizes (see Larsen and Bundesen 1978).

Rotation Transformer

The spatial transformation mechanism located below the synaptic matrix in figure 5.6 operates to rotate an initial pattern of excitation represented retinotopically on the mosaic cell array. As in the case of the size transformer, inputs from the intermatrix neurons that carry a given pattern of stimulation do not activate the rotation transformer until the thresholds of neurons in the transformer array are lowered by a concurrent pulse from an enabling command cell. In this case, the activating pulse is given by the initiate rotation cell. When such a pulse occurs, thresholds are lowered, and the pattern of discharge representing the current retinal image is evoked in the rotation transformer. At the same time, additional input to the transformer is blocked by the inhibitory output of two decoupler cells (as in the case of the size transformer). The pattern "captured" in the rotation transformer can then be neuronally re-represented for learning or recognition at all rotation variations within the capacity of the transformer.

When an initial input pattern is presented and the rotation transformer is activated, the transformer projects this pattern of retinotopic excitation to the second array of intermatrix cells and then to the second detection matrix. However, when any cell on a given transformer ray is fired, it in turn fires the cell that is in the next clockwise ray on its own ring (see figure 5.6). Reversal of the direction of ray-to-ray excitation in an otherwise similar rotation transformer produces successive counterclockwise rotation in the projection of any mosaic cell pattern. Thus, the original pattern is rotated in a clockwise or counterclockwise direction in a succession of projections to the second detection matrix, where it can be learned and recognized over a wide range of angular orientations (see Shepard and Cooper 1982).

The neuronal transformer circuits can accept a single visual pattern and re-afferent the same pattern through the full range of size and orientation transformations that are consistent with the structural constraints and resolution of the attached retina and transformer mechanisms. Since the transforms are projected to a synaptic matrix, each can be stored in memory by the filter cells in accordance with the learning formula (equation 2.3). Thus, the presence of a single stimulus can result in the learning of not only the given stimulus but also that stimulus in a variety of size and orientation manifestations. In order to avoid interference between transformer outputs, it is assumed that the size and rotation transformers are connected in reciprocal inhibition and that only one kind of transformation is performed at any given instant.

The ability to recognize an object despite changes in size and orientation does not require filter cells to be tuned to all possible combinations of size and orientation. It is assumed that filter cells are normally tuned to a range of size transformations of any given object so that on any fortuitous encounter, the object can be quickly recognized despite variations in retinal size. However, where the trade-off of recognition time for storage space in the brain is a reasonable one, filter cells might be tuned to only a few orientation variants. If many retinal sizes of an object are represented in the detection matrix, any veridical orientation later encountered can be rotated internally until its re-afferented orientation conforms to that of its appropriate size representation in the detection matrix. Moreover, given the spatial gradients of ϕ distributions on filter cells (see figure 5.2), exact matches of size and orientation are not required for adequate recognition performance.

Projections from the 3-D Retinoid: Size Constancy

The primate visual system has a large number of separate structures, cortical and subcortical, devoted to the processing of visual information (Livingstone and Hubel 1988). Some nonhuman species have at least 10 to 15 identifiable cortical areas that are responsive to visual stimulation (Van Essen 1985), and it is likely that the human brain has even more anatomically discrete structures, operating in parallel or hierarchical fashion, that represent and process information from the visual world. This abundance of visual processing centers suggests that a single complex stimulus is normally analyzed and represented in the brain in a number of different ways. The capacity of the retinoid model to represent and process concurrently multiple aspects of a current visual stimulus is consistent with these findings.

The perceived constancy in the size of an object over a range of observer-object distance despite large variations in the retinal size of the object (Graham 1951) does not seem to depend on a process of iterative size adjustment like that performed by the size transformer. As an object moves from a position close to an observer to a more distant position, its projected image on the retina becomes progressively smaller as its visual angle decreases (see figure 5.7 and top of figure 5.8). Within the 3-D retinoid as well, the size of the autaptic cell representation of the object decreases accordingly (figure 5.7), yet it is judged to be of constant size. The scheme of axonal projections from principal cells in the 3-D retinoid to a mosaic cell array (bottom of figure 5.8) provides a physical basis for the perception of size constancy. This model assumes that in the central receptive field, there is a structure of 3-D retinoid cell to 2-D mosaic cell connectivity that, in effect, normalizes (roughly) the projected size of an excitation pattern in the 3-D retinoid as a function of the particular Z-plane that the pattern occupies. Principal cells in the nearest 3-D Z-plane are mapped to their corresponding retinotopic coordinates in the mosaic cell array, while cells in more distant Z-planes diverge to project to increasingly more eccentric coordinates on the mosaic cell surface in accordance with the visual distance they represent. Thus, retinal images that become smaller as a function of increasing object distance are magnified in compensatory fashion as they are mapped onto the space represented by the mosaic cell array. (However, the actual

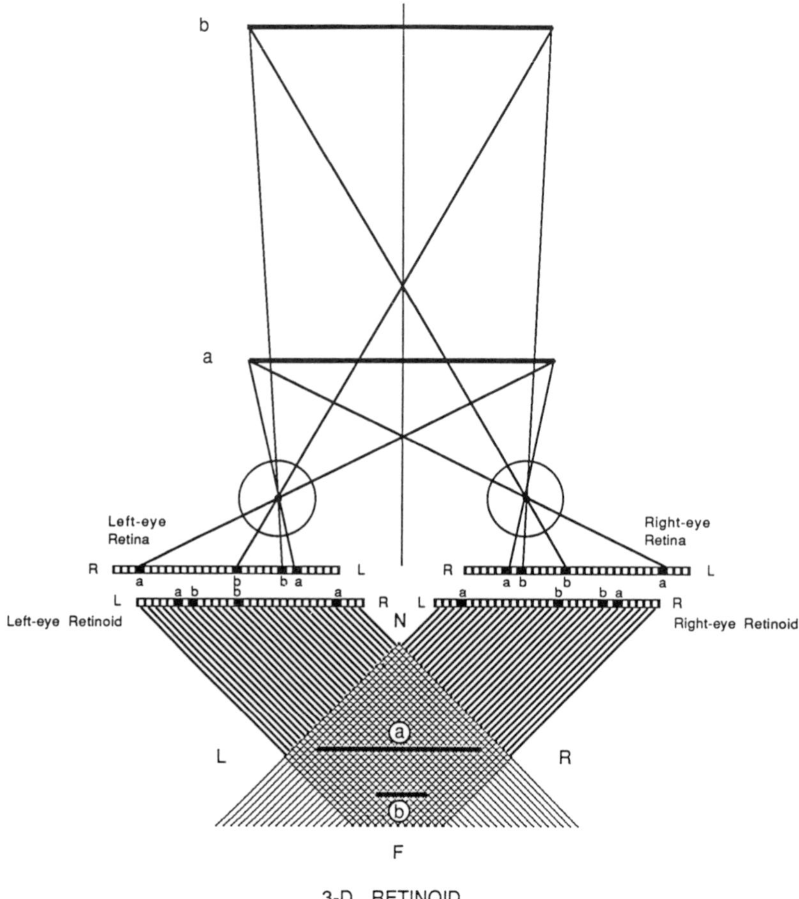

Figure 5.7
Representation in 3-D retinoid of same object at different distances (a and b) from observer.

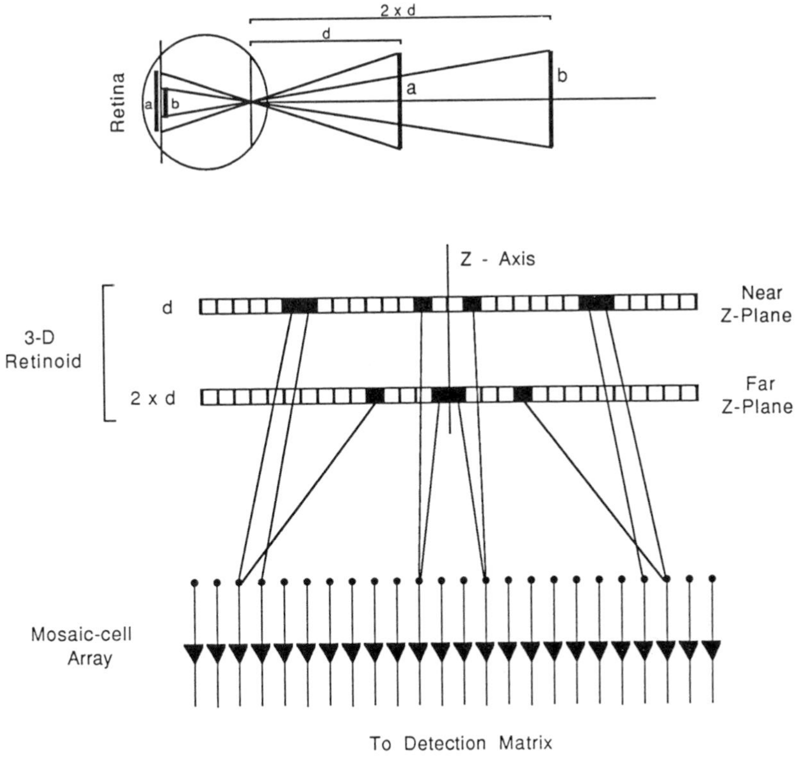

Figure 5.8
Top: Retinal projections of same object at distance d (a) and 2 × d (b). *Bottom:* Normalization of object-size representations on near Z-plane (d) and far Z-plane (2 × d) by compensatory projection of autaptic-cell axons to mosaic cell array.

number of cells activated will always decrease in proportion to object distance, with a corresponding decrease in visual resolution.) This is another instance of the visual system's multiple representation of the properties of objects in the visual world; the relative retinal size of an object is represented in the 3-D retinoid at the same time that its relative inherent size is represented on the mosaic cell array.

This size normalization structure serves a singularly useful purpose for pattern learning and recognition. Since the pattern of excitation on the mosaic cell array will be roughly equivalent for any given object over a wide range of arbitrary distances (although degraded by lower resolution as distance increases), a single filter cell that is tuned to a particular object at a given distance will be an effective detector of that object at other distances. Thus an object need not be learned separately for each distance.

Given the proposed neuronal structure of projection from the 3-D retinoid to the mosaic cells of the synaptic matrix, it is revealing to consider what would happen if the retinal projection of an object to the 3-D retinoid were to remain constant in size as the retinoid representation of the object moved to more distant Z-planes. It would be expected that because of the expanding projection from more distant Z-planes to the mosaic array, the object should be perceived as increasing in size as its distance increased. An anomalous perception of this kind would lend support to the neuronal architecture of the 3-D retinoid and its projections to the mosaic array that I have hypothesized.

To verify that this size illusion does indeed occur, cut out a 1-inch square of black construction paper, and paste it on a sheet of unglossed white posterboard. At normal reading distance, fixate the center of the black square for approximately 1 minute under bright uniform illumination. This will induce a bright after-image of the square on your retinas. If you now shift your gaze to a different region of the posterboard, you will see a square image that is brighter than the surrounding surface. Move the posterboard farther away, and the square will appear to grow larger. Move the posterboard closer than the original fixation distance, and the square will appear to become smaller in size. You can change the perceived shape of the square by tilting the surface of the posterboard after the retinal after-image has formed. If you tilt the fixation surface (the posterboard) away from you on a horizontal axis, the square after-image appears to assume a roughly rectangular shape elongated on the vertical axis. If you tilt it on a vertical axis, you will see a rectangle with horizontal elongation. If the after-image is sharp enough, careful observation reveals that the shape transformations are not quite rectangular; an edge that appears on the near surface of the tilted posterboard is somewhat shorter than its opposite edge on the far surface.

These visual illusions are predictable from the properties of the retinoid system and its projections to the mosaic cell array. It is important to note that the retinal after-image remains constant in size and shape during all the manipulations of fixation. What, then, accounts for the striking changes in the perception of a constant stimulus? The answer lies in the fact that as the fixation surface (the posterboard) is viewed at different distances, the concurrent retinal after-image is necessarily shifted at the same time to the Z-plane that corresponds to the distance of the fixation surface. Thus, with a retinal image of constant size (the after-image), the 3-D retinoid to mosaic array architecture produces an inverse of the size-constancy effect. When the posterboard is slanted, successive slices of the square after-image are shifted to successively distant Z-planes and magnified anisotropically in the direction of slant away from you. Thus, the true retinal image of a square is perceived as a rectangle.

Clock and Sequential Priming Circuit

For many kinds of cognitive operations, the temporal relationships among events plays a crucial role; a substantial part of human learning and memory is episodic in character. Sequences of experience are related and made meaningful by their temporal contiguity within particular time frames (Tulving 1972). The common perception of causal relationships in everyday affairs seems to depend, to a large extent, on the frequency with which distinct events occur in close temporal sequence. In the case of planning a course of action, the order in which the elements of the plan are put into effect is an essential factor. To meet the demands for a timing mechanism in such circumstances, the circuit described here (figure 5.9) can control the timing, registration, and location of episodic learning in a synaptic matrix, as well as the relative temporal locus and sequence of recalled episodic experience (Trehub 1983). It can also serve as a controller for temporal indexing in neuronal programs for behavioral routines.

The mechanism illustrated in figure 5.9 depends on the short-term memory properties of autaptic neurons. The whole circuit consists of two rings of autaptic cells with each pair of principal cells within a ring linked by excitatory and inhibitory interneurons.

Consider the inner (clock) ring. For each pair of autaptic cells, we can establish a clockwise direction around the ring. Each autaptic cell innervates an excitatory interneuron, which innervates its clockwise neighbor. Conversely, each autaptic cell also innervates an inhibitory interneuron, which connects to its counterclockwise autaptic neighbor. If any particular principal cell becomes active (discharges), it will transfer its excitation (via the excitatory interneuron) to its clockwise neighbor, which will inhibit (turn off) its counterclockwise donor. In this way, the clock mechanism will be able to maintain a constant circulation of unitary autaptic cell activity in a single direction (clockwise) around the neuronal ring. With fixed integration slopes for EPSP and uniform discharge thresholds for the neurons in the circuit, the rate at which autaptic cell activity circulates over the ring will depend on the level of diffuse excitation (arousal) within the clock module. The higher the level of excitatory bias is, the faster will autaptic cell activity circulate (the clock will run faster), and vice versa. This mechanism provides a neuronal means for temporal ref-

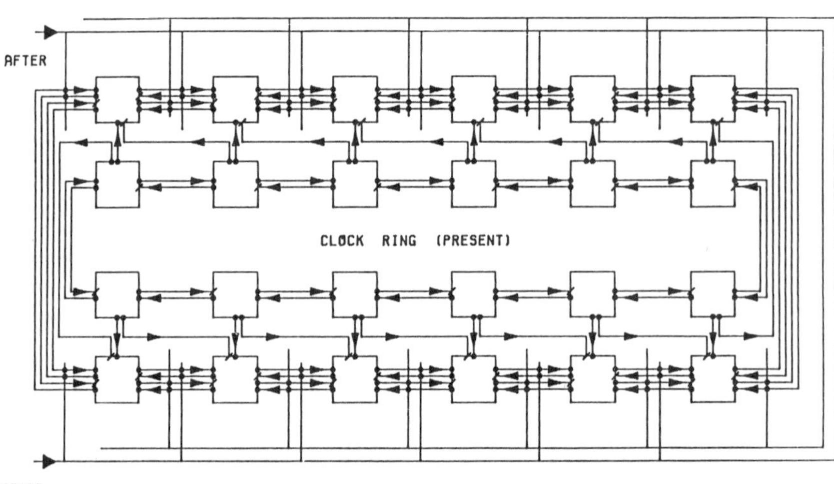

Figure 5.9
Schematic of neuronal clock and temporal priming circuit. Large squares represent autaptic cells that send priming excitatory pulses to synaptic matrix. Small, filled triangles represent control neurons for clock rate and temporal direction (before, after). Inner ring of autaptic cells and interneurons composes clock circuit. Outer ring of autaptic cells and interneurons governs episodic recall. Source: Trehub 1983. Copyright Lawrence Erlbaum Associates, Inc. Reproduced by permission.

erencing and control. If, for example, a particular active autaptic cell should gate the current environmental input in episodic learning, the density of episodically learned experience would be directly proportional to the neuronal clock rate.

The outer ring in figure 5.9, designated the recall ring, provides a means for selective priming or gating of neurons for recalling the images of past experience from memory. In this ring, each autaptic cell receives an excitatory input from a paired clock cell at its corresponding sequential position and an inhibitory input from the clock cell in the next clockwise position. In the absence of any other input, this causes the principal cells in the outer ring to fire in synchrony with the inner neuronal clock. In addition, each pair of autaptic cells in the recall ring is linked by a counterbalanced set of excitatory and inhibitory interneurons. If we take any particular autaptic cell in the outer ring as a spatial and temporal reference, a pulse from the command cell marked BEFORE will bias its local interneurons, causing the transfer of its activity to its counterclockwise autaptic neighbor (going back in time in the sense of an earlier autaptic state). A pulse from the command cell marked AFTER will transfer autaptic cell activity to its clockwise neighbor (going forward in time in the sense of a later autaptic state). The relative direction, rate, and distance of a temporal excursion will be determined by which command cell (BEFORE or AFTER) is discharged, the discharge frequency of the command cell, and the duration of its discharge. (Notice the similarity in the control principles governing operation of this timing module and those for translation of patterns over retinoid surfaces.)

A Network for Episodic Processing

Figure 5.10 illustrates how the clock ring and recall ring are connected to the synaptic matrix so that the system can learn and recall past experiences. The discussion of the basic synaptic matrix in chapter 3 was restricted to a mechanism in which the changes in synaptic transfer weights (ϕ) during the course of learning would be long-lasting; the decay of ϕ over time was not considered as an issue in the initial description of the model. However, synaptic matrices that are involved in episodic processing will have identical filter cells influenced by different afferent patterns on different episodic cycles; consequently, in any given filter cell, the changes in ϕ that occur during learning must decay to approach an initial state before that cell is involved in a new learning cycle. Otherwise the ϕ distributions representing the events learned would be confounded over successive learning cycles.

Each autaptic cell in the clock ring (PRESENT) in figure 5.10 sends an excitatory gating axon to a paired filter cell (f) in the detection matrix. At any given time, only that filter cell that is primed by the output of the neuronal clock can learn the current sensory input. By this scheme, learning (synaptic modification) is transferred over time, sequentially and unidirectionally across the filter cells of the detection matrix, and the sequence of f cell priming is recycled as autaptic cell activity in the clock ring recycles. For any given filter cell, the changes in ϕ due to learning must decay to a base value within an appropriate time period in order to avoid a confounding of learned patterns.

Each autaptic cell in the recall ring (PAST) sends an excitatory axon to its paired class cell (Ω) in the detection matrix. Thus, sequences of Ω discharge can be initiated and synchronously controlled by activity in the recall ring. Because the discharge of any given Ω will evoke its associated (learned) afferent pattern in the imaging matrix, sequences of Ω discharge will recall sequences of learned experiences (images) in their original temporal order, going forward or backward in time

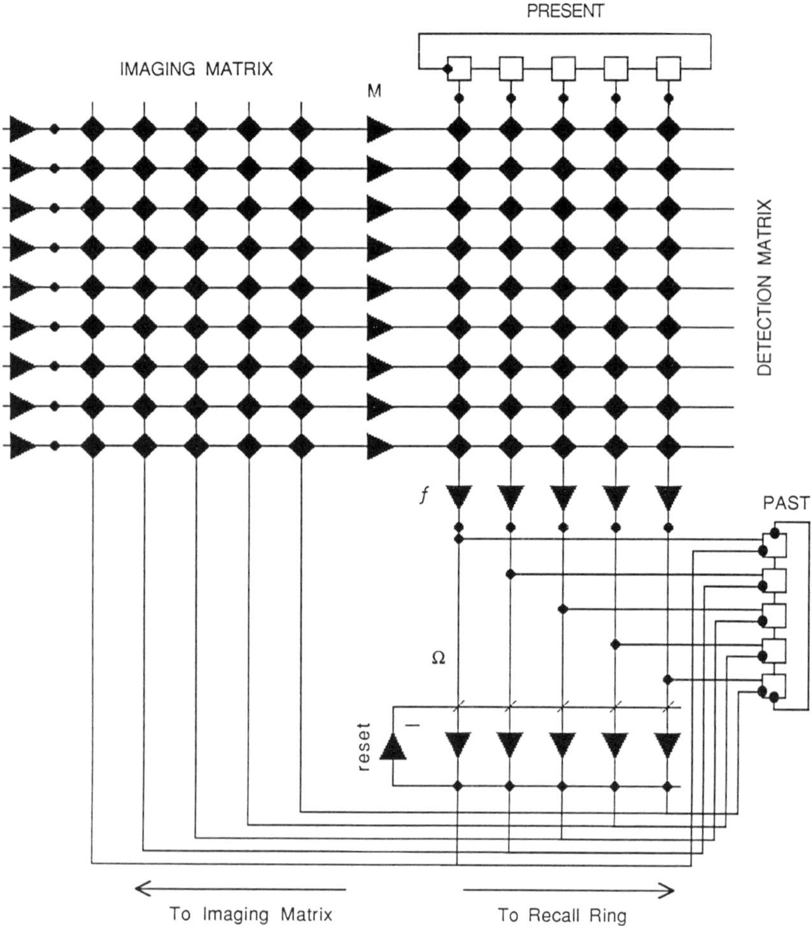

Figure 5.10
Schematic showing synaptic matrix for episodic learning and recall controlled by neuronal mechanism illustrated in figure 5.9. Squares at top represent autaptic cells in clock ring (PRESENT). Squares at bottom right represent autaptic cells governing episodic recall (PAST). Each autaptic cell in the clock ring primes an associated filter cell (f) in the detection matrix. Each autaptic cell in the recall ring can discharge a class cell (Ω), which in turn evokes its related learned afferent pattern in the imaging matrix. The sequence of discharge in the clock ring is unidirectional (forward) in time. The sequence of discharge in the recall ring can vary in direction (forward or backward in "time"). Source: Ibid. Copyright Lawrence Erlbaum Associates, Inc. Reproduced by permission.

from any arbitrary past reference image in accordance with the controlling activity of the recall ring.

If the model were to operate only as described to this point, the initial temporal excursion for the recall of any particular past episode would have to recede sequentially under the control of the autaptic cells in the recall ring starting at the temporal locus that is determined by the currently active principal cell in the neuronal clock (PRESENT). However, a leap back to the beginning of a remembered episode rarely involves a complete sequential playback of intervening images in reverse temporal order from present to past. Rather, a target event is retrieved first, and related episodic recollections are referred to earlier or later times with respect to the temporal locus of the target event. The proposed model can also perform in this way if the clock ring (PRESENT) is momentarily decoupled from the detection matrix while a concurrent increase in diffuse excitation is applied to all filter cells in the synaptic matrix. Under this condition, any input pattern from the mosaic cell array (*M*), whether exogenously or endogenously evoked, will maximally stimulate that filter cell having the highest sum of synaptic products with the given pattern. Its coupled class cell (Ω) will fire first, and this Ω, through its axon collateral to its paired autaptic cell in the recall ring (figure 5.10), will trigger episodic excursions from this point in the ring. Thus, sequential playback through intervening images from the present to a past target episode is prevented, and recall can begin at a target point in "time" that depends only on the distribution of synaptic transfer weights within the synaptic matrix and the concurrent pattern of evocative excitation arriving from the mosaic cell array.

Chapter 6
Building a Semantic Network

A semantic network is a propositional knowledge structure consisting of a set of nodes that are selectively connected to each other by links labeled by the relationship between each pair of connected nodes (Fahlman 1979, 1981; Quillian 1968; Stillings et al. 1987, chap. 4). Links in such networks may assert category membership or a part-to-whole property. These can be described as *is-(a)* and *has-(a)* relationships such as "A trout *is a* fish" and "A trout *has* gills" (figure 6.1). Many other kinds of relationships among nodes may also be represented by labeled links. For example, a link could represent the concept *is made of,* as in "a crowbar *is made of* steel," or a relationship of relative weight, as in "an elephant *weighs more than* a mouse."

When a synaptic matrix serves as a biological instantiation of a semantic network, the word-tokened inputs to its mosaic cells and the tokened class cells of its output correspond to nodes. Selectively augmented synaptic transfer weights (ϕ) on the appropriate filter cells correspond to the links among the nodes. The relationships among connected nodes might be labeled in at least two ways. One way would be to have a separate synaptic matrix devoted to each kind of relationship between nodes—for example, a matrix that processes only *is-(a)* relationships and one that processes only *has-(a)* relationships. The other approach, the one adopted here, is to have the internodal relationship represented by the predicate node. Thus, instead of "A trout (node 1) ‹*has* (labeled link)› gills (node 2)," the synaptic matrix representation would be "A trout (node 1) ‹ϕ link› *has* gills (node 2)." In this scheme, an object and an implication about the object taken together constitute a predicate category that is signaled by the discharge of a single physically indexed cell.

The Synaptic Matrix as a Semantic Network

Consider the following sequence of sentences that could provide the kind of information captured in the network illustrated in figure 6.1:

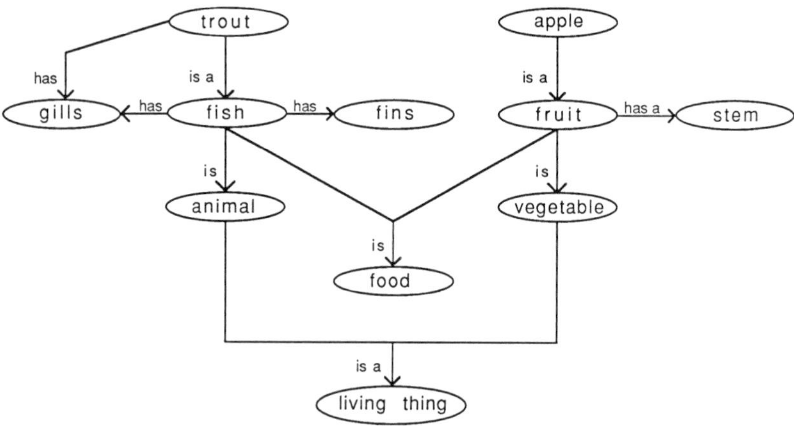

Figure 6.1
A semantic network composed of abstract nodes designating entities and abstract links designating relationships between connected nodes. Notice that if there were no direct *has* link between *trout* and *gills,* traversal of the *is a* link from *trout* to *fish* and the *has* link from *fish* to *gills* allows the proposition *trout has gills.*

(1) A trout is a fish.

(2) A fish has gills.

(3) A fish has fins.

(4) Fish is food.

(5) Fish is animal.

(6) An apple is a fruit.

(7) Fruit has a stem.

(8) Fruit is food.

(9) Fruit is vegetable.

(10) An animal is a living thing.

(11) A vegetable is a living thing.

Each string that composes one of the sentences consists of a sequence of visual or auditory patterns that must be registered, parsed, and subjected to lexical classification by means of neuronal activity. Some kind of analytic brain mechanism, shaped by learning within a particular cultural context, must be able to perform a syntactic decomposition of the string so that subject and predicate can be designated and processed appropriately.

Let us consider how a synaptic matrix might process sentences that are presented as visual stimuli. It is assumed that the pattern of marks that constitute the words of a printed sentence can, like any other visual pattern, be mapped into sets of indexed cells that would be part of a lexical module. When we considered the synaptic matrix in the context of visual processes, retinal stimuli, after translation to the normal foveal axis, were input to an array of cells in the matrix that were designated as mosaic cells (M). The circuitry for semantic processing is somewhat different. It requires a set of autaptic cells that capture the neuronal tokens of words in short-term memory (working memory); it is the activity of these cells, which we shall call word cells (W), that provides the direct afferent excitation to the mosaic cell array (M). Thus, W_1 and M_1 might represent *apple,* and W_2 and M_2 might represent *is (a) fruit.* The designations for filter cell (f) and class cell (Ω) remain unchanged, as do the biological properties of the detection matrix and the imaging matrix.

The objective is to establish within a synaptic matrix a preferred excitation path from W_1 (*apple*) to Ω_2 (*is (a) fruit*) so that upon any subsequent presentation of the word *apple,* the semantically appropriate class cell (Ω_2) will be discharged. This can be done in a simple learning procedure if the filter cell coupled to the class cell token of the predicate *is (a) fruit* were to discharge concurrently with the W-token input that represents the subject *apple.* Because of the sequential nature of sentence strings, however, the required temporal overlap of subject and predicate does not occur naturally; some means must be provided to compensate for this if the proper association is to be learned.

The desired cooccurrence of the tokens for subject and predicate can be ensured if discharge of the word cell (W_i) representing the subject is sustained beyond the duration of its evoking stimulus and terminated after the predicate cell has discharged. This is accomplished by having each word cell in the input array to the synaptic matrix be an autaptic cell and priming the array so that each word token (W_i) continues to discharge (as a latched cell) until the stimulus sentence is completed and the predicate token (Ω_i) has fired.

Illustrated in figure 6.2 is a modified synaptic matrix with the intrinsic capability to organize a semantic network if it is given a series of simple sentences. Initial input to the synaptic matrix is through a set of autaptic word cells (W_i), each of which (if active) stimulates its coordinate mosaic cell and, by means of an axon collateral, a paired

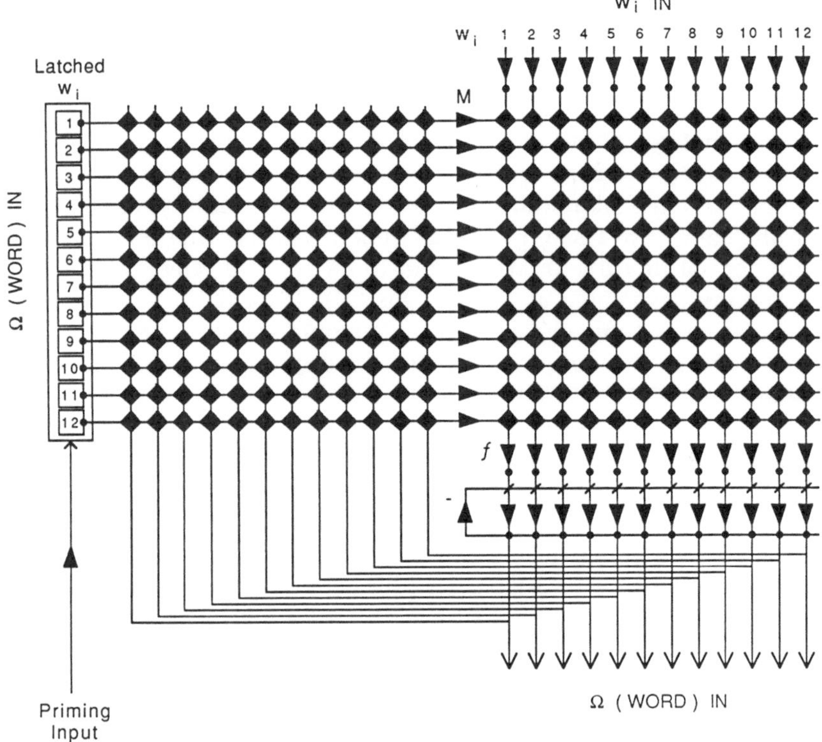

Figure 6.2
Schematic of a semantic network. Open squares (designated W_i) within priming field are autaptic cells that act as lexical tokens. Each autaptic cell connects to a paired mosaic cell (M) and, through an interneuron (not shown), to a paired filter cell (f). Dots represent fixed excitatory synapses; short, oblique slashes represent fixed inhibitory synapses; filled lozenges represent adaptive excitatory synapses. Reset neuron ($-$) generates an inhibitory postsynaptic potential to reset all class cells when discharged.

filter cell (f_i) in the detection matrix. At the start of each sentence, all W_i are primed, enabling the word tokens in the sentence string to be latched. At the completion of each sentence, the priming input is interrupted and all W_i stop firing. The repeated sequence of initiation and interruption of excitatory priming of word cells occurs in phase with the input and completion of successive sentences over any extended lexical message.

Suppose, in the printed sentence *A tiger is a cat,* articles are ignored so that the first recognized character string is *tiger,* which fires W_1, and the second recognized character string is *is cat,* firing W_2. In this case, the mosaic cell M_1 and the filter cell f_1 will discharge concurrently, causing an increase in the efficacy of the synaptic junction between M_1 and f_1 in the detection matrix in accordance with the learning principle. Then mosaic cell M_2 and filter cell f_2 will fire together, causing an increase in the transfer weight of their synaptic junction. At the same time, the synapse connecting M_1 and f_2 will also be modified because M_1 was continuing to discharge (stimulated by the latched autaptic cell W_1) when f_2 fired. In the imaging matrix, the concurrent discharge of class cell Ω_2 and mosaic cell M_1 will raise the efficacy of their synaptic link. After this bit of learning, if *tiger* alone is presented as a stimulus, the response will be *tiger* (Ω_1) *is cat* (Ω_2). If *is cat* is presented alone, it will evoke Ω_2 in the detection matrix, which, in turn, will evoke M_1 in the imaging matrix, resulting in the Ω_1 output *tiger.*

When the semantic network is queried, the discharge of any particular mosaic cell (M_i) is the selected token of a word or phrase taken as the subject of a sentence. The discharge of any particular class cell (Ω_i) is the selected token of a word or phrase taken as the predicate of a sentence—for example, "A *trout* (M_1) is a *fish* (Ω_3)." If we were to ask "What is a trout?" "a fish" would be one of a number of proper replies. If the same question were put to a semantic network previously presented with "A trout is a fish," we expect a similar response. That is, if M_1 (*trout*) is fired, then Ω_3 (*fish*) should fire. Suppose we were to ask, "What is an example of a fish?" The response "a trout" would be appropriate. In this case, the subject *trout* is selected when the predicate *fish* is queried. In terms of the neuronal structure of the semantic network, if Ω_3 (fish) is discharged, then M_1 (trout) should fire.

But we would expect more of a neuronal mechanism that is to serve as a semantic processor in the human brain. In particular, we would expect such a processor to make sense out of combinations of sentences. For example, suppose you were provided the information contained in the following sentences:

(1) A trout is a fish.

(2) A cod is a fish.

(3) A trout lives in freshwater.

(4) A cod lives in saltwater.

If you were asked to give an example of a fish, the responses *trout* and/or *cod* would be appropriate. These could be computed from sentences 1 and 2, where each sentence is treated independent of the other. However, if you were asked to give an example of a fish that lives in saltwater, the information contained in at least two of the four sentences (2 and 4) would have to be combined and used in such a way that the response *cod* is given. From a strictly logical point of view, the fact that a trout lives in freshwater does not preclude the case that it also lives in saltwater. But given the information contained in these sentences and the form of the question asked, the natural inference is that *cod* is the right answer and *trout* is wrong.

If something like this is accounted for by what happens physically in the brain, then the semantic processor must somehow combine and properly relate the information contained in all four sentences. Something roughly corresponding to the following simple bit of reasoning must be taking place: *A trout and a cod are both examples of a fish, but I know only that a cod lives in saltwater, so cod is the right answer.* A semantic network organized by an augmented synaptic matrix can generate "reasonable" inferences of this kind.

An Example of Performance

The following simulation provides an initial example of how the synaptic matrix can perform as a self-organizing semantic network. The neuronal mechanism illustrated in figure 6.2 constituted the processing model that was simulated.

Synaptic changes were based on the same learning principles as presented in chapters 2 and 3. The saturation limit (*Lim*) for the transfer weights (ϕ) was arbitrarily set at a value of 2. All ϕ changes reached the saturation limit during learning because in sentence processing the number of coactive lexically tokened cells is relatively small. Parsing of the words and phrases that composed the sentences typed into the computer was accomplished by a program subroutine that was not part of the simulation of the neuronal model. Thus, input to the word cells (*W*) attached to the synaptic matrix was mediated by an ordinary program for parsing character strings and linking them to *W* cells rather than by a simulated neuronal mechanism for recognizing the actual visual patterns of the character strings. Similarly, initiation and interruption of *W* cell priming were controlled by a standard computer subroutine that responded to the initiation of a sentence and the punctuation at the end of it. However, the essential semantic mechanism for systematically organizing the relationships among biological tokens of words and phrases was a simulation of a dynamic neuronal structure (the augmented synaptic matrix).

For the purpose of simplifying the simulation program, the model ignored the article strings *a, an,* and *the,* as well as the verb *is* when it learned its lexicon from the sentences presented. An *is (a)* relationship was taken as the default characterization of a predicate link to a subject whenever an assertion of relationship was required but was not explicitly specified in the output of the semantic network; for example, the output string *trout fish* was transformed by adding the appropriate articles and the *is (a)* link to make the well-formed expression, "A trout is a fish." Other predicate relationships were expressed directly in the output of the semantic network as predicate phrases (hyphenated in both input and output to facilitate phrase parsing); for example, the output string "fish has-gills" required only the addition of the article to make the well-formed expression, "A fish has-gills."

The following sentences were presented to the neuronal model for semantic processing (a space was left between the last word in each sentence and the period to make it easier for the parsing program to sense the end of the sentence and signal the interruption of *W* cell priming):

(1) A TIGER IS A CAT .

(2) A TIGER HAS-STRIPES .

(3) A TIGER IS WILD .

(4) A TABBIE IS A CAT .

(5) A TABBIE HAS-STRIPES .

(6) A TABBIE IS A PET .

(7) A FLAG HAS-STRIPES .

(8) A FLAG IS AN ARTIFACT .

(9) A CAT IS A MAMMAL .

(10) A MAMMAL IS AN ANIMAL .

(11) A DOG IS A MAMMAL .

(12) A DOG IS A PET .

(13) A DOG BARKS .

From this list of 13 sentences, the model automatically built a lexicon consisting of the following 12 items:

1. TIGER
2. CAT
3. HAS-STRIPES
4. WILD
5. TABBIE
6. PET
7. FLAG
8. ARTIFACT
9. MAMMAL
10. ANIMAL
11. DOG
12. BARKS

The fact that the number of items in the lexicon is many fewer than the total number of words in the 13 stimulus sentences follows from the fact that once a particular word or phrase has been learned, it is no longer novel. The synaptic matrix normally learns a current input (selectively tunes a new filter cell) only when it detects a novel stimulus. Also, recall that the articles and the verb *is* were, for convenience, arbitrarily ignored by the parser.

During the presentation of the stimulus sentences, synaptic weights (ϕ) were changing automatically in accordance with the learning principle. After all 13 sentences were typed in, the ϕ distributions in the detection matrix and the imaging matrix were as represented in figure 6.3.

The semantic network was tested in two different response modes, each appropriate to a different kind of query. In one test mode, the network was asked to define a stimulus word that was the subject of a sentence previously presented to it. In the second test mode, the network was asked to infer the subject(s) of one or more stimulus words that were the predicates of sentences previously presented. When the network was required to define a subject, priming of W cells was sustained, and each activated response token (Ω_i) was assumed to reafferent its word token as the next input to the network—for example, $\Omega_9 \rightarrow W_9 \rightarrow M_9$. When the network was required to infer a subject, priming of W cells was interrupted, and the only continuing activation of the network was mediated by Ω cell

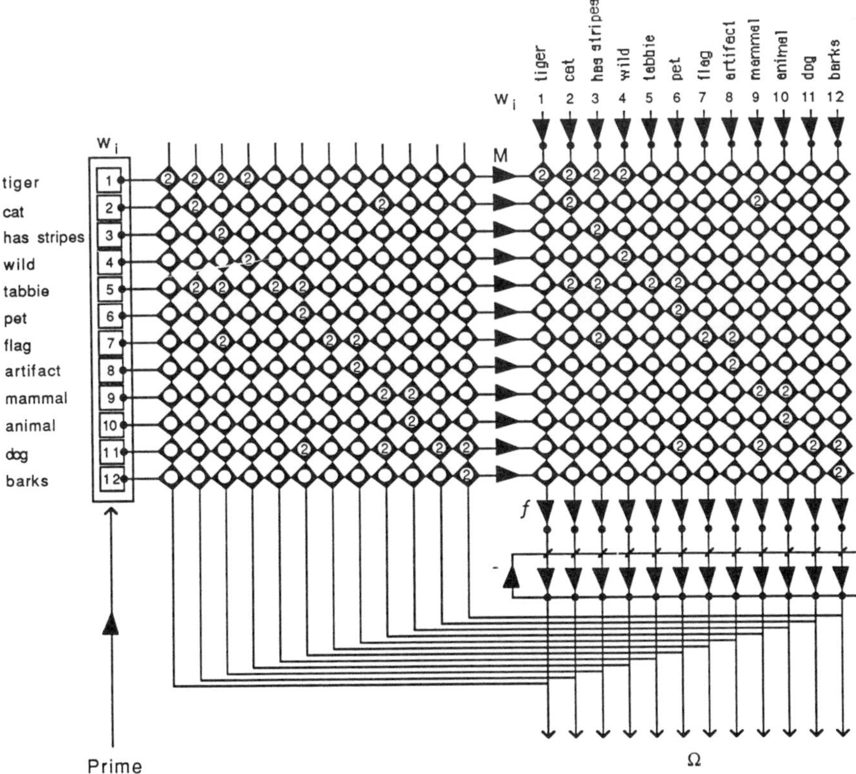

Figure 6.3
State of semantic network immediately after thirteen related sentences were presented to it. Saturation level for synaptic weights (ϕ) = 2. Synaptic junctions without printed weights are those that remained unmodified by learning and are at a uniform low basal value.

feedback through previously augmented synaptic junctions on its mosaic cells—for example, $\Omega_5 \rightarrow M_2$.

In the course of semantic processing, the subject of a sentence is represented by the activity of a mosaic cell (M_i), whereas a predicate is represented by the activity of a class cell (Ω_i). When the semantic network is queried, parallel activation of multiple predicates in response to a given subject can occur only when the synaptic weights (ϕ) that control the respective rates of EPSP integration in Ω cells have the same value (the saturation limit *Lim*). Under such circumstances, it is possible for several class cells to fire together within each Ω reset cycle.

Defining a Subject

After the 13 sentences were presented, the semantic network was asked to define the words in its lexicon that corresponded to the subjects in the sentences. The responses of the model are given in the following listing of questions and answers (phrases in parentheses were not part of the model's lexicon and are added for clarification):

Question: (WHAT IS A) TIGER ?
Response: (A) TIGER (IS A) TIGER
(A) TIGER (IS A) CAT
(A) TIGER HAS-STRIPES
(A) TIGER (IS) WILD
(A) TIGER (IS A) MAMMAL
(A) TIGER (IS AN) ANIMAL

Question: (WHAT IS A) TABBIE ?
Response: (A) TABBIE (IS A) TABBIE
(A) TABBIE (IS A) PET
(A) TABBIE (IS A) CAT
(A) TABBIE HAS-STRIPES
(A) TABBIE (IS A) MAMMAL
(A) TABBIE (IS AN) ANIMAL

Question: (WHAT IS A) FLAG ?
Response: (A) FLAG (IS A) FLAG
(A) FLAG (IS AN) ARTIFACT
(A) FLAG HAS-STRIPES

Question: (WHAT IS A) CAT ?
Response: (A) CAT (IS A) CAT
(A) CAT (IS A) MAMMAL
(A) CAT (IS AN) ANIMAL

Question: (WHAT IS A) MAMMAL ?
Response: (A) MAMMAL (IS A) MAMMAL
(A) MAMMAL (IS AN) ANIMAL

Question: (WHAT IS A) DOG ?
Response: (A) DOG (IS A) DOG
(A) DOG BARKS
(A) DOG (IS A) PET
(A) DOG (IS A) MAMMAL
(A) DOG (IS AN) ANIMAL

The semantic network's responses to the queries are appropriate given the original information (sentences) that it had learned; among its responses to each query was the identity relation ("A TIGER IS A TIGER"); and the model was able to make appropriate inferences from the information provided. Despite the fact that it was not told that a tiger is a mammal or that a tiger is an animal, it was able to infer that if a tiger is a cat and a cat is a mammal and a mammal is an animal, then a tiger is both a mammal and an animal. The same kind of inferences were made about a tabbie. And the model inferred from the fact that a dog is a mammal that it must also be an animal.

The reason that these inferences were made follows from the synaptic structure endogenously organized in the course of learning from the original sentences. When the word cell W_1 corresponding to the character string "TIGER" was discharging, it evoked (through its learning-enhanced synaptic junctions in the detection matrix) the discharge of the following class cell tokens: Ω_1 (TIGER), Ω_2 (CAT), Ω_3 (HAS-STRIPES), and Ω_4 (WILD). These, in turn, were assumed to evoke their word tokens as reafferent stimuli to the synaptic matrix, providing new inputs to the semantic network. In particular, for example, indirect feedback from the active Ω_2 token (CAT) fired W_2 (CAT), which fired M_2 (CAT), and this cell then fired Ω_9 (MAMMAL) (via f_9 in the detection matrix). The response *MAMMAL* was given as part of the definition of *TIGER* though the system was not told that a tiger is a mammal. Moreover, once the response *MAMMAL* was made, the same kind of recursive process induced the discharge of the Ω_{10} token (ANIMAL). So *ANIMAL* was also given as a proper response to the question, "WHAT IS A TIGER?"

A particularly important kind of synaptic change automatically occurs in the semantic network when these recursive neuronal events take place. Since the original subject of the query is latched in an autaptic token in the array of word cells, its coupled mosaic cell remains active and forms an enhanced synapse with each of the filter cells discharged in the inference process. A predicate response that was originally produced by a chain of inference is now directly mediated by a new synaptic link between neuronal tokens of subject and predicate. The self-restructuring of the synaptic matrix that occurred during the course of querying it is revealed in figure 6.4. The synapses marked by asterisks in the figure are the newly formed token-to-token gateways in the semantic network.

Inferring a Subject

In the previous test, the semantic network was asked to define or describe a subject: *WHAT IS A TIGER? WHAT IS A FLAG?* The following test required the semantic network to infer an appropriate subject from a given predicate or a set of predicates. The state of the synaptic matrix corresponded to figure 6.4. Instead of initiating each query by discharging a selected word cell as in the previous simulation, class cells that represented selected predicate tokens were fired either singly or in combinations. Thus, when the model was asked "(WHAT) ANIMAL (IS) WILD? Ω_{10} (ANIMAL) and Ω_4 (WILD) were automatically discharged together. Since the sentences that provided the original information for the naive semantic network contained no plural words, the following queries could be put only in singular form (phrases and letters in parentheses were not part of the model's lexicon and are added for clarification):

Question: (WHAT ARE SOME) ANIMAL(S)?
Response: (A) TIGER
(A) CAT
(A) TABBIE
(A) MAMMAL
(AN) ANIMAL
(A) DOG

Question: (WHAT) HAS-STRIPES?
Response: (A) TIGER
HAS-STRIPES
(A) TABBIE
(A) FLAG

Question: (WHAT) PET HAS-STRIPES?
Response: (A) TABBIE

Question: (WHAT ARE SOME) PET(S)?
Response: (A) TABBIE
(A) PET
(A) DOG

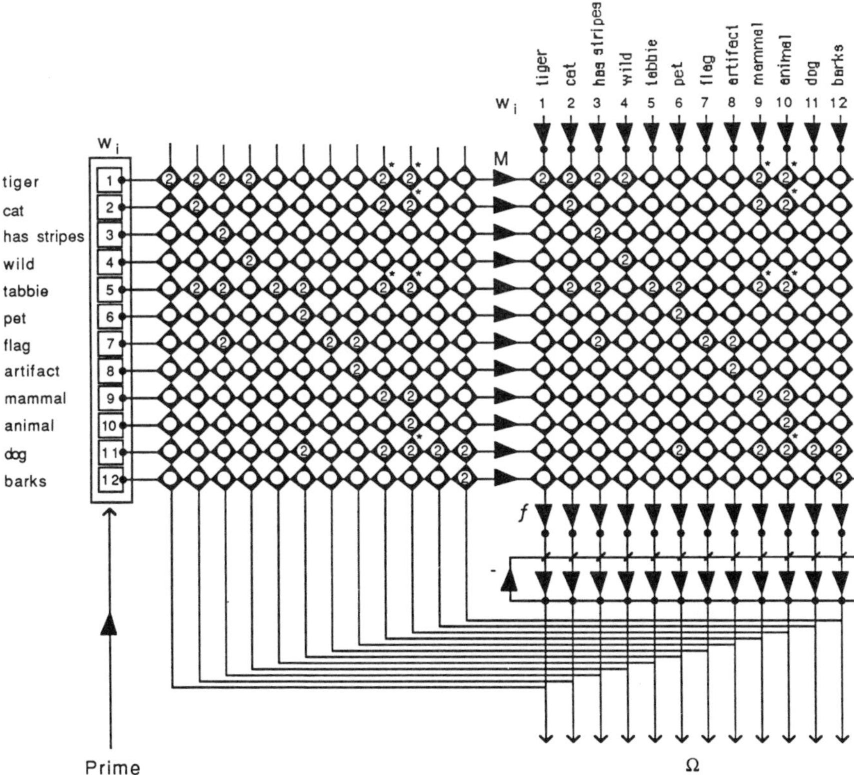

Figure 6.4
State of semantic network after it had been "asked" to define the subjects of the presented sentences. New synaptic changes were automatically induced in the course of responding to queries. The newly strengthened synaptic junctions are marked by an asterisk.

Question: (WHAT) HAS-STRIPES (AND IS AN) ARTIFACT?
Response: (A) FLAG

Question: (WHAT) ANIMAL (IS) WILD?
Response: (A) TIGER

Question: (WHAT) ANIMAL (IS A) PET (AND) BARKS?
Response: (A) DOG

The semantic network that was endogenously organized within the synaptic matrix was able to infer the appropriate subjects on the basis of either simple or complex predicates: *an animal* versus *an animal that is a pet and barks.* And this was accomplished by plausible neuronal mechanisms and architecture.

The reason that the network behaves as it does can be seen in the synaptic structure of figure 6.4. The greater the number of predicate qualifiers (Ω_i) that are "true" of any given subject (W_i), the more learning-enhanced synapses will activate its paired mosaic cell (M_i) when those predicate tokens are fired during a query. It follows that the most appropriate subject tokens (M_i) will exhibit response latencies shorter than those of less appropriate tokens. When a query permits more than one subject as a correct response, all proper M cells are discharged in parallel because each has an equal number of active synapses (see the response to "WHAT ARE SOME ANIMALS?").

Linking the Semantic Network to the Real World

The semantic network model seems to provide a neuronal mechanism that can adaptively organize a lexicon and instantiate logical relationships among lexical items. When it is questioned, it can respond appropriately on the basis of inferences that it makes from previously presented propositional information. But when it asserts that "A TIGER HAS-STRIPES," the word *TIGER* and the phrase *HAS-STRIPES* have no referents other than the character strings that evoke their neuronal tokens. Taken as an isolated module, the semantic network can exhibit logical processing of its physical symbols (tokens), but it can provide no information about their meaning with respect to events in the real world (see Johnson-Laird, Herrmann, and Chaffin 1984).

An appropriate reciprocal mapping is required between the synaptic matrix for pattern recognition at the sensory input level and the lexical tokens within the semantic network. This mapping should provide a neuronal structure wherein a sensory pattern evokes its proper lexical token and the discharge of that token can evoke an afferent image of that sensory pattern. Moreover, the synaptic gateways that instantiate such a mapping between separate processing modules must be able to evolve adaptively in the context of novel sensory environments and new lexical items. A neuronal system that can accomplish the desired mapping for visual-semantic processing is shown schematically in figure 6.5. This architecture is similar to the connectivity scheme illustrated in figure 3.5. It can be adaptively constructed by the backward-chaining mechanism (described in figure 3.6) in the following way.

Mosaic cell analogs (images) of objects at the level of the sensory matrix are mapped to particular object tokens (Ω_i), which provide input to the next processing stage, the synaptic matrix for lexical assignment (designating objects and events by the words that are conventionally used to refer to them). Since, during the learning of a lexical assignment, an object token must be active concurrently with the discharge of its proper lexical token, the axon collateral of the discharging lexical token (Ω'_i) that feeds back to the array of object tokens (Ω_i) will selectively strengthen its synapse with just that object token that was coactive with it (coactivity of Ω_i and Ω'_i). This provides a proper backward mapping from lexical tokens at the stage of lexical assignment to object tokens at the earlier stage of pattern recognition. The same process of backward selection of the proper synaptic couplings occurs between the matrix for lexical assignment and the semantic network because of the coactivity of input tokens from the former and feedback from the output tokens of the latter during the course of building the lexicon. In this fashion, the neuronal architecture shown in figure 6.5 is adaptively constructed as the lexicon is learned and lexical assignments are made. When the semantic network asserts that "A TIGER HAS-STRIPES," it not only states a proposition; it simultaneously evokes internal afferent patterns (images) that are analogs of the objects to which the proposition refers.

When synaptic matrices are organized in this way, the perception of either a specific object in the environment or the character string that names the object will evoke the same lexical tokens in the brain. Conversely, discharge of a lexical token can evoke an image of both its associated object and the object's name. And when lexical tokens are evoked by sentential stimuli, they are automatically related to each other in a logical fashion by selective synaptic coupling within the semantic network. Notice, however, that at the level of the semantic network, some of the components of sentential stimuli could be pictures as well as words, since each (if represented at all) is represented at this stage by its appropriate lexical token. These to-

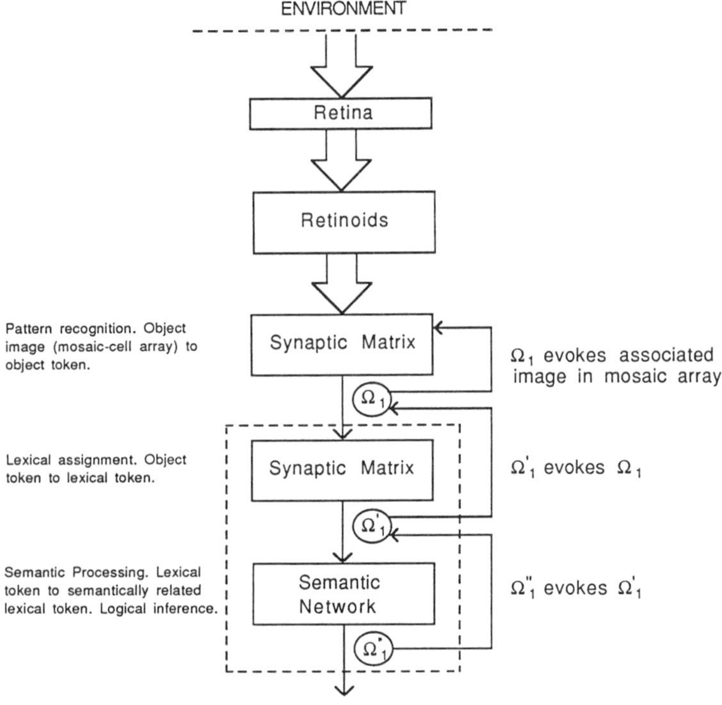

Figure 6.5
Flow diagram depicting forward and backward chaining of Ω tokens. Adaptive mapping binds lexical tokens to appropriate sensory images (including lexical strings).

kens constitute a common conceptual representation for both images and words (Banks and Flora 1977, Guenther and Klatsky 1977, Kroll and Potter 1984, Potter and Faulconer 1975). Thus, the proposed visual-lexical-semantic mechanism behaves in a manner that is consistent with the experimental finding that sentence processing can work directly with internal representations provided by pictured objects as well as with words (Potter et al. 1986).

The Structure of Representation

Fodor and Pylyshyn (1988) have argued persuasively that "mental representations need an articulated internal structure." The properties of the neuronal system suggested here satisfy the requirement for articulated representational structures in a number of ways. First, at the stage where exteroceptive stimulus patterns are learned, filter cells are fully tuned in one exposure to a stimulus. This means that the strength of association between any arbitrary current stimulus and any given class cell token depends on only the correlation between the constituent structures of the current stimulus and the exemplar to which the mediating filter cell was tuned; it is not confounded by the frequency of stimulus occurrence. Second, while individual tokens do not possess constituent structure, they systematically evoke images of their referents (sensory analogs or subsets of other tokens), which can be structurally complex and are decomposable into constituent parts having their own semantic properties. Finally, individual tokens can be activated in combinatorial fashion so that cognitive processing is influenced by the joint effect of separate tokens within a structured representation (as in the query, "What has stripes and is an artifact?").

Moreover, given the capability of retinoid mechanisms to assemble complex, organized representational structures from successive inputs of simpler parts, a visual-lexical-semantic system that incorporates such mechanisms can, in principle, meet the challenge of productivity put by Fodor and Pylyshyn (1988). A system of this kind can not only represent veridical events, but it can inventively synthesize novel images (Trehub 1977, 1987) and sentences. Novel productions can then be projected to synaptic matrices to be learned and stored as newly tuned filter cells in an expanding long-term memory.

In the simulation presented in this chapter, a semantic network was queried by an exogenous source (the tester). Such queries can also be generated endogenously by the appropriate discharge of lexical tokens (self-query). In this way, the neuronal network can monitor the semantic implications of lexical communications in an on-line fashion without mediation or prompting from an outside source.

The communications subject to semantic processing can be self-generated sentences, as well as the lexical productions of others. Because lexical tokens are systematically bound to events in the real world, inferences drawn by the semantic network can provide information on which to base reasonable plans of action. These plans, in turn, can be expressed and learned as new lexical productions—tokened representations of action schemes that are subject to elaboration and interpretation within the semantic network.

Chapter 7
Analysis and Representation of Object Relations

Among the most challenging problems that must be solved by any theoretical model purporting to explain the competence of the human brain for ecologically relevant tasks are those relating to the analysis and representation of the internal structure in an extended spatial layout of multiple objects. For example:

- How can a complex visual environment be effectively parsed into objects that can be learned and represented as cognitive entities?
- How can we selectively remember the location of objects in 3-D space?
- How can we extract and represent spatial relationships among objects?
- How can we represent the movement of a selected object?

In this chapter, we will consider some plausible brain structures that I believe can provide answers to these questions.

Parsing Objects

Try to imagine a person with an intact visual system but absolutely no knowledge about objects in the visual world. In such a case, since any point of gaze would be no more meaningful than another, where would one look? How could the person parse out the articulated objects and parts of the observed environment (Hoffman and Richards 1984, Pinker 1984)? If an individual were unable to capture significant parts of the world as distinct sensory entities, how could they be learned and added to an evolving knowledge base? It is clear that the ability to parse neuronal representations of objects systematically out of a continuous flux of visual stimulation is critical for the development of cognitive competence. The neuronal system described next addresses this problem; it can parse objects in a complex visual environment (Trehub 1986).

Architecture of a Parsing System

Shown in figure 7.1 is a block-flow diagram of the various modular mechanisms already proposed, with the visual parsing system incorporated in this architecture. The principal processing elements in the model can be outlined as follows:

1. Center-surround mechanisms in the retina and lower-level visual nuclei extract contours from the light-intensity distribution of the visual field.
2. There are cells that independently integrate contour excitation within small, discrete regions over the entire visual field. These flux detectors are retinotopically indexed and serve to drive visual saccades to regions of maximum contour flux.
3. A visual field constriction mechanism can limit the effective stimulus input to an area of variable retinal diameter centered on the foveal axis.
4. A postretinal dynamic visual buffer, called a retinoid, can translate patterns of retinal stimulation over an egocentric coordinate space. This module automatically locates and positions pattern centroids on a standard reference axis (the normal foveal axis) within the visual system.

It is assumed that the total visual field is analyzed by an array of retinotopically indexed cells, each of which receives input from a relatively small region of the complete retinal field (figure 7.2). These are the flux detectors, and each of these cells integrates the amount of visual contour excitation in its particular retinal region and discharges with a frequency proportional to its total excitation. It is assumed that the receptive field of each detector overlaps the receptive fields of its neighboring detectors. These contour flux detectors feed a matched array of cells that control visual saccades. The flux detector with the highest discharge frequency captures control of the saccadic apparatus (by the same kind of mechanism that causes the most active class cell to determine the output of the detection matrix) and directs a saccade to the center of the circumscribed visual region that provides its input. Thus, the region of visual space with the highest contour density will be fixated first.

At the start of the parsing process, the visual field aperture is constricted to a small window on the environmental scene, and an initial tolerance level is set for hemifield mismatch in the retinoid system before the centroid of the current effective visual stimulus pattern is shifted to the normal foveal axis. The visual aperture is progressively enlarged in a stepwise fashion and at the same time relaxes its tolerance for hemifield discrepancies (error due to quadrantal-excitation

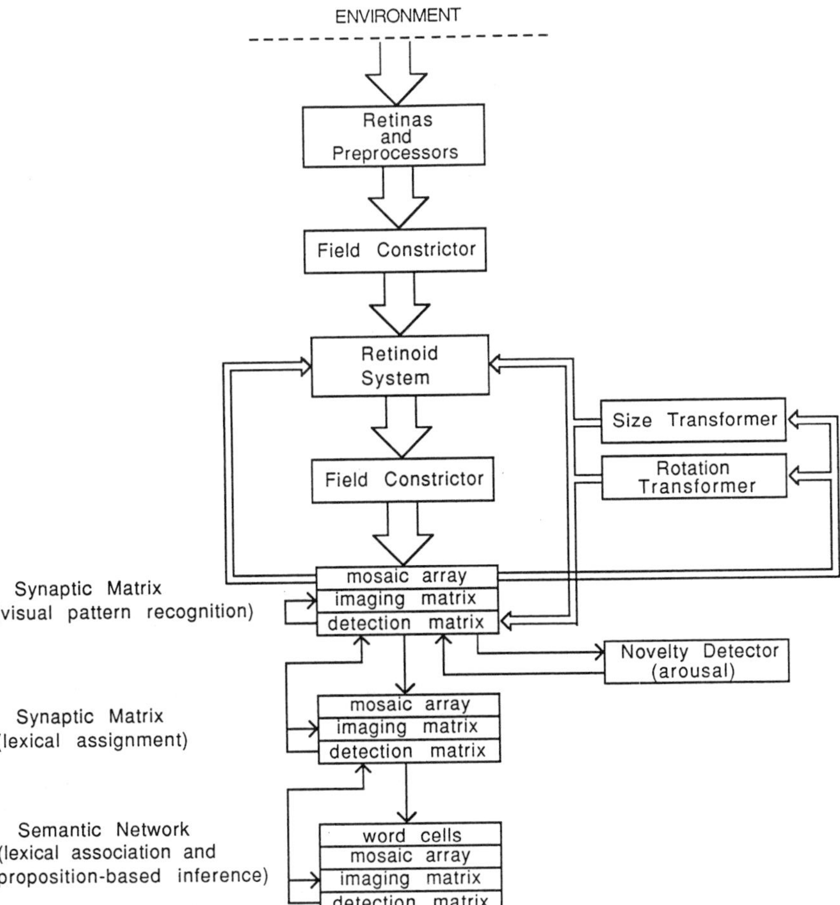

Figure 7.1
Block-flow diagram of visual system and semantic network. Double-lined channels transfer large multicell patterns of excitation. Single-lined channels transfer labeled-line excitation.

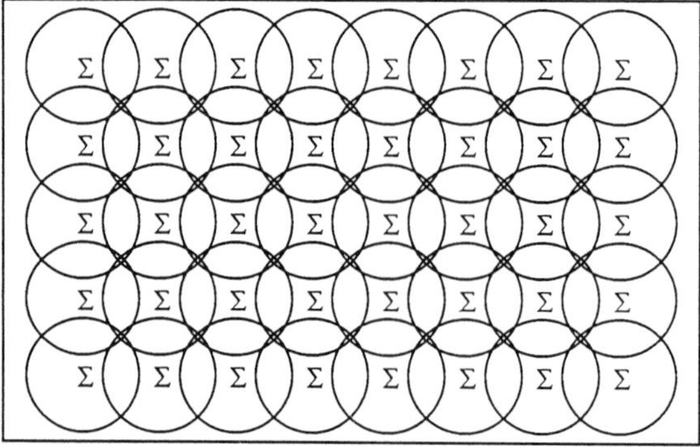

Figure 7.2
Contour flux detectors with overlapping summation fields. Contour excitation is independently integrated over the limited visual field of each detector. The flux detector with the highest output drives a self-locus excursion and a saccade to the retinotopic locus of its visual field.

imbalances). At each step, the system seeks to adjust the current centroid of the stimulus component within the larger pattern aperture so that it lies on the normal foveal axis of the retinoid layer that projects to the synaptic matrix. When the afferent aperture reaches a limiting size, the pattern of retinoid excitation on the normal foveal axis is gated to the synaptic matrix for learning or recognition. Then the currently dominant flux detector is inhibited. This allows the detector with the next highest level of activity to direct the next saccade, causing a new fixation, and the parsing process is repeated. The processing sequence for object parsing is illustrated in figure 7.3.

An Example of Performance

The model was tested for its ability to parse objects from a 2-D projection of the visual environment. In the following simulation, it was provided with a 16 × 16–cell retinal fovea and 20 flux detection cells with overlapping receptive fields that combined to cover the entire visual scene. The exact loci of detection cell fields were distributed in quasi-random fashion over the scene. The initial afferent aperture was arbitrarily set at four retinal units in width, and the fully expanded aperture was limited to 16 retinal units. Initial error tolerance for centroid positioning was arbitrarily set at two units of hemifield disparity. The flowchart for the computer simulation is shown in figure 7.4.

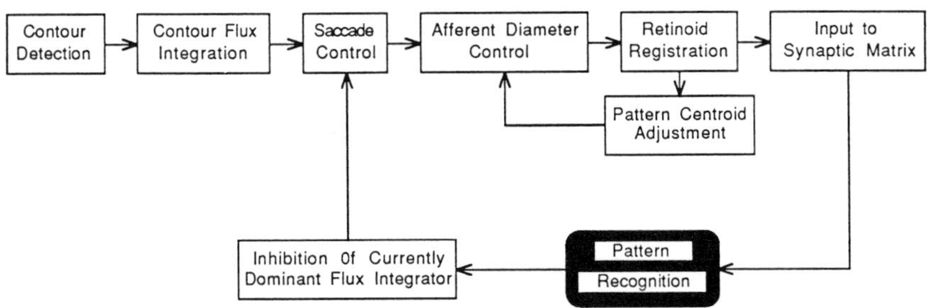

Figure 7.3
Processing sequence for parsing an object in a complex visual environment.

The objects to be parsed were randomly located in a 100 × 40–pixel visual scene. The stimuli were alphabetical characters, a human face, and a person seated at a table with just the head, upper torso, arms, and hands visible. At the start of each scene-parsing operation, the model first made a saccade to the retinotopic locus of the flux detector showing the highest activity. Then initial error tolerance was set (+/− 2 retinal units of hemifield disparity) and the afferent field aperture closed to its initial constriction state (4 retinal units). The centroid of the retinal pattern that fell within the afferent aperture was then moved to the normal foveal axis by the retinoid mechanism described in chapter 4. At any fixed aperture, if error tolerance was exceeded on a given axis, the retinoid pattern shifted in the appropriate direction to reduce disparity on that axis. When the pattern position satisfied error tolerance for one axis, the pattern shifted in the appropriate direction on the other axis unless it was already within tolerance. If shifting the image on the second axis resulted in an unacceptable error on the first, error tolerance relaxed one unit. Whenever the pattern was brought within axial tolerance for both horizontal and vertical disparities, the afferent aperture expanded one unit and the process repeated until full aperture was achieved. This operation was assumed to involve an expenditure of processing effort, and if a retinoid shift over nine consecutive cells on any axis did not reduce hemifield disparity on that axis, the system stopped trying at its current fixation and initiated a saccade to the next highest flux region.

In one test of the parsing system, the letters *A* and *B* were presented at various locations in the visual field, and the ability of the system to isolate and capture these objects on the normal foveal axis

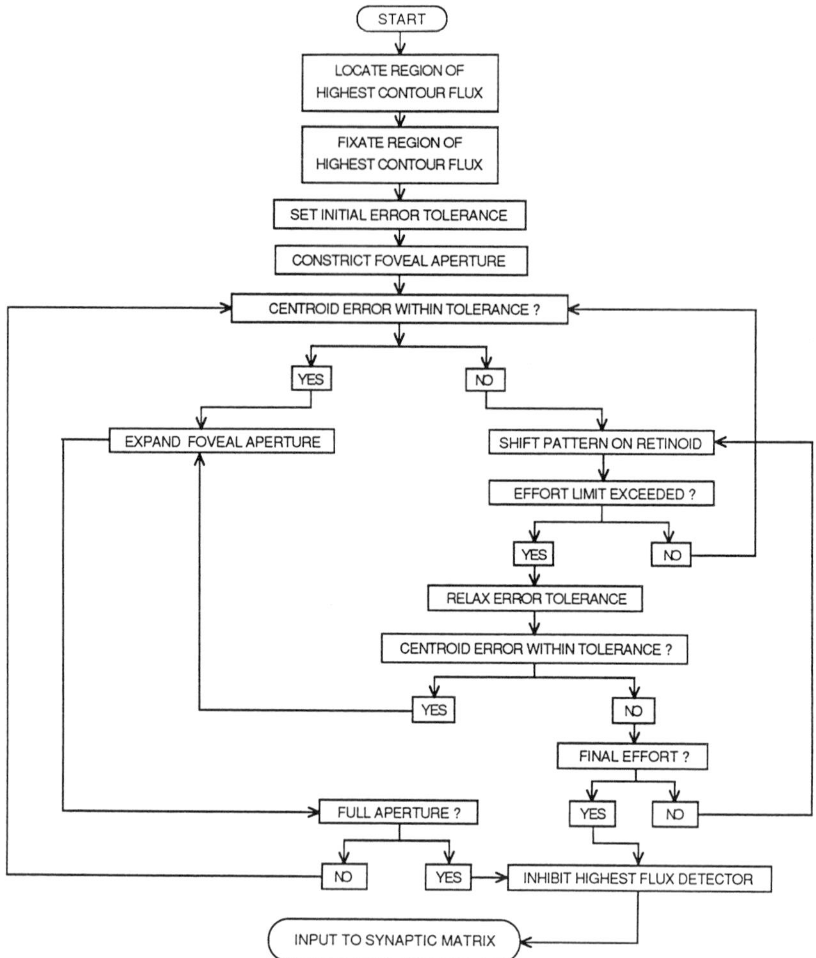

Figure 7.4
Flowchart for object-parsing simulation.

was successfully demonstrated. Another test required the visual system to "look at" and parse displays of a larger number of upper- and lowercase letters. Figures 7.5, 7.6, and 7.7 are printouts taken directly from the CRT. They indicate that even in a visual environment cluttered with many objects, a parsing system of this kind can operate effectively.

These tasks required the visual system to parse individual objects (alphabetic characters) out of a display consisting of a number of randomly located objects, each small enough to be represented in its complete form within the receptive field of the fully expanded afferent aperture. What happens when an object is so large or viewed so near that the visual angle it subtends is much larger than the retinal fovea and the visual projection of its outer bounds extends beyond the afferent aperture? In such cases, we would like the system sys-

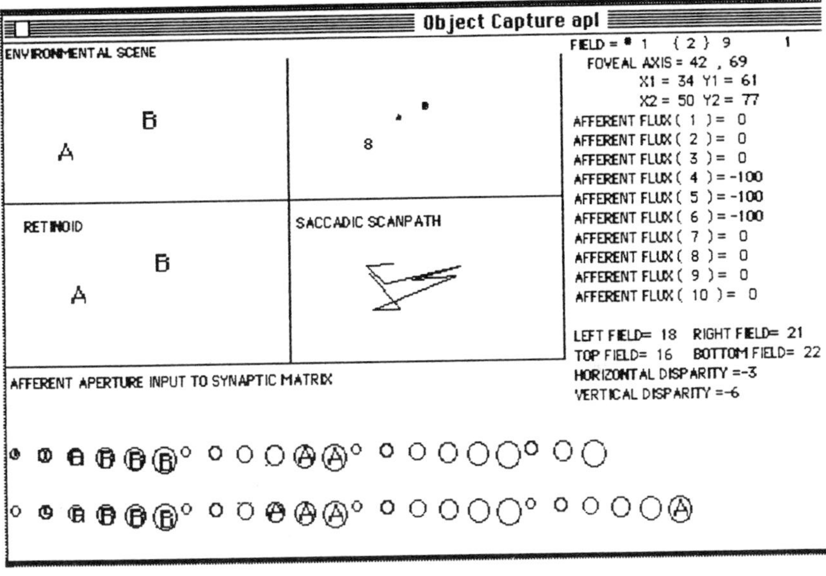

Figure 7.5
CRT display of object-parsing simulation. Upper-left panel shows objects A and B as located in the "environment." Middle panel shows the path of successive saccadic fixations as parsing proceeds. Bottom panel shows successive enlargement of afferent aperture and automatic adjustment of object centroid to normal foveal axis following each of eight saccades. Empty or absent apertures indicate that an object centroid could not be adjusted within tolerance on that fixation at that aperture. An empty maximum aperture indicates that no acceptable centroid adjustment was made before the effort limit was exceeded and a new saccade was initiated. Left-middle panel shows a reconstruction of the visual environment on the scene assembly retinoid.

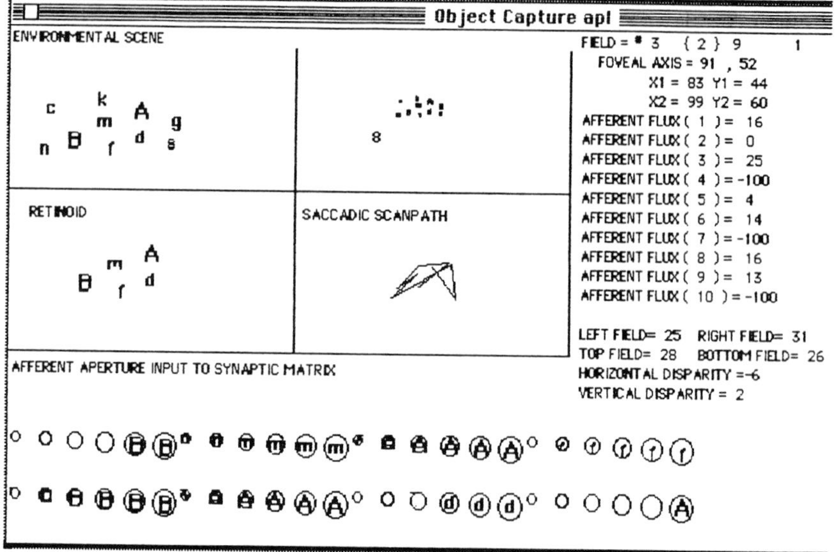

Figure 7.6
CRT display of object-parsing simulation. Upper-left panel shows an "environment" containing 10 objects. Only the five objects that were parsed in the course of eight saccadic fixations are represented on the scene assembly retinoid.

tematically to capture parts of the larger object. To test the behavior of the model in situations of this kind, single stimuli that were much larger than the maximum afferent aperture were presented for parsing—in one case, a human head and face was shown and in another a person seated at a table with the upper part of the body, arms, and hands visible. CRT displays of these simulations are shown in figures 7.8 and 7.9.

When the head and face was presented, the visual system isolated and captured the following parts: left eye (twice); right eye and bridge of the nose (twice); right jaw line, neck, and shoulder; and mouth and lower nose (three times) (figure 7.8). The left-middle panel in figure 7.8 shows the retinotopic excitation pattern that is formed, one part at a time, in the scene assembly retinoid on the basis of the successive saccadic fixations through the afferent aperture. When the figure of a person seated at a table was presented, these parts were isolated: face (twice), hands (three times), edge of table, and right forearm (figure 7.9). Again, notice the image composed on the scene assembly retinoid by successive fixations through the afferent aperture.

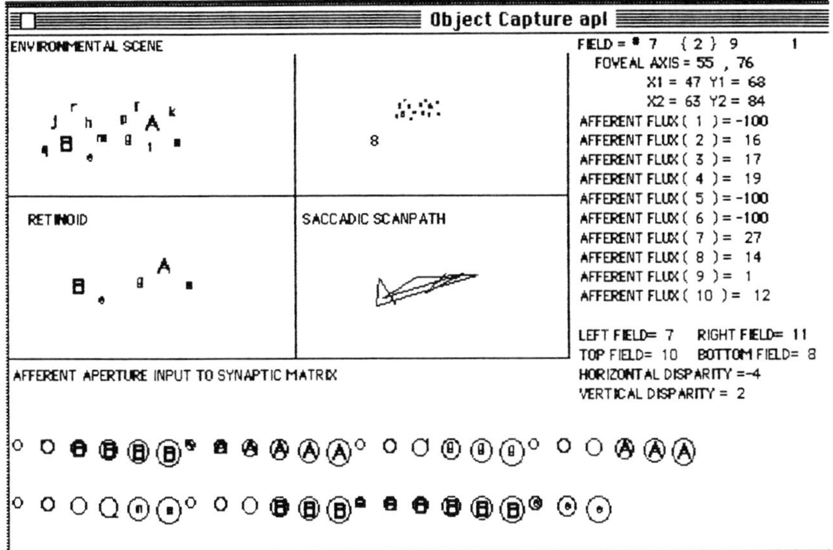

Figure 7.7
CRT display of object-parsing simulation. Upper-left panel shows an environment containing 14 objects. Notice that parsing is effective even in a densely cluttered visual environment.

At each parsing operation, the momentary size of the afferent aperture will limit the size of an object (or part of an object) in the larger visual field that can be projected to the synaptic matrix. For example, if the afferent aperture were limited to a small expansion, an eye or mouth could be isolated as a part of a face to be recognized or learned as a unitary feature. A larger expansion would capture the image of an entire face; this could then be matched as a holistic form against filter cells in the detection matrix or, if novel, provide the excitation pattern for a new profile of synaptic weights in a previously unmodified filter cell.

In this simulation of a minimal parsing mechanism, the relative density of visual contours over segments of the frontal scene served to control successive saccades. It is assumed that in the complete visual-cognitive system, low-level processes such as response to an abrupt change in illumination or to sudden motion and higher-level processes such as a preprogrammed search routine can also select the locus of gaze. But no matter what drives the saccade, the system performs a subsequent fine adjustment that brings the centroid of an aperture-limited image to the normal foveal axis.

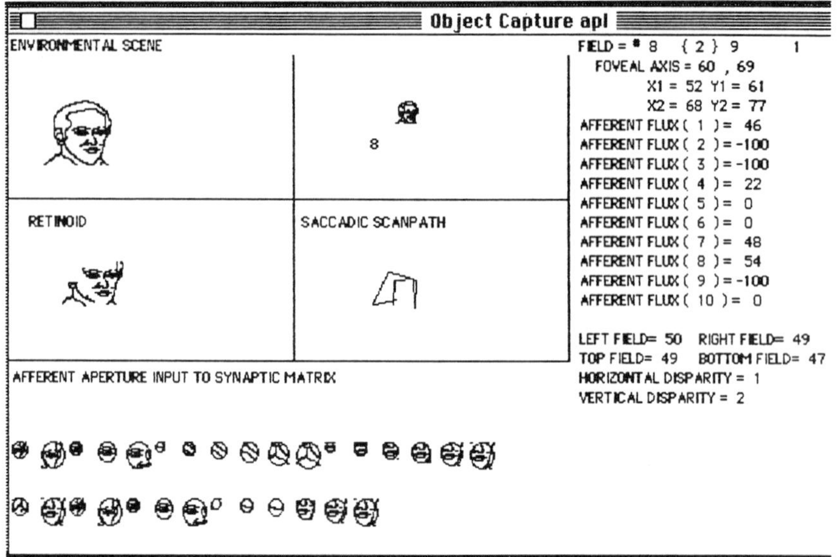

Figure 7.8
CRT display of object-parsing simulation. The stimulus, shown in the upper-left panel, is a three-quarter frontal view of a human head. The bottom panel shows the parts of the head that were parsed after each of eight saccadic fixations: (1) left eye, (2) right eye and bridge of nose, (3) right jaw, neck, and shoulder, (4) mouth and lower nose, (5) mouth and lower nose, (6) left eye, (7) right eye and bridge of nose, (8) mouth and lower nose. Left-middle panel shows the excitation pattern on the scene assembly retinoid. Notice the partial reconstruction of the head and face with the parsed features in proper spatial relation.

Remembering the Location of Objects

There are at least two ways in which the location of objects viewed in an extended environmental scene might be represented in memory for later recall. One is to reduce the size of the scene assembled in the retinoid system. Then it can be projected to the synaptic matrix as a complete spatial layout to be learned and evoked in the imaging matrix when the information is needed. The other is to register the 3-D coordinates of each object in the scene and learn them together with their associated objects. The first procedure would require an appropriate dimensional reduction of the retinoid output by operation of the size transformer (see figure 7.1) so that the entire scene can be captured (within the afferent aperture) by the synaptic distribution on a single filter cell. Although this approach might serve to represent the relative location of objects in 2-D space, location in

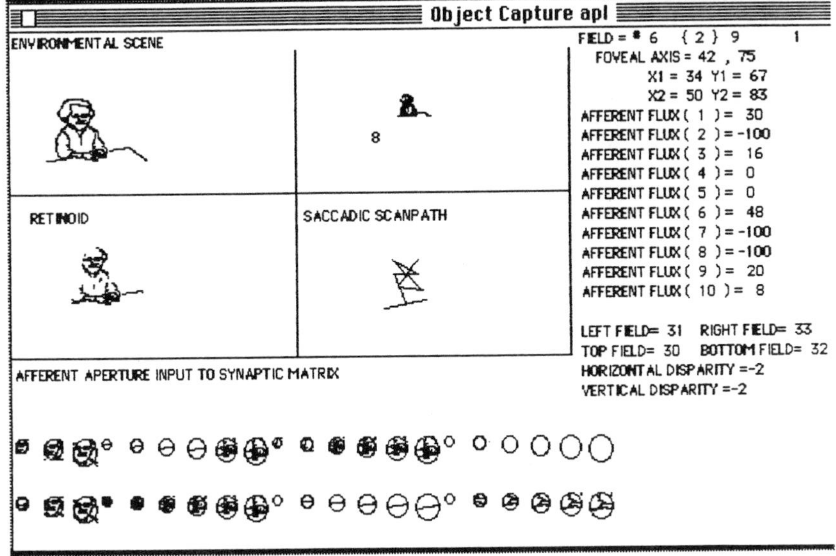

Figure 7.9
CRT display of object-parsing simulation. The stimulus, shown in the upper-left panel, is a person seated at a table. The bottom panel shows the parts of the scene that were parsed after each of eight saccadic fixations: (1) full face, (2) hands, (3) hands, (4) nothing (no centroid adjustment within tolerance), (5) full face, (6) hands, (7) edge of table, (8) right forearm. Left-middle panel shows the excitation pattern on the scene assembly retinoid. Notice the partial reconstruction with parsed features in proper spatial relation.

depth would not be conserved. This follows from the fact that excitation from the 3-D retinoid is a 2-D projection to the mosaic cells of the synaptic matrix. In the second approach, during recall, the imaginal representation of each object or its class cell token would be separately evoked in the imaging matrix, projected to the 3-D retinoid, and then translated in retinoid space to its original autaptic cell coordinates. In this case, because of the connectivity for size constancy in the 3-D retinoid, if the pattern of an object (rather than its token) is projected to the retinoid, its representation would diminish in size in accordance with its distance on the Z-axis

In this routine, it is assumed that focal attention is required to learn the location of an object. Thus, there is an excursion of the self-locus to the retinoid location of each object of interest before it is translated to the normal foveal axis. The model assumes that each autaptic cell in the 3-D retinoid sends out three collateral axons providing selective input to three groups of neurons that sense the planar location of that autaptic cell on the X, Y, and Z axes respectively (if its level of activity is sufficiently high). Activity of autaptic cells at each of the successive target positions of the self-locus is increased by the added input from the self-locus (exogenous stimulation from a retinal pattern or endogenous stimulation from an object token, plus excitation from self-locus discharge). The augmented output from each of the targeted autaptic cells is sufficient to exceed the threshold of a discrete neuron in each of the three groups of labeled lines that sense the location of neuronal activity on the X, Y, and Z axes, respectively. These triplets of labeled lines constitute neuronal indexes to the approximate spatial location of each object or token that is attended to in the scene. Figure 7.10 shows how the position of the self-locus stimulates labeled lines for sensing the X, Y, and Z coordinates that define the retinoid locations of two separate objects. The cell triplets (C_X, C_Y, C_Z) then provide input to a synaptic matrix where object tokens are associated with their appropriate spatial coordinates (figure 7.11).

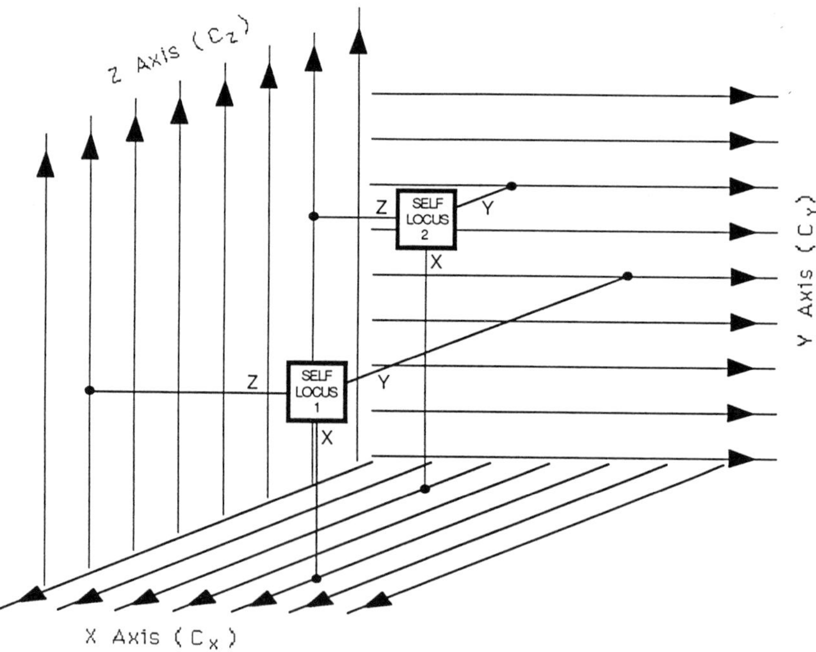

Figure 7.10
Neuronal mechanism for sensing the location of self-locus excursions in retinoid space.

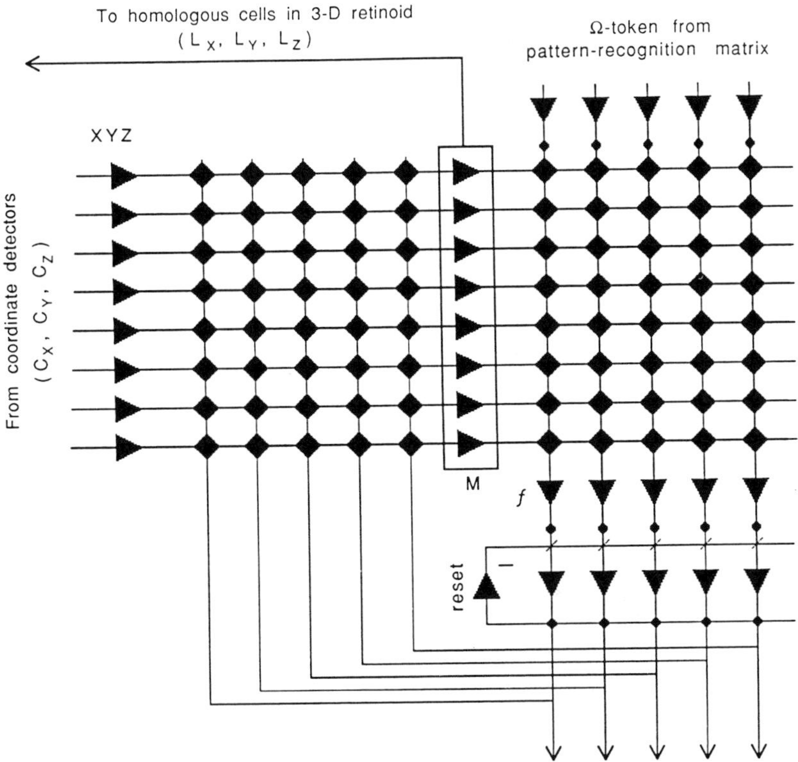

Figure 7.11
Synaptic matrix for associating object tokens with their spatial coordinates in retinoid space.

After the association between a token and its retinoid location has been learned, any evocation of that token alone will induce the discharge of three locator cells (L_X, L_Y, L_Z) via feedback to the 3-D retinoid from their homologous mosaic cells in the imaging matrix (figures 7.11 and 7.12). The function of the locator cells is to activate selected autaptic units at those coordinates within the 3-D retinoid that correspond to the location of each object of interest when the original scene was learned. When positional recall of this kind occurs, the firing of each object token is accompanied by a "brightening" (autaptic cell discharge) at its original location in the 3-D retinoid. This happens automatically because the output from any triplet of locator cells will summate fully and exceed threshold only in the autaptic cell that is at the retinoid coordinate defined and selected by the particular triplet L_X, L_Y, L_Z (figure 7.12).

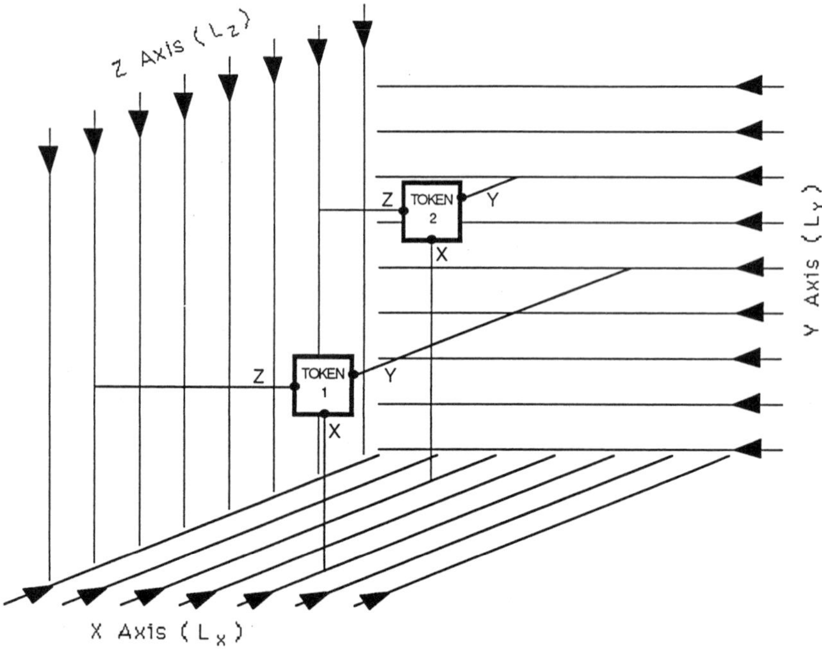

Figure 7.12
Neuronal mechanism for signaling the original location of an object in retinoid space.

A key assumption of this model—that the activity of retinoid cells at the egocentric coordinates of objects of interest in a visual scene will be selectively augmented— is supported by the experimental findings of Andersen, Essick, and Siegel (1985). These investigators report that single neurons in the inferior parietal lobule of behaving monkeys show enhanced spike activity in response to visual stimuli of standard intensity as a systematic function of the angle of gaze. Thus, there is an eye position–dependent tuning of cortical cells for locations in head-centered coordinate space.

Representing Spatial Relationships among Objects

How can the spatial relationships that exist among multiple objects in a scene be analyzed and discretely represented in the brain? How, for example, can we determine the relative distance between object A and object B? Is A above or below B or to the right or left of it? Is A nearer than B or farther away than B to an arbitrary point of reference in space? Quick solutions to such problems are essential for effective action in response to immediate contingencies in the real world. And beyond immediate response, the simplest plans for traveling in an environment that presents multiple constraints on mobility require knowledge of such spatial relationships.

Determining the Position of an Object Relative to Another

Whereas a parallel excitation pattern over the 3-D retinoid can give a holistic neuronal-analog depiction of the spatial layout in a visual environment, a description of the particular pairwise relationships among objects in a scene requires a sequential analysis of the layout. In analyses of this kind, the neuronal triplet C_X, C_Y, C_Z that defines the spatial coordinates of one object must be held in working memory until it can be compared with the triplet that gives the location of the second object. This is accomplished by three separate pairs of autaptic cell buffers that are homologously ordered for C_X, C_Y, C_Z respectively. The corresponding autaptic cells within each pair of buffers have cross-inhibitory coupling. These buffer pairs serve as comparators that signal the relative position among objects on each axis in 3-D space (figure 7.13).

In the example given at the top of figure 7.13, both objects, as represented in their respective buffers, are in the left hemifield of the X-axis. The two autaptic representations are then translated to the right, each inducing a string of excited cells, until the translation of one of them is blocked by cross-inhibition from a leading active cell in the matched buffer. The leading representation, which cannot be blocked by cross-inhibition, continues its extension to the right until it fires the terminal cell in its buffer. When a terminal autaptic cell in either of the two buffers is activated, it discharges a terminal-sensing cell (T_1 or T_2). At this point, the activity of the translation driver *D* is squelched by an inhibitory input from the *T* cell that has fired. In the case shown, T_1 fires, indicating that object 1 is to the right of (leading) object 2 (taking object 2 as the reference) and object 2 is to the left of (lagging) object 1 (taking object 1 as the reference). There are similar buffer pairs for the Y and Z axes, respectively, which operate in the same way. In this fashion, the relative positions of each pair of objects that are the targets of focal attention are individually coded by the output of the *T* cells for each of the three spatial axes (left-right, above-below, nearer-farther).

Determining the Distance between Objects

The buffer comparators that analyze the relative position among objects also generate information about the distance between objects. In figure 7.13, after translation, object 2 occupied just one more au-

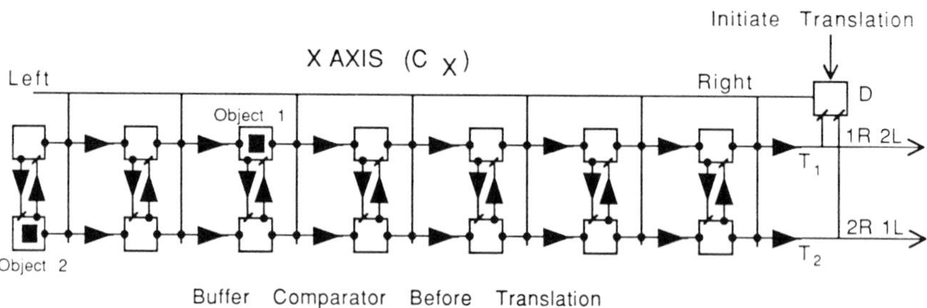

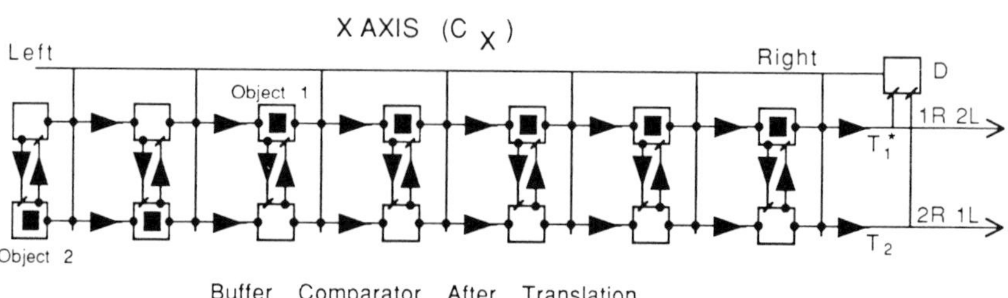

Figure 7.13
A buffer comparator for sensing and signaling the relative position among objects on the X-axis of retinoid space.

taptic cell than before translation. This follows from the fact that in the retinoid analog of the perceived scene, object 2 was separated from object 1 by a single autaptic cell. Had there been a greater distance on the X-axis between the objects, the number of autaptic units activated by object 2 after translation would have been proportionally greater. If object 2 were to the right of object 1, the state of the buffers would be exactly reversed. Thus, the number of active autaptic cells in the buffer that holds the spatial coordinate of the lagging object is an index to the distance between objects. The same principle operates in the buffer comparators for the Y- and Z-axes as well.

One way to capture this information on a labeled line is to sum the autaptic cell activity in the lagging buffer as input to a single "distance" cell for each axis. Figure 7.14 illustrates how this might be done. Output from the *T* cells is inhibitory, and, for each axis, the particular *T* cell that fires is just that terminal-sensing cell activated by the buffer holding the coordinate of the leading object. Activity in each of the buffer pairs is summed independently in two interneurons. The output from these, in turn, is summed in a single output cell. However, inhibitory collateral axons from T_1 and T_2 ensure that

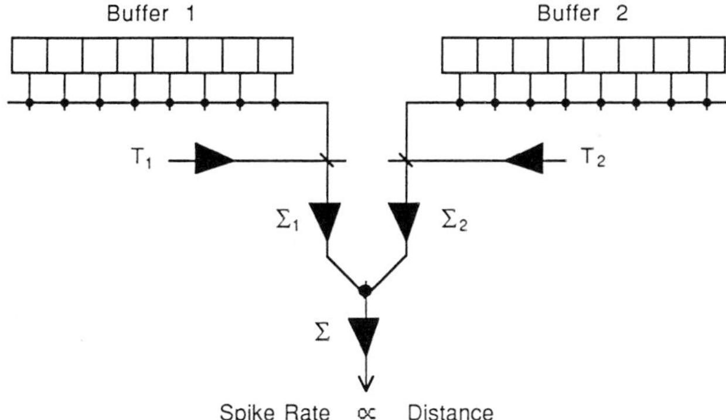

Figure 7.14
Neuronal mechanism for sensing and signaling the relative distance between two objects.

whichever of these is active will block input from the leading buffer, thus allowing only input from the lagging buffer (the desired source) to modulate the frequency of firing of the labeled line that signals the distance between objects. In this scheme, if a triplet is composed of the activity of just one autaptic cell in each of the lagging buffers for the X-, Y-, and Z-axes, the two objects are in contact (or at least so close as to be indistinguishable from the relationship of direct contact). In addition to signaling direct contact between objects, this kind of neuronal information can be used to guide the heuristic movement of the self-locus for tracing and registering the contours of objects or aspects of the environment. The ability to trace and learn significant environmental contours such as barriers and pathways permits the brain to store simple but useful schematic representations of a complex sensory world.

Characterizing the Movement of an Object

We have seen how the relative spatial relationships among different objects in a perceived environment can be analyzed and represented by neuronal mechanisms. The spatial coordinates of a single object at different times can be analyzed and represented in a similar fashion. Instead of comparing a pair of objects, two successive locations of a given object can be captured and compared. In this way, its movement and the direction of movement can be represented.

One might question whether there would be any advantage to having a separate mechanism of this kind when we know that there are motion detectors at lower levels of the visual system (Barlow,

Hill, and Levick 1964). It should be recalled, however, that in the mechanisms under discussion, focal attention (excursion of the self-locus) is required to register the spatial coordinates of objects of interest. This suggests that one advantage of these mechanisms over lower-level motion detectors that are indifferent to stimulus content is that goal-related computations of movement can be selectively performed in an environment that might have a considerable amount of incidental motion. In this account, a person could be well aware of a variety of objects moving about in the immediate environment yet be able to isolate and determine in particular the course of those self-selected objects among them. A recent investigation of motion detection cells in monkey cortex presents some evidence to support such a mechanism. Saito and associates (1986), recording from single cells in the superior temporal sulcus, discovered, near cells that were selective for the direction of image motion but not image content, a cluster of directionally selective cells that responded only to movements of real objects (face, hand). When dot patterns, large spots, or other objects (that presumably did not engage focal attention) were moved in the preferred direction of these cells, they evoked no significant response.

Lexical Assignment

Outputs from the mechanisms described are neuronal tokens of spatial relationships between different objects in the environment or between successive positions of single objects. It is assumed that they provide input to a lexical assignment matrix and are mapped to appropriate words in a language system in the same way that tokens of specific objects are mapped to words. Just as the stimulus provided by a kind of small, furry animal can induce the noun *cat,* so can the stimulus provided by a kind of spatial relationship between objects induce the appropriate adverb, adjective, or preposition (*above* or *below*). Moreover, by the same kind of neuronal architecture for back-mapping that evokes images of specific objects when their lexical tokens are fired, the discharge of a lexical token of a spatial relationship can evoke an analog representation of the relationship that is named.

Cognitive Maps

Knowledge of a particular environment entails more than having an internal representation of the objects in it, their locations, or their individual properties and affordances. It also includes a representation of potential routes—unimpeded pathways that allow personal access to objects and locations of interest. Information of this kind can be learned in the course of experience and stored as a list of propositions about a particular locale, or it can be learned and stored as a schematic analog representation—a cognitive map of a significant place in the world, to be recalled in a single frame and utilized for coping within the environment that is represented. The retinoid system and the analytic mechanisms provide sufficient neuronal means for constructing such cognitive maps. The ability to project heuristic excursions of the self-locus along the routes represented in a recalled map enables one to choose among alternative plans for moving from an initial starting point to successive target regions (or objects) in the associated environment.

In previous discussions of the retinoid system, the normal foveal axis was taken as the reference for direction of translation. This established an egocentric frame for representing the environment. Cognitive maps, however, require an object-centered frame (Marr 1982, Pinker 1984) or geo-centered frame in order to provide useful information for maneuvering in the environment. This can be accomplished by translating a feature (a significant part) of an object or aspect of the environment to a point on the normal foveal axis in retinoid space, fixing its token at this location, and then using this coordinate as the reference origin for controlling subsequent spatial translations. For example, the entrance to a room could be the fixed origin in retinoid space and would be taken as a local region centered on the normal foveal axis at the frontal plane of the room. Front, back, left, and right would be directions in relation to the entrance door. Looking from the doorway at a desk in the front-right corner would entail a direct right excursion of the self-locus. Looking at the same desk from the wall opposite the door would entail an excursion of the self-locus from a back-of-the-room position in retinoid space to a front-left location. Thus, the coordinates of object (room) features are stabilized, and the self-locus is translated with reference to these fixed coordinates.

Figure 7.15 shows the CRT display of a 2-D simulation that illustrates how heuristic excursions of the self-locus during a walk in an unfamiliar building can create an autaptic cell map of the corridors by which particular offices can be reached. The number of autaptic cells that are activated by alternative routes of the self-locus is proportional to the relative distance that must be traveled in the course of each route. Choosing the route with the least total activation ensures that one has selected the shortest route.

In this example, a person (S) is assumed to have exited from a subway station and is facing a large building with two entrances,

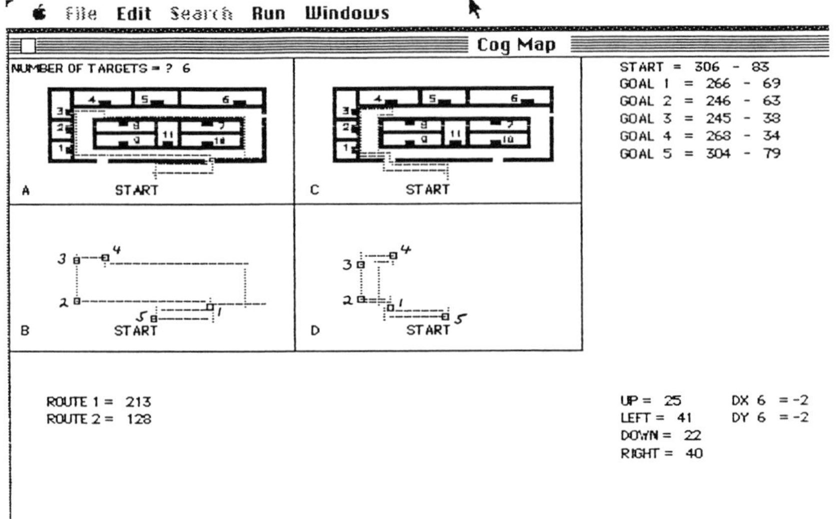

Figure 7.15
CRT display of cognitive map simulation. Panels A and C show the floor plan of an office building. Dotted lines in A and C represent two different routes taken by an individual (S) who transacts business in offices identified as 1, 3, and 4 on two separate occasions. Dotted lines in panels B and D represent the self-locus excursions made in object-centered retinoid space while S walks the routes shown in A and C. Small squares in B and D represent goal regions. Numbers beside squares represent the sequence in which the goals are set. The autaptic cell excitation patterns induced by excursions of the self-locus as shown in B and D are each learned holistically as two possible routes to be taken when transacting business in this building (cognitive maps). The total number of cells traversed and activated by the self-locus over each route is independently summed (bottom panel) and represents the distance traveled in completing each of the routes. This sum is physiologically represented in the relative discharge frequency of a cell that integrates total output from the self-locus retinoid and serves to label each route by its overall distance.

one to the left and the other to the right. The two entrances are approximately equidistant from the subway exit. There are three offices (rooms 1, 3, and 4) in which S must transact business and then return to the subway station for the trip home. S is assumed to be able to recognize and remember whatever is in his visual field (walls, doorways, signs, office numbers).

On the first visit (figure 7.15, panels A and B), the locations of the offices are unknown. S arbitrarily chooses the right-hand entrance because neither entrance is appreciably closer to the subway exit than the other. This entrance is the first goal to be reached and is fixed as the reference locus for the object BUILDING(n). Entering the building,

S is immediately confronted by a long corridor running left and right. The office directly across the entrance (room 10) is not one to be visited. At the far left end of the corridor, however, is room 1, one of the three in which business must be transacted. At this point, none of the other relevant offices is in sight, and room 1 becomes the second goal. Before S walks to room 1, however, the self-locus has already made an excursion to this target region at the end of the corridor in the left-hand part of retinoid space. Thus, the tokens of goal 1 (entrance) and goal 2 (room 1), together with the direction and distance of the self-locus excursion between the two goals, are roughly captured in the retinoid system by the spatial pattern of autaptic cell activity and the number of cells fired (traversed). In this process, each change in direction is determined by change in angle of gaze, and the distance of each leg of the excursion is determined by target location on the Z-axis.

When S reaches room 1, a glance to the right reveals the third goal, room 3, at the end of a corridor extending from the front to the back of the building with reference to the entrance (goal 1). A self-locus excursion is made to that homologous region of retinoid space (in the object-centered frame). Similarly, when S is at room 3, the last office that must be visited (room 4) can be seen. This is goal 4, and the self-locus is translated to the coordinates of this target. After all business has been transacted, S must find an exit from the building and return to the subway station (goal 5). S continues down the corridor where room 4 is located, turns right at the end of the corridor, turns right again, and finds the doorway through which he entered (the first goal). S leaves the building through the same doorway and goes to the subway station (goal 5). The route S traveled in this episode (route 1) is traced by the excitation pattern of the self-locus in its corresponding excursion within object-centered retinoid space (panel B). This pattern is projected to a synaptic matrix and stored as a cognitive map that can be imaged to serve as a possible guide on future visits to the same building.

A second visit to the same offices is shown in panels C and D of figure 7.15 (route 2). In this case, S arbitrarily chooses the left entrance to the building and goes to rooms 1, 3, and 4, as in the first visit. After leaving room 4, however, S turns right, retraces his path, exits through the same door by which he entered the building, and returns to the subway station. The number of autaptic cells traversed and discharged in routes 1 and 2, respectively, represents in a rough way the relative distance traveled for each route. Route 2 is clearly shorter (128 versus 213 autaptic units) and will be the cognitive map followed when the same transactions must be undertaken in the future.

As S walks through the building for the first time, he may note, learn, and relate incidental aspects of the environment to the route traveled. Information of this kind can provide a basis for planning more efficient behavior in the same setting on another occasion. In the example, S made the decision to adopt a particular travel route after he actually followed the route and then compared the result with an earlier course of behavior. An alternative strategy would have S consult (image and analyze) the cognitive map created on the first visit to the building to determine the most efficient route for going to each office. Assuming that he noted and remembered the building entrance close to room 1, all of the information needed is given in the retinoid map of route 1. Before a second trip is undertaken, heuristic excursions of the self-locus (tracing the contours of the map) could reveal that route 2 is better and should be taken as the plan for the next visit.

During each visit, two distinct and parallel representations are constructed in separate registers of the retinoid system: the sequence of visual stimuli observed from S's successive viewpoints and integrated in the scene assembly retinoids and the autaptic cell trace of S's heuristic self-locus as it precedes S's actual motion from each successive goal to the next in an object-centered retinoid space. This trace composes a cognitive map of locomotion affordances among significant regions within the object BUILDING(n).

Given a sufficient level of arousal, the two kinds of retinoid representations can be learned in separate synaptic matrices: one receiving projections from the scene assembly register and the other receiving projections from the register that captures the cognitive map. Because the different object-centered coordinates of the map are temporally correlated with particular visual scenes during learning, class cell tokens of these coordinates in the BUILDING(n) map can be synaptically coupled to class cell tokens of successive scenes (in the same way that lexical tokens can be coupled to visual stimuli). Following the map in imagination (tracing its contour by excursion of the self-locus) will evoke a sequence of self-locus coordinate tokens, which, in turn, can evoke visual images of the sequence of scenes that were originally experienced in BUILDING(n). Alternatively, recalling the class cell token of a particular scene will evoke its coordinate location on the cognitive map of BUILDING(n).

Chapter 8

Composing Behavior: Registers for Plans and Actions

In the conduct of everyday human affairs, the preference of one course of action over another often depends on the perception that the course chosen will tend to maximize or minimize some significant aspect of experience. For example, the decision to wear a coat instead of a light jacket on a fall day might depend on the fact that it is unseasonably cold and wearing a jacket will result in greater discomfort than wearing a coat. The brain must be able to encode and register as neuronal tokens the relative magnitudes of a great variety of experiential parameters, and it must have the capability to recall such tokens as criteria for the selection of episodic adaptive actions—integrated sequences of behavior that can be characterized as the execution of a plan (Miller, Galanter, and Pribram 1960).

Encoding Magnitude

Figure 8.1 shows a schematic representation of a simple neuronal mechanism that receives a pulse of axonal discharge as its input and systematically converts the spike frequency of the input pulse into the discharge of a particular autaptic cell in an ordered string of such cells. This mechanism operates on the same general principles as do the retinoids. In this case, however, the input pulse is of a standard and fixed duration, although its constituent spike frequency will vary according to the intensity of the event that it represents.

The autaptic cell marked 0 is constantly active. Because of the dynamic properties of this kind of neuronal circuit, the extent of excitational translation along the autaptic chain will be proportional to the frequency of the spikes that constitute the input pulse. At the end of the pulse, the ordinal value of the autaptic cell that remains active (in addition to the origin cell 0) will depend directly on the spike frequency of the input pulse. If the input frequency represents the magnitude of an experiential parameter (time or effort to complete a task, for example), then this neuronal analog will be systematically encoded as a particular labeled line (indexed autaptic cell) in an or-

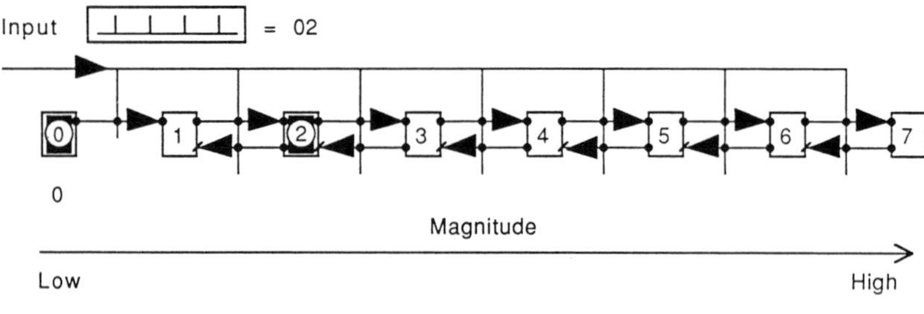

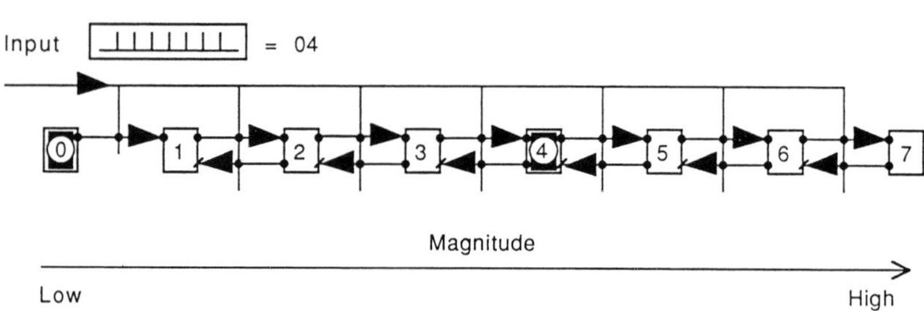

Figure 8.1
A mechanism for encoding magnitude. The degree or intensity of an event that is initially represented by the frequency of neuronal discharge (spike train in inset) is converted to a representation by place in an ordered set of autaptic cells. Each autaptic cell is a labeled line that signals relative magnitude.

dered set. After this transformation, the labeled autaptic line, which is a token (in short-term memory) of the magnitude of its parameter, can provide input to a synaptic matrix to be learned (in long-term memory) as one of the properties of the context in which it was activated.

Binding Consequences to Actions

Chapter 7 gave an example in which two different routes were evaluated for the distance traveled to accomplish the same result. Figure 8.2 illustrates how route and distance can be bound together in a synaptic matrix and represented as a single frame of knowledge that is activated in parallel. The saturation limit (*Lim*) for filter cell transfer weights (ϕ_i) was arbitrarily set at $Lim = 2$. There are two separate but concurrent sources of afferent excitation to the matrix: a labeled-line token of a particular self-locus excursion (route), either current or recalled from memory, and a token output from the autaptic chain that encodes the overall distance of the route. After route and dis-

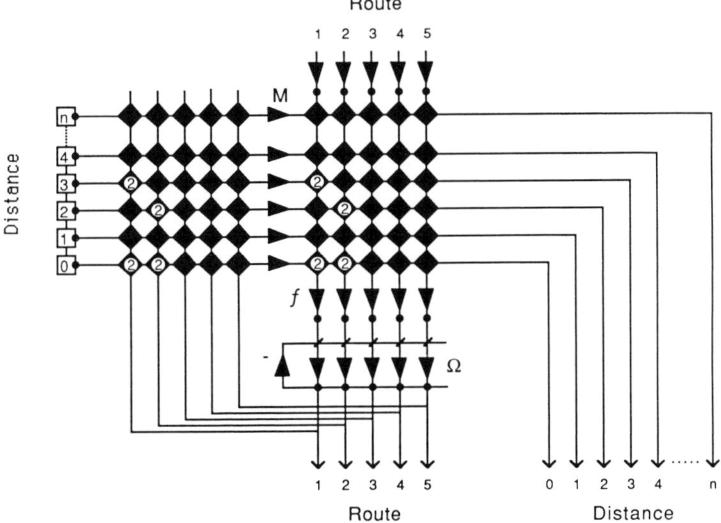

Distance of route 1 = 03

Distance of route 2 = 02

Figure 8.2
A synaptic matrix for binding travel distance to a selected travel route. *Lim* = 2.

tance have been associated during learning, when a filter cell (f_i) and class cell (Ω_i) couplet is selectively discharged by the activity of a particular route token, its Ω collateral to the imaging matrix will discharge a mosaic cell (M_i) representing the distance of the route selected.

Recall the example of the two routes for conducting business within the office building. Suppose S were analyzing the distance of each for the first time. By the mechanisms previously described, activation of route 1 on the self-locus retinoid automatically evokes an analog of its overall distance that is represented in the one-dimensional scale of the autaptic cell input to the synaptic matrix shown in figure 8.2. Thus, the matrix receives two parallel token inputs: one representing the route considered, the other representing its overall distance. This results (in accordance with the learning equation) in the strengthening of two specific synaptic junctions on filter cell 1 (in the filter cell–class cell couplet that signals route 1) and the strengthening of one specific synaptic junction on each of two different mosaic cells. In the example, these are at the inputs to f_1 from mosaic cells representing distance 0 and distance 3. Synaptic enhancement also occurs at the inputs to mosaic cells distance 0 and distance 3 from an axon collateral of Ω_1. When route 2 is analyzed for the first time, the same kind of process takes place. In this case, however, the synaptic junctions on f_2 that are strengthened are from mosaic cells distance 0 and distance 2. At the same time, an axon collateral of Ω_2 strengthens its synapses on the mosaic cells distance 0 and distance 2.

After the synaptic matrix undergoes these changes, discharge of the class cell token of either route will result (via the modified synaptic junctions on the mosaic cells) in the virtually simultaneous discharge of its appropriate token of distance. Thus, recall of route 1 discharges distance token 3, whereas recall of route 2 discharges distance token 2. This provides a neuronal signal that at least one consequence of choosing route 2 is that the distance that must be traveled will be shorter. If minimization of the distance to be traveled (and, indirectly perhaps, time and effort) is a constraint on the selection of behavioral routines, then route 2 will be chosen to guide future behavior in this context. Notice also that discharge of a mosaic cell that signals a particular distance will recall the specific route(s) associated with that distance. On a more general perspective, if there were an opportunity to accomplish one of a variety of necessary errands within a limited period of time, this mechanism enables the selection of an errand that can be completed within the time available.

The example shows how a neuronal token of a particular consequence (distance traveled) can be bound to a token that represents a specific sequence of actions (travel route). The same kind of mechanism that is illustrated in figure 8.2 provides a general means for appropriately binding tokens of action and consequence over a wide variety of instances.

Encoding Plans

A plan consisting of a sequence of self-directed instructions for gating the behaviors required to travel route 2 (starting at the subway exit) and to transact business in the three offices can be listed as follows:

1. Go (left)
2. Find (building entrance)
3. Go (through)
4. Go (left)
5. Find (door to office-1)
6. Go (through)
7. Do (transaction-1)
8. Find (door to office-1)

9. Go (through)
10. Go (left)
11. Find (door to office-3)
12. Go (through)
13. Do (transaction-3)
14. Find (door to office-3)
15. Go (through)
16. Go (ahead)
17. Find (door to office-4)
18. Go (through)
19. Do (transaction-4)
20. Find (door to office-4)
21. Go (through)
22. Go (right)
23. Go (left)
24. Go (left)
25. Find (building exit)
26. Go (through)
27. Go (left)
28. Find (subway entrance)
29. Branch (to subway routine)

On the assumption that substantial components of complex behavior are hierarchically organized (Rosenbaum 1977; Rosenbaum, Kenny, and Derr 1983) commands such as *Go, Find, Do,* and *Branch* are considered to be superordinate and are printed in this listing without parentheses, while specifiers such as *entrance, left, ahead, through, transaction-1* are considered to be subordinate and are enclosed in parentheses. This kind of hierarchical organization is embodied in the model mechanism illustrated in figure 8.3. It is a putative neuronal structure that can encode and initiate plans and control the particular sequence of actions called for by a plan.

In this model, when a plan of action is committed to memory (learned), the cell marked *Initiate Plan (n)* (*IP(n)*) is fired concurrently with the first step (only) of the plan. Discharge of the *IP(n)* line resets the step ring and fires autaptic cell 1 in the step ring. Thus, in figure 8.3 at step 1, when the mode cell *Go* and the specifier cell *left* were first fired during learning, the *Initiate Plan (n)* line was also discharged, and this evoked input from line 1 in the step ring. As each mode and specifier couplet fires, it evokes a stepping pulse that shifts the locus of activity to the next autaptic cell in the ordered sequence of the step ring. After all the behavioral steps that compose the essential elements of the plan have been learned, because of the pattern

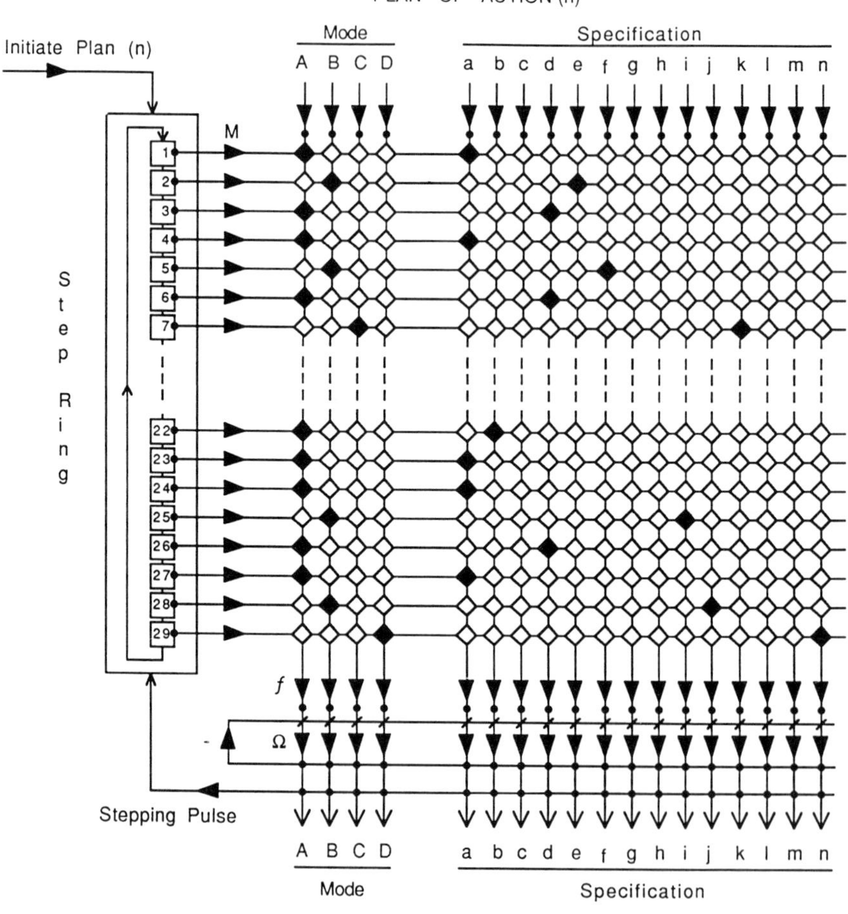

Figure 8.3
A mechanism for registering and recalling a plan of action. Filled lozenges represent synaptic junctions having augmented transfer weights (ϕ_i).

of synaptic enhancement in the detection matrix, if *IP(n)* alone is fired, the entire action sequence represented by the stored plan will be automatically recalled and can be executed under the appropriate circumstances.

The synaptic changes represented in figure 8.3 are the result of successive inputs from the step ring and the sequence of concurrent discharge of mosaic cells (*M*) and filter cells (*f*) that correspond to the first seven and last eight instructions of the plan listed above for conducting business in a particular building. The elements of the overall plan are represented here as follows.

Mode: A = *Go*; B = *Find*; C = *Do*; D = *Branch*.
Specification: a = *left*; b = *right*; c = *ahead*; d = *through*; e = *building entrance*; f = *door to office-1*; g = *door to office-3*; h = *door to office-4*; i = *building exit*; j = *subway entrance*; k = *transaction-1*; l = *transaction-3*; m = *transaction-4*; n = *subway routine*.

During learning, where ⟨=, . . . , =⟩ denotes parallel excitation, the order of activation that established the synaptic structure shown in figure 8.3 is ⟨1, *IP(n)*, A, a⟩; ⟨2, B, e⟩; ⟨3, A, d⟩; ⟨4, A, a⟩; ⟨5, B, f⟩; ⟨6, A, d⟩; ⟨7,C, k⟩; . . . ⟨22, A, b⟩; ⟨23, A, a⟩; ⟨24, A, a⟩; ⟨25, B, i⟩; ⟨26, A, d⟩; ⟨27, A, a⟩; ⟨28, B, j⟩; ⟨29, D, n⟩. The behavioral subroutines represented by steps 1–7 provide for the appropriate actions from leaving the subway to completion of transaction-1 in office-1. The subroutines represented by steps 22–29 provide for leaving the building after final business is accomplished (transaction-4) and finally for branching to the subway routine for the ride home.

The mechanism shown in figure 8.3 does not directly control motor behavior. What it does is organize and store an addressable neuronal representation of action sequences (a plan of action) that can prime a series of motor subroutines competent to accomplish a selected task. Whether the actions represented within any such register dedicated to a given plan are actually expressed in overt behavior depends on the veridical ecological context and neuronal gating (by increase in general excitatory bias) of the specific motor subroutines primed by the plan. In a strictly cognitive review (covert activation) of a plan of action, there are no necessary constraints on the time interval between successive steps. This is clearly not the case when a plan is overtly expressed. The action called for by each subroutine must be completed in real time before the next step is initiated. This suggests that in the overt execution of a plan (as distinguished from its cognitive construction or review), each stepping pulse to the step ring will be initiated by the terminus of each subroutine in the overall plan rather than by discharge of class cell tokens for mode and specifier.

Composing a Plan

Given a neuronal repertoire of *N* different subroutines of action, what controls the composition and initiation of a particular plan? A very general answer might be that a plan is composed and activated by an individual in the belief that it will achieve a particular salient goal in the context of a perceived environmental situation (either current or anticipated). The concept of belief carries the flavor of a resident homunculus, and in the interest of biological explication I will try to characterize it later in terms of a specific kind of neuronal state. For the moment, however, consider some conditions that might account for such a belief. First, real-life experience might have shown that the achievement of a goal was a reliable consequence of executing a particular plan. In this case, a neuronal token that signals the achievement of a goal (say G_1) is bound to the token of a plan (say P_1) by synaptic modification (learning) in a synaptic matrix of the kind illustrated in figure 8.2. Second, covert analysis of a new situation might reveal that out of a set of possible action sequences that can, in principle, lead to the achievement of a goal, only certain individual actions can be performed by the actor but that this subset, if properly chained, can attain the goal. Finally, one might accept a plan of action offered by an outside source in the belief that it will be successful because of relevant expertise attributed to the source.

Consider the microworld schematized by the directed graph at the top of figure 8.4. Each geometric shape represents a particular local situation in which the possible actions of an individual are constrained by local affordances so that the actor can accomplish only those transitions to other situations that are joined to the local one by directed paths. There are three goals (G_1, G_2, G_3). Each can be reached only by means of a particular prior situation-action. Goal 1 is reached by action enabled in the situation represented by the horizontally oriented rectangle; goal 2 by action in the situation represented by the vertically oriented rectangle; and goal 3 from the situation represented by the hourglass figure.

Because of the nature of environmental and behavioral constraints in the natural world, the initial situation at the time an actor (S) first aims to reach a specific goal will determine the particular sequence of actions that can attain the goal. At the bottom-left side of figure 8.4 are two columns—one a list of geometric shapes designating S's starting situation and the second an associated list of goals (G_i), each to be reached from its paired starting situation. For each goal there is a plan of action—a series of action-mediated transitions from one situation to another in a path that should culminate in the attainment

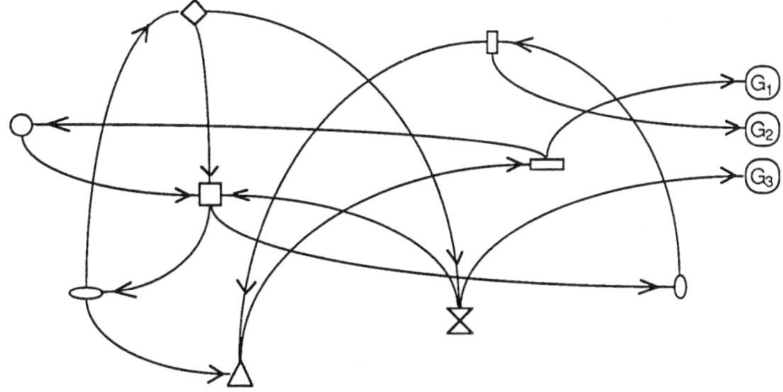

	Start	Goal		Plan of Action
1	△	G_1	1	[△ → ▭ → G_1]
2	○	G_1	2	[○ → □ → ⬭ → △ → ▭ → G_1]
3	△	G_2	3	[△ → ▭ → ○ → □ → ⬯ → ▯ → G_2]
4	⧗	G_2	4	[⧗ → □ → ⬯ → ▯ → G_2]
5	◇	G_1	5	[◇ → □ → ⬭ → △ → ▭ → G_1]
6	◇	G_2	6	[◇ → □ → ⬯ → ▯ → G_2]
7	◇	G_3	7	[◇ → ⧗ → G_3]
8	□	G_1	8	[□ → ⬭ → △ → ▭ → G_1]
9	□	G_2	9	[□ → ⬯ → ▯ → G_2]
10	□	G_3	10	[□ → ⬯ → ▯ → △ → ▭ → ○ → ⊡]
			11	[□ → ⬭ → △ → ▭ → ○ → ⊡]
			12	[□ → ⬭ → ◇ → ⧗ → G_3]

Figure 8.4
Top: Schematic representation of transition affordances among a number of situation actions and finally to one of three separate goals. *Bottom:* Ten states, each characterized by a starting situation action (indicated by a distinctive geometric shape) and a goal to be achieved (G_i). States 1–9 are each followed by a plan of action that leads directly to the goal. State 10 is followed by two ineffective plans (plans 10 and 11, leading back to the starting state), and plan 12, which leads directly to the desired G_3.

of the goal. Plans 1–9 will effectively reach the goals that have been set. Plans 10 and 11 will not; in these two cases, S ends up back in the same situation that he started from, without reaching the goal. Plan 12, however, although starting at the same point as plans 10 and 11, is effective in achieving the goal.

Let us assume that initially S has knowledge of only the local transition affordances of each situation (states from which a target condition can be directly achieved and states that can be directly achieved from a given target condition), including those from which a one-step transition reaches a goal. Given a starting situation from which more than two transitions are required, and in absence of relevant prior global knowledge, there is no way that S can ensure on the basis of local affordances that any particular local transition will be part of a transition sequence (plan of action) that attains a desired goal. Thus, S must engage in either overt or covert trials, testing different chains of situation-action transitions to determine which, if any, provide a continuous path between a current situation (or one known to be attainable) and the desired goal. In a situation-action domain like that depicted in figure 8.4, there is a basic asymmetry in the information available with respect to the attainment of a goal. That is, if one focuses on the local affordances of the starting situation, there is no guarantee that the next step will lie on a path that reaches a desired goal, but if one focuses on the local affordances of the goal, an effective prior state (situation-action on the path to the goal) is revealed with certainty. This suggests that the appropriate strategy for covert testing of possible action sequences in developing a plan is to recall the local affordances at the goal and then, in successive steps, test backward to an acceptable starting condition.

To see how such an analysis might be performed in the neuronal mechanisms of the brain, consider plan 12 shown at the bottom of figure 8.4. The fact that the action represented by the hourglass figure (say A_3) has the immediate consequence of achieving G_3 can be learned and represented by neuronal tokens in a synaptic matrix like the one that serves to organize a semantic network. The same kind of mechanism can represent the local transition consequences of any action depicted in the situation-action domain of figure 8.4. Moreover, because discharge of the class cell token of a consequence will evoke a token of the action that produces the consequence and because each action can be considered as having been enabled by an immediately preceding action, it is possible to evoke a chain of neuronal tokens that represents a backward sequence of transition affordances from any goal state to earlier states on the path to the goal.

All of the situation-action affordances illustrated at the top of figure 8.4 can be captured and represented in a distribution of synaptic transfer weights in a matrix similar to the one shown in figure 6.2. The following sentences presented to the simulated synaptic matrix provided all of the information required for planning in the environment of figure 8.4. The lexical labels for the environmental tokens are self-explanatory except for *hoval* (horizontally oriented oval), *voval* (vertically oriented oval), *hrect* (horizontally oriented rectangle), and *vrect* (vertically oriented rectangle). The word *gets* indicates a transition affordance from a given situation-action to another or else to a goal:

1. Circle gets-square .
2. Hoval gets-diamond .
3. Hoval gets-triangle .
4. Diamond gets-square .
5. Diamond gets-hourglass .
6. Square gets-hoval .
7. Square gets-voval .
8. Triangle gets-hrect .
9. Hourglass gets-square .
10. Hourglass gets-goal3 .
11. Vrect gets-triangle .
12. Vrect gets-goal2 .
13. Hrect gets-goal1 .
14. Hrect gets-circle .
15. Voval gets-vrect .

After this information was learned, the model could formulate a plan of action for reaching a desired goal from any arbitrary starting situation. Consider the problem illustrated at the bottom of figure 8.4: S must compose an effective plan that will achieve goal G_3 from the starting situation designated by the square. S uses the following process of self-query within the matrix module that is automatically initiated when he is first motivated to reach G_3. At the biological level, a self-query corresponds to an endogenously evoked discharge of the class cell token of a predicate *gets-⟨situation-action⟩*. The answer corresponds to the mosaic cell token that is then discharged by the axon collateral of the activated class cell:

Question: What gets-goal3?
Answer: Hourglass gets-goal3.

Question: What gets-hourglass?
Answer: Diamond gets-hourglass.

Question: What gets-diamond?
Answer: Hoval gets-diamond.

Question: What gets-hoval?
Answer: Square gets-hoval.

Discharge of the neuronal token for *square* brings S to the internal state that corresponds to the starting situation, and self-query is terminated. At this point, a series of neuronal tokens has been discharged, beginning with the goal to be reached (G_3) and ending with the situation at which the plan is to start (*square*). It is assumed that this backward chain of situation-action tokens is captured in short-term memory by a string of autaptic cells and then registered in the proper sequence (square → G_3) as a plan of action in the mechanism illustrated in figure 8.3. The plan—square → hoval → diamond → hourglass → G_3—corresponds to plan 12 shown at the bottom of figure 8.4.

Similar simulation tests of the model were run for a variety of planning problems, all designed to determine the sequences of action that will ensure that each selected goal will be reached from arbitrary starting situations. In each case, a satisfactory plan was produced. For example, starting at the situation represented by *triangle,* with G_2 as the goal, the process of self-query was initiated as follows and proceeded until the token for *triangle* was discharged:

Question: What gets-goal2?
Answer: Vrect gets-goal2.

Question: What gets-vrect?
Answer: Voval gets-vrect.

Question: What gets-voval?
Answer: Square gets-voval.

Question: What gets-square?
Answer: Circle gets-square.
Diamond gets-square.
Hourglass gets-square.

Question: What gets-circle?
Answer: Hrect gets-circle.

Question: What gets-hrect?
Answer: Triangle gets-hrect.

On completion of self-query, the plan of action was: triangle → hrect → circle → square → voval → vrect → G_2. A check of this action sequence against plan 3 in figure 8.4 shows that it is correct.

Notice, however, that in response to the query *What gets-square?* there was more than one answer. In addition to *circle, diamond* and *hourglass* provided transition affordances to the situation represented by *square.* As it turned out, querying *circle* led to a direct path back to the appropriate start at *triangle.* But, if instead of *circle,* either *diamond* or *hourglass* were queried, then subsequent transitions would have led to the previously established link in the sequence—*square.* For example,

Question: What gets-square?
Answer: Circle gets-square.
Diamond gets-square.
Hourglass gets-square.

Question: What gets-diamond?
Answer: Hoval gets-diamond.

Question: What gets-hoval?
Answer: Square gets-hoval.

If the same query were repetitively evoked, the system would be locked in an ineffective recurrent loop. It is assumed that in processes of this kind, when a previously established link is repetitively fired before a token of the selected starting situation is evoked, a different candidate for transition to the repeated state is discharged for the next query (*circle*). A neurophysiological basis for such a shift in query might be the fatigue (and associated rise in relative threshold) of repetitively discharged cells.

Storing and Recalling Plans

Effective plans, once composed, are stored as long-term resources in the brain's neuronal networks to serve the efficient pursuit of goals and the solution of diverse ecological problems. A plan is selectively initiated when a current situation is recognized as similar to an earlier situation in which the particular plan (in fact or in imagination) was successful.

Figure 8.5 illustrates a model neuronal register in which plans (discrete action sequences) are selectively associated with the tokens of those situations where they were successfully applied. The states that are mapped to the input tokens each consist of a particular starting situation and a goal to be achieved from that situation. Thus, in figure 8.5 if situations 1, 2, 3, . . . , *n* are identified with the corresponding pairs of *Start* and *Goal* in the lower-left columns of figure 8.4, the

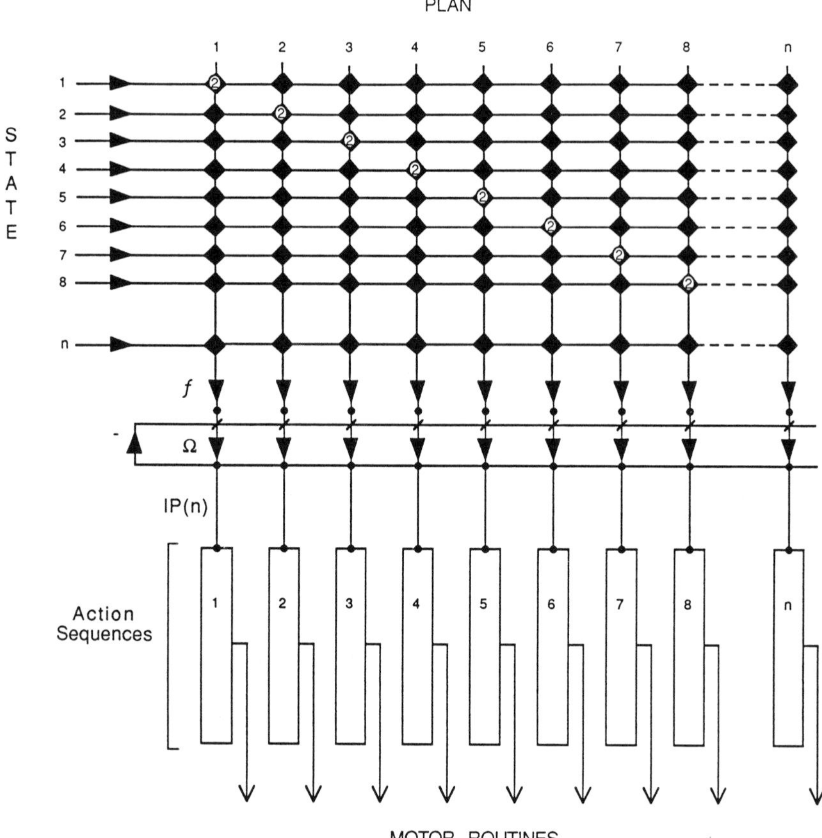

Figure 8.5
A neuronal register for selectively binding plans of action to the states in which they represent effective solutions. Evocation of a particular state recalls the appropriate plan. *Lim* = 2.

action sequences that are selectively initiated by this matrix correspond to the effective plans of action shown in figure 8.4. In figure 8.5, each indexed box triggered by an output *IP(n)* is assumed to contain a stepping ring and a matrix to control the modes and specifications for the proper sequence of actions constituting a plan, as detailed in figure 8.3. Taking state 4 (figure 8.4) as an example, all of the behavioral commands required to move from *hourglass* to *square* to *voval* to *vrect* to G_2 would be represented by the distribution of synaptic weights in box 4 of figure 8.5.

Chapter 9

Set Point and Motive: The Formation and Resolution of Goals

What counts as a dominant problem at any given time in a person's experience? Within the same objective environmental context, two individuals may each initiate behavior directed at the solution of fundamentally different problems. If we are to give a reasonably comprehensive physical explanation of the behavior of an individual in a particular situation, we must not only provide an account of how significant elements of the situation can be perceived, learned, and related to prior experience, we must also explain why formerly neutral aspects are treated as significant, whereas previously significant aspects may be ignored. We must explain the biological bases for the particular complex of cognitive behavior—how it can be selectively initiated, organized, and terminated. In short, we must give a credible account of the processes of motivation.

The commonsense notion of a goal has traditionally served as a core concept for understanding the integrity of intentional behavior. In a domain of arbitrary behavioral affordances, the selection of a goal can serve to organize a whole sequence of neuronal commands (a plan of action) that effectively lead from a given starting situation to the achievement of that goal. Within the framework of the approach taken in this book, this naturally provokes the following questions:

- How do goals develop?
- How are goals represented and stored in the neuronal structures of the brain?
- How is a particular goal selected from the repetoire of stored goals?
- How does an activated goal guide behavior?
- How is the achievement of a goal recognized?
- What happens next?

Set Points and Homeostasis

A commonly presented example of a set point in a physical system is the temperature setting on a home thermostat. If room temperature falls beyond a predetermined margin of tolerance below the set point (temperature setting), the heating system is automatically switched on to bring the temperature back near the set point. When the temperature has risen to within the set point margin, the heating system is automatically switched off. Homeostatic systems in living organisms are mechanisms of this kind (figure 9.1). They initiate processes that tend to maintain internal stability by correcting deviations from a physiological set point.

It is useful to classify homeostatic systems into two kinds, designated here as HS-I and HS-II. HS-I includes, among other mechanisms for maintaining optimal internal states, the vital autonomic mechanisms that ensure the viability of the organism. Type HS-I systems are distinguished from type HS-II by virtue of the fact that the loop of events serving to hold a physiological state near an optimal set point in HS-I does not require that a neuronal token (physical symbol [Newell 1980]) of an external referent be activated.

A clear example of HS-I is the mechanism that causes cardiac output to decrease when there is an increase in arterial pressure and to increase when there is a decrease in pressure (see Cotman and McGaugh 1980), thus reducing possibly dangerous extremes of blood pressure. But consider the hypothesized mechanism for aligning the centroid of an object's visual-afferent representation on the normal foveal axis. While such a system would not ordinarily be called homeostatic, in my view, the automatic balancing of quadrantal excitation on a retinoid can legitimately be regarded as a homeostatic process analogous to that which tends to maintain the stability of arterial pressure. In the case of arterial homeostasis, the set point is normal blood pressure; in the case of centroid homeostasis, the set point is normal quadrantal disparity.

The second type (HS-II), which I will call cognitive homeostasis, contains all of the processes that require the discharge of one or more referential tokens to complete a homeostatic loop that can correct a deviation from an internal set point. Processes of this kind may be entirely covert or may require overt instrumental behavior to close the loop that corrects a deviation from a set point.

Behavior associated with thirst provides a clear example of HS-II. Receptors within the brain that are sensitive to cellular dehydration (osmoreceptors and, possibly, salinity receptors [Cotman and McGaugh 1980]) signal a water deficit and initiate a chain of events

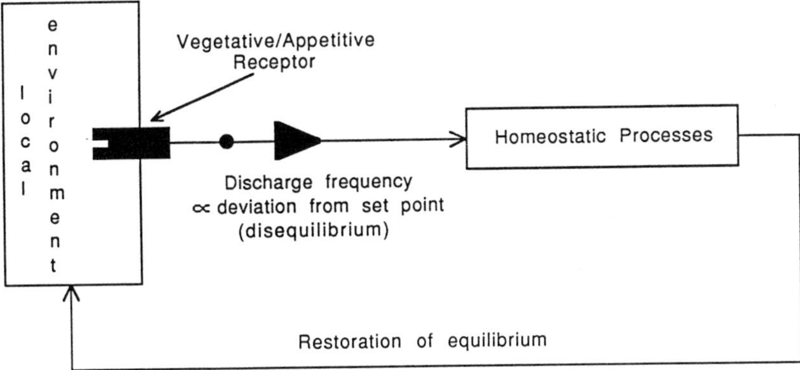

Figure 9.1
A homeostatic system mediated by neuronal discharge proportional to a sensed deviation from a physiological set point.

that correct the deficit. Unlike the homeostatic mechanism for regulating blood pressure, appropriate referential tokens must be discharged and exteroceptive stimulus patterns must be recognized in order to obtain the water needed to bring cellular hydration back to the set point. Thus, if I feel thirsty while sitting in my living room, the neuronal tokens of *kitchen sink, faucet,* and *water glass* must be evoked if I am to take advantage of available utilities. Moreover, I must recognize the exteroceptive patterns of these objects in order to guide the instrumental behavior that quenches my thirst.

The neuronal events that constitute a proper response to self-query provide an important but more subtle example of what I mean by cognitive homeostasis. The virtual set point in such cases is a co-occurrence (balancing) of a subject (*W* cell) and a proper predicate (Ω). If a subject token is discharged, the system is in disequilibrium until a familiar predicate token is fired in addition to the subject identity token (figure 9.2). Thus, for example, if one has a neuronal representation (in a semantic network) of both ⟨*John's-address*⟩ and ⟨*is-43-Maple-Street*⟩ and has learned the correct association, the query "What is John's address?" will evoke the appropriate predicate token with a latency that signals a familiar response. (The predicate response will include at least two activated class cells—one for the identity relationship ⟨*John's-address*⟩ ⟨*is-John's-address*⟩ and the other for the informative predicate ⟨*is-43-Maple-Street*⟩.) The departure from set point that was initiated by the query is corrected by the Ω response. If John's address has not been learned, no second predicate will fire within the latency for a familiar response, and the system

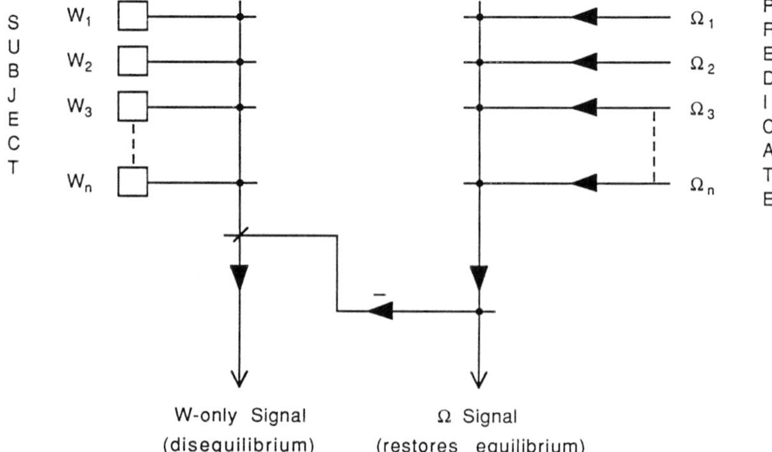

Figure 9.2
Mechanism for restoring equilibrium in self-query.

remains in a state of disequilibrium. In this case, one might resort to overt instrumental behavior to provide the missing predicate and close the homeostatic loop, perhaps by consulting a telephone directory.

Pleasure and Displeasure

The terms *pleasure* and *displeasure* refer to personal and essentially private experiences. There is common agreement about the kinds of overt behavior that indicate the inner experience of pleasure or displeasure and a consensus that these experiences are intimately related to individual motivation. Evidence drawn from experiments in which brain cells are subject to direct electrical stimulation suggests that pleasure and displeasure are modulated by homeostatic events.

During neurosurgical procedures, conscious human patients report electrical stimulation in a variety of deep brain regions (hypothalamus and limbic structures) as pleasurable (Heath 1964; Mark, Ervin, and Sweet 1972). Controlled laboratory experiments provide more detailed information. A rat with an implanted electrode will press a lever thousands of times an hour for many hours simply to receive brief trains of electrical stimulation to a region in its lateral hypothalamus (Olds 1958, 1962). Because of this behavior, together with the observation that the animal will repeatedly cross an apparently painful electrified grid in order to reach the lever, those brain regions that are the targets of self-produced stimulation have been called both pleasure centers and reward centers. It is significant that the rate of lever pressing for self-stimulation is positively correlated with the strength of hunger, thirst, or sexual drive at the time of stimulation (Rolls 1975). For example, animals that are sated with food press at lower rates than when they are hungry and will even press to turn off hypothalamic stimulation that they eagerly worked for when they were deprived. It appears that when the animal is satiated, brain stimulation that was formerly pleasurable can become aversive.

These findings highlight what might seem to be a trivial fact but one that allows us to make sense of a variety of motivated behaviors aimed at the achievement of social goals rather than the gratification of vegetative or basic appetitive needs: the experience of pleasure (activation of its cellular substrate) occurs only when there is a deviation from a homeostatic set point in the brain and dissipates when homeostasis is achieved. A deviation from a set point is not a sufficient condition for pleasure, but it appears to be a necessary condition. What is also required under normal circumstances is some action or event that tends to restore equilibrium to the perturbed system. This implies that for humans to experience pleasure when vegetative and appetitive needs are met, other kinds of homeostatic disequilibria must have been induced in the brain. In addition, these disequilibria must be related to ecological domains in which an individual perceives the possibility of achieving a selected goal, thus reestablishing equilibrium.

The Central Hedonic System

As the human brain matures and interacts with its interoceptive and exteroceptive environment, it constructs new homeostatic systems of the HS-II type that serve an elaborate personalized hedonic economy. The development of new cognitive-homeostatic set points provides the opportunity to tap sources of hedonic currency beyond the basic appetitive ones. We can think of these motivational set points as the neuronal representations of particular goals. A homeostatic imbalance associated with the set point of a goal evokes behaviors that can correct the imbalance (reach the goal), and in the process a pleasure mechanism within the brain is stimulated (figure 9.3). It is parsimonious to assume that this is the same kind of mechanism that is at the core of the cellular systems that receive direct electrical input in the self-stimulation experiments cited.

The biological structures that constitute the vegetative and basic appetitive homeostatic systems are genetically determined. Thus, we

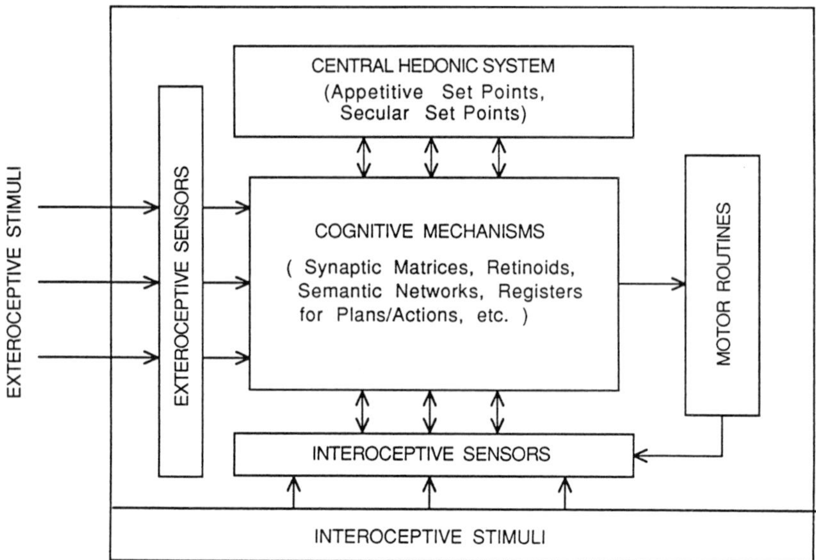

Figure 9.3
Block-flow diagram of the cognitive system of the brain in relation to sensory input, motor routines, and the central hedonic system.

are normally innately endowed with a preset point for benign blood pressure, sensors for detecting potentially destructive changes in vascular pressure, and the physiology for correcting such deviations. Similarly, we are endowed with receptors for glucose and fatty acids that provide hunger signals indicating that concentrations of these substances are below tolerance with respect to our physiological set point (Oomura 1976)—that is, our body cells require nourishment, and we must eat to restore the proper levels of nutrients before the hunger signals will turn off. Homeostatic processes related to thirst and sexual drive are similarly governed by genetically determined factors. But what of the person whose goal is to be a professional basketball player or an entomologist? The set points that represent these goals must somehow be physically instantiated in the brain. Clearly, however, such goals cannot be genetically determined.

Development of Secular Goals

I use the term *secular* to distinguish a special subclass of set points from those that directly serve vegetative and appetitive homeostasis. A secular set point (goal) is an enduring brain state that represents a future imagined worldly situation. As long as the imagined neuronal

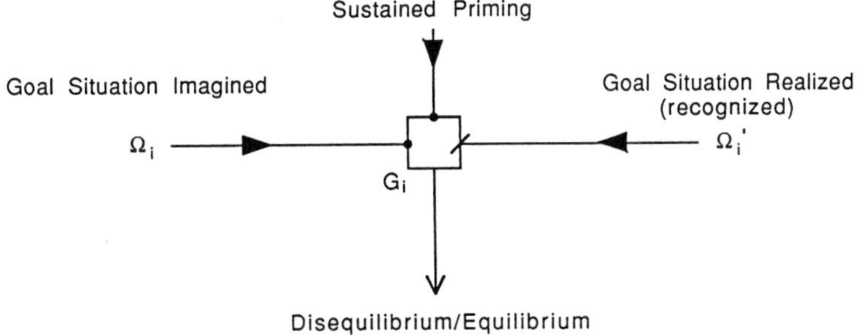

Figure 9.4
Mechanism for activating, sustaining, and terminating a neuronal (autaptic) token of a secular goal (G_i).

representation is not effectively matched by the perception of its corresponding events in the real world, the homeostatic system of which it is a part is in disequilibrium (figure 9.4). This constitutes the neuronal substrate that initiates goal-directed behavior. Those plans and actions that lead to a situation that matches the goal are selectively activated and are said to be motivated by the goal. However, granted that the establishment of a goal can determine a plan to achieve the goal by means of self-query and the intrinsic neuronal logic of a semantic network, what determines the initial establishment of any goal?

The neurophysiological processes and environmental influences that govern the instantiation of a personal secular goal are undoubtedly complex, subtle, and delicately balanced against many competing goal-determining events. I believe, however, that there are some fundamental mechanisms and formative principles that can be reasonably proposed. First, I assume that the instantiation of any secular goal within the microstructure of the brain must be preceded by a heuristic exploration (in imagery) of possible worlds. This kind of fanciful imagery may range over a variety of sensory modalities, and I assume it to be, at least in part, a covert expression of an innate need for exploration and play (Nissen 1951). Under this assumption, one must posit genetically determined homeostatic mechanisms for both exteroceptive and imaginal sensory exploration.

Recall that neuronal tokens can be associatively linked in forward- and backward-going chains. Whatever the signal concomitants of the activation of a pleasure center might be, they too can be represented by a neuronal token and selectively coupled in synaptic matrices to other tokens that are concurrently active. It is assumed that any imagined possible world will be composed of a complex of perceptual tokens. The greater the number and variety of such component tokens that are linked (directly or indirectly) to pleasure centers in the brain during the course of experience, the more likely will pleasure be evoked when that possible world is fantasied. An activated link to a pleasure center does not necessarily result in a pleasurable experience because it is only in those systems in which there is a current homeostatic imbalance that a pleasure signal can be evoked.

In addition to the pleasure centers, we must take account of brain mechanisms that signal pain, discomfort, and many different aspects of displeasure (Kuffler, Nicholls, and Martin 1984; Mark, Ervin, and Sweet 1972). The hedonic system involves the activity of such centers of aversive experience as well as pleasure, and the signal concomitants of the activation of nociceptive cells can, like those in the pleasure centers, be represented by neuronal tokens. Moreover, particular perceptual tokens in the complex of an imagined possible world may be linked in forward and backward chains to displeasure centers in the brain in the same way that other tokens are linked to pleasure centers.

These considerations suggest a neuronal model that can account for the ontogeny of secular goals. In the discussion that follows, I will use the adjectival terms *adiant* (directed toward) and *abiant* (directed away) to distinguish processes and tokens that are linked to the centers for pleasure and displeasure, respectively.

Figure 9.5 illustrates how the summed activity of adiant and abiant tokens modulates the output of an associated autaptic cell (G_i) that is a token of a secular goal. In order for G_i to be instantiated as an active goal in the cellular structure of the brain, it must be stimulated by the token of an imagined goal situation (Ω_i) and receive a priming margin of excitatory input from the sum of associated adiant events sufficient to overbalance the inhibitory input from the sum of associated abiant events. Under these conditions, G_i will fire. Moreover, G_i will maintain its discharge even when Ω_i is no longer active, provided the margin of input from adiant sources (excitatory) over input from abiant sources (inhibitory) is great enough. The continued discharge of G_i represents the departure from the set point (disequilibrium) of a specific secular goal and signals the need to construct an appropriate plan of action for achieving the goal. The recognition of a realized goal results in the discharge of its class cell token Ω_i', which sends an inhibitory input to G_i, squelching its autaptic activity and restoring equilibrium.

Because the brain is a complex hybrid system of quasi-linear and nonlinear processes and threshold gates, very small differences in initial conditions can result in major differences in the evolution of

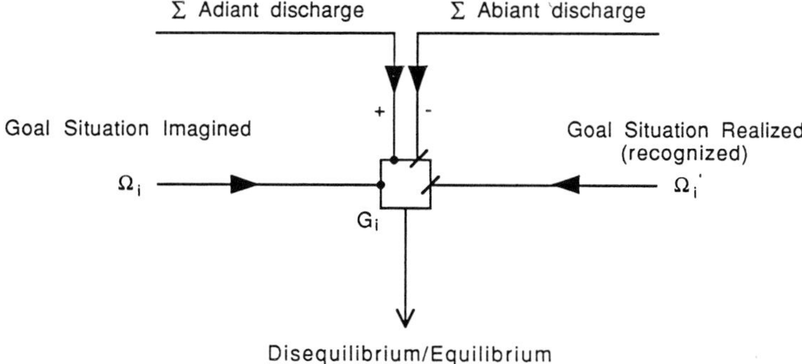

Figure 9.5
Current magnitudes of summed adiant (excitatory) and abiant (inhibitory) inputs to G_i will modulate the moment-to-moment motivational strength (discharge frequency) of the goal represented by G_i. If abiant input approaches the magnitude of adiant input, net excitation will be reduced below the level required to sustain autaptic activity, and G_i will be squelched.

the system. Thus, minor variations in initial neurohumoral and other neurophysiological factors, as well as in subsequent experience, can have profound and unpredictable effects on the selection and expression of personal secular goals. For example, innate physical differences between two individuals can easily result in a different pattern of skills for each, which can affect the development of secular goals. If both individuals initially imagined the same goal situation with the sum of adiant components at the same high level for each, the sum of abiant components might nevertheless be much higher for the individual having the poorer skills related to the goal situation. This is particularly likely to be true if inordinate effort were required for the instrumental behavior needed in the context of the goal or in pursuit of the goal. In this case, the imagined goal might not be instantiated by the person with the poorer skills because net excitatory priming to G_i is insufficient due to an increase in inhibitory abiant input. Or if G_i were instantiated, it might later be squelched before the goal is reached because of an increase in abiant input in the effort to attain the goal.

The role of experience in the setting of secular goals is clear. A goal can be established only on the basis of what can be imagined, and what can be imagined depends on what one has been exposed to and has learned by personal experience. Moreover, the hedonic associations of the neuronal tokens of experience will depend in part on the particular fortuitous coincidences and sequences of the components of experience. In the framework of the model, these associative adiant and abiant links will determine whether a potential secular goal can be instantiated and sustained.

Motivational Biasing of Attention

The hedonic induction of an energetic set point (a labeled autaptic cell) can determine the selection of a plan of action aimed at getting the goal represented by the set point (the biological substrate of motivated behavior). There is, however, another important aspect of motivation in the realm of both appetitive and secular goals: we pay attention to those things that meet our needs.

During the course of daily experience, out of the enormous number of objects and events that stimulate our senses, we respond selectively with a special sensitivity to relatively few. These are the objects and events that must be discriminated to achieve cognitive homeostasis. According to the model, selective perceptual sensitivity results from the associative priming of filter cells (in synaptic matrices) by the output of those set points that happen to be in a current state of disequilibrium. This represents a mechanism of selective attention that augments the attentional effects of self-locus excursion in retinoid systems.

How can particular motivational states and perceptual sensitivity for particular sensory patterns be adaptively coupled? The neuronal network illustrated in figure 9.6 shows how this can be done. In this example, long-term synaptic changes occur according to the basic learning equation. Axon transfer factor (ATF) has been arbitrarily set at $c = 1$; dendrite transfer factor (DTF) has been set at $k = 12$. The saturation limit in the detection matrix has been arbitrarily set at $Lim = 10$. In the other matrices, the setting is $Lim = 2$. The transfer weight (ϕ) at each learning-modified synaptic junction is displayed to the nearest whole number.

Consider the synaptic matrix in the left-hand half of figure 9.6. Five different sensory patterns (objects) have been learned. The presence of each object is signaled by the output of its associated class cell (Ω). The main axon of each class cell token branches to compose two collateral output bundles. One bundle courses back to the imaging matrix; the other carries excitation to a matrix (shown in the right-hand half of figure 9.6) designated O/M Association because it selectively links objects (O) to motives (M). The filter cells in this matrix receive input from three sources: (1) the object-token outputs (Ob1, Ob2, . . . , Ob*n*) from the module for learning and detecting exteroceptive patterns, (2) the output from motivational set points in the brain (G_i), and (3) the output from those pleasure centers (*Pl*) that

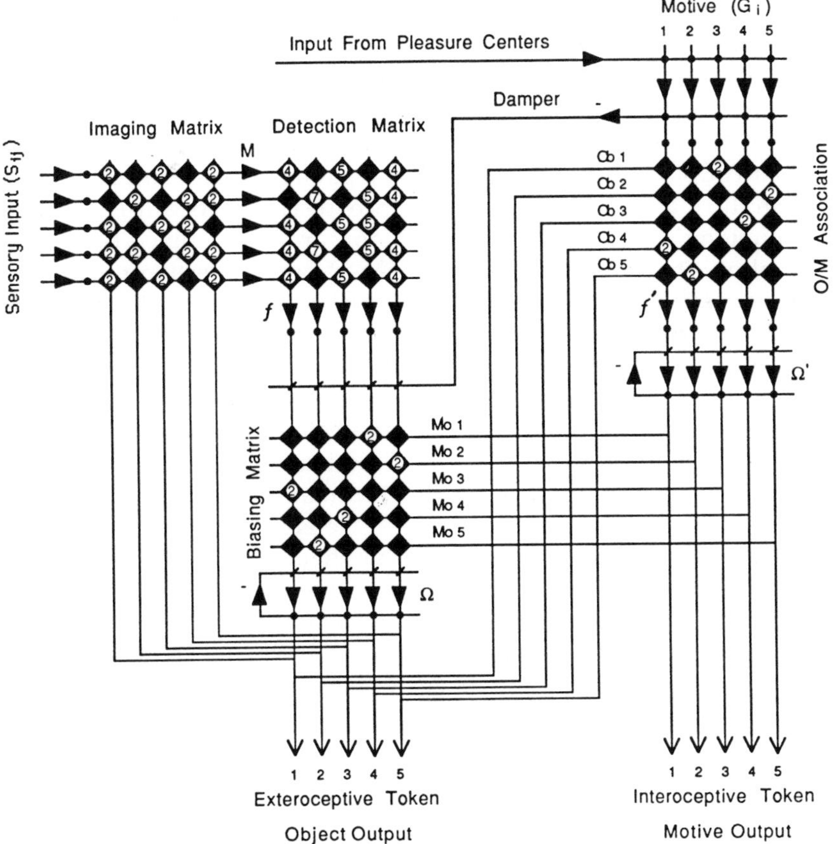

Figure 9.6
Neuronal network that selectively biases perceptual sensitivity in accordance with the strength of a dominant goal.

are activated during the restoration of homeostasis in an energetic motivational system.

Input from motivational set points (G_i) alone is insufficient to fire filter cells (f') in the O/M matrix. Only if there is concurrent biasing input from a pleasure center (*Pl*) can set point inputs (G_i) discharge their coupled filter cells. Thus *Pl* is a gating signal distributed to all f' in the matrix. The frequency of spike discharge for any f' is a joint monotonic function of the level of input from its coupled G_i and the level of concurrent input from *Pl*. As in other detection matrices, if there is simultaneous input from several motivational set points (and if the matrix is gated above threshold by activity from *Pl*), the class cell (Ω_i') that is connected to the filter cell (f') receiving input from the most energetic G_i will fire first and inhibit the discharge of competing class cells. Thus, an active class cell in this module is a token of an individual's strongest current motivational/goal-directed state.

Two kinds of output from the O/M matrix feed back to all class cells of the object-detection matrix. One is inhibitory through fixed synapses (see the cell labeled *Damper* in figure 9.6) and serves to raise the threshold (decrease sensitivity) of the class cells (Ω). The other feedback is excitatory through adaptive synapses (Biasing Matrix in figure 9.6) and serves to couple synaptically the token of a currently dominant motive with the tokens of objects that are at the focus of attention during motivational homeostasis.

Imagine the network without the O/M matrix. The distribution of synaptic weights (ϕ) in the biasing matrix would be at a uniform basal level, and learning and recognition of environmental objects would occur without motivational bias. This would also be true if the O/M matrix were connected as shown in figure 9.6 but without prior concurrent discharge of class cells (Ω) evoked by objects (S_{ij}) and class cells (Ω') evoked by the gratification of motives (G_i). Suppose, however, that a number of objects had been learned and that among these was one (say Ob1) critical for the instrumental behavior needed to gratify a motive (say Mo3). It is assumed that when G_3 is energized and dominant, it will evoke instrumental behavior aimed at homeostasis. In the course of behavior that restores equilibrium, objects with utility relevant to the current state of motivation will tend to be at the focus of perception and will evoke the discharge of their corresponding class cell tokens. Thus, we can assume a high likelihood that the token for Ob1 (Ω_1) will fire at some time during the discharge of the token for Mo3 (Ω_3'). This will result in an adaptive change in the biasing matrix at just that synaptic junction between the axon of Ω_3' and the dendrite of Ω_1. Thereafter, whenever G_3 evokes the discharge of Ω_3', class cell Ω_1 in the sensory detection matrix will receive an excitatory bias through its enhanced synapse with Ω_3'. At the same time, all class cells in the sensory detection matrix will receive an inhibitory bias from the damper cell. It is assumed that the inhibitory bias to all class cells in this matrix is less than the excitatory bias to the cell selectively coupled to Ω_3'.

The general effect, then, is this: when a dominant motive controls behavior that is instrumental in need gratification, there is an automatic and selective facilitation of neuronal response to those objects that have utility in relation to the current motive, and there is an inhibition or dampening of neuronal response to all other objects that are not relevant to the current motive (Moran and Desimone 1985). By neuronal mechanisms like the one proposed in the circuit diagram of figure 9.6, attention can be selectively focused on stimulus patterns (veridical or imagined) important to an individual's governing motives.

The Resolution of Goals

A person will have many different secular goals simultaneously. The output of these energetic set points (G_i) will wax and wane independently according to the momentary relative magnitudes of adiant and abiant input to each. Given this multiplicity of current goals, how can goal-directed behavior be adaptively gated and modulated? What determines which goal will govern during any arbitrary epoch? It would be maladaptive if the various activities motivated by the repertoire of one's goals were unrelated to the perceived or anticipated (imagined) properties of current or future environmental contexts. In situations where there are no affordances that can lead to the achievement of a particular goal (say G_1), persistence of behavior directed toward G_1 would be ineffective and preclude the attainment of other goals.

If the coupling between goals and motor behavior were modulated by the perception of relevant affordances, there would be an increased likelihood that the pursuit of a specific goal will be successful. According to this design, the competition among many different energetic goals to capture and control overt behavior would be resolved on the joint basis of the current relative strength (demand) of each goal and the presence of those affordances needed to continue on a path to a given goal.

From moment to moment, behavior is controlled by plans of action that are initiated and sustained by the most powerful current motive (the G_i with the highest discharge frequency) unless the means for pursuing the goal are initially absent or have become unavailable.

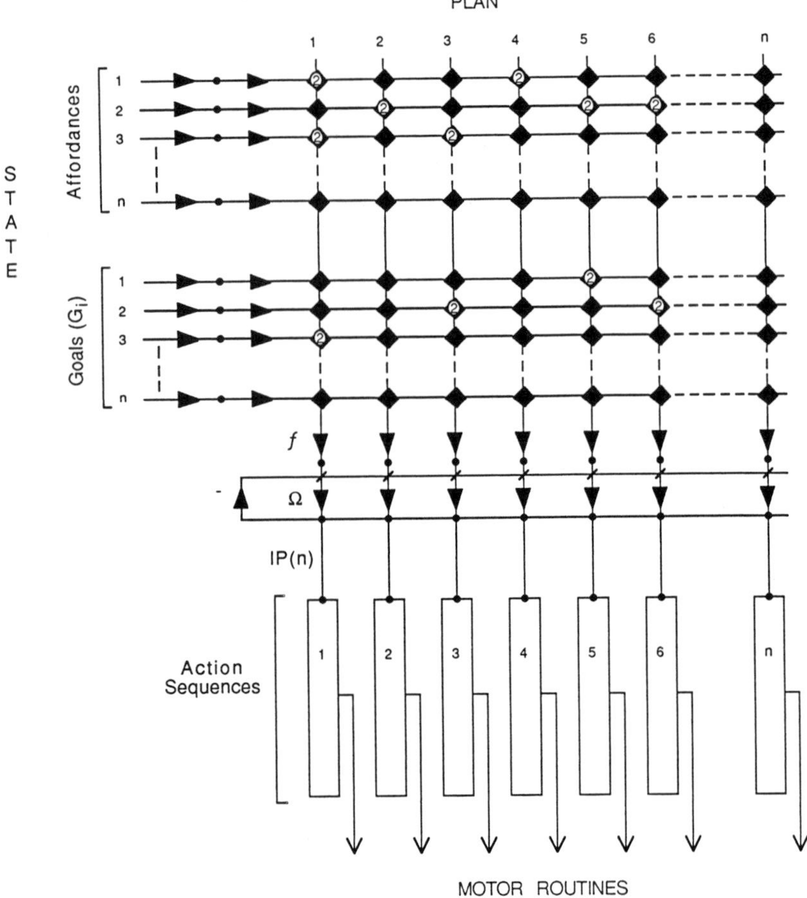

Figure 9.7
Neuronal matrix that selectively activates plans of action in accordance with recognized affordances and the strength profile of current goals. Each numbered box represents a mechanism similar to the one shown in figure 8.3 for sequencing a series of goal-related actions. In this module, activation of filter cells (f) by either goals or affordances alone is insufficient to exceed the threshold of their coupled class cells (Ω). Only joint excitation of a filter cell by both kinds of input can fire its paired class cell.

When this happens, supporting tokens of critical affordances are no longer active, and the current peak of motivational excitation alone is insufficient to dominate class cell output. Control of behavior is then captured by the strongest motive having the supporting bias of available affordances. The pursuit of goals that have been interrupted can be resumed at the proper step in the sequence of situation-action transitions when the appropriate affordances are encountered. Of course, behavior governed by secular goals will also be periodically interrupted by more urgent appetitive needs (hunger, thirst) and harm-avoiding action evoked by abiant signals.

Figure 9.7 shows a schematic of a neuronal matrix that is stimulated in parallel by active tokens of recognized affordances and the outputs of the motivating autaptic set points (G_i) that represent the relative strengths of current goals. Given the particular distribution of synaptic weights shown in this example, it is possible to determine the governing goals and their associated plans that will be induced under a variety of state contingencies.

A sampling of possible goal-affordance conditions and their outcomes is presented in table 9.1. In accordance with figure 9.7, there are three goals and three affordances. For each of the 22 states in this example, the values within the cells for the goals represent the relative discharge frequencies of the set points of the goals (their relative motivational strengths). Cells that represent affordances have a value of 1 if the designated affordance is recognized; otherwise the cell has a value of 0. The bottom two rows of table 9.1 show which goal controls behavior and which plan is evoked under the designated state. With identical patterns of motivation, different goals can con-

Table 9.1
Output of the network shown in figure 9.7

STATE	1	2	3	4	5	6	7	8	9	10	11	12	13	14	15	16	17	18	19	20	21	22
Goal 1	5	5	5	6	6	6	3	3	3	4	4	4	5	5	5	9	9	9	1	1	1	5
Goal 2	3	3	3	7	7	7	5	5	5	2	2	2	8	8	8	3	3	3	3	3	3	0
Goal 3	2	2	2	9	9	9	4	4	4	8	8	8	2	2	2	1	1	1	9	9	9	0
Affordance 1	1	0	0	1	0	0	1	0	0	1	0	0	1	1	0	1	1	0	1	1	0	1
Affordance 2	0	1	0	0	1	0	0	1	0	0	1	0	1	0	1	1	0	1	1	0	1	0
Affordance 3	0	0	1	0	0	1	0	0	1	0	0	1	0	1	1	0	1	1	0	1	0	1
Controlling Goal	3	1	2	3	2	3	3	2	2	3	1	3	2	2	2	1	2	2	3	3	2	*
Plan Evoked	1	5	3	1	6	1	1	6	3	1	5	1	6	3	3/6	5	3	3/6	1	1	6	*

* = none

trol behavior and evoke different plans because of the recognition of different affordances. Moreover, the same controlling goal can evoke different plans depending on which affordances are recognized (states 8 and 9). Under some conditions, a controlling goal can evoke one of a number of appropriate plans with equal probability (state 15). In such a case, the final selection among the suitable plans would depend on chance or on biasing factors outside the mechanisms considered here. Finally, even if there is an energetic goal having no competition from other goals, it will not control behavior, and no plan of action will be evoked without the recognition of a related affordance (state 22).

The examples presented derive from just six state parameters. If similar mechanisms govern secular motivation in the human brain, it is clear that idiosyncratic behavioral contingencies of great depth and complexity will evolve as the number of goals and affordances increases and as adiant and abiant processes ramify through learning in the course of personal development.

Chapter 10

Learning and Recalling Canonical Visual Patterns

Various aspects of the proposed brain model have been simulated to provide initial assessments of the basic competence and operating characteristics of the component mechanisms. The tests described in this chapter involve the synaptic matrix, either in isolation or working together with some of the accessory circuits and the retinoid system. All of the stimuli used in these tests were visual objects with nonvarying shapes. They were projected to a simulated retina not only in pristine form but also presented as multiple objects in superposition, degraded by visual noise, or rotated away from the angular orientation at which they had been learned.

Pattern Recognition and Associative Sequential Recall

One of the more intriguing aspects of human cognitive activity is that of associative sequential recall. The stream of passive thought is often not constrained by the principles of deduction or the application of rules of inference; the succession of conscious impression seems to proceed rather along analogical and metaphorical links. A given situation may evoke a wide variety of imaginal recollections. Some may be obviously similar to the immediate stimuli; other recalled images may be so dissimilar to the initial perception as to be surprising and seemingly completely fortuitous. Useful insights and creative ideas often occur without our awareness of logical precession (see Shepard 1978 for an extended treatment of this topic). The following simulation yielded results suggesting that the synaptic matrix can generate associative relationships rich enough to provide a biological mechanism for such phenomena.

In an early test of the model (Trehub 1979), a synaptic matrix that received visual input from a 6 × 6–cell retina was simulated. Two different modes of recall were examined. The stimuli consisted of 25 scenes, each composed of a combination drawn randomly from a set of four objects (patterns) or an empty space and randomly assigned to each quadrant of the scene (figure 10.1). Filled regions designated

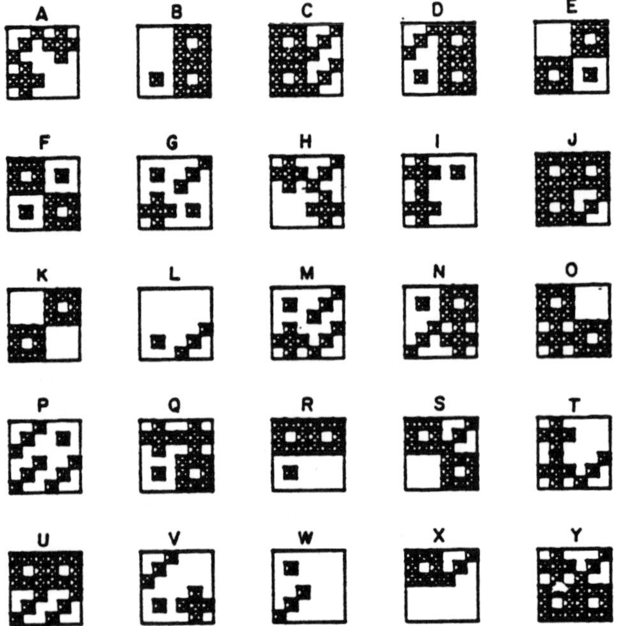

Figure 10.1
Scenes presented for learning and subsequent recall. Letters A–Y represent associated class designations. Source: Trehub 1979. Copyright Academic Press (London) Ltd. Reproduced by permission.

points of stimulation to the retina and thence through the afferent channel to their coordinate mosaic cells in the synaptic matrix. Each scene was arbitrarily centered on the normal foveal axis. Scenes were learned in accordance with equation 2.3 but without assuming a dendrodendritic spread of excitation in the mosaic cell layer. In this simulation, the learning parameters were arbitrarily set as follows: $b = 1$ (although it is not necessary to assign b in a simulation because b is assumed to be uniform over all adaptive cells); $c = 2$; $k = 100$. The products of active stimulus points (pixels constituting an afferent scene) and their coordinate synaptic transfer weights were summed for each scene on each of the 25 output classes (Ω_i) and ordered in terms of descending magnitude. This procedure yielded a table of associative rank, or hierarchy of recall, which is reflected in the relative latency of class cell discharge (figure 10.2).

For a given stimulus, if a class cell (Ω_i) remains inhibited immediately after it fires, the Ω that is next highest in the associative hierarchy will have an opportunity to fire. Thus, sequences of associative

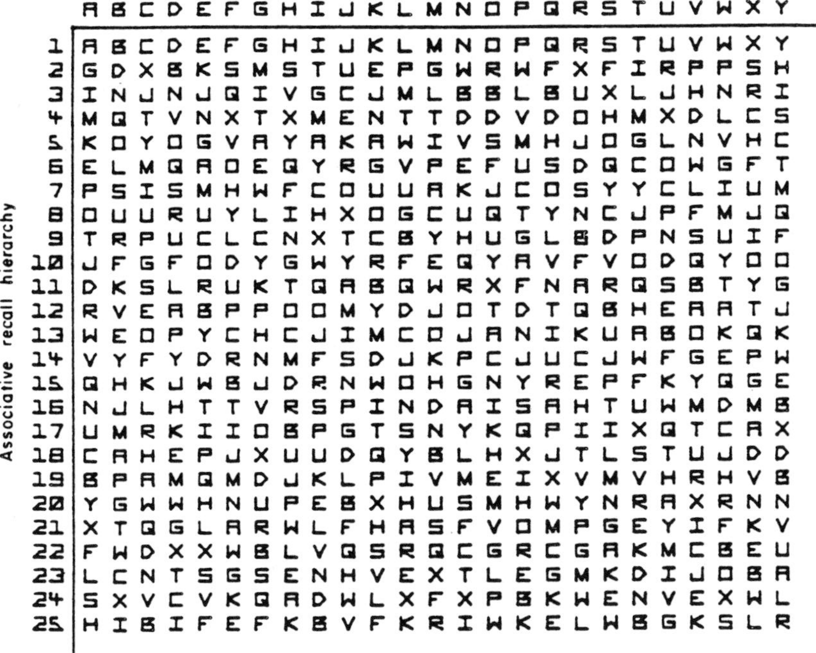

Input scene

Associative recall hierarchy

	A	B	C	D	E	F	G	H	I	J	K	L	M	N	O	P	Q	R	S	T	U	V	W	X	Y
1	A	B	C	D	E	F	G	H	I	J	K	L	M	N	O	P	Q	R	S	T	U	V	W	X	Y
2	G	D	X	B	K	S	M	S	T	U	E	P	G	W	R	W	F	X	F	I	R	P	P	S	H
3	I	N	J	N	J	Q	I	V	G	C	J	M	L	B	B	L	B	U	X	L	J	H	N	R	I
4	M	Q	T	V	N	X	T	X	M	E	N	T	T	D	D	V	D	O	H	M	X	D	L	C	S
5	K	O	Y	O	G	V	A	Y	A	K	A	W	I	V	S	M	H	J	O	G	L	N	V	H	C
6	E	L	M	Q	A	O	E	Q	Y	R	G	V	P	E	F	U	S	D	Q	C	O	W	G	F	T
7	P	S	I	S	M	H	W	F	C	O	U	U	A	K	J	C	O	S	Y	Y	C	L	I	U	M
8	O	U	U	R	U	Y	L	I	H	X	O	G	C	U	Q	T	Y	N	C	J	P	F	M	J	Q
9	T	R	P	U	C	L	C	N	X	T	C	B	Y	H	U	G	L	B	D	P	N	S	U	I	F
10	J	F	G	F	O	D	Y	G	W	Y	R	F	E	Q	Y	A	V	F	V	O	D	Q	Y	O	O
11	D	K	S	L	R	U	K	T	Q	A	B	Q	W	R	X	F	N	A	R	Q	S	B	T	Y	G
12	R	V	E	A	B	P	P	O	O	M	Y	D	J	O	T	D	T	Q	B	H	E	A	A	T	J
13	W	E	O	P	Y	C	H	C	J	I	M	C	O	J	A	N	I	K	U	A	B	O	K	Q	K
14	V	Y	F	Y	D	R	N	M	F	S	D	J	K	P	C	J	U	C	J	W	F	G	E	P	W
15	Q	H	K	J	W	B	J	D	R	N	W	O	H	G	N	Y	R	E	P	F	K	Y	Q	G	E
16	N	J	L	H	T	T	V	R	S	P	I	N	D	A	I	S	A	H	T	U	W	M	D	M	B
17	U	M	R	K	I	I	O	B	P	G	T	S	N	Y	K	Q	P	I	I	X	Q	T	C	A	X
18	C	A	H	E	P	J	X	U	U	D	Q	Y	B	L	H	X	J	T	L	S	T	U	J	D	D
19	B	P	A	M	Q	M	D	J	K	L	P	I	V	M	E	I	X	V	M	V	H	R	H	V	B
20	Y	G	W	W	H	N	U	P	E	B	X	H	U	S	M	H	W	Y	N	R	A	X	R	N	N
21	X	T	Q	G	L	A	R	W	L	F	H	A	S	F	V	O	M	P	G	E	Y	I	F	K	V
22	F	W	D	X	X	W	B	L	V	Q	S	R	Q	C	G	R	C	G	A	K	M	C	B	E	U
23	L	C	N	T	S	G	S	E	N	H	V	E	X	T	L	E	G	M	K	D	I	J	O	B	A
24	S	X	V	C	V	K	Q	A	D	W	L	X	F	X	P	B	K	W	E	N	V	E	X	W	L
25	H	I	B	I	F	E	F	K	B	V	F	K	R	I	W	K	E	L	W	B	G	K	S	L	R

Figure 10.2
Hierarchical associative order of all scenes in response to each stimulus scene. Source: Ibid. Copyright Academic Press (London) Ltd. Reproduced by permission.

recall are produced by inhibiting for the duration of a recall sequence each Ω immediately after it has discharged and signaled the scene that it has detected and classified. If an initial retinal pattern is maintained as a continuing stimulus to the mosaic cells in a synaptic matrix while class cells are successively inhibited immediately after their activation, the sequence of associations is called a stimulus-bound recall sequence. If an initial pattern is not maintained as a stimulus and subsequent excitation of mosaic cells is provided only by the brief class cell collateral volleys back to the imaging matrix, the sequence of associations is called an image-bound recall sequence.

Figure 10.3 shows a comparison of the two modes of recall in response to the presentation of scene S as the initiating stimulus. In both modes, the first pattern class and image recalled are those correctly matched to the initiating scene, as one would expect in an accurate perceptual system. The second response of the network is also the same for both modes: the class and image recalled are those

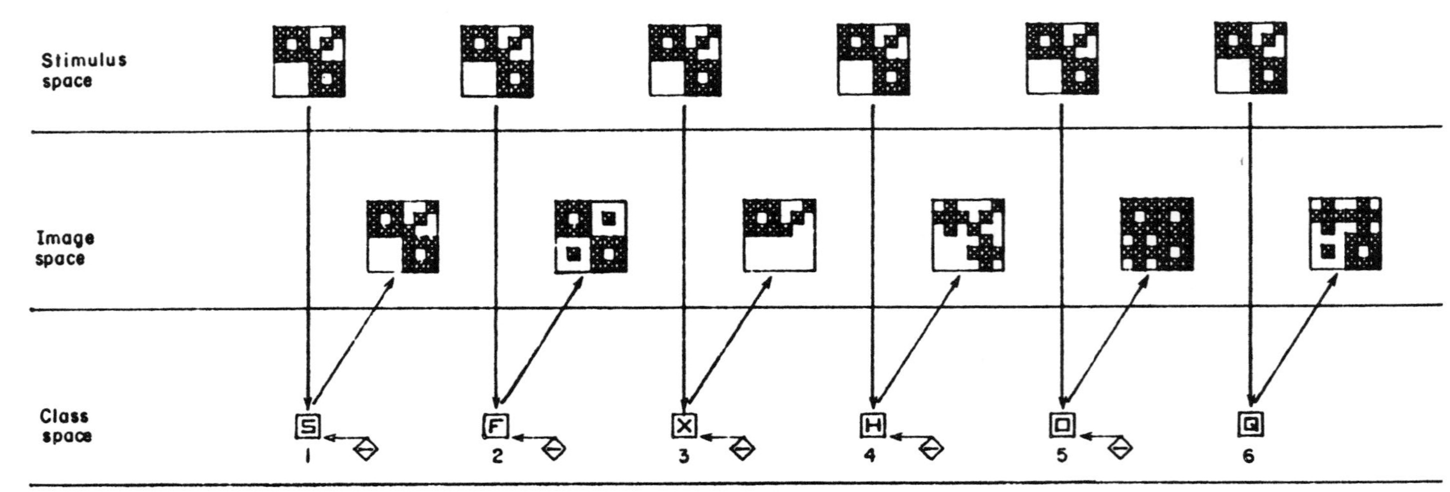

Stimulus-bound recall sequence

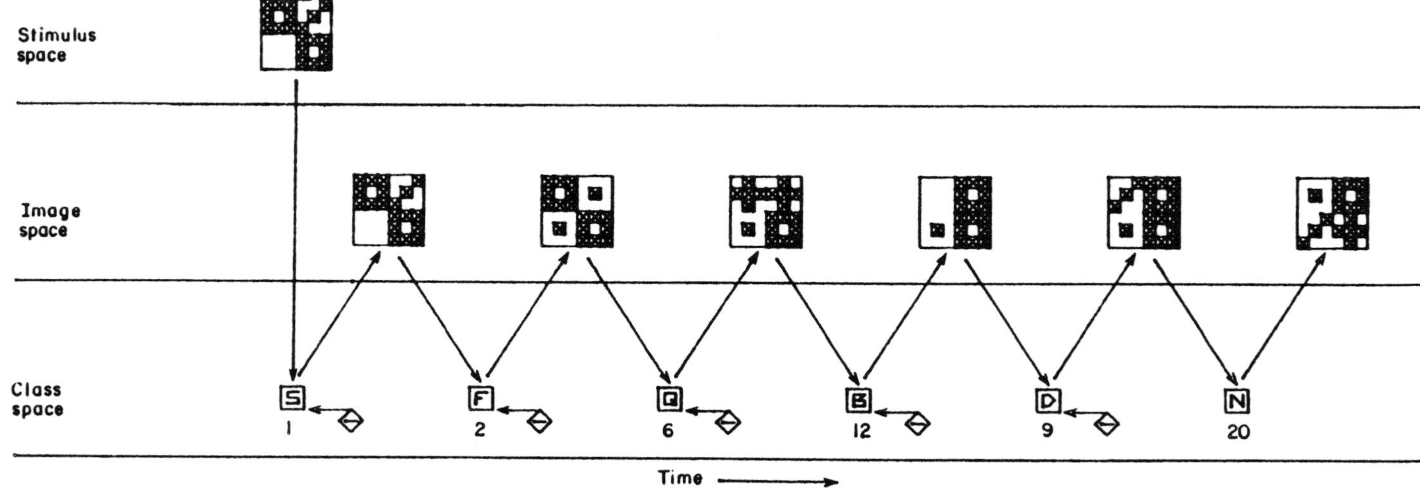

Figure 10.3
Example of two modes of recall in response to scene S. Numbers below class designations represent associative rank relative to S. Source: Ibid. Copyright Academic Press (London) Ltd. Reproduced by permission.

standing at rank order 2 in associative strength with scene S. This outcome is also to be expected because the image that generates the second response (class F) in the image-bound sequence is identical to the external scene in the stimulus-bound sequence (see figure 10.1). Thereafter, however, the chain of association is distinctly different in the two modes of recall.

Whereas the stimulus-bound sequence proceeds monotonically down the associative hierarchy (orders 1, 2, 3, 4, 5, 6) with respect to the initial scene, the image-bound sequence defies monotonicity and ranges widely over the associative hierarchy of the initial scene (orders 1, 2, 6, 12, 9, 20). Yet despite its random appearance, this latter sequence of associative recall is systematically determined by the functional characteristics and learning history of the synaptic matrix.

The first six recollections of the synaptic matrix in response to each of the 25 scenes were examined, and the median and range of associative ranks were derived (figure 10.4). In the stimulus-bound recall mode, associative rank relative to the initial scene was always identical to the order of recall. For the image-bound recall mode, however, after the second recall, median associative rank departed markedly from recall order, and the range of associations within the first six recollections spanned almost the entire hierarchy.

These data show that sequential recall in a synaptic matrix can exhibit, on the basis of this module's intrinsic properties, characteristics of orderliness or looseness of association that appear to conform with human associative behavior.

Recognition under Noisy Conditions: I

In this simulation (Trehub 1987), a microworld was constructed in which three motivated characters moved about and interacted within an environment that had a number of objects and "natural" features relevant to a number of goals arbitrarily installed in each of the characters. The microworld consisted of David, Lisa, a dog named Wolf, David's house, Lisa's cottage, a restaurant, a pond, a pine tree forest, and a rabbit. Here we will consider only the visual-cognitive aspects of the simulation and ignore the motivations that shaped each character's travel route in the simulated environment.

The principal character, David, was endowed with a synaptic matrix so that he was able not only to move among the objects in his world, as the other characters could, but also to learn and later recognize the visual world about him. After David learned the individual elements of his world, the simulation program projected to his 21 ×

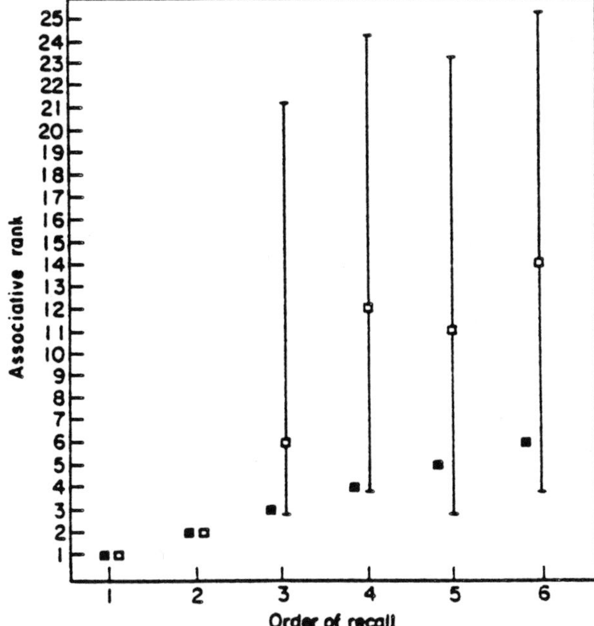

Figure 10.4
Median and range of associative rank of recalled scenes relative to initiating scenes through six sequential recollections. Filled squares designate stimulus-bound recall; open squares designate image-bound recall. Source: Ibid. Copyright Academic Press (London) Ltd. Reproduced by permission.

21–cell retina all objects that happened to be close to him (within an arbitrary distance) during the course of his activities. The visual stimuli were arbitrarily centered on the normal foveal axis, and he was programmed to make a "verbal" response appropriate to the objects encountered. If two or more objects happened to be close enough to be "seen," their patterns were arbitrarily superposed on the retina. When this occurred, the synaptic matrix had to disambiguate the complex image for each of the superposed objects to be correctly recognized. The network was able to respond to each of the constituent objects in succession because any class cell that signaled the presence of its associated object auto-inhibited immediately after its discharge. This released other class cells, enabling a different cell to fire and signal the presence of a different object (top, figure 10.3).

The program allowed the investigator to introduce controlled amounts of visual noise into the environment. Noise was both additive and subtractive; an active pixel (pixel = 1) in the visual field would either be erased (pixel = 0) or remain unchanged, and an inactive pixel (pixel = 0) would be activated (pixel = 1) or remain unchanged. Pixels affected by noise were selected on a random basis, with the overall proportion of affected pixels determined by the percentage of noise introduced. Under the condition of 100 percent noise, each pixel in the visual field had a 50 percent chance of changing from *on* (active) to *off* (inactive) or from *off* to *on*.

Figure 10.5 shows a moment from the dynamic simulation in which David has encountered Lisa at the restaurant. The divided inset at the upper left shows the image of Lisa superposed on the image of the restaurant as they would appear on David's retina if there were no visual noise and as they actually appeared, degraded by the introduction of 40 percent noise. The verbal responses show that, under this condition of pattern superposition and visual noise, David correctly recognized both Lisa and the restaurant. Examination of records over extended periods of simulation indicate that, even with superposition of objects, errors in recognition are rarely made until the noise level exceeds approximately 70 percent. In the initial learn-

2(.4)LISA
2(.4)RESTAURANT

I HOPE THEY SERVE SEAFOOD CHOWDER TODAY.......
HI!..LISA!.....

Figure 10.5
One frame of the microworld simulation copied directly from the CRT display. David has just encountered Lisa at the restaurant (far right). At the upper left of the display, the divided graphic inset shows, on the left, the image of Lisa superposed on that of the restaurant as it would appear to David if there were no visual noise. On the right side of the inset is the same image degraded by 40 percent random visual noise, which is the actual stimulus projected to David's retina. David's verbal responses at the bottom of the CRT display show that he has correctly identified both the restaurant and Lisa despite superposition and substantial image degradation.

ing situation, David was exposed to only one character or object at a time. Thus, the ability of the synaptic matrix to disambiguate and properly recognize later each superposed component of a complex of patterns, degraded by substantial levels of visual noise, represents a powerful generalization of the original learned response.

Recognition under Noisy Conditions: II

In the previous simulation, visual patterns were arbitrarily centered on the normal foveal axis. In the test described in this section, stimuli were presented in the visual field at locations eccentric to the initial point of fixation. Thus, the network had to initiate a visual saccade to each stimulus, and the stimulus pattern had to be adaptively shifted on a retinoid in order for its centroid to fall on the normal foveal axis.

The network was simulated with a 16 × 16–cell retina. The learning parameters were arbitrarily set at $c = 1$; $k = 100$. A gradient coefficient of 0.6 was set for dendrodendritic transfer to neighboring cells in the mosaic array. Base error tolerance (ET) for centroid alignment on the normal foveal axis was set at three retinoid units.

Test stimuli consisted of four different alphabetic characters in uppercase Geneva font: G, L, O, and Q. First, a quasi-random jumble of lines was presented as a separate stimulus and learned as "NOLETTER." Then the model learned to recognize and identify each of the four letters in their pristine form (no noise degradation). Figure

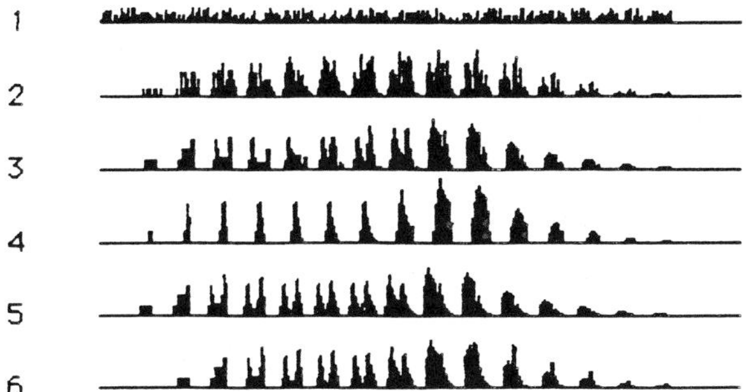

Figure 10.6
Distribution of synaptic transfer weights (ϕ) on the dendrites of filter cells following learning. Each point on the dendritic line represents the relative magnitude of transfer weight for that synapse. The stimuli that were learned in the examples shown are as follows: 1 = random visual pattern; 2 = quasi-random scribble (NOLETTER); 3 = G; 4 = L; 5 = O; 6 = Q.

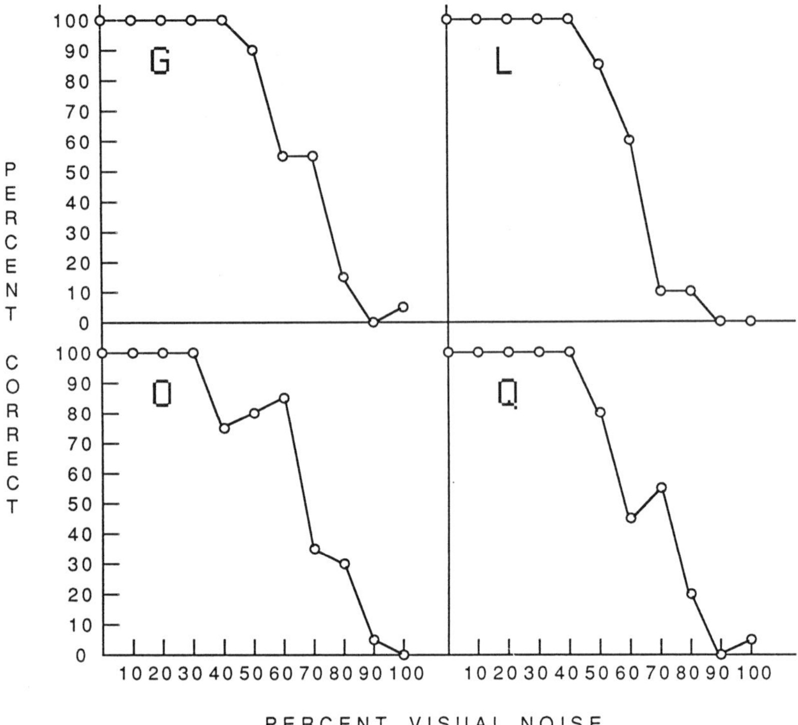

Figure 10.7
Recognition performance for each of four test stimuli as a function of level of visual noise.

10.6 shows the distribution of synaptic transfer weights (ϕ) on filter cells that had been modified in the course of learning the stimuli used in this simulation. Recognition tests were then performed in 10 blocks of 20 trials for each letter, with a different level of visual noise (additive and subtractive) introduced for each block of trials. Noise ranged from 10 to 100 percent, where the magnitude of noise indicates the proportion of stimulus pixels affected.

As each letter was presented, the model network was required to identify it. Response on each trial could be one of the following: G, L, O, Q, or NOLETTER. Because a letter was always presented, though it might be distorted by 100 percent noise, the response NOLETTER was always counted as an error. The four histograms in figure 10.7 show the percentage of correct responses for each of the four letters as the level of visual noise increased from 0 to 100 percent. In each case, there were no errors in recognition until visual noise

Table 10.1
Number of instances of false recognition under noisy condition

Letter Presented		Recognized As: G	L	O	Q
	G	-	0	4	5
	L	1	-	2	0
	O	2	0	-	5
	Q	3	0	15	-

exceeded at least 30 percent. Performance remained better than 50 percent correct until noise exceeded 60 percent.

The stimuli were deliberately selected to include three with substantially similar shapes (G, O, Q) and one with a shape unlike the others (L). Table 10.1 shows the number of false recognitions of each letter as a function of the letter presented. The pattern of confusion in recognition conforms in general with what one might intuitively expect. The greatest number of misidentifications occurred when the letter Q was presented. In the context of high levels of noise, it was incorrectly "seen" as the letter O 15 times. The specific vulnerability of the letter Q is apparently due to the fact that its discrimination from O depends on the presence of a tiny visual feature—the diagonal stroke at the bottom right of the figure. Interestingly, O was misidentified as Q only five times. (One wonders if the same task presented to humans would yield a similar asymmetry in confusions between O and Q.) The letter G was confused with O and Q in approximately equal measure. And the letter L exhibited the least number of misidentifications, a result that might be expected given its distinctive shape in the memory set.

Recognition under Rotation

The simulations just described demonstrate the robustness of the putative brain mechanisms when learned stimuli must be recognized despite degradation by visual noise. Now suppose that a visual stimulus is learned at a particular angular orientation in the frontal plane and is then presented at a different orientation. How robust will the network be in recognizing learned exemplars that undergo such rotational transformation? One way to ensure recognition under rotation is to transform input patterns covertly until they match the orientations of previously learned exemplars. Another way of dealing with recognition under rotation would not necessarily ensure successful recognition but might be ecologically efficient for many purposes:

to learn an object in enough different angular orientations so that exemplars of the object at intervening orientations would, with high probability, be more closely matched to their appropriate filter cells than to incorrect *f* cells. If this were the strategy, how would performance degrade as a stimulus departed from the angular orientation at which it was learned? How many different orientations would have to be learned to provide reasonably adequate performance with arbitrary stimulus rotations? The following simulation was run to provide some clues.

A 16 × 16–cell retina provided input to the system. Parameters for learning were $c = 1$; $k = 100$. The gradient for dendrodendritic excitation was set at 0.6. Base error tolerance (ET) for automatically shifting pattern centroids to the normal foveal axis was set at three retinoid units. The uppercase letters L, O, and G (Geneva font) were the stimuli used in this test.

Each letter was learned at its normal vertical orientation (0 degree) and at a clockwise rotation of 22 degrees. Figure 10.8 shows the distribution of synaptic transfer weights on filter cells that were tuned to the stimuli at their standard orientation and at a clockwise rotation of 22 degrees. Because the letter L is an asymmetrical yet relatively simple stimulus, with a single vertical and horizontal stroke, it was used to see how a filter cell, having learned the pattern at its normal

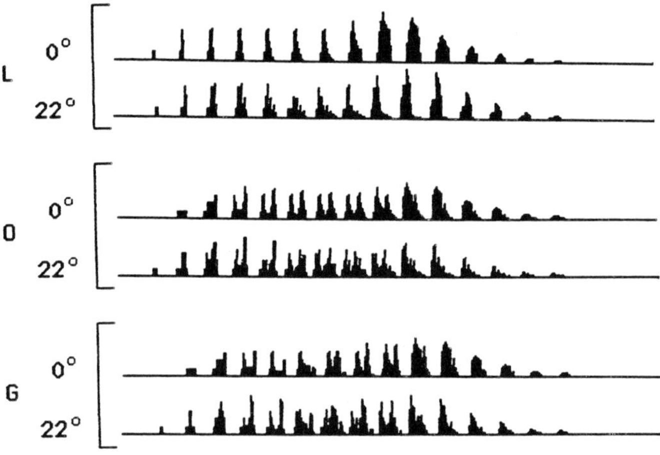

Figure 10.8
Comparison of synaptic transfer weight profiles on the dendrites of filter cells for each of three stimuli learned at normal (0 degrees) and rotated (22 degrees) orientation.

vertical orientation, would respond to exemplars of L at different angular orientations.

Figure 10.9 shows how the discharge of a filter cell that has learned a vertical L (0 degrees) changes when it is stimulated with the same letter at angular orientations ranging from −55 to +55 degrees. The responses of the cell over the range of stimulus orientations are plotted as an output proportional to its discharge when it is presented with the letter that it has learned. When the stimulus was rotated away from its normal representation, the filter cell response did not fall abruptly but rather exhibited a graded decrement analogous to the response of a band-pass filter in the frequency domain. Indeed, when the stimulus was tilted as much as 22 degrees in either the clockwise or counterclockwise direction, filter cell discharge declined to no less than 52 percent of its maximum.

In a test of recognition under rotation, each of the three letters was rotated clockwise from 0 to a maximum of 55 degrees in incre-

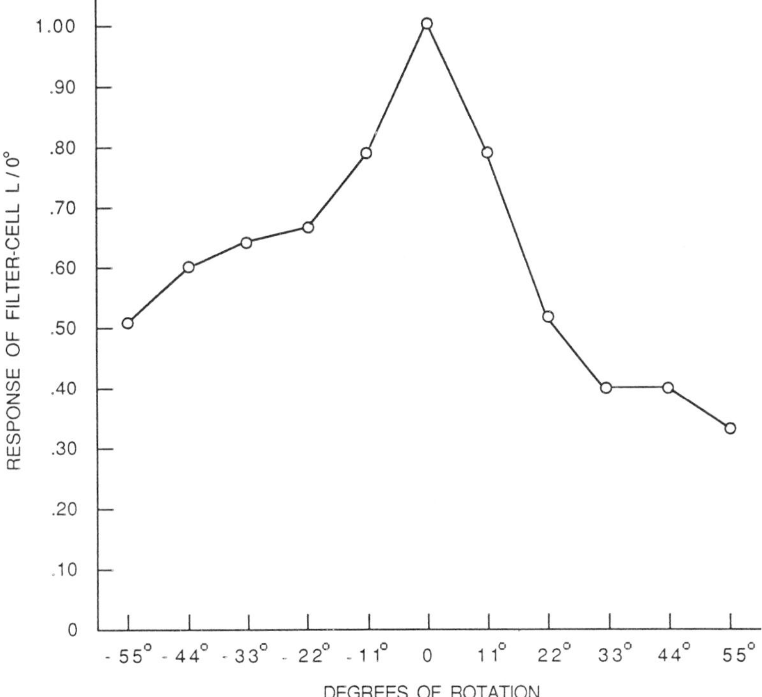

Figure 10.9
Response of a filter cell (L/0°) to rotation of its learned exemplar.

ments of approximately 11 degrees (figure 10.10). Each letter was presented for recognition in blocks of 20 trials for each of its angular orientations.

The percentage of correct responses for each of the six different orientations is given in table 10.2. Recall that the letters were learned at their standard orientation (0 degrees) and at a rotation angle of 22 degrees. It is not surprising that recognition performance was 100 percent correct for all letters at the two learned orientations. However, recognition was also at the 100 percent level for all letters at the intermediate orientation of 11 degrees, which had not been learned. Moreover, for the letters L and O, there were no errors at the novel orientation of 33 degrees. As clockwise rotation increased, recognition of the letter L decreased to 35 percent at the 55 degree orientation, while recognition of O remained at or near the 100 percent level. Recognition of the letter G was 75 percent correct at 33 degrees and declined to 55 percent at 55 degrees.

When we examine the nature of the errors made in this test (table 10.3), we see that L was confused with G 22 times but was never confused with O. There was only one confusion of the letter O, and that was with G. The letter G, on the other hand, was confused with

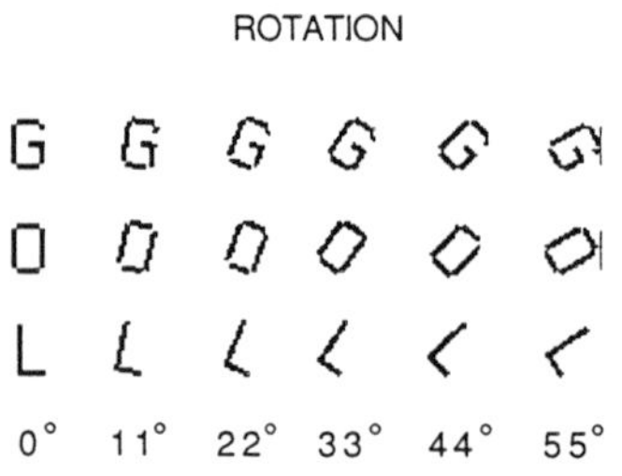

ROTATION

0° 11° 22° 33° 44° 55°

Figure 10.10
Stimuli used in test of recognition under rotation.

Table 10.2
Recognition under rotation

Letter Presented		DEGREES ROTATION 0°	11°	22°	33°	44°	55°
	L	100	100	100	100	55	35
	O	100	100	100	100	95	100
	G	100	100	100	75	70	55

Note: Cells indicate percentage of correct responses to test stimuli. Shaded cells show where exemplars were learned.

Table 10.3
Number of instances of false recognition under rotation

		Recognized As		
		L	O	G
Letter Presented	L	-	0	22
	O	0	-	1
	G	0	20	-

O 20 times but was never confused with L. The striking resistance of the letter O to confusion is most likely due to its relative symmetry under rotation, a property shared somewhat less by G and least by L. However, given the rough similarity in shape between G and O, it is impressive that recognition performance was 100 percent correct for these stimuli as well as for L when rotation was 11 degrees in angular distance from their bounding learned exemplars (0 degrees and 22 degrees).

More parametric work should be done to examine the performance of the model with rotated stimuli, but these results suggest that the proposed neuronal mechanism is robust under rotational transformation, as well as with visual noise. If, in fact, exemplars of a rotated object need only be learned at approximately 11 degree intervals to ensure adequate recognition with arbitrary rotation, then the issue of neuronal resource constraints becomes a less thorny one.

Episodic Learning and Recall

In chapter 5, a model neuronal mechanism was described that was able to control the timing, registration, and location of episodic learning in a synaptic matrix. It was also shown how this mechanism, composed of a clock circuit and a recall circuit, could serve to determine the temporal locus and sequence of recalled episodic experience. In the following simulation of episodic learning (Trehub 1983), the model was tested with some added assumptions concerning the effects of fluctuating levels of arousal and the time course of memory decay.

Learning proceeded according to the basic formula for synaptic modification (equation 2.3) in the matrices for stimulus detection and imagery, with the additional assumption of transfer weight (ϕ) modulation according to the momentary level of randomly fluctuating arousal. This assumption was made on the grounds that increased diffuse priming of filter cells (f) by higher levels of arousal would induce a more vigorous response in those cells that were undergoing modification in the learning process and, as a result, the amount of free DTF (represented by the coefficient k) would increase. Thus,

$$\phi_{0 \atop b \to Lim} = (b + S\,(c + kN^{-1}))\,L \tag{10.1}$$

where L is a normal random variable with $\bar{x} = 1.0$ and $\sigma = 0.2$ (arbitrarily chosen) and represents a randomly fluctuating arousal context for each instance of learning.

A long-term decay function for synaptic transfer weights (ϕ) was chosen on the basis of Wickelgren's (1974) proposal for memory decay. Thus, for ϕ decay in episodic learning,

$$\phi_t = \phi_0\,(1 - \beta t)^{-\psi} \tag{10.2}$$

where ϕ_0 = synaptic transfer weight immediately after learning; t = time elapsed since initial learning; β = first parameter for decay rate; and ψ = second parameter for decay rate. In this simulation, the two parameters were arbitrarily set with $\beta = 2.0$ and $\psi = 0.5$.

It was assumed that in order to recall any given component image in a contiguous sequence of learned stimuli (an episode), the sum of ϕ_t values (equation 10.2) supporting that image must exceed a concurrent threshold value. It was further assumed that recall threshold would change from moment to moment as an inverse function of the level of randomly fluctuating arousal (L). Thus,

$$\theta = L^{-1} + \tau \tag{10.3}$$

where θ = recall threshold; L = level of arousal; and τ = base threshold level. Note that L (which modulates recall threshold at each instance of recall) is taken as a normal random variable with $\bar{x} = 1.0$ and $\sigma = 0.2$.

Assuming an appropriate repertoire of language to characterize component images during an epoch of learning, figure 10.11 presents the set of primitive images and associated language that was used in the simulation. Figure 10.12 shows the results of testing the neuronal network for episodic learning and recall. A complete episode was learned via successive input on a 6 × 6–cell retina. The sequence of stimuli is shown in figure 10.12 beside ELAPSED TIME 00. Episodic recall was tested at elapsed times corresponding to 1–14 days following the original learned experience. Failure to recall particular details of the episode increases as time passes. Occasional recovery of memory for forgotten details is also seen in figure 10.12.

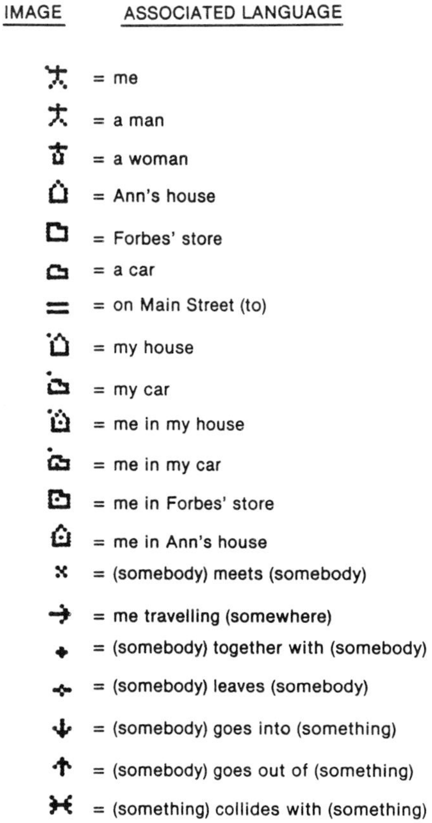

IMAGE ASSOCIATED LANGUAGE

= me
= a man
= a woman
= Ann's house
= Forbes' store
= a car
= on Main Street (to)
= my house
= my car
= me in my house
= me in my car
= me in Forbes' store
= me in Ann's house
= (somebody) meets (somebody)
= me travelling (somewhere)
= (somebody) together with (somebody)
= (somebody) leaves (somebody)
= (somebody) goes into (something)
= (somebody) goes out of (something)
= (something) collides with (something)

Figure 10.11
Primitive images and associated language. Source: Trehub 1983. Copyright Lawrence Erlbaum Associates, Inc. Reproduced by permission.

In order to convey the flavor of episodic learning and recall as exhibited by the model, a protocol of descriptive language appropriate to the original episode and to later "verbalized" recollections is presented below (figure 10.11). Oblique lines separate underlying component images (patterns evoked in the imaging matrix). Words bracketed by ⟨ and ⟩ indicate the absence of a specific image. Words in parentheses were arbitrarily added to improve the narrative flow of the protocols. Word tense was arbitrarily changed wherever it was grammatically appropriate.

Elapsed Time = 00

/I am in my house/. /I/ go out of/ my house/ (then) go into/ my

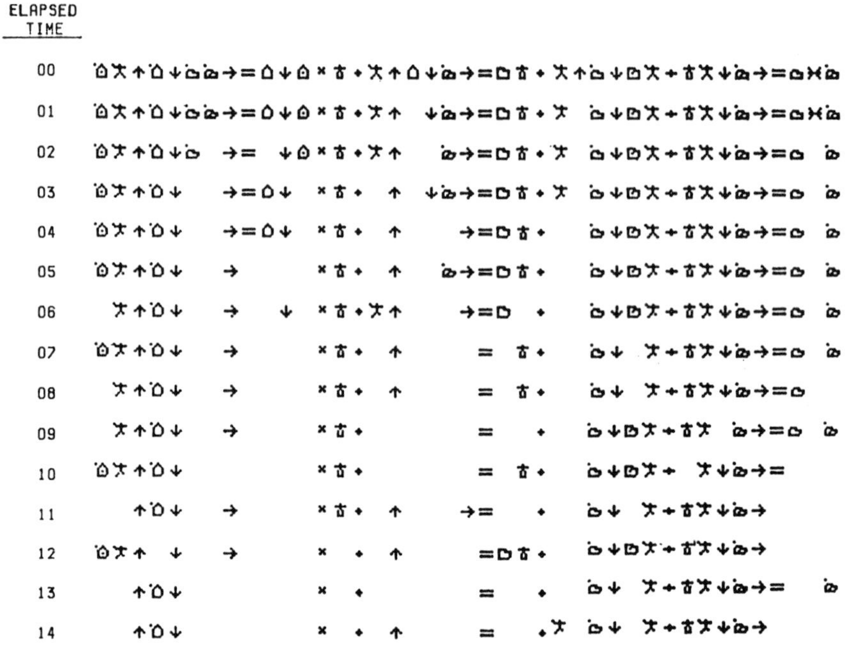

ELAPSED TIME

00
01
02
03
04
05
06
07
08
09
10
11
12
13
14

Figure 10.12
Simulation test. *Top row:* Complete sequence of learned images in the original episode. *Following rows:* Recalled episodic images at indicated elapsed times. Source: Ibid. Copyright Lawrence Erlbaum Associates, Inc. Reproduced by permission.

car/ (and) travel/ on Main Street to/ Ann's house/ (and) meet/ Ann/. /I/ together with/ Ann/ go out of/ Ann's house/ (and) go into/ my car/ (and) travel/ on Main Street to/ Forbes' store/. /I/ together with/ Ann/ go out of/ my car/ (and) go into/ Forbes' store/. (Then) I/ leave Ann/ (and) I/ go into/ my car/ (and) travel/ on Main Street/. /A car/ collides with/ my car/.

Elapsed Time = 01

/I was in my house/. /I/ went out of/ my house/ (and) got into/ my car/ (and) travelled/ on Main Street to/ Ann's house/ (then) went into/ Ann's house/ (and) met/ Ann/. /Ann/ (and) I/ left ⟨somewhere⟩/ (and) went into/ my car/ (and) travelled/ on Main Street to/ Forbes' store/. /Ann/ was with me/. /(I remember) my car/ (and) going into/ Forbes' store/. /(Then) I/ left/ Ann/ (and) I/ got into/ my car/. /I/ travelled/ on Main Street/. /A car/ collided with/ my car/.

Elapsed Time = 07

/I was in my house/. /I/ went out of/ my house/ (and) got into ⟨something⟩. /I travelled/ ⟨somewhere⟩. (Then I remember) / ⟨somebody⟩ met Ann/. /Ann/ (was) together with/ ⟨somebody⟩. (I remember) /my car/ (and) going into/ ⟨something⟩. (I remember) / leaving/ Ann/ (and) /getting into/ my car/ (and) travelling/ on Main Street/. (I remember) /another car/ (and) being in my car/.

Elapsed Time = 14

(I remember) ⟨someone⟩ /leaving/ my house/ (and) going into ⟨something⟩. (Then) ⟨someone⟩ /met ⟨somebody⟩/ (and) together/ (they) got out of/ ⟨something⟩. (I remember) /Main Street/. /⟨Somebody⟩ was with/ me/. (I remember) /my car/ (and) ⟨somebody⟩ /going into/ ⟨something⟩. (Then I remember) /I/ left/ Ann/ (and) got into/ my car/ (and) travelled/ ⟨somewhere⟩.

The behavior exhibited by this network can be elaborated in a number of interesting ways. For example, if the component images in an episode were to evoke different hedonic values linked to the magnitude of arousal (L), then the relative temporal density of particular episodically linked images and the individual probabilities of their recall would vary accordingly over an episode. Two different individuals experiencing the same episode might well give two quite different accounts depending on their personal emotional response during the experience. As an example of excessive arousal inducing psychopathological behavior, suppose an individual is in a heightened state of arousal for an extended period of time. Under this condition, the neuronal clock will run very fast for a long time due to arousal priming of the clock ring. Given a constant ϕ decay function (equation 10.2), ϕ changes in the filter cells (f) of the detection matrix might not have sufficient time to decay close to initial values before the f cells are recycled and primed for learning. If this happens, component episodic images would be confounded with earlier memories, and, if the confounding is extreme, one might characterize the individual as being in a pathologically confused state.

Not all episodic memories must be controlled by a single clock ring. It is more likely that there is a hierarchically structured system of clock rings and recall rings with short (high frequency) to long (low frequency) priming-pulse intervals for temporally organized learning. In such a network, we would assume that the high-frequency circuits would recycle over short periods of time, and low-frequency circuits would exhibit long recycle periods.

Chapter 11
Learning and Recalling Objects with Naturally Varying Shapes

Computer simulations described in the previous chapter demonstrated that the putative visual-cognitive system can learn and recall canonically shaped objects that are presented on the normal foveal axis or at eccentric locations in the visual field. Furthermore, the tests provided evidence that recognition performance of the model is robust under conditions of visual noise and rotational transformation. In the simulations described in this chapter the proposed centroid-finding mechanism works with the synaptic matrix to enable the system to fixate and learn visual stimuli that are not canonical and presented at random locations in the visual field. Figure 11.1 is a block-flow diagram summarizing the processing sequence. The mechanisms within the labeled blocks embody the neuronal properties described in earlier chapters.

The performance of the model with noncanonical stimuli was tested by presenting it with handprinted lowercase letters, freely written on a digitizing tablet as one might write in a notebook but without the usual guiding lines. Handprinted lowercase letters are well suited as stimuli because each sample conserves the distinguishing underlying characteristics of the letter it represents and at the same time varies from one instance to another in its exact shape, size, angular orientation, and location with respect to a fixed reference axis (the normal foveal axis). The first test required the model network to learn and recognize letters printed by one person (Trehub 1990). In a second test, the system was given the task of learning and recognizing letters printed by five different individuals. Clearly, in the latter case, one would expect a much wider range of variation in shape, size, and slant over the sample of stimuli. Although performance of the network would be enhanced if each letter presented to the retina were normalized for variation in size and angular orientation, none of the simulations embodied size and rotation transformers to correct for such variations.

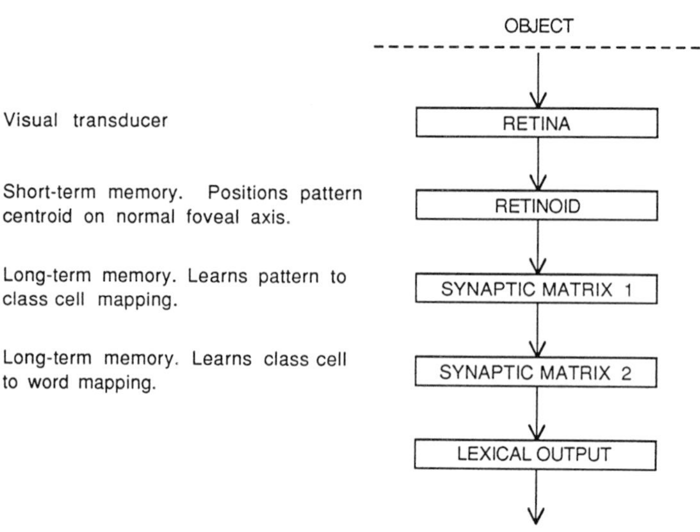

Figure 11.1
Block-flow diagram of simulated pattern recognition subsystem.

Test Procedure 1

A neuronal subsystem consisting of a retina, retinoid, synaptic matrix, and afferent aperture circuit was simulated in a digital computer. The gradient coefficient of dendrodendritic transfer to neighboring cells in the mosaic cell array was arbitrarily set at 0.5. The constant b (representing the initial transfer weight of filter cells) was disregarded because it is assumed to be very small and uniform for all such cells in the synaptic matrix. The constant c (representing the axon transfer factor) was set at 2.0. The coefficient k (representing the dendrite transfer factor) was set at 38.0. Error tolerance (ET) for centroid alignment on the normal foveal axis was set and held constant at 3 retinoid units.

Input to the retina was provided by a graphics digitizing tablet. Lowercase letters were handprinted in normal size on an unlined sheet of paper that overlay the digitizing tablet, which converted the pressure of the pencil trace to a spatially conforming digital signal pattern. This two-dimensional binary pattern constituted the stimulus to a 15 × 15–cell retina in the simulated network.

During the initial learning phase, each letter of the alphabet was presented one at a time. Because the letters were freely drawn within the fixed visual field of the system, most stimuli happened to project to parafoveal positions on its retina. Where the fixation tolerance was exceeded, the retinoid mechanism attempted to translate its representation of the letter pattern to the normal foveal axis before the letter was learned. Despite this effort to fixate each stimulus representation on the standard learning axis, the coarse resolution of the retina resulted in an inability to satisfy error tolerance for horizontal and/or vertical axes in about half of the stimulus presentations. When this happened, the model printed the message "CANNOT FIXATE THIS OBJECT," and another exemplar of the same letter was printed. This phase of the procedure was completed after each letter of the alphabet had been fixated once and then learned, which resulted in the synaptic "tuning" of 26 filter cells in the detection matrix. The discharge of any class cell was then taken to indicate the presence of the letter previously learned by its synaptically coupled filter cell.

In a correction phase following the initial learning sequence, letters were printed, one at a time, starting from the beginning of the alphabet. The model was required to fixate and recognize (by appropriate class cell discharge) the letter presented. If the response was correct, the next letter was written. If the response was wrong, the misidentified letter was learned (that is, an additional filter cell was synaptically modified) as another exemplar of its stimulus class. The model was then required to recognize another printing of the same letter. If the response was correct, the next letter of the alphabet was presented; if incorrect, the current letter was learned as a new exemplar of its class. This procedure was repeated until 33 lowercase exemplars had been learned, at which point recognition performance was tested without correction.

In the uncorrected test sequence, each letter of the alphabet was presented for fixation and recognition. Each stimulus-response pair was recorded for all 26 letters, and the entire procedure was repeated through five runs of the alphabet. Thus, 130 letters were drawn and 130 recognition responses were made with no corrective learning. Similar uncorrected test sequences were run after 36 and 46 exemplars had been learned in interspersed correction phases.

Upon completion of the learning routines, the distributions of synaptic transfer weights (ϕ) on 46 filter cell dendrites had changed in accordance with the basic learning mechanism. Figure 11.2 shows the synaptic profiles of a few selected filter cells in the detection matrix together with the alphabetic character associated with each learning-induced synaptic distribution. The selectivity of recognition response is determined by the differences among such ϕ distributions over the population of filter cells in the detection matrix.

The graph in figure 11.3 shows the improvement in recognition performance in the uncorrected test sequences as the number of

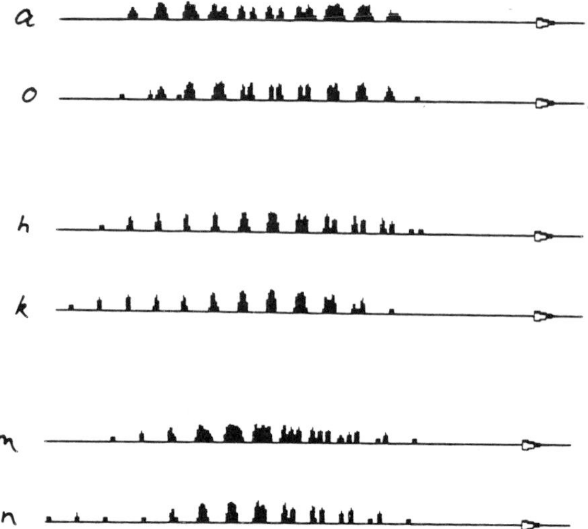

Figure 11.2
Examples of the distribution of synaptic transfer weights (ϕ) on the dendrites of filter cells that learned handprinted letters in test procedure 1. Each point on the dendritic line represents the relative magnitude of transfer weight for that synapse. Letters learned are shown to the left of each filter cell. Source: Trehub 1990. Copyright Lawrence Erlbaum Associates, Inc. Reproduced by permission.

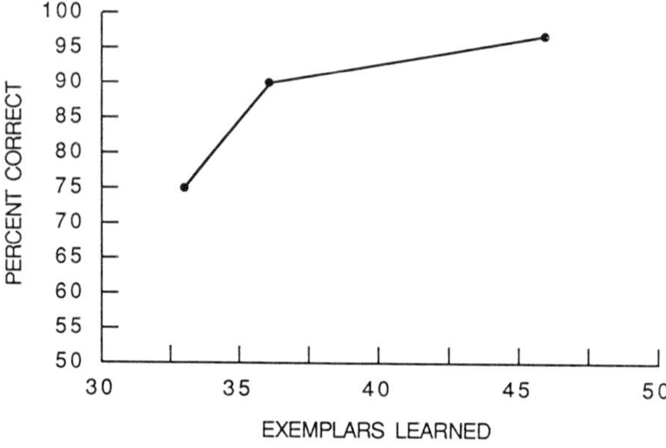

Figure 11.3
Graph showing the percentage of correct letter recognition responses during the test trials plotted against the total number of exemplars learned before each test. Source: Ibid. Copyright Lawrence Erlbaum Associates, Inc. Reproduced by permission.

learned exemplars increased from 33 to 46. Each point on the graph is based on 130 stimulus-response pairs. When 33 exemplars were learned, response was 75 percent correct. With 36 learned exemplars, response was 90 percent correct. After 46 exemplars had been learned, response was 97 percent correct.

Confusion matrices based on all stimulus-response pairs in the initial uncorrected test sequence and in the last test sequence are presented in figures 11.4 and 11.5. For most letters, confusions occur when the stimulus and response share similar graphic features.

Test Procedure 2

In the second test, the task of learning to identify handprinted letters was made more difficult: the network was required to learn and recognize lowercase letters printed by five different individuals, and it was not permitted to reject stimuli with centroids that it could not align within a tolerance of plus or minus three retinoid units from the normal foveal axis. Thus, unlike the previous simulation, an attempt at recognition was required for each stimulus presentation.

The neuronal subsystem consisted of a retina, a retinoid, and a synaptic matrix, with the retina dimensioned at 16 × 16 cells. The gradient coefficient for dendrodendritic transfer to neighboring cells in the mosaic cell array was set at 0.6. The axon transfer factor (c) was set at 1.0 and the dendrite transfer factor (k) at 100.

Test stimuli were obtained from the writing of five individuals. In the first sample, each writer printed all lowercase letters of the alphabet in three complete sequences on the page of a notebook, providing an initial total of 78 stimuli per individual (figure 11.6). In the second sample approximately two months later, each writer again provided three complete printings of the alphabet.

Stimulation to the retina was provided by digitized tracings of the handprinted letters. Most letters projected to parafoveal positions on the retina as before, but in this case, instead of rejecting stimuli that could not be fixated within a constant error tolerance, the system worked to minimize fixation error before attempting to recognize each stimulus. It first tried to align the stimulus centroid to within plus or minus two retinoid units of the normal foveal axis. If quadrantal disparities exceeded this limit, the model relaxed its error tolerance by one unit (to plus or minus three units). This process was iterated until the minimum tolerance was established within which fixation could occur (figure 7.4). At this point, the letter pattern was gated through to the synaptic matrix to be recognized, and if the response happened to be incorrect, that stimulus was learned.

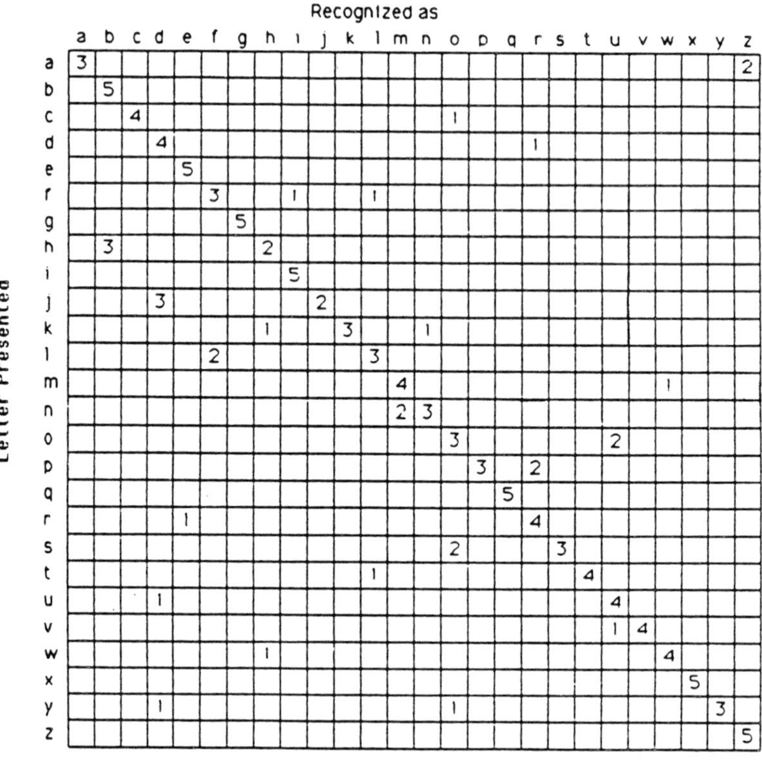

Response to Handprinted Alphabetic Characters

Recognized as

Letter Presented	a	b	c	d	e	f	g	h	i	j	k	l	m	n	o	p	q	r	s	t	u	v	w	x	y	z
a	3																									2
b		5																								
c			4												1											
d				4														1								
e					5																					
f						3			1			1														
g							5																			
h		3						2																		
i									5																	
j				3						2																
k								1			3			1												
l						2						3														
m													4										1			
n													2	3												
o															3						2					
p																3		2								
q																	5									
r					1													4								
s															2				3							
t												1								4						
u				1																	4					
v																					1	4				
w								1															4			
x																								5		
y				1											1										3	
z																										5

Number of Exemplars = 33 Correct Responses = 75%

Figure 11.4
Confusion matrix following the learning of 33 exemplars. Source: Ibid. Copyright Lawrence Erlbaum Associates, Inc. Reproduced by permission.

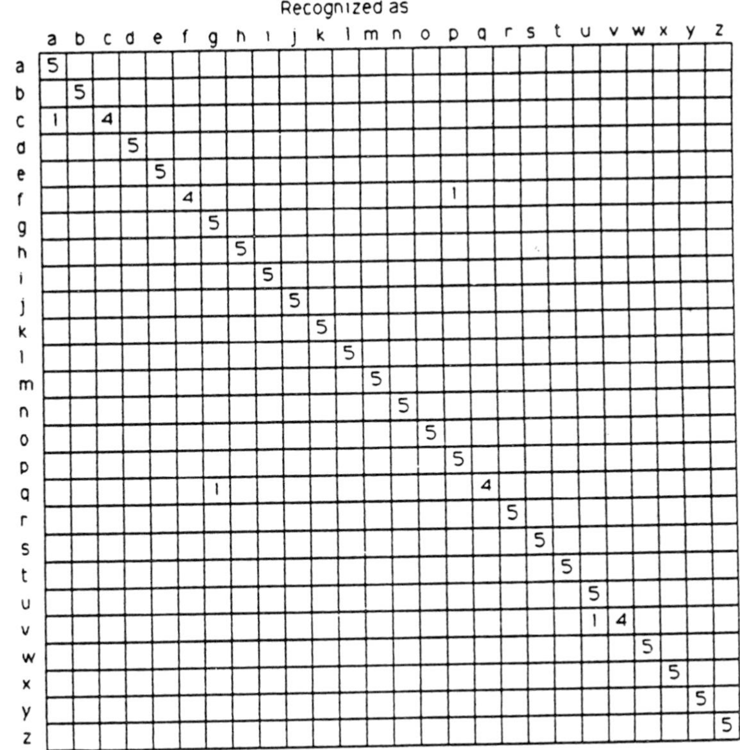

Response to Handprinted Alphabetic Characters

Recognized as (columns) / Letter Presented (rows)

	a	b	c	d	e	f	g	h	i	j	k	l	m	n	o	p	q	r	s	t	u	v	w	x	y	z
a	5																									
b		5																								
c	1		4																							
d				5																						
e					5																					
f						4										1										
g							5																			
h								5																		
i									5																	
j										5																
k											5															
l												5														
m													5													
n														5												
o															5											
p																5										
q							1										4									
r																		5								
s																			5							
t																				5						
u																					5					
v																					1	4				
w																							5			
x																								5		
y																									5	
z																										5

Number of Exemplars = 46 Correct Responses = 97%

Figure 11.5
Confusion matrix following the learning of 46 exemplars. Source: Ibid. Copyright Lawrence Erlbaum Associates, Inc. Reproduced by permission.

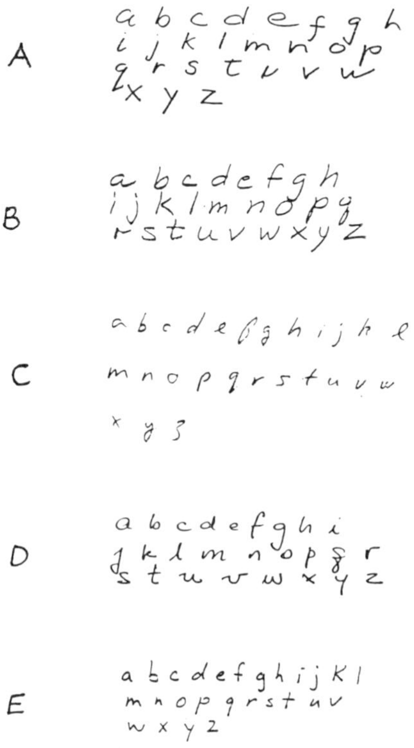

Figure 11.6
Samples of the handprinted stimuli produced by each of the five writers in test procedure 2.

All of the letters from the first sample provided by individual A were presented to the model. At each presentation, if the response was correct, the next letter of the alphabet was presented; if the response was wrong, the misidentified letter was learned, and then the next letter was presented. This procedure was repeated until all letters provided by source A in the first sample had been presented. Stimulus presentation, recognition response, and learning (if an error was committed) continued in the same fashion for the letters from each source until all stimuli in the first sample had been shown. Thus, three successive runs of the lowercase alphabet printed by each of five individuals were presented to the network. At this point, the entire procedure was repeated with the second sample of letters. In all, 780 stimulus-response trials were obtained in this simulation.

Figure 11.7 shows the synaptic transfer weight (ϕ) profiles of the

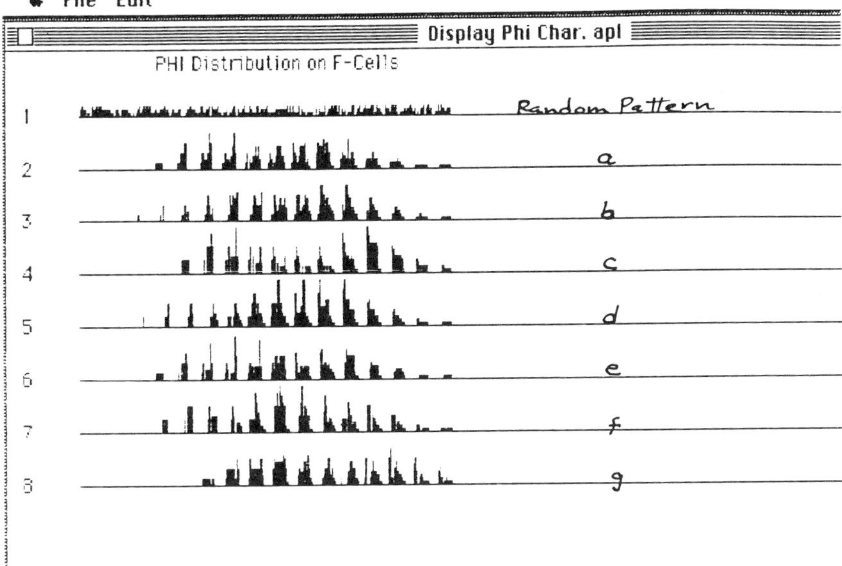

Figure 11.7
Synaptic transfer weights on the dendrites of the first eight filter cells modified during learning in test procedure 2. The synaptic profile on filter cell 1 is the result of learning a random visual pattern.

first eight filter cells that were modified during the learning procedure and the alphabetic character associated with each.

The proportion of correct responses made by the model for each complete presentation of the lowercase alphabet (the number of correct identifications divided by 26) was plotted against the number of exemplars that had already been misidentified and learned just before each new test of the alphabet began. These data are shown in figure 11.8 as percentage correct against exemplars learned. There was a generally progressive improvement in the model's performance as it was exposed to more stimuli despite the fact that for each character there were natural variations in size and orientation as well as shape, the model was not permitted to reject stimuli with centroids that could not be aligned within narrow error tolerance, and the letters to be identified were produced by five individuals with clearly different writing styles.

For the inputs in the second sample, when the model had to identify the writing of a given individual, it had already learned something about the writing of four other individuals. One might wonder

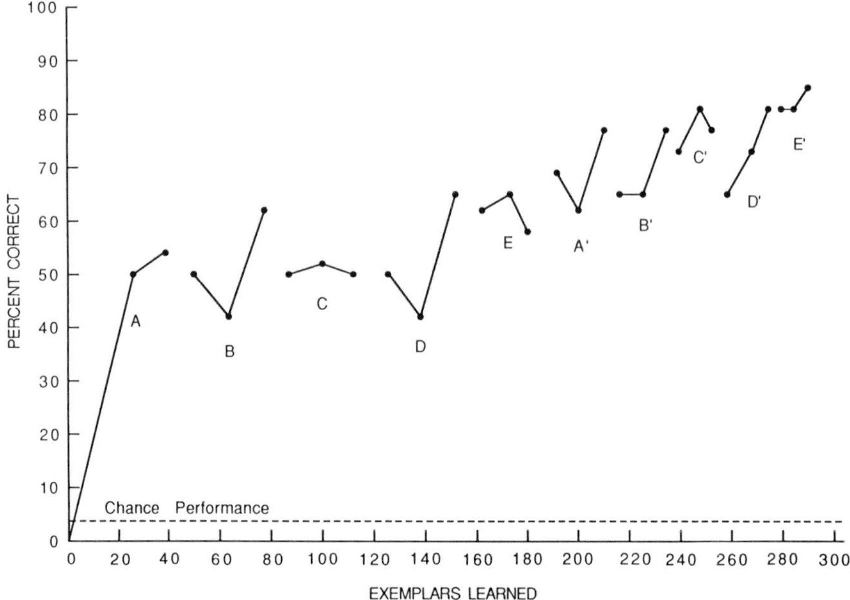

Figure 11.8
Graph showing the percentage of correct letter recognition responses over each run of the alphabet presented by each of the five writers, plotted against the number of exemplars learned at the start of each test run. Letters A–E indicate stimuli produced by the different writers. Letters without primes indicate sample 1. Primed letters indicate sample 2.

if the addition of filter cells tuned to the differing letter characteristics of other writers would interfere with the recognition of new exemplars. If, indeed, this is the case, then table 11.1 shows that any interference effects that might exist are more than offset by a positive generalization effect from the exposure to other exemplars, which results in a substantial improvement in performance. The gain in the percentage of correct identifications from the first to the second sample over the five stimulus sources ranges from 18 to 34 percent, with an overall average gain of 24 percent.

Comments

In these tests, the model does not depend on feature extraction or feature processing for learning or recognition. This differs significantly from models requiring preprocessed critical features for their input or innate "feature detectors" (Hinton 1981). The system simply

Table 11.1
Change in correct recognition responses

	Percentage Correct		
Writer	Sample 1	Sample 2	Percentage Gain
A	35	69	34
B	51	69	18
C	51	77	26
D	52	73	21
E	62	82	20

Average gain = 24%

learns its current pattern of retinal excitation after it has been shifted on the retinoid so that the pattern centroid is as close as possible to the normal foveal axis, given the physical constraints of the system. Objects that subtend large visual angles will naturally be partitioned by the visual apparatus before they are learned one part at a time, whereas small objects like alphabetic characters may be learned at once as holistic patterns.

Given the coarse resolution of the retina in the simulation, the lack of compensation for variations in size and slant, and substantial variability in the shape of each handprinted letter, the level of recognition performance exhibited by the model suggests that natural pattern recognition can proceed very well without prior feature extraction when the objects to be recognized are small.

These results also bear on the issue of representation by an average-based prototype versus representation by a subset of exemplars. The system modeled here does not compute a single prototypical distribution of synaptic transfer weights to represent a given letter of the alphabet. Instead, filter cells are separately tuned to different exemplars of each object (letter) class. The robust generalization exhibited in the simulation tests follows naturally from the intrinsic ordinal logic of the synaptic matrix. This mechanism ensures that even in the absence of a good match between an input pattern and its appropriate filter cell, if there is no better match with an inappropriate cell, the correct recognition response will occur.

The mode of internal representation used by the putative brain system (storage of exemplar instances in the form of distinct synaptic weight distributions on distinct filter cells) can explain another aspect of letter recognition: we are often able to identify the person who did the writing. This would not be possible if all instances of a particular object were represented by some normative prototype. When exemplars are stored, however, one can associate the name of the person producing a letter with the individual characteristics of the pattern that is learned. In a more general and important sense, when objects are represented discretely in the brain, any contextual events that might be significant can be associated with a particular experiential instance.

A fundamental question that can be asked of any quantitative model concerns the range of variation its parameters can tolerate before the model loses its effectiveness. The narrower the tolerable range is, the less robust is the model. In the simulations described here, two different sets of values were assumed in the learning formula. For the first simulation, the coefficient for dendrodendritic transfer was 0.50, the axon transfer factor (c) was 2.0, and the dendrite transfer factor (k) was set at 38.0. In the second simulation, the corresponding values were 0.60, 1.0, and 100. The fact that recognition performance was satisfactory with either set of parameter values is additional evidence of the robustness of the postulated learning mechanism.

Chapter 12
Self-Directed Learning in a Complex Environment

It has been conjectured that a template-filter model for cognitive processes such as pattern learning and recognition would not be able to operate effectively in a complex visual environment because nearby or partially occluding objects would cause insurmountable interference with the processing of target objects (Pinker 1984). Early tests of this conjecture suggested that the limitations attributed to mechanisms of this kind were not as severe as they were represented to be (Trehub 1986). Additional evidence has been provided in simulations of the brain model, where the operation of adaptive filter cells (comb filters) in the detection matrix is critical. These simulations indicate that the hypothesized parsing and filtering mechanisms for pattern learning and recognition can perform effectively in a complex environment. The results also demonstrate that when a novelty detection circuit modulates the excitatory bias of a synaptic matrix, the model is able, in a completely self-directed fashion, to learn, recall, image, and find the objects that compose its fortuitous visual environments.

Parsing and Learning

The simulated brain system consisted of a 16 × 16–cell retina, the neuronal modules for scene representation and visual parsing described in chapter 7, a basic synaptic matrix for pattern detection and imaging, and a novelty detector. The contribution of axon transfer factor (ATF) to synaptic modification was arbitrarily set at $c = 1.0$. The contribution of dendrite transfer factor (DTF) was set at $k = 100$. The gradient coefficient of dendrodendritic excitation of neighboring cells in the mosaic array was set at 0.6.

Outdoor (far) and indoor (near) visual "environments" were created in sketch-to-pixel conversions. These complex scenes were then presented to the simulated neuronal system for parsing, learning, and object recognition.

Simulation 1
The model was exposed to a succession of different outdoor environments, each consisting of a variety of trees, houses, buildings, cars, and animals and some including the outline of distant hills (figure 12.1). Because the actual coordinate projections from a 3-D retinoid to the mosaic cells of a synaptic matrix maintain size constancy as viewing distance changes, the distance of an object as well as its retinal image will determine the pattern of synaptic transfer weights (ϕ) on any filter cell that is modified at the time of learning. Since the simulation did not incorporate mechanisms of stereopsis or visual accommodation, the viewing distance to the major elements of each scene was assumed to be constant.

Environmental scenes were presented in a frame of 4000 pixels. Thus, there would be 4000 potential fixation points during the viewing of each scene if there were no principled constraints on fixation in an extended visual environment. Given the proposed brain model, however, the number of potential fixations on any complex scene is greatly reduced by contour flux control of saccadic action and by the centroid-finding properties of the retinoid system. A significant consequence of this is to reduce the number of object exemplars that must be learned for adequate recognition performance in new visual environments.

In the previous simulations, visual learning occurred only when a teacher (the operator) indicated that an incorrect recognition response was made by the detection matrix. In this simulation, visual learning was initiated solely by the model brain mechanism whenever it "judged" an object (or a part of an object) to be novel. If the latency of discharge for the first class cell (Ω) in the detection matrix to respond to a simulus exceeded the delay time of the novelty detector, then the synaptic matrix received a pulse of excitatory bias and the current exemplar was automatically learned. Feedback from a teacher or from an error-detecting module was not required, nor was it given.

Another aspect of the model's performance that should be noted is the manner in which it associated common names to the object tokens that it had learned. Periodically, after the exploration of each new environment, the system drew an image (on the CRT screen) of each object (or part of an object) that it had learned to represent by a biological "name" (a class cell token) but for which it had no common name. It then asked what that object is called. If a name was provided, the neuronal network automatically entered that name (character string) in its lexicon and assigned it to the class cell token of its referent.

At the start of each scene-parsing operation, the model first fixated

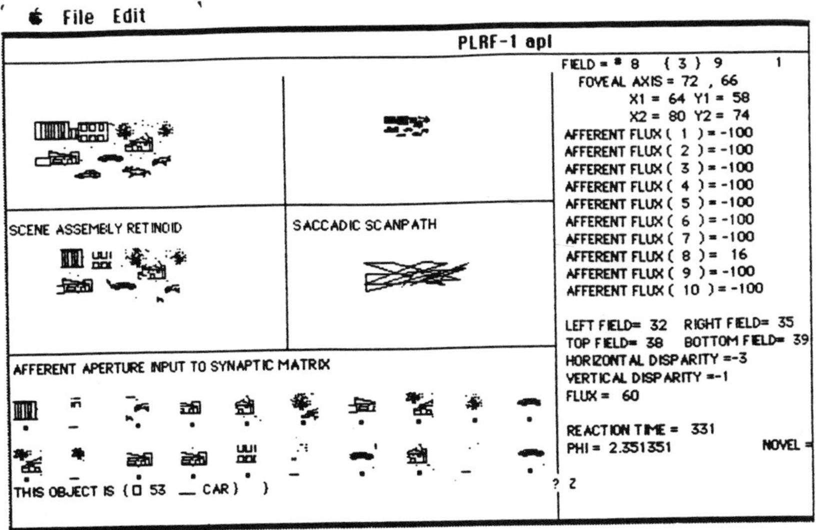

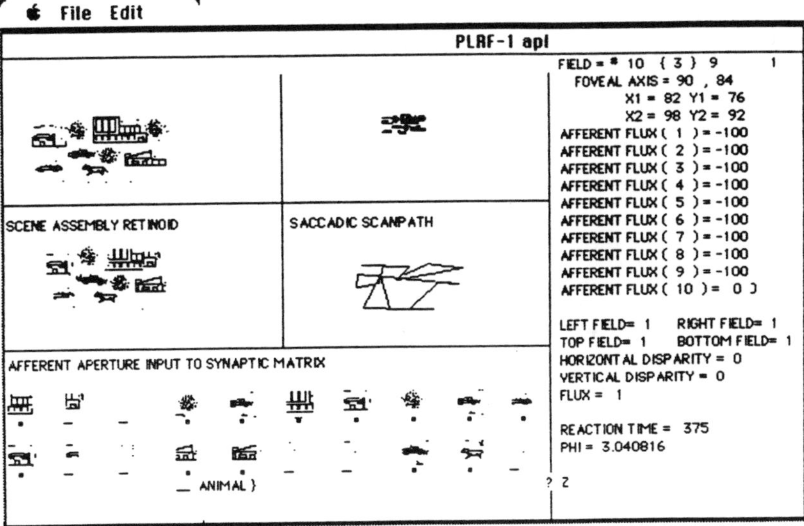

Figure 12.1
Visual exploration of two outdoor scenes (printout of CRT displays). Upper left panel in each display shows scene presented. Central panel shows scanpath of 20 saccades. Middle left panel shows reconstruction on scene assembly retinoid. Bottom panel shows images parsed after each saccade. Dots mark images that were captured and gated to synaptic matrix to be recognized and (if novel) learned. Short horizontal lines mark parsed images that were not captured.

on the retinotopic locus of the flux detector with maximum output. The afferent field aperture then closed to its fully constricted state, arbitrarily set at six retinal units in width and height. The fully expanded afferent aperture was limited to 16 × 16 retinal units. Starting error tolerance for quadrantal disparity over either horizontal or vertical axes was set at three units. At any fixed aperture, if error tolerance was exceeded on a given axis, the pattern of excitation on the retinoid was automatically shifted in the appropriate direction to reduce hemifield disparity on that axis. When pattern position satisfied error tolerance for one axis, the pattern was automatically shifted on the other axis unless it was already within tolerance. If shifting the image on the second axis now resulted in an unacceptable error on the first, error tolerance was automatically relaxed one unit. Whenever the retinoid pattern was brought within tolerance for both horizontal and vertical disparities, the afferent aperture expanded one unit, and the process repeated automatically until full aperture was achieved. This operation was assumed to involve an expenditure of processing effort; if a pattern translation of nine units on any retinoid axis did not bring disparity within tolerance, the system stopped trying at its current fixation and initiated a saccade to the next highest flux region. Whenever the afferent aperture reached the state of full expansion with an input flux of at least 25 active cells and with disparity within tolerance on both axes (thus centered on the normal foveal axis), the excitation pattern on the retinoid was gated to the synaptic matrix for recognition. Thus, each excitation pattern projected to the synaptic matrix was a discrete image parsed out of the complex visual field.

The simulated visual system was allowed to make 20 saccades during the presentation of each scene. Because of the requirement for quadrantal balance before gating from the retinoid module to the synaptic matrix, an image that falls on the line of sight at the terminus of a saccade is rarely the image projected to the mosaic cell array of the synaptic matrix. Here, it will be useful to make a distinction between visual fixation, which refers to any resting locus of gaze in the visual field, and visual capture, which refers to the bringing of an object's visual centroid to the retinoid's normal foveal axis, within tolerance for error and effort. Only images that have been captured are gated to the synaptic matrix (where they can be learned if filter cells and mosaic cells receive sufficient excitatory priming).

Threshold for stimulus novelty varied from moment to moment in a random fashion and corresponded to a recognition latency (first-order class cell [Ω] response) ranging from 330 to 360 milliseconds. If the recognition response time exceeded the current novelty threshold, the synaptic matrix was primed, and the captured exemplar was learned.

Through learning during the course of the simulation, the model visual system was building a repertoire of class cell tokens (labeled lines in the detection matrix) and latent images (class cell collaterals on mosaic cells in the imaging matrix), which represented the objects or parts of objects parsed and captured in each environment. In order to facilitate communication by providing a common name as well as a biological name for the things it had learned, the model performed as follows. After completing the exploration of each scene, it traced from its imaging matrix one image at a time on the CRT screen. The images traced were those exemplars that it had just learned but for which it had no common name. After drawing an image, it asked what that object is called (figure 12.2). When the name (character string) was provided, it was linked to the currently active class cell, the neuronal token of the object in question. As the simulation progressed, the model was able to signal recognition of an increasing number of objects by their common names as well as by their neuronal tokens.

The simulation was terminated after 160 exemplars (objects or parts of objects) were captured. At this point, 12 different outdoor scenes had been presented, and, of the 160 exemplars that had been captured, 82 had exceeded the novelty threshold and had been learned. The examples given in figure 12.1 are two printouts of the CRT screen during the simulation. The upper left panel in each printout shows the actual scene presented to the model system for visual parsing, recognition, and learning. The central panel shows the scanpath of the 20 saccades that were initiated in the course of visual exploration. The middle left panel shows the partial neuronal reconstruction of the full visual field on a scene assembly retinoid. This fragmentary visual representation was created by the reassembly of the excitation patterns (images) that the model had parsed during the course of 20 successive saccades over the current scene. In the large bottom panel are the successive images that were parsed after each saccade. Only images marked by a dot beneath them were actually captured and transmitted as input to the synaptic matrix for recognition and, if novel, for learning. Images marked by a short horizontal line beneath them were those retinal stimuli that the system was unable to capture within the constraints of centroid tolerance or parsing effort.

Of 20 saccadic fixations over each of the outdoor scenes, the number of images captured ranged from 9 (45 percent) to 17 (85 percent), with an overall capture rate of 67 percent. Because 82 of these stimuli had exceeded the threshold of novelty, a corresponding number of

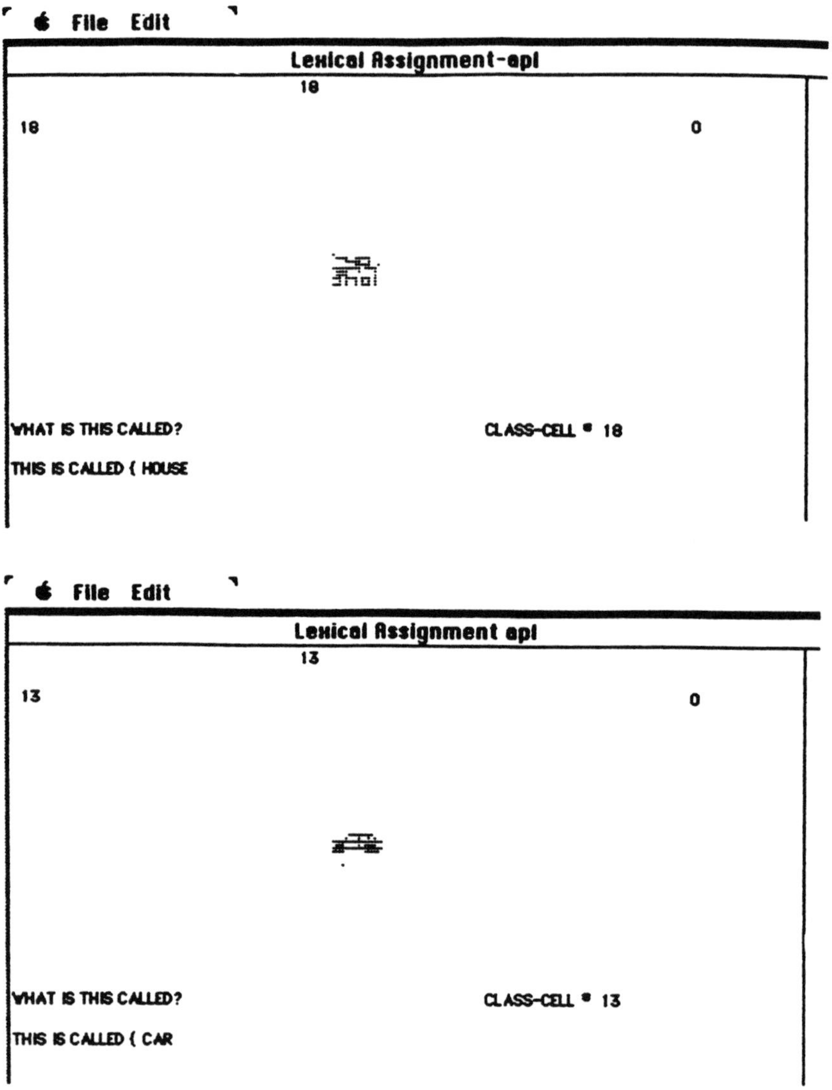

File Edit

Lexical Assignment-apl

18

18 0

WHAT IS THIS CALLED? CLASS-CELL = 18

THIS IS CALLED { HOUSE

File Edit

Lexical Assignment apl

13

13 0

WHAT IS THIS CALLED? CLASS-CELL = 13

THIS IS CALLED { CAR

Figure 12.2
Two instances of lexical assignment. Model displays the image evoked by discharge of each class cell token for which it has not yet learned a common name and asks what the image is called. Operator provides the appropriate name (bottom left).

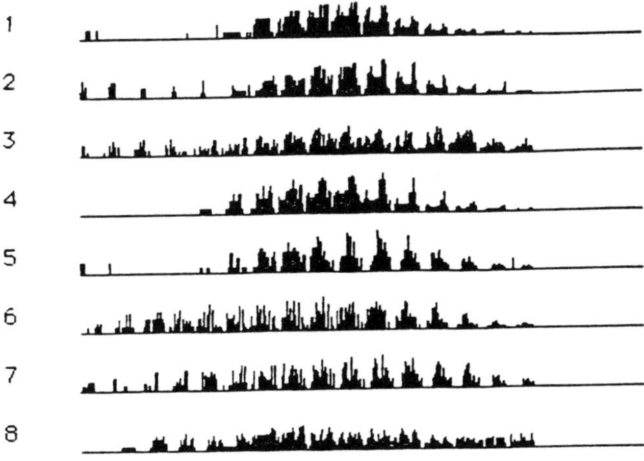

Figure 12.3
Examples of the distribution of synaptic transfer weights (ϕ) on dendrites of filter cells that have learned images captured during exploration of outdoor scenes. Each point on the dendritic line represents a particular synaptic location. Amplitude of each vertical line represents relative magnitude of ϕ for that synapse. The objects learned by these cells are as follows: (1) a car, (2) an animal, (3) a house, (4) a different exemplar of a car, (5) a different exemplar of an animal, (6) a tree, (7) a different exemplar of a tree, (8) a building.

filter cells in the detection matrix had been synaptically modified in accordance with the learning formula. Figure 12.3 shows the synaptic transfer weight (ϕ) profiles of an arbitrary sample of the 82 learning-modified filter cells. Differences among the ϕ distributions over the population of filter cells in the detection matrix determine the selectivity of object recognition. Associated ϕ distributions in the imaging matrix shape the images that are evoked on the mosaic cell array by active class cell collaterals.

The course of recognition performance was assessed by examining the percentage of correct responses in successive blocks of 20 captured images. Figure 12.4 shows the improvement in recognition as the number of objects parsed and captured increased to the simulation limit of 160. The curve of performance increases rapidly and appears to reach a plateau at a level between 80 percent and 90 percent correct recognitions.

Simulation 2

In the second test, the model visual system was exposed to a succession of cluttered desktop scenes, each having different exemplars and arrangements of books, bookmarks, telephones, ashtrays, and

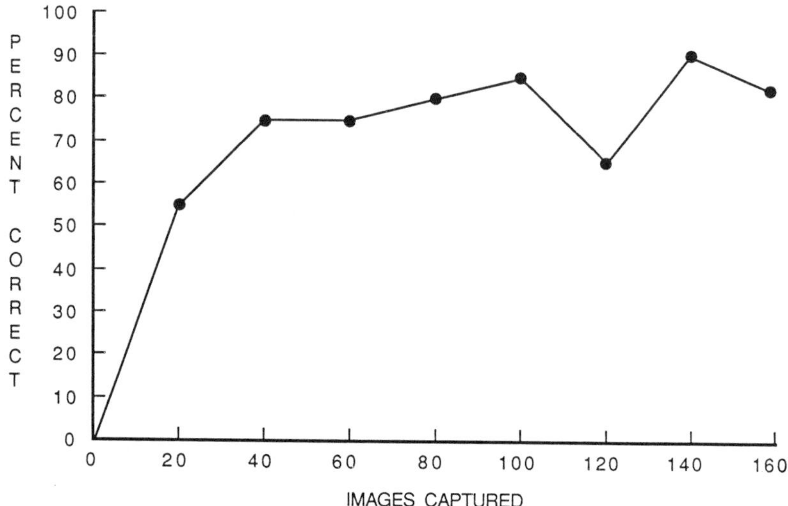

Figure 12.4
Graph showing the percentage of correct object recognition responses in successive blocks of 20, plotted against the cumulative number of images captured in the outdoor scenes.

pencils. The model was required to parse, learn, and recognize the objects that composed its visual environment. Like the previous simulation, learning was automatically initiated by the model whenever its class cell response time exceeded the delay time (threshold) of its novelty detection circuit. Common names were provided in response to the model's queries on the basis of images drawn after the exploration of each new scene. All characteristics of the neuronal mechanisms (number of retinal cells, parameters for parsing and capture, learning) were the same as in the first simulation.

After 13 different desktop scenes had been presented, the model had captured 160 images, and the simulation was terminated. Of the 160 exemplars that had been captured, 61 had exceeded the novelty threshold and had been learned. Figure 12.5 shows two printouts of the CRT screen during this simulation test.

The number of images captured during the 20 saccadic fixations on each of the desktop scenes ranged from 8 (40 percent) to 15 (75 percent). The overall capture rate was 62 percent. Because 61 of these stimuli had exceeded the threshold of novelty, a corresponding number of filter cells in the detection matrix were synaptically modified. Profiles of synaptic transfer weights (ϕ) on a sample of eight of the 61 learning-modified filter cells are shown in figure 12.6.

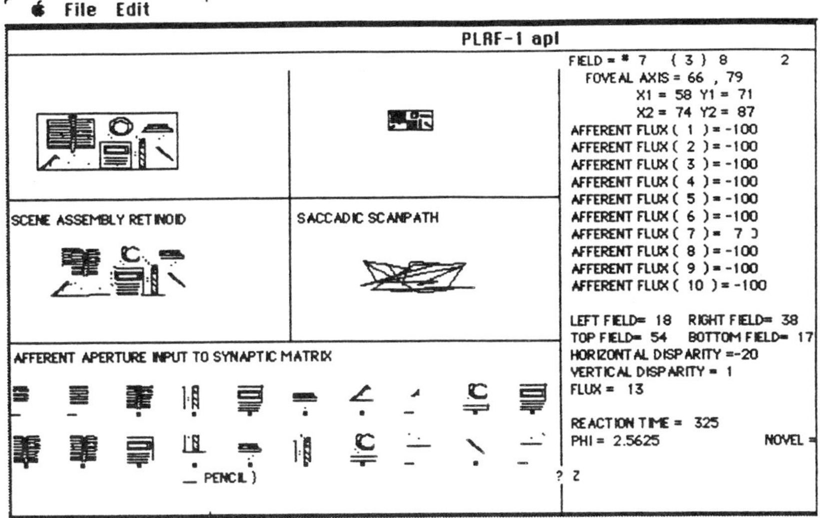

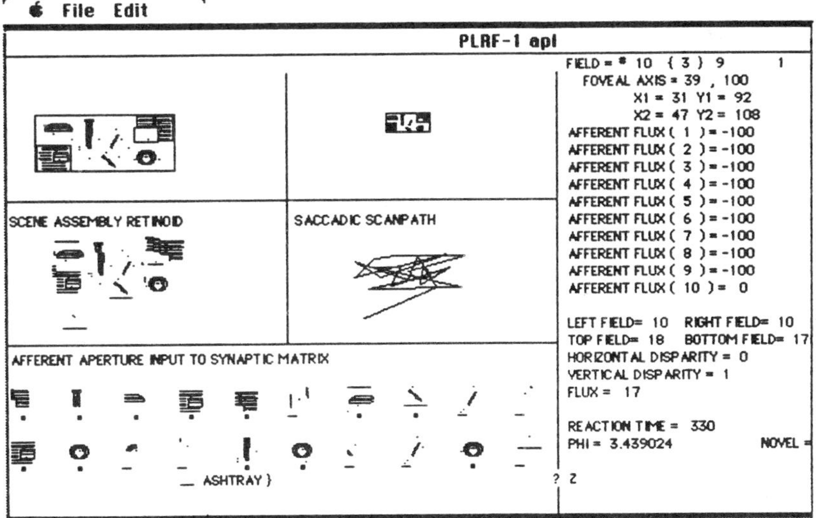

Figure 12.5
Visual exploration of desktop scenes (printout of CRT displays). Upper left panel in each display shows scene presented. Notice that books are partially occluded by a bookmark (upper display) and a sheet of paper (lower display). Central panel shows scanpath of 20 saccades. Middle left panel shows reconstruction on scene assembly retinoid. Bottom panel shows images parsed after each saccade. Dots mark images that were captured and gated to synaptic matrix to be recognized and (if novel) learned. Short horizontal lines mark parsed images that were not captured.

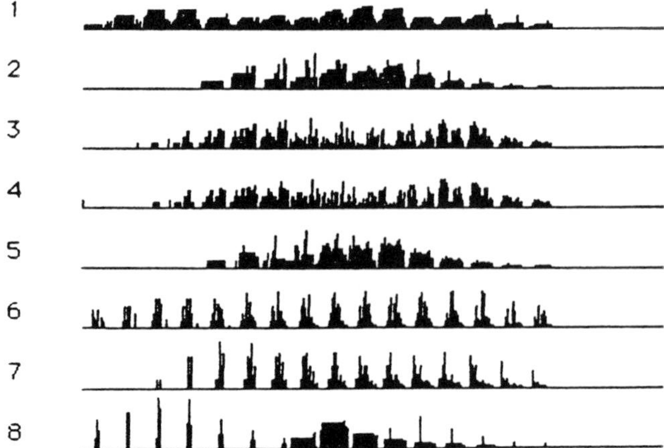

Figure 12.6
Examples of the distribution of synaptic transfer weights (ϕ) on dendrites of filter cells that have learned images captured during exploration of desktop scenes. The objects learned by these cells are as follows: (1) a book, (2) a telephone, (3) an ashtray, (4) a different exemplar of an ashtray, (5) a different exemplar of a telephone, (6) a bookmark, (7) a pencil, (8) an edge of the desk.

The course of recognition performance was assessed by examining the percentage of correct responses in successive blocks of 20 captured images. Figure 12.7 shows the improvement in recognition as the number of objects parsed and captured increased to the simulation limit of 160. The curve of performance increases rapidly and then tends to flatten, reaching a level of 95 percent correct recognitions.

Searching for Objects

The ability of the model visual system to search for and find named objects in complex scenes was also demonstrated. In the simulations of search behavior, two neuronal processes were automatically triggered. First, whenever the model system was in a search mode, all cells in the mosaic array received a sustained increment of inhibition (-1 on each cell). Second, when the name (character string) of an object to be found matched a common name linked to class cell tokens in the detection matrix, those class cells that corresponded to the named object received a sustained increment of excitation, causing their axon collaterals to induce a pattern of net positive bias on just those mosaic cells in the imaging matrix that composed their associated images. These neuronal processes have the joint effect of suppressing the response of filter cells that are not tuned to the object

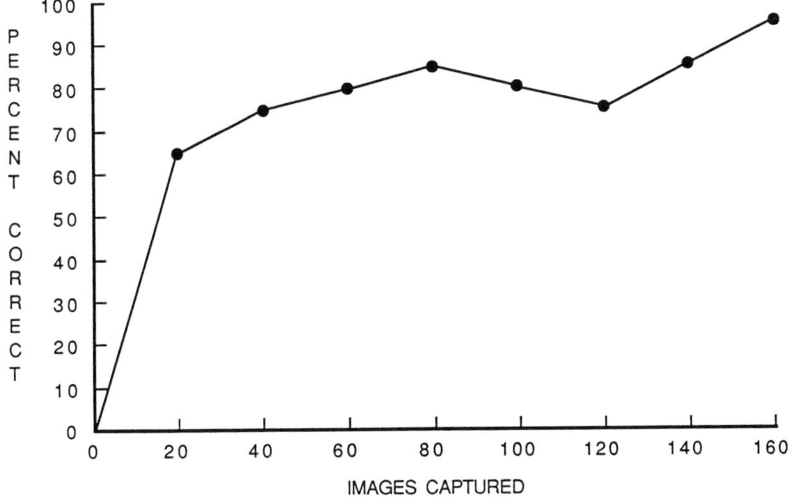

Figure 12.7
Graph showing the percentage of correct object recognition responses in successive blocks of 20, plotted against the cumulative number of images captured in the desktop scenes.

of search and facilitating an appropriate response to the searched-for object.

Saccadic activity, object parsing, and capture proceeded in the same way as in the previous simulations. However, if a captured image was not identified as the object of search, a new saccade was immediately initiated, and search continued. When a captured image was recognized as the object to be found, it was named, and its neuronal representation and relative spatial location were marked on the scene assembly retinoid. Figure 12.8 shows two CRT screen printouts when the model was "asked" to find a car and a tree in outdoor scenes. Figure 12.9 shows the model's responses on the CRT when it was asked to find an ashtray and a telephone in desktop scenes.

Comments

The simulated brain mechanisms parsed objects out of complex environments and learned to recognize them at a level of accuracy between 80 and 95 percent without the assistance of a teacher or feedback from an error-detecting source; reconstructed rough representations of environmental scenes by assembling, at their relative

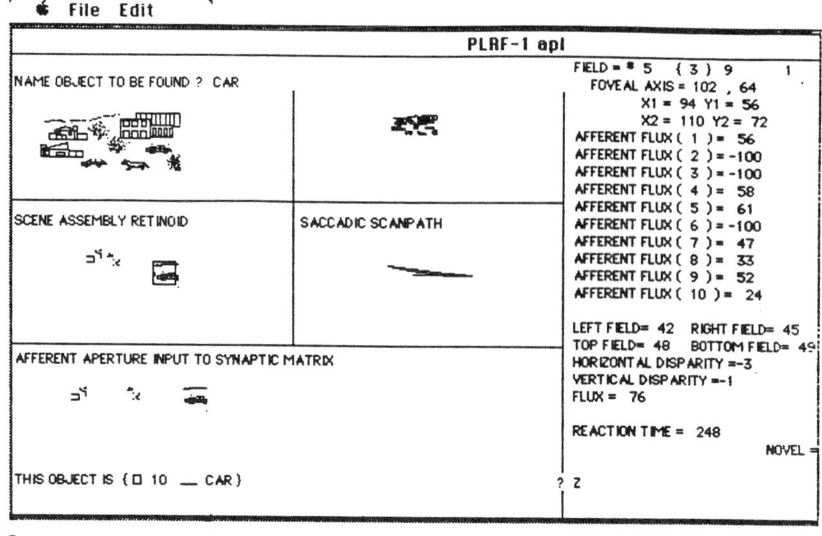

File Edit
PLRF-1 apl
NAME OBJECT TO BE FOUND ? TREE
FIELD = * 10 { 3 } 9 1
FOVEAL AXIS = 72 , 65
X1 = 64 Y1 = 57
X2 = 80 Y2 = 73
5
AFFERENT FLUX (1) = 50
AFFERENT FLUX (2) = 52
AFFERENT FLUX (3) = -100
AFFERENT FLUX (4) = -100
AFFERENT FLUX (5) = 33
AFFERENT FLUX (6) = -100
AFFERENT FLUX (7) = 9
AFFERENT FLUX (8) = -100
AFFERENT FLUX (9) = 50
AFFERENT FLUX (10) = 57
SCENE ASSEMBLY RETINOID
SACCADIC SCANPATH
LEFT FIELD= 41 RIGHT FIELD= 35
TOP FIELD= 39 BOTTOM FIELD= 37
HORIZONTAL DISPARITY = 6
VERTICAL DISPARITY = 2
FLUX = 63
AFFERENT APERTURE INPUT TO SYNAPTIC MATRIX
REACTION TIME = 278
NOVEL =
THIS OBJECT IS { □ 19 __ TREE }
? Z

Figure 12.8
Active search. Small rectangular frame around parsed object on the scene assembly retinoid indicates that a searched-for object has been found and its spatial location registered. In these examples, the model was asked to find a car (top display) and a tree (bottom display).

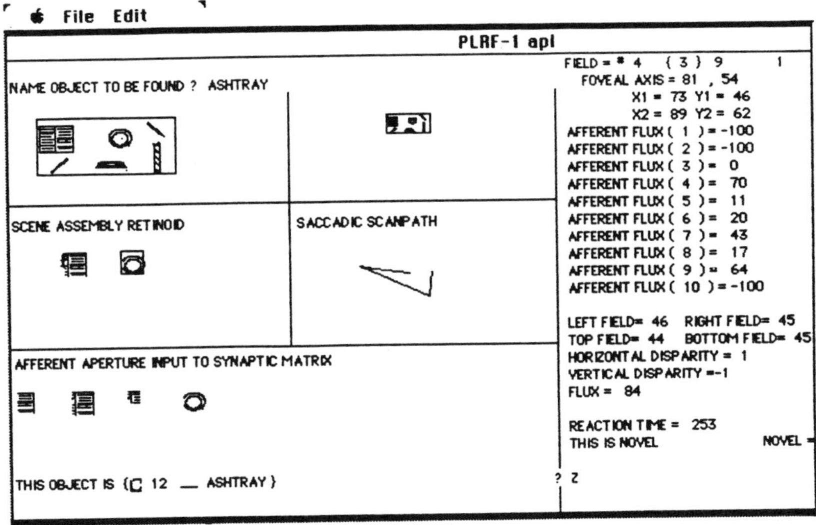

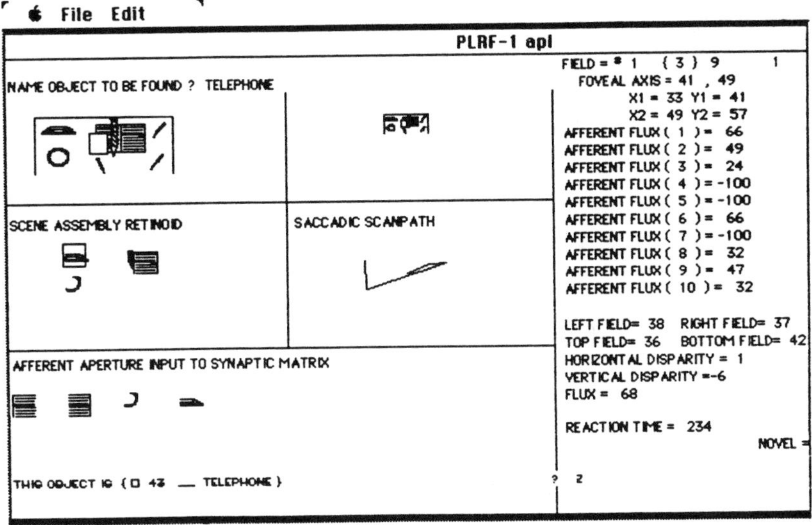

Figure 12.9
Active search. The model finds an ashtray (top display) and a telephone (bottom display).

spatial coordinates on a retinoid, the successive images of objects that it had parsed; and searched for, found, and represented in retinoid space the location of objects in its visual environment when they were designated by name. Given these results, it seems fair to conclude that brain mechanisms of the template-filter kind can effectively serve pattern learning and recognition in complex visual environments.

The processes by which the model assembles a spatially integrated neuronal representation of a frontal scene from a sequence of disparate fixations on the environment might provide an explanation for the clinical findings of hemispatial neglect in some brain-injured patients (Bisiach, Luzzati, and Perani 1979; Bisiach and Berti 1989). Suppose there were selective damage to a hemifield of autaptic cells in the retinoids or neuronal failure for one direction of the shift control mechanism. In the former case, the individual would be unable to experience beyond the retinal level any representation of environmental space homologous with the damaged area of the retinoids. In the latter case, an individual would be unable to translate to the normal foveal axis any image evoked on one of the retinoid hemifields. For example, if the shift-right circuit were damaged, an autaptic image in the left hemifield could not be shifted rightward to the normal foveal axis. Inability to bring an image to the normal foveal axis means that the image cannot be recognized in the detection matrix.

The demonstrated ability of the putative brain system to construct a neuronal analog of the spatial layout of objects in a visual environment supports the theory that candidate plans of action can be instantiated and tested covertly by heuristic excursions of the self-locus in retinoid space. Significant spatial locations, paths to goal objects, relative distances between objects, barriers to direct access, and so forth can be computed and represented analogically by patterns of autaptic cell activity on the retinoid substrate. Such representations can then be learned in synaptic matrices and stored as part of an enduring knowledge base.

In these simulations, the tasks of parsing, learning, and recognition were performed in artificial 2-D visual environments. One might question how well the model would perform in complex 3-D environments. It would clearly be desirable to run simulations in natural settings using photosensitive binocular sensors for retinal input. Such tests would require a computer powerful enough to model effectively the hypothesized 3-D brain mechanisms as integral parts of the simulated visual-cognitive system.

Chapter 13
Narrative Comprehension and Other Aspects of the Semantic Network

Chapter 6 described the neuronal structure of a self-organizing semantic network based on the operating principles of the synaptic matrix. A simulation of the network showed that exposure to a set of simple sentences resulted in the automatic learning of lexical tokens (M_i, Ω_i), and when the lexical tokens were evoked by sentential stimuli (queries), they were automatically related to each other in a logical fashion through selective synaptic couplings induced by the intrinsic operations of the network. Thus, after learning a body of information conveyed by sentences that characterized the properties of named objects, the model was able to respond correctly to questions about the material learned. The simulations presented in this chapter test the performance of the putative semantic network with somewhat more complex semantic tasks.

When the semantic network is stimulated by proper sentences (character strings), it builds a lexicon and selectively organizes an internal pattern of synaptic enhancement. The distribution of synaptic weights established during learning then determines the input-output routing for neuronal activity later induced by word stimuli that correspond to items in its lexicon. In its basic form, the semantic network simply establishes privileged neuronal links between the subject (initial character string) and predicate (following character string) of each sentence presented to it. If there is a true logical structure in what the network is "told," it can capture that structure and make valid inferences that are reflected in its response to queries.

Unlike the visual model, which can parse objects out of a complex visual field, a neuronal mechanism for parsing lexical strings has not yet been formulated for the semantic network model. In all simulations of the semantic network, parsing is accomplished by a subprogram that detects alphabetic characters, spaces, and sentence terminators. After lexical strings are parsed, however, subsequent processing is carried out by the intrinsic neuronal properties of the simulated network.

Comprehending a Narrative

There are many formidable problems to be solved in the effort to develop even an abstract computational model of natural language processing (Clifton and Ferreira 1987, Miller and Johnson-Laird 1976, Stillings et al. 1987, chap. 11). The difficulty is compounded if we constrain our theorizing within the bounds of biological plausibility. The neuronal (semantic) network detailed in chapter 6 is by no means a broadly competent processor of natural language, but it does display some essential capabilities that make it a strong candidate for one of the modules in the brain's language processing system.

One of the central problems in comprehending a narrative relates to the assignment of pronoun reference. In normal discourse, pronouns are commonly used to achieve economy of expression and to convey a sense of continuity. For example, "Laura went to the library. *She* was looking for a particular book. *She* recalled that *it* had an unusual fifteenth-century map of the world. *This* was *her* special interest." If we are to understand these sentences as more than a sequence of independent assertions, we must be able to assign the pronouns to their appropriate references. We must know that *she* refers to *Laura* and not to *the library; it* refers to *a particular book; this* refers to *fifteenth-century map of the world* and probably to old maps in general; and *her* refers to *Laura.* This means that before the passage can be understood as a narrative, one must have prior knowledge of at least the rough equivalence classes for the pronouns used. However, in the general case, determining the reference of a pronoun can be a difficult problem because, except for number and gender, there are no exact criteria for pronoun substitution (Miller and Johnson-Laird 1976). Context and prior knowledge determine what a given pronoun can stand for in a narrative passage. Suppose we teach the semantic network some general facts about the meaning of words (including pronouns) that it will later encounter. Can we then present it with a simple narrative, ask it questions, and get responses that correspond to what one would expect if the passage were understood? The following simulation test demonstrates that, after it is given relevant general information, the semantic network can be "shown" a narrative passage and respond appropriately when it is later questioned about the passage.

The same neuronal mechanism that was described in chapter 6 was simulated, and the following list of sentences was typed in to be learned for background knowledge:

A MAN IS A HE .

A WOMAN IS A SHE .

BOB IS A MAN .

JENNY IS A WOMAN .

JENNY-AND-BOB IS A THEY .

A NON-HUMAN IS AN IT .

A CAR IS NON-HUMAN .

These sentences provided the network with information about the gender attachment of two proper names (Bob, Jenny) and two pronouns (he, she), the impersonal attachment of one pronoun (it), the plural attachment of another pronoun (they), and the impersonal nature of a common noun (car). Following the presentation of this essential general information, the following brief narrative was typed in:

> BOB DID NOT HAVE TO WORK THAT EVENING . HE PHONED JENNY . HE SUGGESTED A MOVIE . SHE SUGGESTED DINNER AND A MOVIE . SHE OFFERED TO DRIVE . HE INSISTED ON DRIVING . SHE SUGGESTED THAT THEY EAT AT BUB'S RESTAURANT . SHE HAD WINE WITH HER MEAL . HE HAD BEER . THE GLOBE WAS THE THEATRE THEY WENT TO . CABARET WAS THE MOVIE THEY SAW . THE CAR WAS OLD . IT BROKE DOWN ON THE WAY BACK . SHE WENT HOME BY TAXI . HE TOOK A BUS . THEY LAUGHED ABOUT IT LATER .

After the passage was presented to the semantic network, it defined all subjects of the input sentences by discharging each of the word cells (W_i) that constituted autaptic tokens of its learned lexical items. This resulted automatically in additional selective synaptic modification that constrained the network to make proper chains of inference on the basis of the sentences it had learned. Then the model was asked questions about the narrative:

Question: WHO DID NOT HAVE TO WORK?
Response: BOB DID NOT HAVE TO WORK

Question: WHO PHONED JENNY?
Response: BOB PHONED JENNY

Question: WHO SUGGESTED DINNER AND A MOVIE?
Response: JENNY SUGGESTED DINNER AND A MOVIE

Question: WHO JUST SUGGESTED A MOVIE?
Response: BOB SUGGESTED A MOVIE

Question: WHO OFFERED TO DRIVE?
Response: JENNY OFFERED TO DRIVE

Question: WHO INSISTED ON DRIVING?
Response: BOB INSISTED ON DRIVING

Question: WHAT WAS OLD?
Response: (THE) CAR WAS OLD

Question: WHO SUGGESTED THAT THEY EAT AT BUB'S?
Response: JENNY SUGGESTED THAT THEY EAT AT BUB'S

Question: WHO HAD BEER?
Response: BOB HAD BEER

Question: WHO HAD WINE?
Response: JENNY HAD WINE

Question: WHAT WAS THE THEATRE THEY WENT TO?
Response: (THE) GLOBE WAS THE THEATRE THEY WENT TO

Question: WHAT WAS THE MOVIE?
Response: CABARET WAS THE MOVIE

Question: WHAT BROKE DOWN?
Response: (THE) CAR BROKE DOWN

Question: WHO WENT HOME BY TAXI?
Response: JENNY WENT HOME BY TAXI

Question: WHO TOOK A BUS?
Response: BOB

Question: WHO LAUGHED ABOUT IT?
Response: JENNY-AND-BOB LAUGHED ABOUT IT

After learning the relevant lexical concepts, the semantic matrix was able to comprehend a simple narrative, judged by the appropriateness of its answers. Notice, though, that the passage permitted no ambiguity about the referents of *he* or *she*. These pronouns could only refer to Bob or Jenny. Similarly, *they* could refer only to *Bob-and-Jenny*. The pronoun *it* was less constrained but posed no problem in the context of the questions asked. What would happen if different nouns shared common characteristics for pronoun substitution? The following passage was presented to the semantic network, and its responses to two queries revealed its inadequacy in understanding narratives in which pronominal reference is ambiguous:

JIM MET FRED AT THE BALL PARK . THE YANKEES WERE PLAYING THE RED-SOX . THE GAME WENT INTO EXTRA INNINGS . JIM WAS AN AVID FAN . HE STAYED UNTIL THE END OF THE GAME . FRED WOULD RATHER WATCH FOOTBALL . THE PATRIOTS-AND-MIAMI WERE ON TV THAT NIGHT . HE LEFT AFTER THE NINTH INNING . THE GAME ENDED IN THE TWELFTH INNING .

Question: WHO STAYED UNTIL THE END OF THE GAME?
Response: JIM STAYED UNTIL THE END OF THE GAME
FRED STAYED UNTIL THE END OF THE GAME

Question: WHO LEFT AFTER THE NINTH INNING?
Response: JIM LEFT AFTER THE NINTH INNING
FRED LEFT AFTER THE NINTH INNING

A person reading such a passage resolves the ambiguity in pronominal reference by employing the heuristic of searching for and finding the most recent appropriate antecedent of each pronoun encountered. This means that the narrative must be learned and stored (at least in short-term memory) as an episodic sequence to allow a backward search for proper antecedents. A competent brain model must have the same capability.

Such a capability is provided by linking the semantic network to a synaptic matrix for episodic learning and recall by means of an adaptive interfacing matrix. In this case, words that evoke lexical tokens in the semantic network will, at the same time, establish corresponding class cell tokens within the matrix for episodic learning, and the temporal sequence of these episodic tokens will necessarily follow the order of lexical stimulation. In addition, since the discharge of each token in the semantic network will be paired with the concurrent discharge of its corresponding token in the episodic matrix, these tokens will be synaptically coupled through the interfacing adaptive matrix. When the semantic network is later queried about a narrative, its intrinsic logic evokes each of the lexical tokens that could be proper antecedents for pronoun substitution (see the responses *JIM* and *FRED*). The system then initiates a backward search (activation of successively "earlier" autaptic cells in the recall ring) over the episodic matrix starting at the location of the queried (activated) predicate. When it discharges the first token that matches one of the proper antecedents evoked in the semantic network, that nominal token in

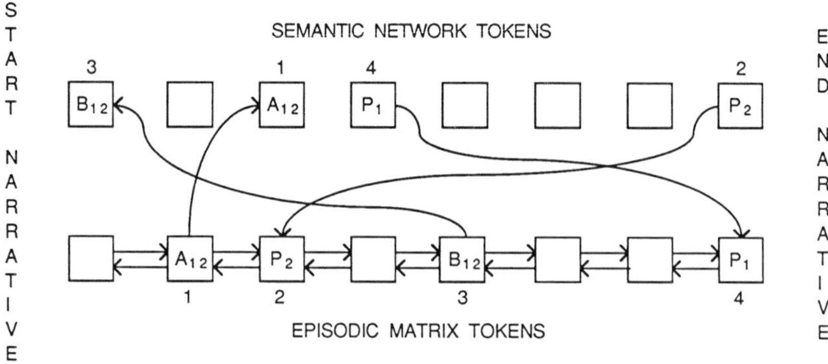

Figure 13.1
Semantic network augmented by episodic matrix. Modules are synaptically linked through an interfacing adaptive matrix by the normal coactivation of corresponding lexical tokens (represented by squares) during the learning of a narrative passage. Lexical tokens in semantic network are logically related but not temporally organized. Lexical tokens in episodic matrix are temporally organized but not logically related. P_1 and P_2 are pronominal predicates. A_{12} and B_{12} are different subjects, but each is a logically proper referent of both P_1 and P_2, and both subject tokens are evoked in the semantic network when either predicate is queried. Numbers above and below the tokens indicate the relative temporal order in which each occurs in a narrative passage. If predicate P_1 is queried, a backward search over the episodic matrix encounters B_{12} first. Discharge of B_{12} in episodic matrix elevates output of B_{12} (the appropriate antecedent) in the semantic network. If predicate P_2 is queried, a backward search encounters A_{12} first. Discharge of A_{12} in episodic matrix elevates output of A_{12} in the semantic network.

the network (the most recent with respect to the predicate that is activated) will receive an increment of stimulation that raises its activation level above its competing token(s), and the final (overt) response will be the correct one. The dynamic coupling between the semantic network and the episodic matrix is schematized in figure 13.1. The constraints on lexical response imposed by this hypothesized neuronal subsystem correspond to the natural heuristic for pronominal reference.

The augmented system was simulated and its comprehension of the narrative passage about Jim and Fred at the ballgame was tested again:

Question: WHO MET FRED AT THE BALL PARK?
Response: JIM MET FRED AT THE BALL PARK

Question: WHO WERE PLAYING THE RED-SOX?
Response: (THE) YANKEES WERE PLAYING THE RED-SOX

Question: WHO STAYED UNTIL THE END OF THE GAME?
Response: JIM STAYED UNTIL THE END OF THE GAME

Question: WHO LEFT AFTER THE NINTH INNING?
Response: FRED LEFT AFTER THE NINTH INNING

Question: WHO WERE ON TV THAT NIGHT?
Response: (THE) PATRIOTS-AND-MIAMI WERE ON TV THAT NIGHT

The responses to the questions "Who stayed until the end of the game?" and "Who left after the ninth inning?" show that the previous failure to disambiguate pronominal reference was corrected when the temporal processing capability of the episodic matrix was utilized with the logic of the semantic network. The competence of the augmented model resulted from its ability to instantiate the heuristic of selecting the most recent one of different logically appropriate pronominal antecedents.

Negation

In all of the sentences considered so far, each predicate or predicate phrase asserted the existence of an attribute, an action, or an event—*is a man, took a bus, were on TV*. The meaning of a sentence can be fundamentally changed by negating a stated predicate—for example, "Fred was not an avid fan." "What has feathers but does not fly?" "He had no tickets to the concert." The words *not* and *no* are general-purpose lexical signs that assert that the next word or phrase is false with respect to its referent. The negational modifier is an important aspect of human communication and reasoning and must be instantiated in the neuronal mechanisms of the brain's semantic network.

Figure 13.2 presents an elaboration of the basic semantic network that provides it with an intrinsic competence for the logical processing of negation. During learning or when a subject (W_i) is to be defined, the autaptic cell *S* (top left of figure) is automatically activated. This inhibits discharge of the autaptic cell *N* if the negators "NOT" or "NO" are encountered in a sentence, and these words will have no privileged effect on lexical processing. However, if a predicate token is initially activated in order to infer a subject, the *S* cell will be bypassed, and, thus, it cannot inhibit the *N* cell. In this case, recognition of the lexical string "NOT" (or "NO") fires the autaptic cell *N*, which gives an excitatory bias to all of its target autaptic cells (*n*), each discretely paired with a cell in the mosaic array (*M*). A short collateral excitatory output from each *M* cell synapses with its paired *n* cell. Each *n* cell makes an inhibitory synapse on its paired *M* cell.

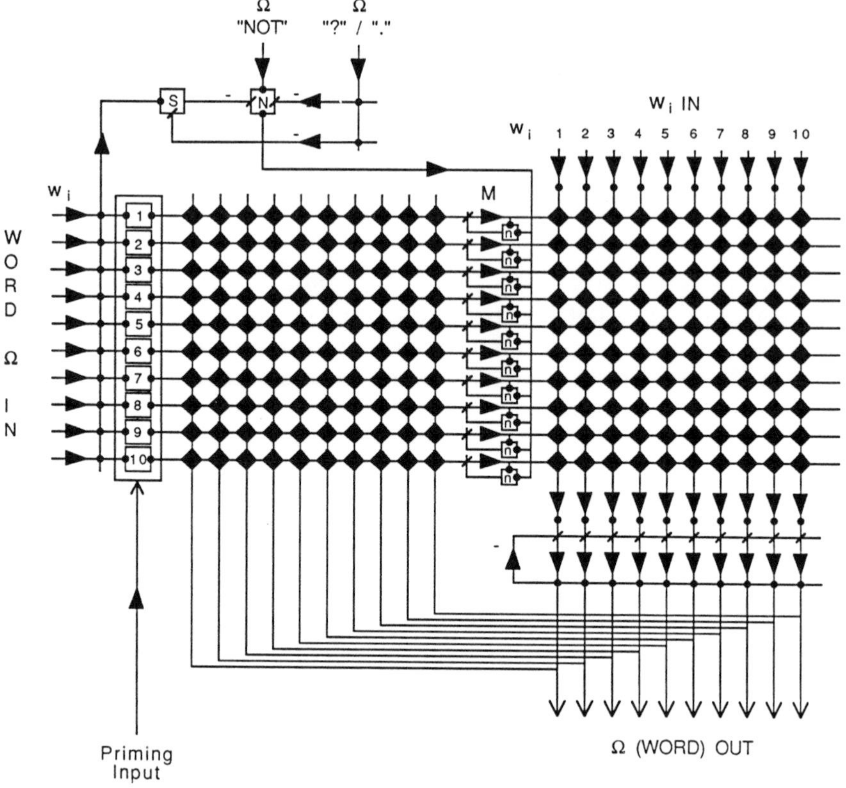

Figure 13.2
Semantic network for the logical processing of predicate negation.

When the network is queried by activating one or more predicate tokens (Ω_i) and before "NOT" is encountered, the predicate collaterals in the imaging matrix will discharge those mosaic cells corresponding to their associated subject tokens (via previously learned synaptic links). The activation of each subject will proceed in normal fashion. As soon as "NOT" is detected, however, all *n* cells are automatically primed. Because of the priming, the discharge of the next mosaic cell (subject) by its proper predicate token will then fire its linked inhibiting *n* cell, and that subject token will immediately be squelched. Notice that negation does not inhibit the negated predicate but does inhibit any subject evoked by that predicate. Thus, if the network has learned no more than "An apple is a fruit" and is then asked "What is a fruit?" it will respond "(An) apple"; but if it is asked "What is not a fruit?" it will give no response because the proper subject, "apple," will have been squelched. Notice at the top of figure 13.2 that detection of a sentence terminator inhibits both the *N* cell and the *S* cell. This resets the negation circuit to its initial condition by removing excitatory bias from all *n* cells and allows subject tokens to discharge normally until the next "NOT" is encountered in the context of a predicate query.

The semantic network, including the neuronal circuitry for processing negation (figure 13.2), was simulated. The following list of sentences was presented to the model:

JUMBO IS AN ELEPHANT .

AN ELEPHANT IS BIG .

AN ELEPHANT IS A MAMMAL .

A MAMMAL IS AN ANIMAL .

AN ANIMAL IS A LIVING-THING .

A MOUSE IS A MAMMAL .

A MOUSE IS SMALL .

AN ELEPHANT IS GRAY .

A MOUSE IS GRAY .

A CUCUMBER IS A VEGETABLE .

A CUCUMBER IS GREEN .

A VEGETABLE IS A PLANT .

A PLANT IS A LIVING-THING .

A POPPY IS A FLOWER .

A FLOWER IS A PLANT .

A POPPY IS RED .

A DANDELION IS A PLANT .

A DANDELION IS YELLOW .

A ROCK IS A MINERAL .

A MINERAL IS A NON-LIVING-THING .

A RUBY IS A GEM .

A GEM IS A MINERAL .

A RUBY IS RED .

A GEM IS VALUABLE .

After these sentences were typed in and the definitions of all subjects had been tested, the network was queried as follows:

Question: WHAT IS RED?
Response: (A) POPPY
(A) RUBY
(A) GEM

Question: WHAT IS RED AND IS A NON-LIVING-THING?
Response: (A) RUBY
(A) GEM

Question: WHAT IS RED AND IS NOT A NON-LIVING-THING?
Response: (A) POPPY

Question: WHAT LIVING-THING IS RED?
Response: (A) POPPY

Question: WHAT LIVING-THING IS NOT RED?
Response: JUMBO
(AN) ELEPHANT
(A) MAMMAL
(AN) ANIMAL
(A) MOUSE
(A) CUCUMBER
(A) VEGETABLE
(A) PLANT
(A) FLOWER
(A) DANDELION

Question: WHAT IS GRAY?
Response: JUMBO
(AN) ELEPHANT
(A) MOUSE

Question: WHAT IS GRAY AND SMALL?
Response: (A) MOUSE

Question: WHAT IS GRAY AND NOT BIG?
Response: (A) MOUSE

Question: WHAT IS GRAY AND NOT SMALL?
Response: JUMBO
(AN) ELEPHANT

Responses were correct not only when the network was required to infer a subject on the basis of negated predicates after exposure to a list of definitions. Negation was also appropriately processed by the network when it was tested for narrative comprehension. For example, the following passage was presented to the model:

> LARRY LOOKED FORWARD TO THE CONCERT . ANN LOOKED FORWARD TO THE CONCERT AS WELL . LARRY ARRANGED TO MEET ANN AT THE AUDITORIUM . THEY HAD BOUGHT THEIR TICKETS IN ADVANCE . ANN ARRIVED ON TIME . LARRY ARRIVED A BIT LATER . ANN HAD A TICKET WHEN THEY MET . LARRY WAS EMBARRASSED . HE HAD FORGOTTEN HIS .

Question WHO LOOKED FORWARD TO THE CONCERT?
Response: LARRY LOOKED FORWARD TO THE CONCERT
ANN LOOKED FORWARD TO THE CONCERT

Question: WHO BOUGHT THEIR TICKETS IN ADVANCE?
Response: LARRY-AND-ANN BOUGHT THEIR TICKETS IN ADVANCE

Question: WHO ARRIVED WITH A TICKET?
Response: ANN

Question: WHO ARRIVED WITH NO TICKET?
Response: LARRY

In answering the last question, the semantic network did not have enough background knowledge to base its response on the meaning of "embarrassed" or "forgotten." Thus, it could not infer from the fact that "Larry was embarrassed" or that "he had forgotten" that it was Larry who did not have a ticket when he arrived for the concert. When the network responded correctly to the question "Who arrived with no ticket?" it reached its decision simply because it had information that Ann arrived and had a ticket, but it had no information that Larry had a ticket when he arrived. Therefore, the intrinsic logic of the semantic network did not suppress the response "Larry" as a possible subject for one who had arrived and had no ticket, whereas the response "Ann" was inhibited because it contradicted the predicate condition of having no ticket.

If the sentences "Larry was embarrassed" and "He had forgotten his" were not included in the narrative passage, the semantic network would still have said "Larry" in response to the question "Who arrived with no ticket?" But in this case, the question posed would have been inappropriate or deceptive.

Chapter 14

Illusions and Ambiguous Shapes: Epiphenomena of Brain Mechanisms

In the early days of radio, it was often possible to guess the method of signal amplification and the kind of power supply used in a receiver by characteristic whistles, howls, hums, and low-frequency throbbing sounds called motorboating. These audio effects would occur under certain conditions as intrusive epiphenomena associated with particular kinds of circuits and were telltale clues to their design. In the same way, illusions and other anomalous perceptions may provide clues to some fundamental mechanisms in the human brain and lend selective support to particular candidates among competing theories of brain design. For example, it was shown in chapter 5 that the postulated neuronal wiring scheme connecting the 3-D retinoid to the mosaic cell array is able to account for size constancy in human visual perception, a normal process with obvious ecological utility. But it was also demonstrated on the basis of the same brain circuitry that accurate predictions would be made about a variety of visual illusions involving the perceived size and shape of retinal after images as a function of the distance and slant of fixated surfaces—phenomena with no apparent utility. In this chapter, we consider other examples of anomalous visual phenomena and show how they can be explained by the natural operations of the hypothesized brain mechanisms.

Seeing More Than Is There

If a vertically oriented slit in an otherwise occluding screen is fixated while a visual pattern is moved back and forth behind it, much more of the pattern can be seen at a given instant than is physically present within the aperture of the slit. For example, with a screen aperture of 0.1 degree of visual angle in width, it is possible to see a complete figure having a true width of 2.0 degrees (20 times as wide the aperture) if it is in horizontal oscillatory motion behind the masking screen. This phenomenon of anorthoscopic perception was reported as long ago as 1862 by Zöllner and by Helmholtz in 1867. More recently, it has been called the seeing-more-than-is-there effect (McCloskey and Watkins 1978). Efforts to understand this interesting phenomenon continue, and it remains the subject of active investigation (Casco and Morgan 1984; Parks 1965, 1970; Rock et al. 1987; Shimojo and Richards 1986).

The retinoid system can solve a number of fundamental problems in the realm of cognitive ecology. Moreover, it can be shown that the same putative brain mechanism is able to account in a straightforward fashion for the seeing-more-than-is-there (SMTT) effect—as an epiphenomenon of retinoid dynamics, with no apparent ecological utility.

Explaining SMTT

The ability of the retinoid system to capture a fleeting image in short-term memory and translate its neuronal representation in an egocentric spatial frame is central to the physical explanation of SMTT. On this account, the SMTT phenomenon occurs in the standard experimental paradigm when the successive pattern segments, directly observed through a narrow aperture, evoke autaptic excitation that is swept across a retinoid surface driven by signals from the visual system's motion detection cells. This explanation depends on the detection of the velocity and direction of the stimulus pattern on the basis of information available in the screen aperture and the short-term memory properties of the retinoid that enable it to assemble a unified representation of the stimulus from the sequence of partial inputs that are registered in its aperture region and then shifted stepwise across adjacent autaptic cells.

The significant factors in the SMTT paradigm are shown in schematic form in figure 14.1. The stimulus pattern (depicted in the figure as a triangle) is moving to the right, with its leading edge just entering the aperture in an otherwise occluding screen. The symbols in figure 14.1 are to be interpreted as follows:

S = complete stimulus pattern behind occluding screen.

s = input from stimulus contour appearing in aperture.

$\dot{\mu}$ = autaptic cell in aperture field of retinoid excited by stimulus segments.

μ = autaptic cell in retinoid beyond aperture field.

ι = excitatory interneuron in retinoid.

ρ = retinoid shift control cell (shift right).

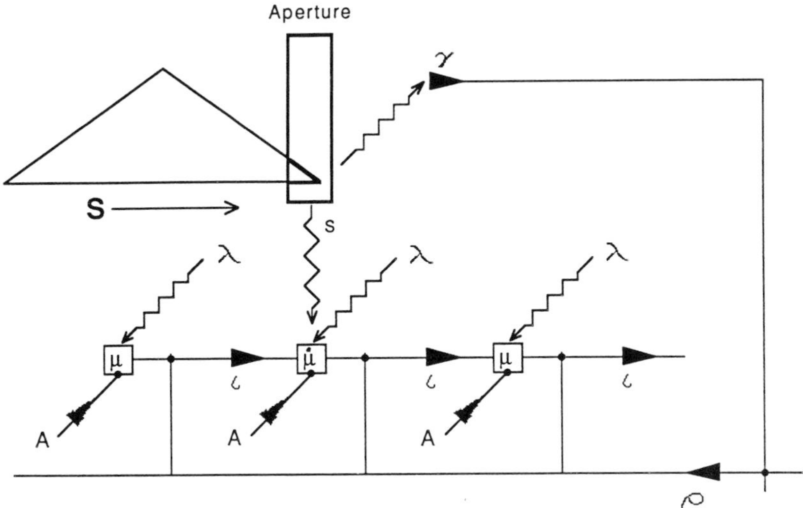

Figure 14.1
Schematic showing significant elements and parameters in the SMTT paradigm. After Trehub and Pollatsek 1986.

γ = motion detector (senses velocity of motion to right).

A = diffuse excitatory bias from arousal.

λ = diffuse excitatory bias from ambient illumination.

To consider how the factors relate to the performance of a retinoid network, notice that the subset of autaptic cells ($\dot{\mu}$) "looking at" the stimulus segments receive their input from stimulus excitation (S), arousal excitation (A), ambient illumination (λ) and excitation from active interneurons (ι). Since neurons integrate all EPSP over time, the slope of integration and thus the frequency ($F_{\dot{\mu}}$) of cell discharge in $\dot{\mu}$ will be a positive monotonic function of the dwell time of S on $\dot{\mu}$, the magnitudes of A and λ, and the discharge frequency of ι. For the subset of autaptic cells (μ) outside the direct stimulus (aperture) field, their discharge frequency (F_{μ}) will be a positive monotonic function of input from their associated interneurons (ι) and the magnitudes of A and λ. These relationships can be expressed as follows:

$$F_{\dot{\mu}} \propto (s, A, \lambda, \iota)$$

$$F_{\mu} \propto (A, \lambda, \iota)$$

The discharge frequency (F_{ι}) for any interneuron (ι) is a positive monotonic function of the input pulse rate from its shift control driving cell (ρ) and the spike frequency of its donor autaptic cell ($\dot{\mu}$ or μ). Thus

$$F_\iota \propto (\rho, \dot{\mu}) \qquad \text{or} \qquad F_\iota \propto (\rho, \mu)$$

Given any arbitrary pulse rate from a shift control cell (say ρ), variation in the actual velocity of translation of an excitation pattern across the surface of a retinoid will be a positive function of the discharge frequency (F) of those retinoid cells carrying the pattern. This follows from the fact that the latency of discharge in each successive cell on the translation route of the image is inversely related to the F of its donor cell. If the translation velocity of an assembled retinoid image is equal in direction and velocity to the stimulus pattern S (in degrees of visual angle per second), then it is assumed that the perceived proportions of the pattern will correspond to the veridical proportions of the stimulus. If, however, translation velocity on the retinoid is less than stimulus velocity, then the stimulus pattern will be perceived as shorter along its axis of motion in relation to its other dimensions. As a corollary, it follows that if translation velocity on the retinoid should somehow be greater than stimulus velocity, the stimulus pattern would be perceived as longer along its axis of motion.

The dynamic properties of the retinoid system not only explain the sheer occurrence of this phenomenon but also predict certain systematic changes in SMTT perception as experimental parameters vary. In a series of SMTT experiments, Trehub and Pollatsek (1986) made predictions about the effects of change in stimulus velocity, aperture width, and ambient illumination on the basis of the SMTT-retinoid paradigm presented above.

General Method

Visual stimuli were presented on a CRT screen that was partially masked by a sheet of gray posterboard with a narrow, vertically oriented aperture in its center. The height of the aperture was fixed and was greater than the height of the stimulus pattern. The width of the aperture was adjustable and always much less than the width of the stimulus, so that only a small segment of the stimulus pattern could be seen by the subject at any given moment. The subject was provided with a hand-held controller. The controller had a potentiometer knob that allowed the subject to vary the rate of stimulus motion across the face of the CRT from 1.0 degree per second to a maximum velocity of 12.5 degrees per second at the viewing distance used in this study. The subject could press a button on the controller to signal when a perceptual criterion was met. After instructions were read, all experimental trials were controlled by a computer. Stimulus presentation, recording, and analysis of the subjects' responses were performed automatically according to a preprogrammed protocol.

Experiment 1

Hypothesis 1 Given a horizontally oscillating figure in the SMTT paradigm, the perceived width of the figure will contract as stimulus velocity increases.
This follows from the fact that the dwell–time of S on $\dot{\mu}$, hence $F_{\dot{\mu}}$, will decrease with an increase of stimulus velocity, causing the rate of translation over the retinoid to decrease relative to the true stimulus velocity.

Hypothesis 2 For any given stimulus velocity, the perceived width of the figure will increase as aperture width increases.
This follows from the fact that the proportion $\Sigma\dot{\mu}/\Sigma\mu$ will increase as the aperture for direct stimulation increases. Since $F_{\dot{\mu}} > F_{\mu}$, the velocity of translation over the retinoid will be greater for the larger aperture.

Procedure The subject was seated approximately 58 centimeters from the CRT. A laterally oscillating triangle on the face of the CRT was exposed to the subject through the narrow aperture in the masking screen. The triangle disappeared behind the screen at the terminus of both left and right excursions. The height of the triangle was fixed at 0.7 degree in visual angle, and the base of the triangle varied randomly on each trial within a range of 0.8 degree to 1.9 degrees in visual angle. Incident illumination on the CRT mask was set at approximately 8.0 foot-candles. The subject was instructed to fixate the center of the aperture on each stimulus presentation and to adjust the controller knob until the width of the perceived triangle was equal to its height. As soon as this occurred, the subject was to press the controller button, which recorded the current rate setting, cleared the CRT screen, and terminated the trial.

Data were collected from four subjects under two aperture conditions in five 20-trial blocks for each condition. Two subjects were first tested on five blocks with a 0.1 degree aperture, followed by five blocks with a 0.2 degree aperture. During each block of trials, there was an interstimulus interval of 5 seconds following each trial response of the subject. A rest interval of 90 seconds was given after each block of trials.

Results In this experiment, the independent variables were the height-width ratios of the stimulus patterns and the width of the viewing aperture. The dependent variable was the stimulus velocity set by the subject to give the perception of height-width equivalence. At each velocity setting required to meet the criterion of equivalence, the ratio of perceived width to true width was computed and expressed as a contraction ratio. Figure 14.2 shows the results plotted separately for each of the four subjects. Hypothesis 1 was confirmed by a statistical test of the response curves obtained from each of the subjects under the two aperture conditions.

To test hypothesis 2, we analyzed the stimulus velocity settings selected by the subject to achieve the contraction ratios required to perceive height-width equivalence for the 0.1 degree versus 0.2 degree viewing aperture. If the subject sees a wider triangle given a wider aperture, then the subject must increase the velocity of the stimulus to perceive equivalence. Hypothesis 2 was confirmed by a statistical test of the differences in the response curves obtained from each of the subjects under the two aperture conditions (figure 14.2).

Experiment 2

Hypothesis 3 For a given aperture, the perceived width of the stimulus figure will increase as ambient illumination increases.
This follows from the assumption that ambient illumination increases both $F_{\dot{\mu}}$ and F_{μ}. Thus velocity of translation over the retinoid should be greater with higher general illumination.

Procedure The apparatus, instructions, and procedure were the same as in experiment 1, except the width of the aperture was fixed at 0.2 degree and data were collected under two different intensities of ambient illumination. Two subjects were tested with 8.0 foot-candles of incident illumination followed by 2.0 foot-candles. For the remaining subjects, the order of illumination conditions was reversed.

Results In this experiment, the independent variables were the height-width ratios of the stimulus patterns and the level of ambient illumination. The dependent variable was the stimulus velocity set by the subject to give the perception of height-width equivalence. Figure 14.3 shows the results plotted separately for each of the four subjects. Hypothesis 3 was not confirmed in this test since only one of the subjects showed the predicted effect of an increase in the perceived width of the figure under higher ambient illumination.

Experiment 3

Hypothesis 4 In the SMTT paradigm with stimulus parameters held constant, the absolute number of stimulus sweeps required to squelch the SMTT effect will increase as ambient illumination increases (one sweep equals one complete excursion of the figure behind the aperture).

This follows from the assumption that the small interneurons (ι) in the retinoid will fatigue under prolonged driving. Cells of this type have a relatively high ratio of surface membrane to internal volume and are therefore more easily fatigued than are the larger autaptic neurons (Shepherd 1974). Thus, F_ι will decrease to the point that it no longer adds sufficient excitation to the target autaptic cells (μ) for them to reach discharge threshold. When this occurs, pattern translation over μ will cease, and SMTT will be squelched. Since the theoretical model assumes that ambient illumination (λ) adds biasing excitation to μ, it follows that SMTT squelching should occur later (more successive stimulus sweeps will be required) under higher ambient illumination. This prediction is opposite to what might be expected given the reduction in stimulus contrast on the face of the CRT screen when ambient illumination increases.

Procedure The apparatus in experiment 3 was the same as used in experiments 1 and 2. The screen aperture was fixed at 0.2 degree in visual angle. The stimulus presented on each trial was a triangle with a height of 0.7 degree and a base of 1.7 degrees in visual angle. The triangle oscillated horizontally at a constant rate of 10.0 degrees per second and disappeared beyond the aperture on both left and right excursions. In this test, however, the subject could not vary the rate of stimulus motion. The subject was instructed to fixate the center of the aperture and to press the controller button as soon as the perceived pattern shifted from a horizontally oscillating triangle to a short, vertically oscillating line segment above a short, stable line segment (the veridical retinal input). When the button was pressed, the number of stimulus sweeps required for the perceptual shift (squelch of SMTT) was automatically recorded. The screen was then cleared and, after a 5-second interval, a warning buzzer sounded and was followed a second later by another trial.

Each subject was given 10 consecutive trials under each of two intensities of ambient illumination. Two subjects were tested first with 8.0 foot-candles, followed by 2.0 foot-candles. The order of illumination was reversed for the other two subjects. A rest interval of 5 minutes was allowed between the illumination conditions.

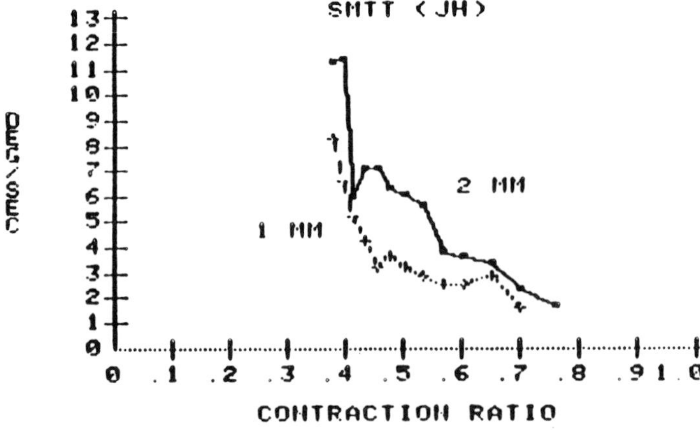

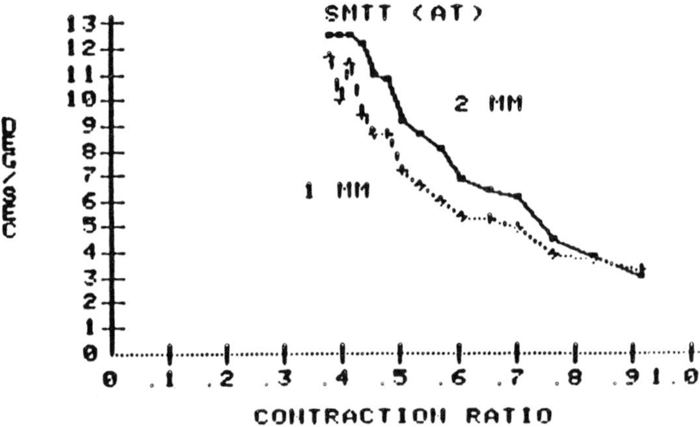

Figure 14.2
Experiment 1: Adjusted stimulus rates plotted against contraction ratios needed to achieve a perceived width-to-height match for each of four subjects. Aperture width = 0.1 degree (1 MM) and 0.2 degree (2 MM). Source: Trehub and Pollatsek 1986.

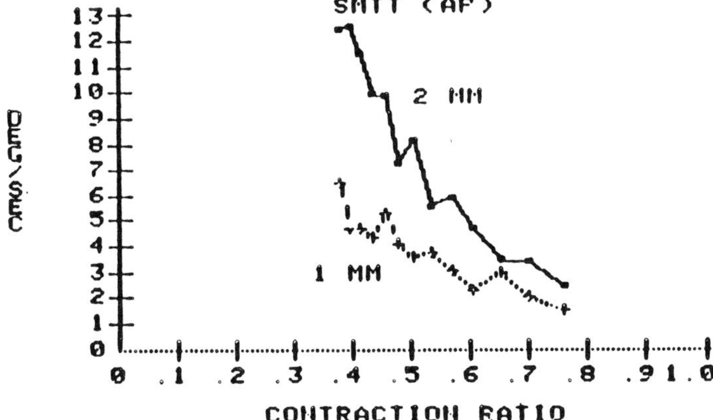

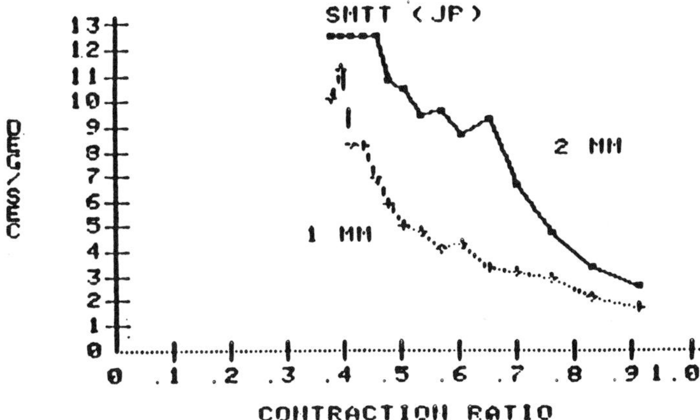

Figure 14.2 (continued)

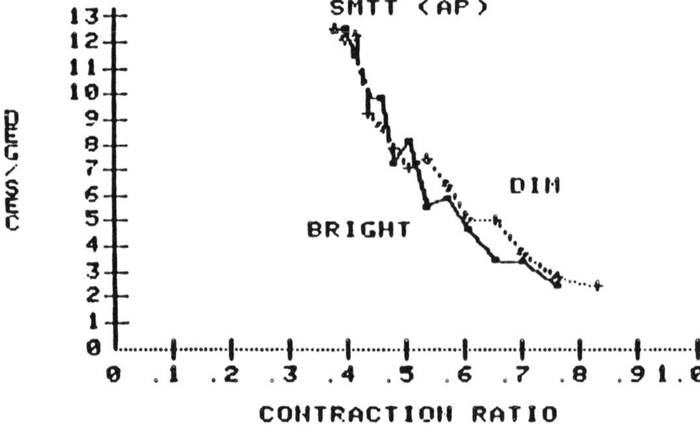

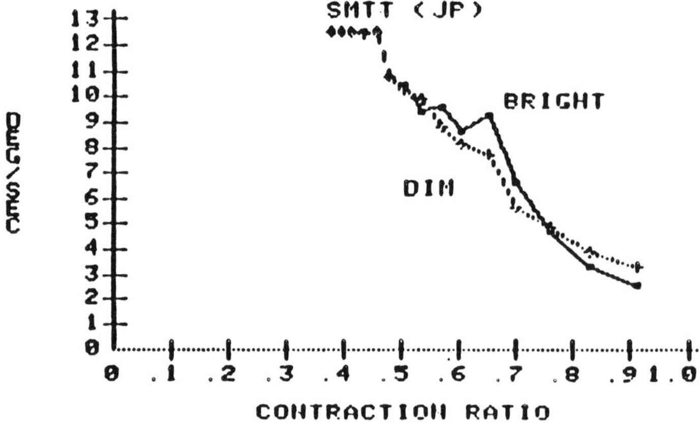

Figure 14.3
Experiment 2: Adjusted stimulus rates plotted against contraction ratios needed to achieve a perceived width-to-height match for each of four subjects. Ambient illumination = 2.0 foot-candles (DIM) and 8.0 foot-candles (BRIGHT). Source: Ibid.

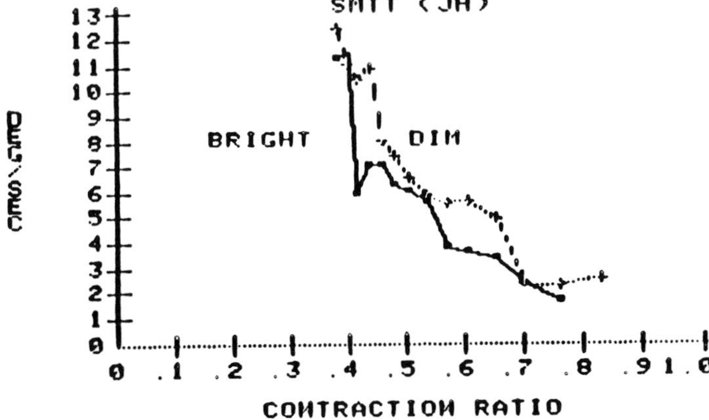

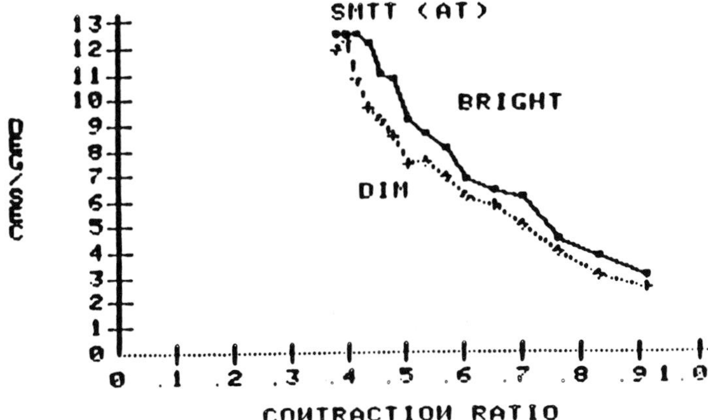

Figure 14.3 (continued)

Results In this experiment, the independent variable was the level of ambient illumination. The height-width ratio of the stimulus pattern, as well as its velocity, were held constant. The dependent variable was the number of successive stimulus sweeps required to squelch the SMTT effect. Figure 14.4 shows the results plotted separately for each of the four subjects. Hypothesis 4 was confirmed by a statistical test of the differences in the response curves obtained from each of the subjects under the two illumination conditions.

Comments

SMTT provides a strong argument against a static representation in visual short-term memory and argues for a dynamic form of postretinal storage (McCloskey and Watkins 1978). The retinoid system (Trehub 1977) offers a biologically plausible model of what such a dynamic storage mechanism would look like. It explains the SMTT effect as an epiphenomenon of the retinoid system and makes several confirmed predictions about the effects of changing parameters in the standard paradigm.

The retinoid model predicted an effect of ambient illumination on perceived width in SMTT (experiment 2, hypothesis 3) that was not confirmed. According to the model, an increase in the level of ambient illumination should increase the perceived width of a stimulus pattern by adding excitatory bias to autaptic cells in the retinoid network. This, in turn, should increase, to some extent, the rate of translation of the autaptic representation of the figure on each of its sweeps across the viewing aperture. While this assumption of the model might be incorrect, it is also possible that the difference in ambient illumination in the experiment was too small to exert a reliably detectable influence on translation velocity over the retinoid at each sweep. In contrast, the prediction of resistance to SMTT squelching under higher ambient illumination (experiment 3, hypothesis 4) was confirmed, and this depends on the same assumption that an increase in ambient illumination will add excitatory bias to autaptic cells in the retinoid network. However, the effect observed in experiment 3 does not depend on the ambient light intensity at each single sweep but on a cumulative influence over the entire trial (typically thirty to several hundred sweeps). Thus, it appears that ambient illumination has a real but relatively weak influence on retinoid dynamics.

A New Visual Illusion

In the standard SMTT demonstration, a rectangular aperture provides the observer with a continuous sequence of fragmentary views of a moving stimulus pattern. Because of the rectangular shape of the slit in the occluding screen, the width of the stimulus field is uniform along the vertical axis. This results in the direct stimulation (via retinal afferents) of a uniform number of autaptic cells ($\dot{\mu}$) on each horizontal plane along the vertical axis of the retinoid. Suppose that the aperture were triangular in shape. In this case, the number of autaptic cells that would be directly stimulated ($\dot{\mu}$) by the oscillating figure would be much greater at the base of the triangular aperture than at its vertex. Since the number of $\dot{\mu}$ collinear with the horizontal direction of stimulus motion will change as a function of the triangular shape of the aperture and since $F_{\dot{\mu}} > F_{\mu}$, the rate of horizontal translation of a retinoid representation should increase from the vertex to the base of the aperture. This property of retinoid dynamics implies that if a rigid shape were to be presented as an SMTT stimulus behind a triangular aperture instead of a rectangular one, the observer should experience an illusion of a figure swinging in pendular fashion as though pivoting near the vertex of the triangle rather than moving in simple reciprocating translation (the veridical situation).

The predicted pendulum illusion was confirmed (Trehub 1985). It can be clearly seen with simple materials. Near the top of a strip of white cardboard, draw a heavy black circle approximately 25 millimeters in diameter with a vertical line through its center. On a sheet of gray cardboard, cut out an isosceles triangle approximately 30 millimeters high and 15 millimeters wide. Holding the gray cardboard screen at normal reading distance, position the circle on the white strip behind the triangular aperture and slide it laterally back and forth at a rate of about 2 cycles per second, taking care to move the circle beyond the aperture in each direction. If the center of the cutout is fixated, an egg-shaped figure will be perceived swinging like a pendulum within the aperture (figure 14.5). The apparent contraction of the figure along the axis of motion occurs because the rate of image translation on the retinoid is less than the veridical rate of stimulus motion. Moreover, in accordance with the retinoid model, the rate lag is greater near the vertex (narrower aperture) than near the base (wider aperture), which accounts for the egg-shaped transformation of the circle.

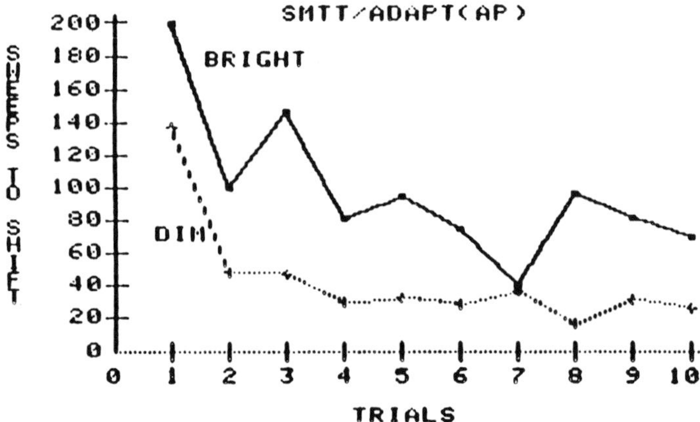

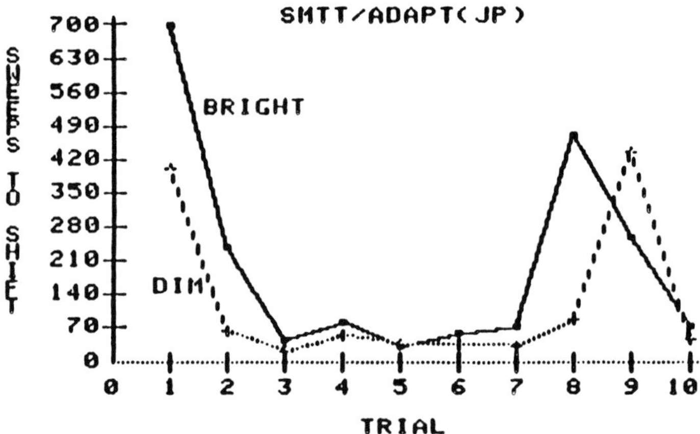

Figure 14.4
Experiment 3: Plot of the number of successive stimulus sweeps required to squelch the SMTT effect over 10 successive trial blocks for each of four subjects. Ambient illumination = 2.0 foot-candles (DIM) and 8.0 foot-candles (BRIGHT). Source: Ibid.

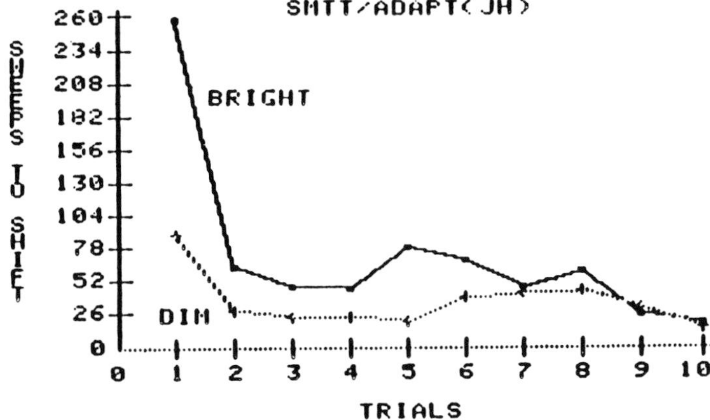

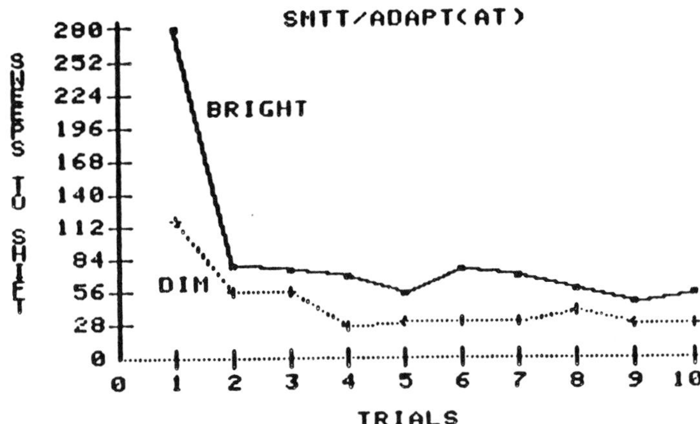

Figure 14.4 (continued)

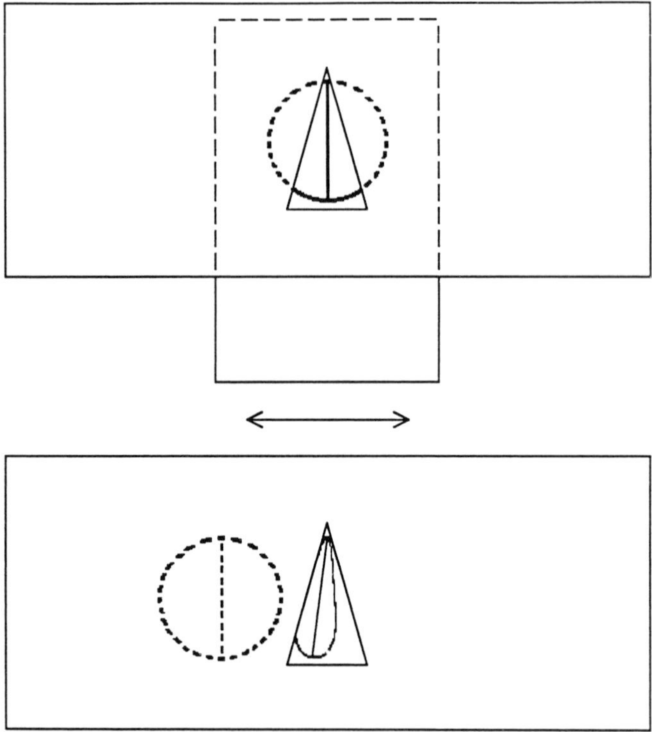

Figure 14.5
Top: Opaque screen with triangular aperture through which a part of the stimulus pattern (circle with vertical line) can be seen. *Bottom:* Appearance of pendulum illusion when stimulus is moved back and forth at approximately 2 cycles per second.

The Moon Illusion

Surely the oldest and one of the most striking and puzzling illusions—a false perception on a truly cosmic scale—is the so-called moon illusion (Reimann 1902, Schur 1925, Holway and Boring 1940, Boring 1943). In this illusion, the moon, or any other celestial body, when viewed at or near the horizon is perceived as much larger than when it is at its zenith, though its true visual angle (~0.5 degree) remains unchanged. The kind of process that might account for this phenomenon, even in the most general terms, has long been a subject of vigorous dispute (Boring 1962, Rock and Kaufman 1962, Wallach 1962, Reed 1984). The debate has remained in the arena of psychophysics, and, to date, no theoretical explanation of the illusion has been proposed at the level of neuronal structure in the visual system.

Here I will show how a plausible anisotropy of the 3-D retinoid system provides a simple biophysical explanation of the moon illusion.

Explaining the Moon Illusion

A guiding premise motivating the models that I have proposed is that the structure of the human cognitive brain has been shaped by evolution to cope with the ecologically significant demands of the human environment. In this process, we can imagine a principle of neuronal economy at work. We would expect limited genotypic neuronal resources to be allocated for specific kinds of cognitive representation and computation in rough accordance with their importance to the survival of the species. In the visual system of lower animals, there are clear examples of this principle (Ingle 1968, Fite 1976, Spinelli 1987). If the location of objects in particular regions of egocentric space is a matter of little ecological importance, then we might expect a reduction in neuronal resources devoted to the representation of those regions, the savings invested (by evolutionary competition) in more useful brain structures.

Can regions of human egocentric space be characterized as having more or less ecological value? If so, how might this fact shape those genotypic visual mechanisms that must be involved in the moon illusion? While we cannot assign precise ecological value to sharply defined extrapersonal regions, there are considerations that persuasively suggest the relative ecological value of broadly specified regions in egocentric space. For example, the space within the immediate reach of an individual is critically important for a wide variety of vital behaviors. Beyond that, space within the range of quick natural locomotion contains objects and features that may demand immediate response. As the regional locus of terrestrial space increases in distance from the observer, the objects contained tend to diminish in ecological urgency. Thus, the brain's reduction in distance discrimination with the increasing distance of visual targets entails no serious loss of the ability to cope in the natural environment. In addition, with respect to the location of objects with ecological significance, as egocentric distance increases, the maximum vertical angle of regard tends to decrease. For example, an apple on a tree branch that is within reaching distance may be directly overhead, a vertical sighting angle of 90 degrees; but any earthbound object at a horizontal distance of 1000 feet would have to be 1000 feet tall at the point of fixation to demand an angle of regard of even 45 degrees.

If evolution has conserved neuronal resources in mechanisms for 3-D viewing of horizon-limited terrestrial space, why should it not devote even fewer biological resources for the 3-D discrimination of

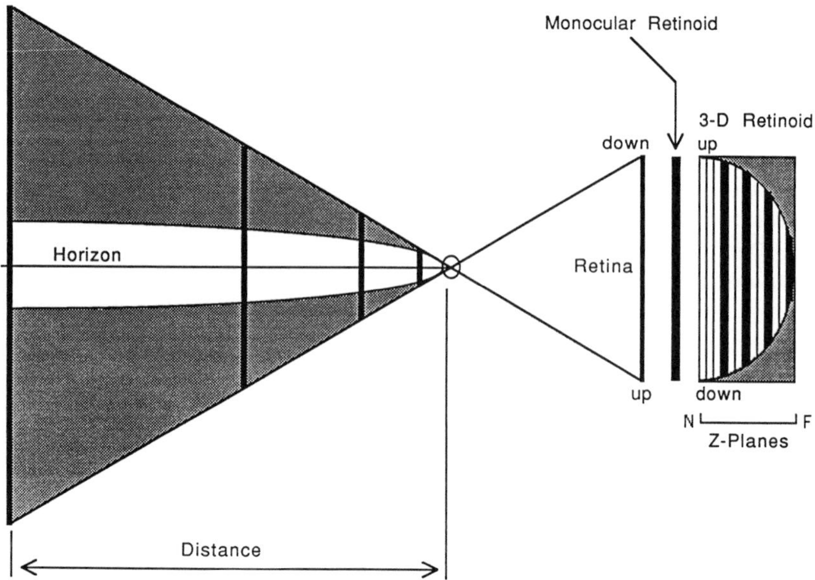

Figure 14.6
Schematic illustration of anisotropic representation of egocentric space within 3-D retinoid. Shading indicates the region in egocentric space that is represented in the 3-D retinoid on progressively nearer Z-planes as the vertical angle of regard departs from the horizon and as distance increases. Shaded area in 3-D retinoid indicates absent neuronal substrate for spatial representation.

objects in extraterrestrial space? After all, these are phenomena that, except for the briefest (modern) period of human experience, were beyond the scope of possible contact and demanded only philosophical speculation. I argue that egocentric space is anisotropically represented in the brain's 3-D retinoid system so that representations of objects within regions of increasing distance are progressively collapsed onto nearer Z-planes as the elevation in their lines of sight departs from the plane of the normal horizon (figure 14.6). Thus, valuable neuronal tissue is conserved for more important matters.

Recall the connectivity scheme from the 3-D retinoid to the mosaic cell array that was discussed in chapter 5 (figure 5.8). Principal cells in the nearest Z-plane are mapped to their corresponding retinotopic coordinates in the mosaic cell array while the axons of cells in the more distant Z-planes diverge to project to increasingly more eccentric coordinates on the mosaic cell array in accordance with the visual distance they represent. This provides a neuronal circuit for magnifying (or reducing) images in rough compensation for the change in retinal size at different viewing distances.

Since the distance of the moon from an observer on earth, as well as its retinal size, remain effectively unchanged whether it is viewed at the horizon or at its zenith, one might not expect a mechanism for size constancy to play a role in the moon illusion. However, the hypothesized brain architecture predicts size constancy (Emmert's law) (Boring 1940) for all vertical angles of regard at all distances only if it is assumed that the structure of the 3-D retinoid is functionally isotropic over all Z-planes. If the combined effect of viewing distance and angle of regard results in the shift of an excitation pattern of constant size from a distance Z-plane in the 3-D retinoid to a nearer Z-plane, then the axonal projection of the image on the mosaic cell array will shrink correspondingly in size. I propose that this is precisely what happens when the moon is seen after it has departed from the horizon (figure 14.7). Because of the great distance of the moon, it is always represented on the most distant Z-plane in the 3-D retinoid that can provide a neuronal medium for the moon's current angular position in egocentric space. As the moon rises above the horizon, the most distant Z-planes that have a substrate to represent its increasing elevation correspond to progressively nearer regions of 3-D space. Thus, the image projected to the mosaic cell array is that of a rising moon diminishing in size.

Comments

The neuronal architecture of the 3-D visual system described can not only explain the moon illusion but can account as well for at least two other previously unexplained classical psychophysical observations. Even before the writings of Ptolemy, many observers reported that the "dome of the sky" appeared to be flattened from horizon to horizon (Smith 1738). The vertical distance of the sky is perceived to be closer than its horizontal distance. But notice that this perception is just what one should expect if the properties of the 3-D retinoid model accurately reflect the corresponding visual-cognitive mechanisms in the human brain. Since egocentric space is represented within the limits of the 3-D retinoid, the outer representational bounds of the retinoid structure will define the outer bounds of perception of the limitless sky. Thus the anisotropy of retinoid space that is characterized by representation on closer Z-planes as the vertical angle of regard is elevated will result in a corresponding anisotropy of spatial perception when the sky is scanned. The sky above will appear closer than the sky beyond the horizon.

One might raise the objection that the phenomenon is experienced even in a starless and cloudless (empty) sky. What then would be the targets of visual regard? And if there were no visual stimuli repre-

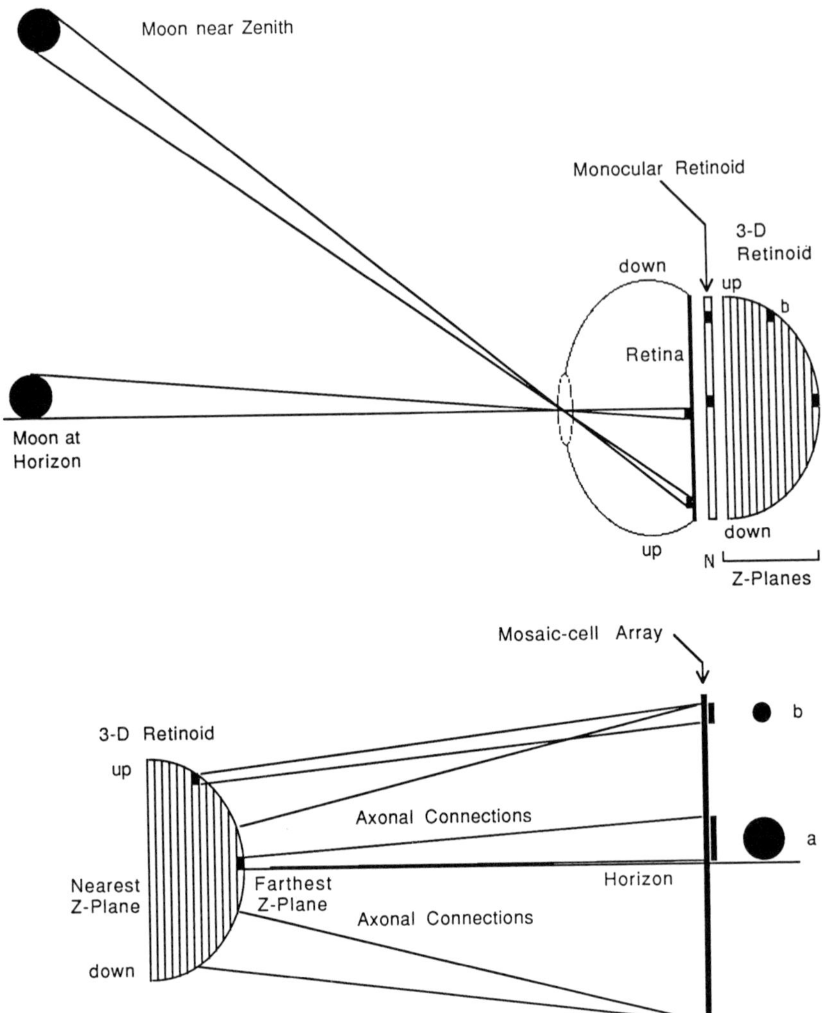

Figure 14.7
Moon illusion. *Top:* N = near; F = far. Moon at horizon is represented on farthest Z-plane (a). Moon near zenith is represented on nearer Z-plane (b), which is the farthest Z-plane available for the representation of an object at its distance and elevation. *Bottom:* Expanding axonal connections from Z-planes in 3-D retinoid to mosaic cell array that normally preserve size constancy evoke a larger representation of the horizon moon (a) than the zenith moon (b).

sented in the anisotropic space of the 3-D retinoid system, how could such a brain structure shape our perception of the sky? But notice that even when we scan an empty sky, binocular convergence relaxed and lens accommodation at infinity, the locus of our attention moves in accordance with our visual search. In the retinoid model, shifts in attention are real neuronal events—excursions of the self-locus (autaptic cell discharge) over selected coordinates of retinoid space. When we visually scan an empty sky, neuronal excitation provided by the corresponding excursion of the self-locus traces the outer bounds of retinoid space—closer as the line of sight approaches the vertical axis, more distant as the line of sight approaches the horizontal axis (the horizon).

The same anisotropic properties of the retinoid model and the circuitry for size constancy explain the results of an early psychophysical investigation of perceived size and angle of regard reported by Schur (1925). Working in a large, dark room, she presented two projected disks of light to subjects, one in a horizontal direction and the other above the subject and always at the same distance as the horizontal disk. Both stimuli were presented at distances varying from 3 to 33 meters. It was found that as the viewing distance increased, there was an increase in the perceived size of the stimulus in front of the observer relative to the stimulus above. The advantage in the ratio of perceived size for the frontal stimulus relative to the overhead stimulus was 1.16 to 1 at 3 meters, 1.71 to 1 at 22 meters, and 1.87 to 1 at 33 meters. These results are consistent with my assumption of an anisotropy in the representation of visual distance within the brain (figure 14.6), which is related to elevation of gaze and is based on the argument of evolutionary economy.

Other Visual Illusions

Many other kinds of visual illusions can be explained by the intrinsic properties of the retinoid system and accessory mechanisms. A few more examples will show how a variety of other illusions that have had no satisfactory physical explanation will occur as natural consequences of the structure and dynamics of the proposed brain model.

The Waterfall Illusion

When we look at a stationary pattern of vertical bars under ordinary conditions, we see no more than the stimulus itself—a stable pattern of vertical bars. If we look at the same stimulus after prolonged viewing of a pattern moving, for example, to the left, the stationary bars are perceived as streaming to the right. The illusion of motion of the stationary test pattern is an aftereffect of a prior moving stimulus and is always in a direction opposite to that of the prior inducing motion. This phenomenon is commonly called the waterfall illusion. (If the motion of the inducing stimulus is upward, the stationary stimulus is seen as streaming down like a waterfall.)

According to the retinoid hypothesis, the illusion of motion is experienced because the neuronal representation of the stimulus pattern evoked on the retinoid actually moves a small distance in the direction perceived, though the stimulus itself is stationary. The reason that it happens is a straightforward consequence of retinoid structure, the known properties of the ocular-motor system, and the physiology of nerve cells.

Even while we are fixating a visual target, our eyes are in constant motion, which can be characterized as a high-frequency, low-amplitude tremor. The tremor movements occur with a magnitude of less than 0.5 minute of arc and at a rate of up to 150 cycles per second (Ratliff and Riggs 1950; Riggs, Armington, and Ratliff 1954). Movements of the eye normally drive shift control cells in the retinoid, with the result that a retinoid image is translated in the direction of eye movement. However, the micro-oscillations of the eye change direction at high frequency; thus, under normal conditions, their directional influences on the retinoid offset each other during fixation so that there is no false representation of stimulus motion. But if one fixates a stimulus that is in constant unidirectional motion for a prolonged period, the small interneurons within the retinoid that are part of the activated translation circuit become selectively fatigued (Shepherd 1979) and a significant bias is induced in the dynamic properties of the retinoid. The bias consists of a loss of efficacy for translation in the direction served by the fatigued interneurons. It is this bias, caused by the moving induction stimulus, that produces the waterfall illusion.

Figure 14.8 illustrates what happens in the retinoid when the illusion is induced. After shift-left interneurons have been fatigued by prolonged fixation of a pattern in constant motion to the left, the stationary test pattern appears to stream to the right. This occurs because the phase of eyeball tremor that would normally drive the retinoid representation of the pattern in offsetting motion to the left does not elicit a corresponding response from the fatigued shift-left interneurons. At the same time, right-going movements of the oscillating eyes are effective in eliciting small successive right-going translation of the retinoid image, which decays as it traverses more autaptic cells beyond the microfields of direct excitation by stimulus contours.

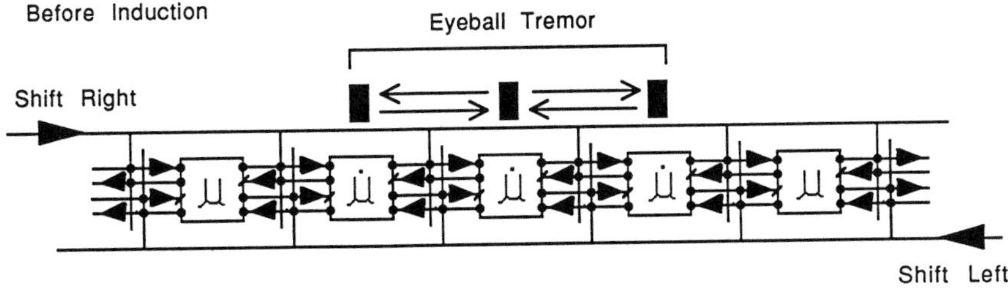

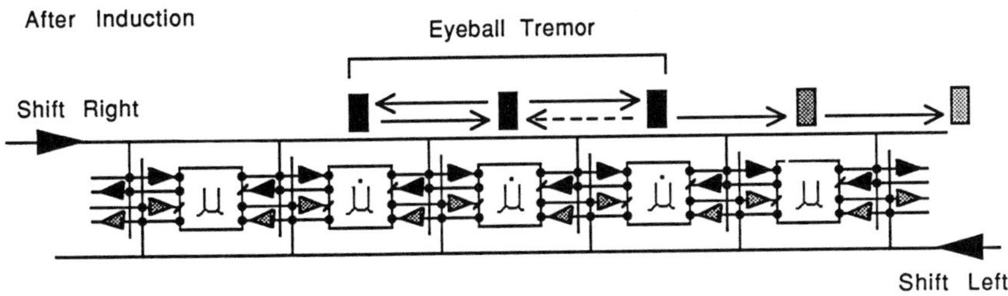

Figure 14.8
Waterfall illusion. *Top:* Normal eyeball tremor shifts a stationary stimulus back and forth over adjacent autaptic cells with no net motion of the stimulus in either direction. *Bottom:* During the induction phase, after prolonged viewing of a pattern in constant motion to the left, shift-left interneurons are fatigued (stippled cells). Given a stationary test pattern after induction, normal tremor-related shifts of the pattern to the right are not offset by corresponding shifts to the left, resulting in an illusory streaming of the stimulus to the right. Streaming decays as the illusory image traverses autaptic cells beyond the field of direct stimulus excitation.

Illusory Motion as a Resultant of Orthogonal Induction

In the standard waterfall illusion, the direction of illusory motion is always opposite to the motion of the inducing stimulus; it is rotated 180 degrees from the angular direction of the inducing motion. Thus, motion to the left (180 degrees, where up is 90 degrees and down is 270 degrees) produces the illusory aftereffect of a pattern moving to the right (0 degree).

Suppose one were exposed to two inducing stimuli moving alternately in orthogonal directions. What would be the direction of the illusion? On the basis of the retinoid explanation proposed, we should be able to predict the perceived motion of the stationary test pattern. The directions of the orthogonal induction patterns should evoke discharge in retinoid shift control cells at a frequency proportional to the vectorial component of stimulus motion for each of the four shift control directions. The relative degree of fatigue for each set of directionally oriented interneurons will then correspond to the

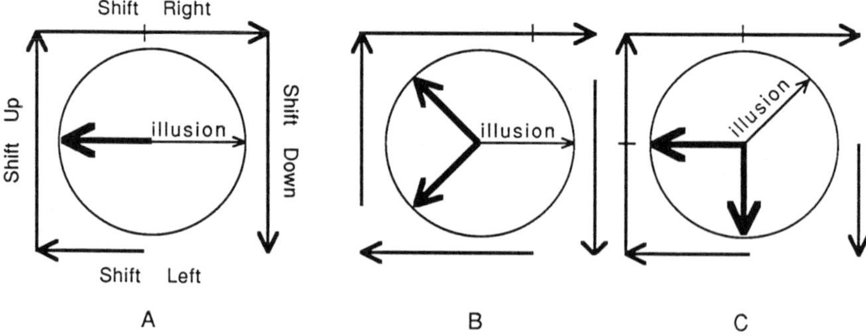

Figure 14.9
Retinoid states after simple and orthogonal induction according to theoretical model. Relative length of each of the outer four directional shift lines indicates relative efficacy of interneurons serving translation in the corresponding direction. Distance from short tick mark to arrow head indicates net advantage in translation efficacy for the direction shown. Within circles, thick arrows indicate direction of inducing motion and thin arrows the expected direction of illusory motion. *A:* Direction of illusion following simple induction. *B:* Direction of illusion following orthogonal induction of 135 degrees and 225 degrees. *C:* Direction of illusion following orthogonal induction of 180 degrees and 270 degrees.

relative frequency of discharge in the shift control cell that drives that set of interneurons. Thus, perceived motion of the stationary test pattern should stream in a direction that is the resultant of the relative efficacy of each set of interneurons considered as a vectorial component for retinoid translation. Figure 14.9 illustrates how the directions of inducing stimuli jointly determine the direction of translation on the retinoid and therefore the direction of illusory aftermotion.

In an experiment reported by Riggs and Day (1980), a visual aftereffect of motion was induced by bars moving alternately at two different angles in the frontal plane. During the 10 minutes of induction time, the angle of motion was alternated every 10 seconds. When the angles of inducing motion were 135 degrees and 225 degrees, the direction of illusory aftermotion was 0 degree. When inducing motion was presented at 180 degrees and 270 degrees, the direction of illusory aftermotion was 45 degrees. These results are exactly as predicted by the retinoid model (see examples B and C in figure 14.9).

The Mueller-Leyer Illusion

One of the classical illusions of visual extent is the Mueller-Leyer illusion (Mueller-Leyer 1889, Coren 1986). If two line segments of equal length are each attached at both ends to short angles, one line to the vertices of angles pointing out and the other to the vertices of

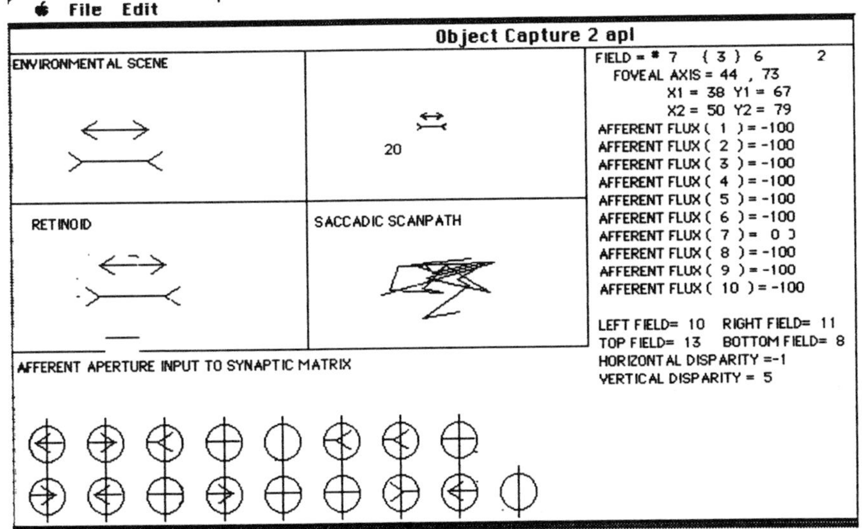

Figure 14.10
Simulation of Mueller-Leyer illusion. Stimulus parts captured on successive saccades are displayed in the bottom frame. Circles indicate afferent aperture. Vertical lines bisecting circles represent vertical plane along normal foveal axis.

angles pointing in (top left frame of figure 14.10), the line with the angles pointing out is perceived as shorter than the other. This illusion can be explained as a normal consequence of the mechanisms for parsing aspects of the visual environment, marking location, and representing distance between objects.

In a comparison of the length of the two lines in the Mueller-Leyer paradigm, the length of each line from one terminus to the other must be registered and the two linear extents compared. Chapter 7 shows how this is done by excursions of the self-locus that are registered in neuronal comparator circuits. The illusion arises because of errors in locating the ends of each line, which are systematically caused by the shapes of the stimuli used in the illusion. The direction of the appended angles biases the centroid location of the terminating line segment. When the end angles point out, the terminating centroids of the attached line are closer together than they are when the end angles point in. This results in a mismatch of the two self-locus traces that are made when the lengths of the lines are compared.

Figure 14.10 shows the result of a simulation of the Mueller-Leyer illusion. Standard stimuli (top left frame) were presented to the model visual system. Twenty saccades were allowed (middle frame). The bottom frame shows the centroids of stimulus segments that were captured over the course of 20 saccades. For the figure with the angles pointing out, extreme right and left centroids were closer to the center of the figure than they should be. For the figure with the angles pointing in, extreme right and left centroids were either at the terminus of the horizontal line or somewhat beyond it (farther from the center of the figure than they should be). The direction of the results is consistent over a variety of trials using different afferent apertures and initial error tolerances, although the magnitude of centroid error is reduced with smaller apertures and tolerances. However, the trade-off in such cases is that for a small improvement in the accuracy of registering the ends of the horizontal lines, there is a great increase in perceptual effort. Many more saccades must be made and a more extended sequence of retinoid hunting must be tolerated to achieve a modest reduction in the extent of the illusion.

Ambiguous Shapes

Certain well-recognized shapes evoke unstable perceptions. At one moment the stimulus is clearly recognized and classified as a particular kind of object, while at the next moment it is just as clearly seen as a completely different kind of object. I propose that the ambiguity in the perception of such shapes is systematically related to the part of the shape that falls on the normal foveal axis at the moment of visual capture. Given the hypothesized visual mechanisms for finding a centroid and aligning it on the normal foveal axis, if an extended shape has multiple centroids and if the constituent parts within the afferent aperture for the different centroids are also distinctive parts of different objects or different exemplars of an object, then the object that is "seen" at any moment will depend on the particular centroid of the extended shape that has been aligned to the normal foveal axis at that moment. With stimulus patterns having multistable centroids, small saccadic shifts will normally result in the capture of different centroids when a change in gaze is of sufficient magnitude.

The Necker Cube

A common example of an ambiguous figure, in this case one that evokes the perception of bistable perspective, is the Necker cube (Necker 1832). The stimulus is a 2-D projection of a cube with no hidden edges (top left frame of figure 14.11). As the cube is viewed, it is typically seen to "jump" unpredictably between two perspec-

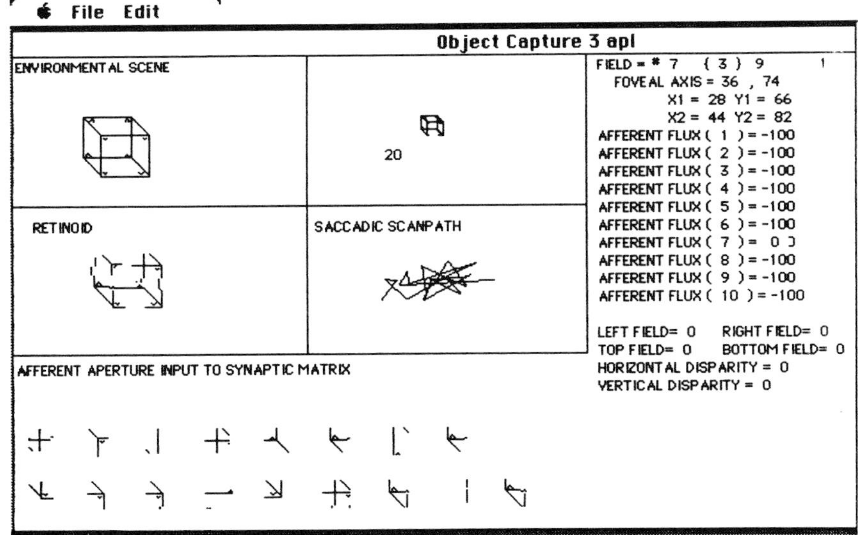

Figure 14.11
Simulation of response to Necker cube. Stimulus parts captured on successive saccades are displayed in the bottom frame.

tives. One is a cube, seen from above front, with the lower square as its front plane and the upper square as its back plane. The other perspective is a cube, seen from below front, with the lower square as its back plane and the upper square as its front plane. Confronted with the same stimulus, will the model visual system perform in a way that would constrain perception to one or the other of the two geometric interpretations, and will there be natural alterations in the captured patterns that can account for the shifting perspective?

Figure 14.11 shows the result of a simulation with the Necker cube as the visual stimulus (upper left frame). In order to facilitate interpretation of the results, the two squares that form the front or back faces of the cube are marked at their corners. The lower square has a small V at each corner. The upper square has a small inverted V at each corner. Twenty saccades were allowed. The center frame displays the scanpaths of all saccades. The bottom frame displays the parts of the stimulus that were successively captured by the visual system during the 20 saccades. A partial reconstruction of an image of the whole cube on the scene assembly retinoid is displayed in the left center frame.

Each captured pattern that represents a corner of the cube uniquely determines one of the possible visual perspectives on an opaque cube (the exterior form of a solid cubic object). Whenever a corner is captured within the afferent aperture and projected to the synaptic matrix, any image of a remembered (previously learned) cubic object that is evoked in the imaging matrix must correspond in perspective to the angular properties of the current effective stimulus (the captured corner). When the eye moves, the current effective stimulus can change, and a different corner can be captured. Thus, the two different perspectives on the cube can each be evoked at different times even though the whole stimulus pattern is static.

In this simulation run, there were 17 captures of parts of the cube over the course of 20 saccades. We can see from the bottom frame of figure 14.11 that the model first "perceived" a cube from above (first corner captured, top row). At the fifth captured part, the perspective changed to a cube seen from below (second corner captured, top row). This perspective was maintained until the ninth capture (bottom row) and reversed again at the fifteenth capture. Thus, the perceptual experience of a "spontaneously" shifting perspective in the Necker cube paradigm can be explained as a natural consequence of visual mechanisms embodied in the proposed brain model.

Figure Reversal

In the case of the Necker cube, the part of the figure that had been captured (centered within the afferent aperture) was the effective stimulus that determined the perspective from which the figure was viewed. Other kinds of figures will evoke the recognition of entirely different objects depending on which of their parts are captured as effective stimuli. A well-known example is displayed in the top left frame of figure 14.12. When this drawing is viewed, there is typically a spontaneous alternation in the perception of the figure. One moment it is recognized as a vase and at another moment as two faces. The explanation for such figure reversals is that perception is constrained by the effective stimulus within the afferent aperture. Since the parts of the figure around different centroids are proper parts of different well-known objects and because small saccades will often lead to the alignment of different centroids on the normal foveal axis for projection to the detection matrix, the particular object that is perceived will vary from time to time within a common visual field.

The simulation shown in figure 14.12 displays the responses of the model visual system in the vase-face paradigm. The pattern in the upper left frame is the stimulus presented to the system. Saccades are displayed in the center frame. The bottom frame displays the parts of the stimulus that were successively captured by the visual

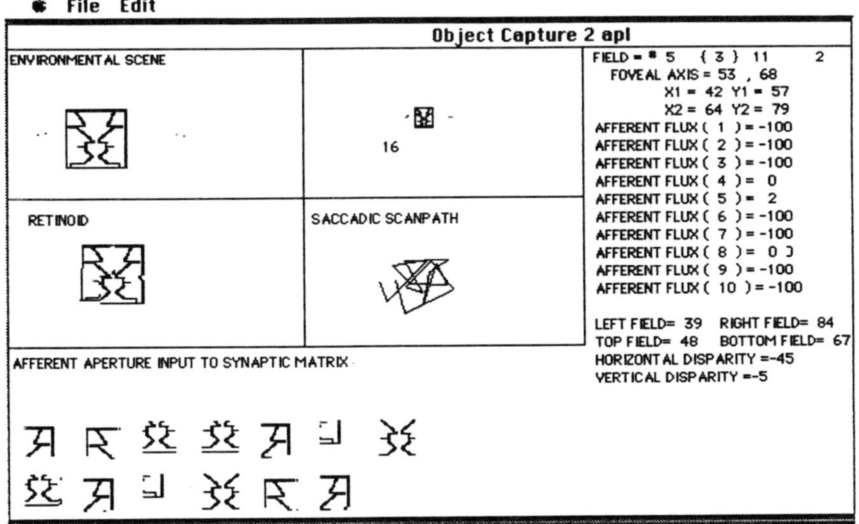

Figure 14.12
Simulation of response to ambiguous figure: Vase-face reversals. Stimulus parts captured on successive saccades are displayed in the bottom frame.

system during the simulation. A reconstruction of an image of the stimulus is displayed in the left center frame.

The sequence of the stimulus parts that were captured (effective stimuli) and projected to the synaptic matrix is consistent with the perception of either of two different objects appearing at differing times within the same visual field. For example, the first pattern that was captured (bottom frame, figure 14.12) corresponds to the brow, eye, and nose in the profile of a face looking to the left. Next is the same profile facing right. This is followed by two successive patterns corresponding to a large part of a vase, and so forth. Although the whole figure is ambiguous, its component parts, captured at different centroids, are unambiguous and clearly associated with different objects. Thus our perception of the object that is "depicted" shifts back and forth between a vase and two faces.

Chapter 15

Other Experimental and Clinical Evidence

This chapter presents additional findings from neurophysiological, psychological, and clinical studies that support the biological plausibility and explanatory competence of the model's principal component mechanisms.

Synaptic Plasticity

In a technically elegant study, the factors responsible for the associative properties of long-term potentiation (LTP) were investigated directly in a hippocampal-slice preparation (Gustaffson et al. 1987). The EPSPs of individual cells resulting from single-volley, low-frequency stimulation of their afferent axons were recorded by an intracellular electrode. The preparation also allowed depolarizing current pulses to be injected through the recording microelectrode in the postsynaptic cell. It was demonstrated that:

1. EPSPs became potentiated when they were paired with depolarizing pulses of sufficient magnitude.
2. The potentiation (LTP) generally reached a peak after 20 to 30 single presynaptic volleys were paired with depolarizing pulses in the postsynaptic cell.
3. LTP was specific to the paired inputs (the coactive synaptic junction).
4. For LTP to occur, the EPSP had to be induced together with the postsynaptic depolarizing pulse or precede it by less than ~100 milliseconds. There was no potentiation when the EPSP immediately succeeded the postsynaptic pulse.
5. LTP was blocked by the application of the NMDA-receptor antagonist 2-amino-5-phosphonovalerate (APV).
6. If an EPSP occurs together with a large postsynaptic depolarization, not much additional LTP can be induced by subsequent coactivation at the modified synapse.

These relatively recent findings extend and clarify earlier notions about LTP, and they provide support for a number of assumptions I made in my proposed model of neuronal plasticity. First, synaptic enhancement is spatially restricted on the postsynaptic dendrite. Second, a long-term increase in synaptic weight (learning) occurs only if there is coactivation of the pre- and postsynaptic cells or if postsynaptic activation follows the EPSP by less than ~100 milliseconds. Finally, the efficacy of an adaptive synapse can approach its maximum value (saturation) during a single learning exposure if the activation (depolarization) of the postsynaptic cell is high enough. In the synaptic matrix model, the excitatory bias of arousal is a necessary condition for learning and serves to ensure a high level of postsynaptic activation of filter cells (f) and mosaic cells (M) when stimulus-evoked EPSPs occur. Thus, my theoretical assumptions about the selective locus of synaptic modification, the necessity for the interaction of ATF and DTF within the postsynaptic dendrite, one-trial learning during high arousal, and synaptic saturation seem to be confirmed by microelectrode measurements of LTP processes in single hippocampal neurons.

In an effort to determine whether the effective process underlying LTP is presynaptic or postsynaptic, Kauer, Malenka, and Nicoll (1988) studied synaptic transmission in the CA1 region of the hippocampus. They found that presynaptically released glutamate activates both NMDA and non-NMDA postsynaptic receptors on pyramidal cells, which produces an EPSP with two distinct components. When LTP is induced, there is a selective increase in the non-NMDA component of the EPSP. Thus, it appears that while activation of NMDA receptors is necessary to initiate LTP, the persistence of LTP is caused specifically by a long-lasting increase in the sensitivity of non-NMDA receptors in the postsynaptic neuron (dendrite) to glutamate that is released at spike-activated presynaptic axonal terminals. This finding provides additional physiological support for the proposed learning mechanism essential for the adaptive competence of the synaptic matrix.

A number of the cognitive processes that I have described have required adaptive synaptic coupling between different more or less modular neuronal mechanisms. This is true, for example, in the feed-forward and feed-backward adaptive chaining of class cell tokens (figure 3.6), the linking of motivation to the detection matrix for pattern recognition (figure 9.6), and the cross-coupling between the semantic network and the matrix for episodic learning (figure 13.1). A recent series of studies (Laroche, Jay, and Thierry 1989) provides direct evidence of this kind of adaptive synaptic coupling between anatomically distinct systems in the neocortex of the rat. Single unit recordings were obtained from 120 neurons in the prelimbic region of the prefrontal cortex. Of these, 42 percent exhibited excitatory responses to single-pulse stimulation of the hippocampal CA1-subicular region, indicating an excitatory pathway between hippocampal cells and these prefrontal neurons. Stimulation of the hippocampus with a high-frequency pulse train (tetanic stimulation) resulted in a significant and persistent potentiation of evoked response (LTP) and a reduction of onset latency in the recorded cells of the prefrontal cortex.

The Synaptic Matrix–Retinoid System

Physiological Evidence

A central architectural feature of the synaptic matrix is the abundance of dynamic cellular junctions created by the intersection of bundles of axons (presynaptic lines) with a large population of orthogonally oriented dendrites (postsynaptic lines). Such an anatomical arrangement requires relatively long cellular processes to accommodate multiple inputs and outputs. The neuronal architectures of the hippocampus and the cerebellum provide clear examples of long dendrites that are transversed and synaptically innervated by long axonal projections. Dendrites range from 500 to 1000 microns in length on hippocampal pyramidal cells and are ~400 microns long on cerebellar Purkinje cells. Apical dendrites of pyramidal cells in the sensory regions of the neocortex range in length from 200 to 1600 microns (Shepherd 1979).

In a recent study of the striate cortex of the macaque monkey, Blasdel, Lund, and Fitzpatrick (1985) established by darkfield microphotography that axonal projections intrinsic to this visual region can extend laterally (parallel to the cortical surface) at least 5000 microns in length. Pyramidal cells in the cortex are tightly packed and oriented with their dendritic shafts orthogonal to the cortical surface. Because of this kind of crossed orientation of axons and dendrites, a single 5000-micron axon can contact the dendrites of many thousands of cells in its lateral passage. Thus, it appears that a basic structural requirement of the synaptic matrix is met in the neuronal architecture of the neocortex.

In a systematic survey employing both simple and complex visual stimuli, the responses of many individual neurons in the inferior temporal (IT) cortex of the macaque were recorded and analyzed (Desimone et al. 1984). A subpopulation of cells was discovered in this brain area that responded selectively to faces. The magnitude of response in these cells was dependent on the configuration of specific facial features. The selectivity of response was reported to be maintained over a wide range of stimulus sizes, angular orientations, and location in the receptive field. These findings demonstrate that there are individual neurons in the visual system selectively tuned to the holistic patterns of complex stimuli and that serve as detectors of objects characterized by such patterns. Recall that the synaptic matrix model assumes the visual detection mechanism can be thought of as a comb filter within which individual filter cells are selectively tuned to the complex stimulus patterns of significant objects. In addition, pattern recognition in the synaptic matrix occurs after the centroid of an object's representation on a retinoid has been shifted to the normal foveal axis, differential response in tuned filter cells appears to be rather robust over pattern rotation, and the model includes explicated neuronal mechanisms for normalizing pattern size before input to the detection matrix. Thus, the selective responsivity of a filter cell can be effectively maintained despite changes in the position, size, or rotation of an object in the visual field. These properties of the putative synaptic matrix–retinoid system are consistent with the response characteristics of individual neurons in the inferior temporal cortex reported by Desimone and his co-workers.

Damage to the hippocampus or fornix is known to impair the performance of a conditional spatial response task in both monkey and humans. A task of this kind was used together with direct microelectrode recording to investigate the response properties of single neurons in the hippocampus of rhesus monkeys (Miyashita et al. 1989). The animal learned to make a particular spatial (motor) response when one visual stimulus was presented on a video monitor and a different response when a different stimulus was shown. Of 905 single hippocampal cells studied, 14 percent fired differentially to one or the other of the visual-stimulus spatial response associations. Responsive neurons were found throughout the hippocampal structure but were particularly concentrated in the subicular complex and in area CA3. The investigators concluded that single hippocampal neurons respond selectively to combinations of visual stimuli and the specific motor responses with which they must become associated. This finding gives strong support to the proposed model for selective association of an arbitrary sensory input and a discrete motor routine gating output through the adaptive interface of a synaptic matrix.

Motter and Mountcastle (1981) conducted an extensive single-unit study of light-sensitive (LS) neurons in the inferior parietal lobule of the monkey. They found that the LS cells are sensitive to stimulus movement and the direction of movement over a wide range of velocities. Response was specific to motion that was directed either inward toward the center of the visual field or outward toward the perimeter of the field. In cells with bilateral response fields, motion vectors commonly pointed in opposite directions in the two visual hemifields.

On the basis of their findings, Motter and Mountcastle suggested that LS neurons in the inferior parietal area of the brain "contribute to a continual update of a central neural image of the spatial frame of the immediate behavioral surround and to the perceptual constancy of that space that obtains during body movement." They concluded, "The light-sensitive neurons possess properties suitable for the attraction of gaze and attention toward objects and events in peripheral visual fields." It is clear that the response properties of these parietal neurons meet the dynamic requirements for an environmentally linked input to the shift control mechanism of the retinoid system that will translate images and move the focus of attention (self-locus excursion) within an egocentric frame.

The spatial memory functions of neurons in the dorsolateral prefrontal cortex were investigated in an oculomotor delayed-response task (Funahashi, Bruce, and Goldman-Rakic 1989). Rhesus monkeys were trained to fixate a central target during the presentation of a brief (0.5 second) peripheral visual cue and through a subsequent delay period of 1 to 6 seconds, which was terminated by the extinction of the fixation target, and then to make a saccade to the remembered location of the peripheral cue. Recordings of the activity in single cells within the prefrontal cortex were obtained during the performance of the task. A large proportion of the neurons within and around the principal sulcus and in the frontal eye fields exhibited significant changes in activity during the delay period between the offset of the cue and the visual saccade to its remembered location. Of these cells, most were directionally selective; they exhibited a significant response only following cues in localized regions of the visual field. The investigators concluded that:

1. Prefrontal neurons possess information about the location of visual cues.
2. Information provided by these neurons "appears to be in a labeled line code: different neurons code different cue locations and the same neuron repeatedly codes the same location."
3. These cells exhibit mnemonic activity over a 1- to 6-second interval in the absence of any overt stimuli or movements and

the activity ceases upon the execution of the required behavioral response.
4. "These results strengthen the evidence that the dorsolateral prefrontal cortex participates in the process of working or transient memory and further indicate that this area of the cortex contains a complete 'memory map' of visual space."

The hypothesized neuronal mechanisms of the retinoid system provide just this kind of representation of visual space in short-term memory. Moreover, the retinoid's spatial map is organized in egocentric coordinates—a necessary property for effective visuomotor behavior. In addition to supporting the putative retinoid system, the short-term mnemonic activity of labeled-line cells that has been reported by Funahashi and co-workers lends physiological credence to the other postulated neuronal circuits in the cognitive brain that are organized around short-term memory registers (see, for example, figures 5.9, 8.1, and 8.3).

Excursion of the self-locus over autaptic cells in the retinoid system is assumed to be the biophysical substrate of directed attention over egocentric visual space. Translation of the self-locus to a target region of interest serves (among other functions) to increase the sensitivity of neuronal response to stimuli in the attended region and to direct visual saccades to the target. Andersen and Mountcastle (1983) reported experimental results that link directed visual attention and angle of gaze to the excitability of light-sensitive neurons in the posterior parietal cortex of the macaque monkey. Following up on this work, Andersen, Essick, and Siegel (1985) conducted additional studies of the response properties of neurons in the inferior parietal lobule of rhesus monkey. Their results provide physiological support for the self-locus mechanism of selective attention in the retinoid model of visual representation. With the animal's head restrained and a fixation light straight ahead (coordinates 0,0 on a tangent screen), they first established the retinotopic receptive fields of single cells by briefly flashing a second light at various locations on the tangent screen. After this mapping was completed, the animal fixated at different locations on the screen while the same stimulus that was used for mapping was presented at the center of the receptive field of each cell. It was found that the visual sensitivity of the retinotopic receptive fields changed systematically with the angle of gaze. There was an eye-position-dependent tuning for stimulus location in a head-centered (egocentric) coordinate space. In the retinoid model, the angle of gaze is normally systematically related to the target coordinates of a self-locus excursion, and simple reversal of these coordinates translates an eccentric target to the normal foveal axis. Since retinoid cells around the spatial coordinates of the self-locus automatically receive biasing excitation, the observed selective enhancement of neuronal response as a function of the direction of gaze in a head-centered coordinate space would be expected on the basis of the model.

I have hypothesized that heuristic excursions of the self-locus over retinoid space account for what is commonly called the searchlight of attention. Under certain task demands, the normal coupling of visual fixation to the locus of attention can be interrupted so that the coordinates of fixation and those of the self-locus are dissociated. If the retinoid model of selective attention is correct, it should be possible selectively to facilitate the neuronal response to visual stimuli at targets of attention in arbitrary regions of visual space even while eye position is held constant. A study by Spitzer, Desimone, and Moran (1988) provides direct evidence in support of the retinoid model. Rhesus monkeys were trained on a visual discrimination task with two levels of difficulty. The monkeys maintained fixation on a central target while pairs of visual stimuli (small colored bars) were presented in succession within the receptive fields of single neurons in area V4 of the extrastriate cortex. A sample stimulus appeared for 200 milliseconds, and 400 to 600 milliseconds later a test stimulus was presented at the same location. The animal was required to make one response if the test stimulus was an exact match to the sample and a different response if the test stimulus differed from the sample. In the "easy" discrimination trials, nonmatching test stimuli differed from the samples by either 90 degrees in orientation or 77 nanometers in wavelength. In "difficult" trials, nonmatching test stimuli differed from the samples by 22 degrees in orientation or 19 nanometers in wavelength. An analysis found that the responses of just those neurons mapped to the location of the test stimuli were selectively more vigorous in the difficult task, while at the same time, the monkey's ability to make difficult discriminations improved. The investigators concluded that "increasing the amount of attention directed toward a stimulus can enhance the responsiveness and selectivity of the neurons that process it."

The conditions of this experiment and the conclusions drawn from it support the view that excursions of the self-locus, in the absence of corresponding eye movements, can selectively enhance neuronal responsiveness in the retinoid target region of the self-locus (focal attention). Moreover, if the increased arousal induced by a more difficult task were to increase the excitation of the autaptic cell source of the self-locus (home position at the normal foveal axis), then we would expect a corresponding spatially selective increase in neuronal response in the difficult task (the empirical finding) when the self-locus makes its excursion to the egocentric coordinates of the test stimulus.

Gnadt and Mays (1989) recorded from single neurons in the posterior parietal cortex and superior temporal sulcus of trained rhesus monkeys during task-driven visual-motor behavior. They manipulated the task demands of ocular vergence, accommodation, and binocular disparity and measured vergence and accommodative responses. They found the following kinds of cells:

1. Disparity-sensitive visual tracking cells, related to binocular disparity during visual tracking in depth.
2. Velocity-sensitive motor cells, which reflected the velocity of either ocular vergence or lens accommodation.
3. Visual fixation cells, which modulated their firing rate during changes in conjugate and disjunctive eye position and their response did not depend on the presence of a visual target.
4. Eye-position-dependent visual cells, which were visually responsive cells in which the response was modulated by the conjugate and disconjugate position of the eyes, even though the stimulus fell on the same locations on the two retinae.

These findings demonstrate the existence of cortical neurons with response properties consistent with the assumed properties of shift control cells in the monocular retinoids and in the 3-D retinoid system. The eye-position-dependent visual cells are of particular interest with respect to the putative 3-D retinoid because they provide direct evidence of visually responsive cells tuned in an egocentric three-dimensional coordinate frame of reference.

In the 3-D retinoid model, the egocentric distance of a target is represented by the selective activity of different distance-ordered populations of autaptic cells (Z-planes). For any given distance, the egocentric direction of a target is represented by the selective activity of autaptic cells within the appropriate Z-plane. A recent experiment utilizing chronic microelectrode implants in single cells of the premotor cortex (Karluk and Ebner 1989) supports the hypothesized neuronal architecture of the 3-D retinoid. Rhesus monkeys were trained to move to targets arranged in concentric circles at three distances from a central start box. Analysis of the single-unit responses in relation to target distance and direction revealed that for a given target direction, different populations of cells are recruited for different target distances, and for a given target distance, roughly the same population of cells is activated, while the magnitude of cell discharge within the population varies with the direction of the target.

These findings are consistent with the representation of different distances in the 3-D retinoid by the activation of different populations of cells in their respective Z-planes (Z-plane brightening) and with the representation of different directions by the increased activation of selected cells within a Z-plane population.

Psychological Evidence

All of the work reported in this section studied normal human subjects with no known brain lesions or other significant sensory or motor impairment.

In a follow-up to an earlier study concerning the duration and specificity of memory for events occurring during the first year of life (Myers, Clifton, and Clarkson, 1987) two groups of children who had one learning experience at the age of 6.5 months were tested one or two years later (Perris, Myers, and Clifton 1988). During the original learning occasion, each child had reached in the light and in the dark for a sounding toy that was positioned at five different locations in front of the child: midline, 30 and 60 degrees left, and 30 and 60 degrees right. After an interval of one or two years, the children were tested in the dark only for memory of this experience. It was found that both groups of these children were significantly more likely to reach and grasp the sounding toy than age-matched control groups of children without the single early experience. The investigators concluded that, after a single infant experience, children retain memory for that experience at least as long as two years later. These results are consistent with the rapidity and long-term stability of synaptic modification (learning) in my model of the synaptic matrix.

Object recognition by the visual-cognitive mechanisms that I have proposed can be accomplished solely on the basis of the stimulus contours or edges that are extracted from the brightness distribution of the retinal image by center-surround processes at the retina and other low-level visual preprocessors. Biederman and Ju (1988) performed a series of experiments aimed at uncovering the principle determinants of visual recognition. They presented to their subjects slides of common objects to be named or verified against a target name as quickly as possible. Each object was shown as a full-color photograph (all surface properties displayed) and as a simplified line drawing of the object's major components (only contours displayed). Mean reaction times and error rates were found to be virtually identical for the two types of stimuli. Surface features such as color, brightness, and texture did not contribute to the speed or accuracy of recognition performance. The investigators concluded that "initial access to a mental representation of an object can be modeled as a matching of an edge-based representation of a few simple components." This conclusion is clearly in agreement with the processes of object recognition in the synaptic matrix.

Shepard and Metzler (1971) conducted a landmark experiment that probed an important aspect of the mental transformation of visual objects. Subjects were shown pairs of perspective line drawings of unfamiliar three-dimensional objects at various orientations. Half of the pairs of objects could be rotated so that their shapes would be congruent with each other (objects the same). The other half of the object pairs differed by a reflection as well as rotation and could not be rotated into congruence. Half of the pairs differed by rotation about a vertical axis; the other half differed by rotation in the picture plane. Angular differences between the paired objects ranged from 0 to 180 degrees. At the presentation of each stimulus pair, subjects were required to signal as quickly as possible whether the objects were the same or different. It was found that the time required to recognize two perspective drawings as depicting an object of the same three-dimensional shape was a linearly increasing function of the angular difference between the two depicted objects. Subjects seemed to perform actual mental rotations of analog representations of the objects in order to test for congruence of shape. Shepard and his co-workers explored phenomena of this kind in many different experiments. The findings consistently suggested an internal process that actively transforms spatial analogs of perceived objects within a two- or three-dimensional spatial frame (Shepard and Cooper 1982). These results and other related studies (Koriat and Norman 1988) lend support to the analog nature of visual representation in the retinoid system and in the mosaic array, the 3-D to 2-D axonal projection from the 3-D retinoid system to the mosaic array, and the local mechanisms for stepwise spatial transformation of excitation patterns in the retinoid system and in the rotation transformer.

Imagination is a powerful and extremely important cognitive faculty that distinguishes the human species (Ferguson 1977, Shepard 1978). The putative neuronal circuitry of the synaptic matrix provides an essential mechanism for the basic processes of imagination. Discharge of a class cell token of a previously learned object or scene can evoke a retinotopically organized pattern of afferent excitation that corresponds to the afferent pattern induced at the original perception of the object. This happens because of a selective reorganization of synaptic transfer weights that automatically occurs in the imaging matrix during learning. Thus, in my proposed model of the cognitive brain, imagination is a neuronal process having the retinotopic spatial coherence (but not normally the intensity or detail) of ordinary vision (Trehub 1977, 1987).

Over the past two decades, the nature of imagery has been a focus of considerable experimental effort and lively theoretical controversy (Paivio 1971, Pinker and Kosslyn 1983, Pylyshyn 1973, Sheikh 1983). Kosslyn (1980) has undertaken a long-term program of research devoted to the study of imagery. He and his research collaborators have contributed an extensive experimental literature that is relevant to the hypothesized imagery mechanisms in my model of the cognitive brain.

A series of experiments by Kosslyn, Ball, and Reiser (1978) demonstrated that as the distance across a visual image increases, more time is required to scan across the image. This was true even when the amount of visual detail between the starting focus on the image and the final target focus was the same. It was found that the relationship between scanning time and the relative distance between target objects is a linear one. Subjectively larger images required more time to scan than similar but subjectively smaller images. These results are precisely what one would expect according to the neuronal model. An image is first evoked on the array of mosaic cells in the imaging matrix, projected to the retinoid system, and then scanned by translating the retinoid image over the afferent aperture to the detection matrix that is centered on the normal foveal axis (Trehub 1977).

The relationship between the subjective size of an imaged object and the imagined distance at which it is "viewed" was explored in a number of experiments (Kosslyn 1978). Subjects were instructed to imagine an object far off in the distance and then to imagine moving toward it until all of the object could not be seen in a single image (overflow). It was found that as subjects "approached" objects, their subjective size increased, and the larger the imaged object was, the farther away it seemed at the point of overflow. Thus, subjects could imagine moving closer to a beaver than to an elephant before experiencing subjective overflow. In terms of the visual-cognitive mechanisms that I have modeled, overflow would occur when the size of an image exceeds the bounds of the afferent aperture. The progressive expansion of the subjective size of the image would result from a neuronal linkage of the self-locus with the size transformer. When an object is first imagined far in the distance, one of its exemplars is evoked in the imaging matrix reduced in size, and projected to a distant Z-plane in the 3-D retinoid. Moving toward an object in imagination corresponds to a self-locus excursion to the Z-plane coordinate of the imagined object. As the self-locus crosses successive Z-planes in its movement toward the "distant" object, it activates the size transformer at each crossing, causing a corresponding succession of incremental expansions in the size of the imaged exemplar. Since the size of the initial image will vary with the intrinsic size of the object imaged, the number of Z-planes crossed by the self-locus in "approaching" the object before the size transformer causes an image overflow will be inversely proportional to the intrinsic size of the imagined object. Thus, the self-locus can get closer to a beaver than to an elephant before overflow is experienced. Put another way, the larger the imaged object is, the farther away it will seem at the point of overflow.

Another series of experiments (Kosslyn et al. 1983) explored the process of amalgamating image units that are stored in memory into a composite form or scene. The principal findings were that:

1. Mental images can be constructed by assembling separate images of individual parts.
2. An increment of time is required to add each additional part to an image.
3. Verbal description can be used to coordinate parts into an imaged scene.
4. Multipart images are assembled by the inspection of parts already in the image.
5. The time required to integrate an image part into a larger image is not a constant.

All of these results can be explained by normal operation of the neuronal mechanisms detailed in earlier chapters. Parts of images (called image units by Kosslyn et al.) are stored in the distribution of synaptic weights (ϕ) over mosaic cells (M) in the imaging matrix. These image parts are activated one at a time by the discharge of their associated class cells (Ω) in the detection matrix and then projected from the mosaic cells to the retinoid system. Each successive part of a complex image is captured on the autaptic cells of a retinoid layer, translated to its proper spatial coordinate, and projected to the scene assembly retinoid where the complete image is constructed (finding 1 above). For multipart images, iteration of the neuronal operation is required. Thus, it is clear that an increment of time will be needed to integrate each additional part within the larger image (finding 2). Given the connective architecture between the synaptic matrix and the networks for lexical assignment and semantic processing, lexical descriptions can evoke selected image components as well as their relative coordinate locations on the scene assembly retinoid surface (finding 3). As a complex image is being constructed, it can be inspected (analyzed) by parallel projections from the retinoid system to the synaptic matrix and to the mechanisms for analyzing object relations (finding 4). Inspection of this kind can signal what parts are missing (to be recalled for image completion) and where they should be located with respect to the parts already assembled. One would expect that the more complex the image is to be assembled, the longer will be the inspection time to determine what parts are still missing, what the next image part should be, and where it should be located. Thus, the time required to integrate an image part into a larger image would not be a constant (finding 5).

The results of Cave and Kosslyn's (1989) study of size-scaling processes in visual selection fit nicely with the specific properties of the neuronal scaling mechanisms that I have assumed to exist in the visual system. Subjects were required to evaluate visual stimuli of varying sizes under conditions designed to influence their expectations about the stimuli. The general finding was that when an upcoming stimulus is expected to be a certain size, response time increases with the disparity between the expected size and the actual size. At any given time, the visual system seems set to process information at a particular scale, which can be adjusted to match the size of an object. Beyond this basic result, however, the data indicated that two different kinds of size adjustment processes are involved in size scaling: a slow type of size scaling that is shape specific and can filter out a visual object from a superimposed distractor (see Trehub 1977, 1987) and a faster type that is not shape specific.

Cave and Kosslyn's conclusion that there are two different kinds of size-scaling processes in the visual system conforms to the two kinds of size transformation mechanisms that I have hypothesized. Recall that in my neuronal model of the visual-cognitive system, the size transformer iteratively expands or contracts a ring-ray representation of an object (Trehub 1977, 1987). This is done by transferring a shape-specific pattern of excitation to progressively larger or smaller afferent rings one step at a time. Stepwise size transformations of this kind are necessarily time-intensive processes. However, there is a second size-scaling mechanism with different properties—the neuronal circuitry between Z-planes in the 3-D retinoid system and the mosaic cell array that accounts for size constancy. Any object represented on a given Z-plane will automatically project to the mosaic array at a scale factor associated with that retinoid plane. The nearer the Z-plane is, the smaller is the scale factor, and vice versa. If we assume that visual information is optimally processed at some standard representational size, then small stimuli should be scaled up to standard and large stimuli should be scaled down to standard. On these grounds, when a small object is expected, a distant Z-plane is primed to capture its excitation pattern so that it will be relatively larger at its projection on the mosaic cell array; when a large object is expected, a near Z-plane is primed so that the projected pattern will be relatively smaller at the mosaic cell array. Because each Z-plane can be independently addressed and primed without requiring the sequential transfer of excitation over neighboring cells on the Z-axis, scale adjustment can be much faster than in the size transformer mechanism.

The influence of parafoveal information on response to foveal information was explored in a series of experiments aimed at gaining a better understanding of cognitive processing during reading (Rayner, McConkie, and Ehrlich 1978; Rayner, McConkie, and Zola 1980). Subjects were presented with a word or letter string in the parafoveal visual field and then, during the saccade to this location, the initial display was replaced by a word that the subject was asked to read. Thus, a parafoveal stimulus was replaced by a word that stimulated the fovea and that the subject had to pronounce as quickly as possible. The visual, lexical, and semantic similarity between the initial parafoveal stimulus and the word to be named was varied. It was found that certain kinds of parafoveal information facilitated the naming of the target word. In particular, facilitation depended on the match between the first two or three letters in the first string and the subsequent word. The matching letters did not have to be the same shape or size to produce facilitation. For example, if the target word was presented in lowercase letters, the preceding parafoveal string would facilitate naming even if it was an uppercase display provided that its initial letters signified the same substring of alphabetical characters that formed the beginning of the target word. The finding that parafoveal lexical information can be integrated with subsequent foveal lexical information is consistent with the operating characteristics of the retinoid–synaptic matrix system. According to the model, the results can be explained as follows:

1. Initial parafoveal letter strings are captured on a retinoid and translated to the normal foveal axis.
2. The translated parafoveal letter patterns are projected to the detection matrix where they selectively excite filter cell–class cell couplets (object tokens) that have previously learned those patterns.
3. Object tokens of letter patterns provide the input to the matrix

for lexical assignment where they selectively excite their associated word tokens.
4. Excitation of a word token provides a facilitating bias (prime) for that word.
5. The initial letter strings of foveal target words are also processed by steps 1–4. If the initial letters of a target word match those of the immediately preceding parafoveal string, its appropriate word token will have been primed by the preceding string, and word naming will be facilitated (the empirical finding).

Similar neuronal processes can explain the integration of pictorial information across eye movements. In a series of experiments (Pollatsek, Rayner, and Collins 1984), line drawings of objects were presented in peripheral vision. During the saccade to the peripheral stimulus, the initially presented picture was replaced by another that the subject was instructed to name as quickly as possible. There was a significant facilitation in response time when the first and second pictures were identical compared to conditions in which the second picture was a different object or to a control in which only the target location was specified on the first stimulus. Changing the size of the picture from the first to the second stimulus had little effect on naming time. When two differently shaped pictures represented the same concept, there was also a significant facilitation effect. The results are consistent with the priming of object tokens in the detection matrix and word tokens in the matrix for lexical assignment on the basis of similarity of stimulus shapes and/or conceptual equivalence.

Morrison and Rayner (1981) asked subjects to read sentences presented on a CRT at different viewing distances while their eye movements were monitored. Sentences at different distances contained different lexical items, but they were matched for word length and grammatical class. It was discovered that there was no significant increase in the number of character spaces traversed by each visual saccade over viewing distances of 36, 53, and 71 centimeters. The average saccade traversed approximately 5.5 characters at each distance. The mean saccade sizes corresponded to visual angles of 3.81, 2.48, and 2.00 degrees at the three distances respectively. Thus, there was a roughly linear inverse relationship between the length of a saccade and the distance of the visual targets. If, during reading, the parsing of five or six characters at a time is optimal for word recognition and comprehension, one would expect saccade size to decrease as the viewing distance of a text increases. This fits in well with the 3-D retinoid–synaptic matrix mechanisms. The more distant lexical characters would normally be represented by autaptic cell activity on a more distant Z-plane. The particular Z-plane that is activated during reading can provide a neuronal signal that regulates saccade length. Long saccades for near Z-plane activation; short saccades for far Z-plane activation. At the same time, the size-constancy scaling from the 3-D retinoid to the mosaic array of the synaptic matrix will maintain a pattern of input to the detection matrix that will be near optimal size for word recognition despite differences in reading distance.

Additional support for the 3-D retinoid and its accessory mechanisms is provided by a series of experiments undertaken to explore the sort of medium that underlies imagery for 3-D scenes (Pinker 1980, Pinker and Finke 1980). The time that a subject took after viewing a 3-D scene to scan between objects in a mental image of the scene was used to infer the kind of geometric information preserved in the image. On the basis of clear performance differences associated with different kinds of imagery instructions, it was concluded that 3-D information must be preserved in images, 2-D distance information in the original perspective view must also be preserved, and images can be transformed to display 2-D distance information in perspective views never experienced in the stimulus situation.

Pinker (1980) proposed that these results can be explained by a model in which 3-D structure is encoded in long-term memory in a 3-D object-centered coordinate system and mapped onto a 2-D "display" when imaged. Perspective properties specific to a given viewing angle would then be depicted on the 2-D display. The 3-D retinoid–synaptic matrix system and the putative neuronal mechanisms for analyzing and representing object relations conform to this kind of model. The full retinoid system has the capability of representing veridical or imagined objects and scenes and transforming these representations through 3-D space. It has intrinsic axonal projections that map from the 3-D Z-planes to the 2-D mosaic cell array. The mechanisms for analysis and representation of object relations that are specified in my brain model provide 3-D coordinate tokens that can be selectively attached to the visual objects stored in the long-term memory of the synaptic matrix. When objects in the original 3-D scene are later imaged, these X-, Y-, and Z-axis tokens govern the placement coordinates of the object images in 3-D retinoid space. Excursions of the self-locus to the targets at these coordinates and the reverse translation of target objects to the normal foveal axis provide the neuronal means for scanning over the metric distances between objects in 3-D and 2-D retinoid space.

In an investigation of another aspect of mental imagery, subjects were shown an array of dots followed by an arrow in an otherwise blank field and asked to determine if the arrow pointed to any of the previously seen dots (Finke and Pinker 1983; Pinker, Choate, and Finke 1984). Instructions to form or scan a mental image were never given; nevertheless, subjects almost always reported that they scanned a mental image to make a judgment. Response times were linearly related to the metric distance between the arrow and the nearest dot. After conducting a number of control variants of the basic experimental paradigm, the investigators concluded that "mental scanning along a straight path can be performed on images reconstructed from memory." They also concluded that such mental extrapolations over image patterns did not depend on the perception of a continuous surface or on eye movements.

A neuronal explanation for these findings is provided by the intrinsic properties of the retinoid–synaptic matrix system and the ability of the heuristic self-locus to trace the contours of objects in retinoid space. According to my proposed model, when the array of dots is briefly shown to subjects, it is learned as an arrangement of objects (dots) at a particular egocentric location in the visual field. After the delay period, when the arrow alone is shown, subjects recall the previous dot arrangement as a pattern of excitation in the imaging matrix and project it at its original coordinates in retinoid space. The retinoid surface will now hold a spatially integrated representation of the imaged dots together with the current arrow stimulus within the same coordinate frame. A straight-line trace in the direction of the arrow head along and beyond the shaft of the arrow by an excursion of the self-locus will either hit (response "yes") or miss (response "no") one of the dots in the imaged array. Assuming a uniform rate of self-locus translation, the time taken to give a correct "yes" response should be a linear function of the distance between the arrow head and the imagined dot that it points to (tracing distance), a prediction confirmed by the experimental results. Thus, the proposed brain model can explain in neuronal terms how people can make mental extrapolations in visual patterns constructed from memory.

Two experiments employing somewhat different paradigms (Jolicoeur, Ullman, and MacKay 1986) give additional support to the self-locus model of contour tracing. In the first experiment, several complex, interdigitated curves were displayed, and the subject's task was to determine as quickly as possible whether two Xs in the display lay on the same or different curves. It was found that the mean response time for a "same" response increased monotonically as the distance along the curve between the Xs increased. In the second experiment, the subject's task was to decide as quickly as possible whether a complex curve joining two Xs was unbroken or had a gap.

Again, response time increased as the length of the curve joining the Xs was increased. According to Jolicoeur and his co-investigators, "The results of both experiments suggest that people can trace curves in a visual display internally at high speed (the average rate of tracing was about 40 degrees of visual angle per second)."

An underlying constraint of the putative retinoid–synaptic matrix system is that environmental scenes are normally learned and stored in memory within an egocentric frame of reference. Experiments by Fredrickson and Bartlett (1987) tend to confirm that people learn and recall scenes within an egocentric frame. In one experiment, subjects first verbally encoded and then verbally recalled the lateral location of objects within scenic pictures that were projected in a room with a door on one side and a window on the other. Object location was encoded in two ways: using an egocentric frame (left or right) and an environmental frame (near the window or near the door). Significantly fewer errors were made when recalling locations in egocentric terms (left or right) than when recalling in environmental terms (near the door or near the window), even if the latter proximities had been verbalized at input.

In a second experiment, subjects first viewed half of a set of projected pictures directly, while the remainder of the pictures, together with their near environment in the room (door, window, post), were viewed in a mirror reflection. Subjects were shown (in direct view) a set of pictures of which half had been seen in the first phase (old items) and half were new items. They were required to detect the new items and to classify the old items in terms of their orientation (same or reversed) with respect to their appearance in the original set. Subjects were divided into two groups. One group (the egocentric group) was told that *same* and *reversed* referred to whether what had been to the right (left) of their visual field was still to the right (left). The other group was told that *same* and *reversed* referred to how the picture was presented on the screen without regard to how it looked to them previously. Performance was found to be much better when orientation was egocentrically defined. The investigators concluded that "encoding lateral orientation of complex pictures is cognitively impenetrable in at least one respect: It is strongly constrained, perhaps absolutely constrained, by a viewer-centered reference frame."

Shulman, Remington, and McClean (1979) performed several experiments to determine whether shifts of visual attention can occur in a continuous analog fashion across the visual field in the absence of eye movements. In their experimental paradigm, four light-emitting diodes (LEDs) were positioned 8 degrees and 18 degrees to the left and to the right of a central fixation point. Subjects were instructed to press a key as soon as any one of the four LEDs was turned on. An arrow pointing left or right was presented at the fixation point. The arrow served as a cue informing the subject that the far LED on the indicated side had a very high probability of being the target light. Thus, the far light on the indicated side was always the expected target light. Subjects were instructed to pay attention to that light but to maintain their fixation on the center. Eye movements were recorded by electrooculograms, and any trial showing eye movement was discarded. Target lights were illuminated at a randomly determined interval following each onset of the cue (arrow). The difference between the reaction time to the far expected light (18 degrees) and to the intermediate light (8 degrees) was measured and plotted as a function of the delay time between the cue and the onset of a target light. Analysis of the data indicated that an intermediate delay time facilitated response to the intermediate light relative to the far (expected) light, whereas a longer delay time facilitated response to the far light relative to the intermediate light. This result suggests that the focus of visual attention moves through space in a continuous analog fashion.

In a variation of the experimental paradigm employed by Shulman and colleagues, Tsal (1983) confirmed and extended their conclusions. Tsal's data suggest that when attention is directed to a peripheral target, it moves through visual space at a constant velocity of ~1 degree per 8 milliseconds. The results of both studies are consistent with the neuronal mechanism of directed attention that I have proposed: heuristic excursions of the self-locus evoke a "spotlight" of local excitatory bias that moves over retinoid space in a continuous analog fashion from the normal foveal axis (the home position of the self-locus) to the peripheral target.

Experiments by Chambers and Reisberg (1985) and by Finke, Pinker, and Farah (1989) provide interesting examples of both a specific limitation and a high degree of flexibility in manifestations of human imagery, which can be seen as natural consequences of the putative retinoid–imaging matrix mechanism. In the study reported by Chambers and Reisberg, subjects were shown ambiguous figures that have been traditionally employed to demonstrate multistability in visual perception. They were then instructed to form mental images of these shapes and to try to see reversals in their images. It was found that reversals of the imaged figures that are normally experienced under the condition of direct perception were never reported by the subjects. Why should this be the case? Recall that perceptual reversal of ambiguous shapes is fully explained by shifts in the capture of pattern centroids during visual parsing of the overall figure. Normal operation of the hypothesized neuronal mechanisms results in the alignment of different centroids of an extended figure on the normal foveal axis as a consequence of shifts in the locus of visual fixation on the stimulus pattern at different times. In the usual perception of unstable figures, the partial pattern that is automatically parsed (captured within the afferent aperture) in association with a particular centroid will trigger an object token (class cell) appropriate to its particular shape and different pattern parts will evoke different object tokens (figure reversal). However, whenever a single object is imaged, it can be represented only on the mosaic array oriented around one centroid—the one at which it was learned and stored in the synaptic memory of the imaging matrix. Thus, in simple imagery, there are no alternative parsings of the object pattern that can spontaneously evoke alternative object interpretations.

It would be a mistake, however, to conclude from Chambers and Reisberg's study that new patterns cannot be "seen" in the form of an image. When the full capabilities of the transformer circuits, the retinoid system, and aperture control are utilized, then spatial transformations, analytical decomposition of unitary image patterns, constructive and destructive modification of a source pattern, controlled assembly of multiple component images, and retinoid tracings of the self-locus can all contribute to reconstruals of old images or the creation of entirely novel images. The series of experiments by Finke, Pinker, and Farah (1989) clearly demonstrated that initial visual patterns in mental imagery can be transformed and combined with other images in response to verbal instructions so that emergent imaginal objects are induced and recognized. In their most rigorous procedure, subjects were first instructed to imagine a familiar pattern—for example, a square or the capital letter H. Then they were instructed to perform a series of changes of the original imagined figure such as spatial transformations and pattern additions or deletions. After each instructional step, subjects were asked to inspect their images and guess the identity of the final emergent pattern—for example, "Imagine a capital letter 'D'. [Guess 1] Rotate the figure 90 degrees to the left. [Guess 2] Now place a capital letter 'J' at the bottom. [Final identification]."

The complete set of transformations for this experiment is illustrated in figure 15.1. It was found that emergent patterns were never identified at the end of the first step and were identified only 4.2 percent of the time at the end of the second step. But when the sequence of imaginal transformations was correctly performed (48 trials), a significant proportion of correct identifications were made

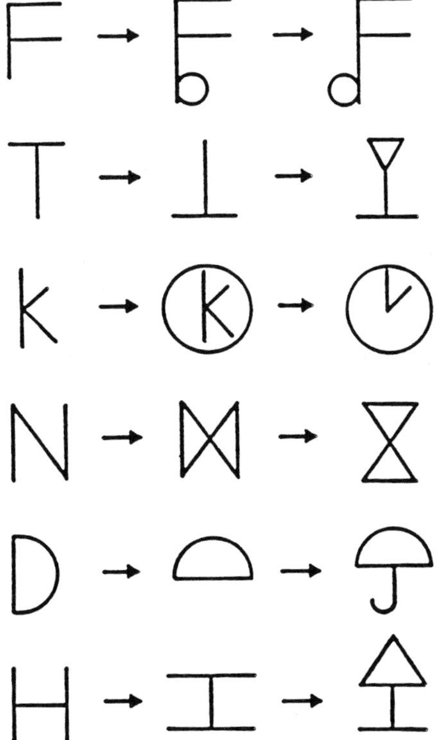

Figure 15.1
Subjects were instructed to begin by imagining the patterns shown at the left of each row and then to imagine transforming the patterns as the illustration depicts. The final patterns in each sequence are the emergent patterns that subjects were to try to recognize. Source: Finke, Pinker, and Farah 1989. Copyright Cognitive Science Society, Inc. Reproduced by permission.

after the third step (44 percent). These results are consistent with the capability for imaginal transformation, reconstruction, and recognition inherent in the putative neuronal mechanisms that I have described.

Clinical Evidence

Clinical investigations of the effects of localized brain pathology on cognitive performance can illuminate both the functional topology of the brain and the issue of functional modularity—the degree to which an identified cognitive process can be dissociated from other related processes. My cognitive brain model is a complex biological system composed of many intercommunicating special-purpose neuronal mechanisms. A system of this kind is characterized by a high degree of modularity in distinction from systems that might operate on the basis of global distributed processes. When there is localized damage in such a modular brain architecture, one would expect that dissociated functional loss would often occur, and, in fact, there is abundant evidence in the clinical literature that this is the case (Brown 1989).

In a review of specific deficits of visual gnosis, Benson (1989) cites a variety of dissociated failures of function associated with brain damage. For example, patients having apperceptive visual agnosia are unable to name, copy, or recognize visually presented objects but can immediately identify the object if they are given tactile or auditory cues. At the same time, they are able to identify light intensity and the direction and dimension of visual stimuli. This disorder can be explained by discrete damage of neurons in the detection matrix or to its afferent channel. In another class of disorders, patients are able to copy words but unable to read them (alexia).

In terms of the synaptic matrix model, such a condition can arise if filter cells that have been tuned (in prior learning) to the visual pattern of words or their coupled class cells that constitute word tokens are damaged. The same syndrome would also result if the cellular interface between word tokens in the synaptic matrix and mosaic cells in the lexical assignment matrix were disconnected by brain pathology (localized lesion, neoplasm, or vascular deficit). Another specific clinical deficit cited by Brown is in the ability to make simple constructions on the basis of visual stimulus patterns. He reports a relatively pure visual-spatial discrimination loss in patients with focal damage in the right parietal-occipital area of the brain and a language-dependent construction loss with left parietal damage. Pure visual-spatial deficits would be expected to occur with damage to the mechanisms for coordinate location on the representational surfaces of the retinoid module, while a specific loss in language-dependent construction would result from an interruption of normal projections from lexical matrices to the cells that govern object location on the scene-assembly retinoid.

Topographagnosia and environmental agnosia are two interesting pathologies that would seem to implicate the accessory control mechanisms of the retinoid system in one disorder and the recollection of previously schematized spatial representations in the other. Individuals with topographagnosia are typically able to perform normally in real-life situations (drive long distances, navigate city streets) but are unable to interpret artificial displays of topography. They cannot place their own location on a map, draw a plan of their own house, or identify rooms on a plan drawn for them. These patients typically show right parietal lobe damage. In chapter 7, I detailed the neuronal mechanisms that work together with the retinoid system to enable analysis and schematic representations of visual space. It would appear that topographagnosia results from damage to these mechanisms.

Patients with environmental agnosia are able to read maps and house plans but are unable to find their way in familiar environments. They can get lost even in their own homes. In this case, brain pathology always involves the medial aspects of the right occipital lobe (Landis et al. 1986). The phenomenon can be explained by an interruption of axon collaterals from the detection matrix for local stimuli to the imaging matrix of another module, which normally evokes the previously associated schematic representation of the spatial-environmental context.

Riddoch and Humphreys (1989) report patients who appeared to have lost all experience of 3-D vision although their 2-D vision remained intact. These individuals perceive the world as utterly flat. In such cases, one would expect that the 3-D retinoid system is severely damaged or disconnected while the monocular retinoids function properly.

A striking as well as informative example of a specific representational deficit in patients with brain lesions involving the right temporal-parietal-occipital junction has been reported by Bisiach and Luzzatti (1978). These patients were asked to imagine they were standing in a very familiar setting, the main square in Milan. They were first to imagine themselves facing the cathedral and to describe what they could see in their mind's eye. They reported a greater number of details to the right than to the left of their imaginary line of sight and often neglected salient aspects on the left side. They were then asked to perform the same imagery task facing in the opposite direction, away from the cathedral. In this case, they were able to report previously neglected details within the right half of the new imaginal perspective but ignored items in the left half that they had reported a few moments before. This example of unilateral neglect indicates that the deficit is not due to a loss of sensory input, a fault in sensory processing, or a discrete memory loss but rather to a failure in the internal representation of egocentric space or in the ability to classify objects represented within a particular region of egocentric space. The cognitive deficit can be explained by damage to the left hemifield of the retinoid system (representational loss), selective damage to that part of the shift control mechanism that translates retinoid images from left to right in order to bring them to the normal foveal axis for detection and classification in the synaptic

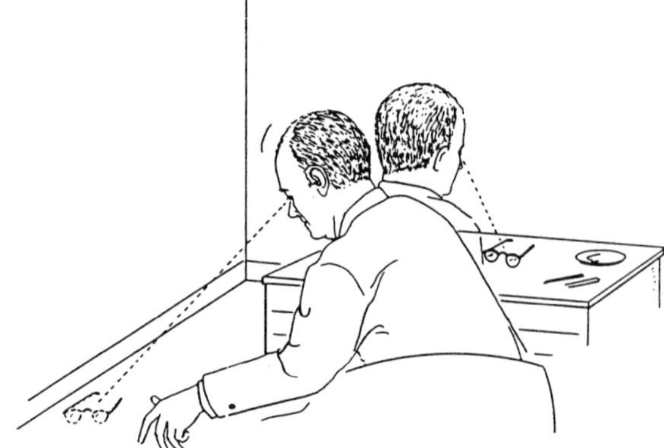

Figure 15.2
Palinopsia. Patient initially viewed his eyeglasses placed horizontally on a desk in front of him. Seconds later he looked away but continued to see an image of the eyeglasses to his left on the floor. Source: Jacobs 1989. Copyright Lawrence Erlbaum Associates, Inc. Reproduced by permission.

matrix (analytical loss), or selective damage to that part of the shift control mechanism that drives the self-locus into the left hemifield of retinoid space (attentional loss).

While perceptual-cognitive deficits constitute the typical sequelae of brain damage, intrusive perceptual anomalies can also occur. Palinopsia is a particularly interesting instance of such an anomaly in the visual domain. It is characterized by the persistence or recurrence of a visual percept after the exciting stimulus object has been removed and is usually associated with lesions in the parieto-occipital region (Bender, Feldman, and Sobin 1968; Jacobs 1989; Michel and Troost 1980). An example of the kind of intrusive visual experience typical in the palinopsic patient is given in the following case report (Jacobs 1989):

> On one occasion he initially saw his eyeglasses placed horizontally before him on a desk. Seconds later, after turning away, the eyeglasses were no longer in view, but he continued to see an image of them off to his left on the floor (figure 15.2). The illusory eyeglasses appeared so realistic that he reached out attempting to pick them up from the floor before he realized that they were still there on the desk in front of him. He continued to see an image of the eyeglasses in his left visual field wherever he looked for the next five minutes.

If one were still undecided about the essential visuo-spatial nature of visual imagery (Farah 1988), the evidence of palinopsia leaves little doubt that images share the spatially extended property of normal visual perception. But can palinopsia be explained in neuronal terms—specifically by the properties of the mechanisms in our putative cognitive brain model?

What mainly distinguish the palinopsic image from normal imagery are its vividness (to the point of being mistaken for an actual visual percept) and its involuntary persistence; in addition, the image seems to be located wherever the focus of gaze comes to rest in the immediate environment. Recall that an image is normally evoked in the synaptic matrix when an axon collateral of an activated class cell induces the pattern of discharge in the mosaic cell array that was present at the time the original stimulus object was learned. Suppose that local cell irritation associated with a lesion in the visual system were to result in phasic hyperexcitation of the synaptic matrix. Under this abnormal condition, a perceived object would immediately be learned; it would be stored in the synaptic transfer weights of a filter cell and on the mosaic cells in the imaging matrix through a coupling class cell. Moreover, the lesion-induced hyperexcitation would induce a more vigorous response in the imaging matrix than one would experience in normal imagery, and this could account for the abnormal vividness of the palinopsic image. In addition, the class cell that evokes the palinopsic image would be locked in sustained discharge during the phase of hyperexcitation, and the patient would be unable to exercise voluntary control of the intrusive image. In accordance with the ordinary operation of the visual-cognitive mechanisms, the visual pattern on the mosaic array would consist of the vivid palinopsic image superposed on normal perceptions transmitted from the retina. Thus, the intrusive object would be "seen" wherever the patient looked. The fact that in palinopsia a visual object can be captured as a vivid memory during a single brief exposure provides strong support for the learning principle of one-trial reorganization of synaptic efficacy that I have assumed to be true of the human brain (Trehub 1975a, Lewis 1979).

Other Mechanisms

In chapters 8 and 9, I presented the circuitry of neuronal mechanisms that are competent for composing, storing, and recalling plans, as well as initiating actions in accordance with concurrent motivational states. These mechanisms are variants of the basic synaptic matrix and adaptively couple sensory tokens with motor-control circuits to construct sequenced plans of action. They are characterized by multimodal inputs representing the convergence of complex multisensory information that defines tokens of environmental affordances, tokens of simple motor commands, and tokens of concurrently activated goals. Outputs serve to select plans of action (latent sensory motor sequences) on the basis of affordances and goals. These neuronal structures, in turn, project to motor regions for the initiation of overt action sequences. Recent investigations by Joaquin Fuster and his co-workers provide direct neurophysiological evidence that tends to support these putative brain mechanisms.

In a study of cross-temporal integration of sensory and sensory motor information, the activity of 295 single neurons was recorded in the dorsolateral prefrontal cortex of rhesus monkeys (Quintana, Yajeya, and Fuster 1988). The monkeys were given two visual discrimination tasks: a delayed matching to sample that required the animal to remember a colored cue to be matched 18 seconds later and a delayed conditional position discrimination that required the animal to remember the color of a cue so that a correct spatial response could be made 18 seconds later. On the basis of their analysis of single unit responses, the investigators concluded:

1. During visual delay tasks, neurons in the dorsolateral prefrontal cortex may process both spatial and nonspatial information.
2. Because of their protracted differential discharge during the delay between cue and response, some units seem involved in the transfer of sensory information across time.
3. The findings suggest that prefrontal neurons have a role in the representation of multiple attributes of sensory stimuli, including their associated motor connotations.
4. The findings are consistent with the role of the prefrontal cortex in the cross-temporal mediation of sensory motor contingencies and the temporal organization of behavior.

The observed properties of cells in the prefrontal cortex fit well with the neuronal details of my hypothesized register for plans and actions; for example (figure 8.3), sustained stimulation of register cells by input from autaptic cells in the step ring would account for their protracted discharge during the delay between cue and response (conclusion 2). Multiple sensory attributes would normally be represented by the activity of register cells that compose specification of the *find* mode, and particular outputs from the register are selective for particular motor routines (conclusion 3). Finally, the hypothesized mechanism provides an explicit neuronal basis for mediating sensory motor contingencies over time and achieving effective temporal organization of behavior (conclusion 4).

A follow-up study was performed to explore the role of behavioral significance on the neuronal representation of stimulus attributes during delay tasks (Yajeya, Quintana, and Fuster 1988). Rhesus monkeys were given two visual discrimination tasks requiring a delayed response after 18 seconds. In both tasks, the correct response depended on the color of a visual cue. Red and green guided the response in one task, yellow and blue in the other. A fifth color (violet) was not relevant to either task and was presented at random in the same location as the significant cues. As in the previous experiment, the activity of 294 single units in the dorsolateral prefrontal cortex was recorded and analyzed. It was found that cellular reactions to the insignificant stimulus were of lesser magnitude than the reactions to the significant cues. Cell response differences as a function of stimulus significance outnumbered and overshadowed differences as a function of cue color or any other task variable. The investigators concluded that neurons in the prefrontal cortex differentiate stimuli by their behavioral significance as well as by other stimulus attributes and that "these results support the notion that the prefrontal cortex integrates motivational inputs into the structure of behavioral action."

Mechanisms detailed in chapter 9 can clearly account for these empirical findings. For example, the neuronal network shown in figure 9.6 selectively enhances cellular response to significant stimuli by providing discrete excitatory bias to just those cells that are relevant to a currently activated motive and by inhibiting the response of other sensory tokens. Figure 9.7 and table 9.1 illustrate how motivational inputs are integrated into the structure of behavioral action by the putative brain mechanisms. Thus, the activity of individual cells in the prefrontal cortex reported by Yajeya and colleagues is consistent with the model.

I have described neuronal mechanisms that can analyze the visually perceived environment, represent pathways within the environment, and formulate plans for navigating the environment, but I have not explicitly dealt with processes whereby the representation of spatial properties of the physical environment might be mediated by nonvisual information. An example of the latter kind of cognitive ability is highlighted in a study by Landau, Gleitman, and Spelke (1981) who demonstrated in a series of experiments that a congenitally blind 2½-year-old child, as well as sighted but blindfolded children and adults, were able to determine the appropriate path between two objects in a room (on a route never before followed by

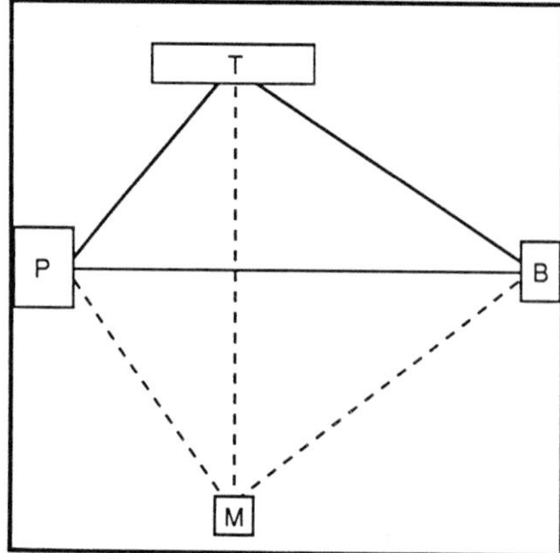

Figure 15.3
Room layout for spatial inference experiment. Dashed lines indicate trained routes. Solid lines indicate test routes. Landmarks: M = mother; P = pillows; T = table; B = basket. After Landau, Gleitman, and Spelke 1981.

the subjects) after traveling under guided locomotion to each of those objects from a third object (figure 15.3). The distances and angular relationships of paths between the initial pairs of target objects were detected and internally represented without visual input, solely on the basis of locomotion. Moreover, potential paths between objects in the environment were apparently "deduced" from the internal motor-generated representation.

This finding can be explained if we assume that the retinoid system may be spared even in congenitally blind individuals and feedback signals from the motor system and/or signals of motion from the vestibular system can control excursions of the self-locus in retinoid space. If these assumptions are true, then the location of objects will be usefully (if not precisely) represented in egocentric retinoid space despite the absence of visual input, and all potential paths among the represented locations can be traced by heuristic excursions of the self-locus. Now we need only assume that these new cognitive-neuronal representations can govern locomotion.

Recall that while the neuronal mechanism of the semantic network is normally accessed by the words of a culture-bound lexicon and its output normally selects words from the contents of such a lexicon, semantic knowledge and the making of logical inferences are intrinsic to the mechanism. It is assumed to be independent of any particular lexicon. A recently reported clinical experiment supports this aspect of the hypothesized semantic network mechanism (Anderson et al.

1989). A left tempero-parietal infarct in a 28-year-old man caused severe aphasia for English. Although the patient had no prior knowledge of American Sign Language (ASL), he was able to acquire ASL at a rate equal to that of an age-matched normal control. This finding was replicated in another patient with left tempero-parietal damage and severe aphasia. The fact that specific semantic knowledge can be readily expressed by a visual-gestural symbolic system after damage to posterior language–related cortices and profound aphasia for English indicates that semantic knowledge is represented in the brain independently of any particular lexicon. This conforms with the assumption of the model.

The logical structure of the semantic network enables two modes of query: (1) defining a subject (evoking a predicate, given a subject) and (2) inferring a subject (evoking a subject, given a predicate). A query of the first kind depends on a direct input to a selected mosaic cell (subject token) in the semantic network. A query of the second kind depends on a direct input to a selected class cell (predicate token) in the network. Because each mode of query is served, in part, by a discrete bundle of neurons, selective brain damage might disrupt the ability to answer one kind of question while sparing the ability to answer the other kind of question. For example, having learned that a bird flies, an individual with focal brain damage that interrupts extramodular excitation of predicate tokens might be able to answer "flies" in response to the question "What does a bird do?" yet be unable to answer "bird" when asked "What flies?" This, at least, is an implication of the brain mechanism for semantic processing that I have hypothesized.

Interestingly, a patient described by Damasio and Tranel (1989) seems to exhibit just this kind of semantic dissociation when tested for his knowledge of cities in states. When the patient was given the names of cities and asked to tell what state each city is in (defining a subject), his performance was accurate. However, when given the names of the states and asked to tell what cities were in the states (inferring a subject), he was almost completely unable to do so. This clinical observation is clearly consistent with the operating principles of the putative semantic network mechanism.

Chapter 16
Overview and Reflections

The goal is to understand in as much detail as possible the biophysical mechanisms and systems of the human brain that account for our cognitive capacities. I presented a partial list of basic cognitive tasks that confront us in our day-to-day activities and that we are able to perform with apparent natural ease. A credible theoretical model of the cognitive brain must specifically address these ecologically relevant tasks and provide evidence of its operational competence in the appropriate cognitive domains. At the same time, the fundamental biophysical and structural assumptions of the model must be plausible in the light of current neurophysiological and neuroanatomical knowledge.

Although the brain model I have proposed does not cover the full range of cognitive processes in each modality, it does explicate a number of plausible neuronal mechanisms serving a variety of essential functions. These mechanisms and systems were shown to be competent for tasks that are critically important in human cognition. In addition, the same putative brain mechanisms predict classical visual illusions and other anomalous perceptions as epiphenomena of their normal operating principles. Moreover, a large and diverse body of experimental and clinical findings can be explained by the biophysical and structural properties of these mechanisms.

The principal functions mediated by the hypothesized mechanisms can be subsumed under the following broad headings: learning and long-term memory, short-term phasic representation, visual cognition (including imagery), semantic processing, planning and composing behavior, and motivation. Neurons are the primitive biological units of which the entire model system is composed. A block-flow diagram of the integrated cognitive brain system is shown in figure 16.1.

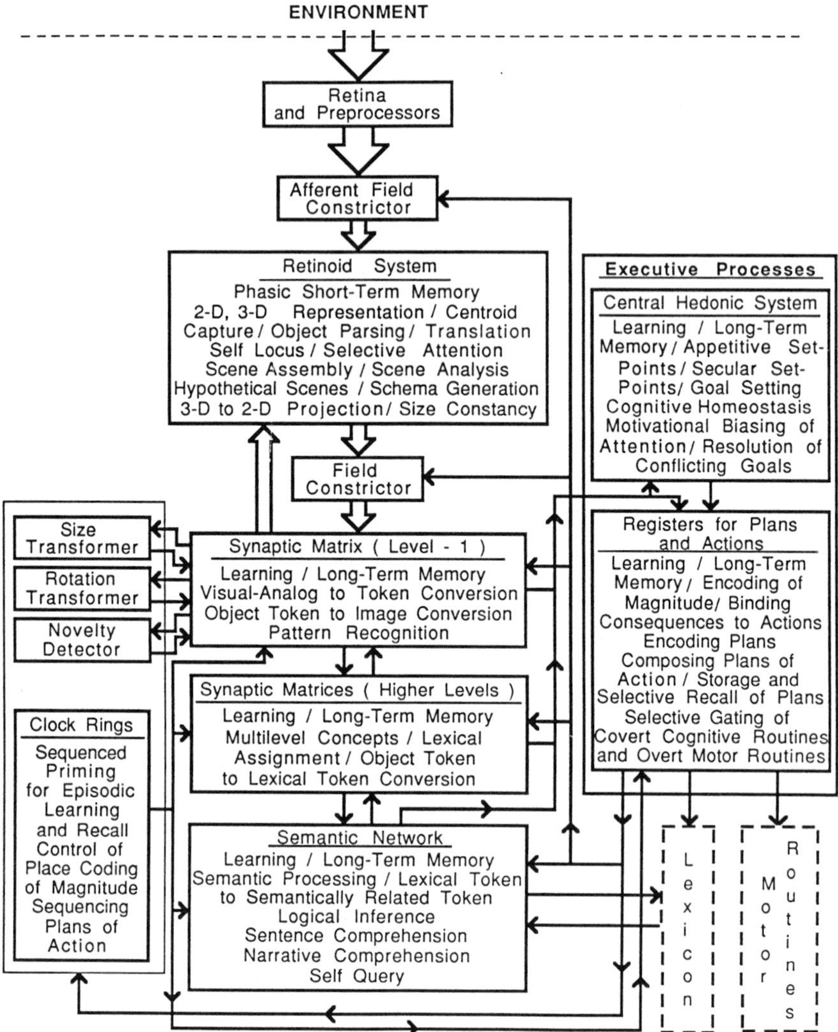

Figure 16.1
Block-flow diagram of the cognitive system.

Learning and Long-Term Memory

The biophysical aspect of learning is a long-term modification (increase) of synaptic transfer weights (ϕ) in selected synapses of adaptive neurons. Learning will occur if and only if coactivation of a pre- and postsynaptic cell results in postsynaptic activity sufficient to result in a reaction between an axon transfer factor (ATF) and a free dendrite transfer factor (DTF) within the postsynaptic dendritic matter. During an ATF-DTF reaction in an adaptive cell, ϕ increases occur only at active synapses, and the peak magnitude of ϕ at each synapse is limited by the amount of DTF that can be utilized at the local receptor region. Whenever learning occurs, ATF makes a small, fixed contribution to the transfer weight of its locally active synapse, whereas a limited store of DTF is distributed over all active synapses and makes a contribution to each that is, up to the local saturation limit, inversely proportional to the number of concurrently active axonal inputs. This latter property causes intrinsic quasi-normalization of the synaptic weight distribution on an adaptive cell and is critical for effective pattern learning and subsequent recognition. These assumptions are reflected in the basic learning formula represented in equation 2.3.

The distribution of synaptic transfer weights on each adaptive cell constitutes its latent memory for the stimulus that it learned (its pattern of axonal inputs). We can think of such a cell as having been tuned to a particular stimulus, which will be more effective than any other in activating the adaptive cell. For this reason, I call a neuron that has been synaptically modified in the course of learning a labeled line.

Another point should be emphasized: learning will not normally occur simply on the basis of coactivation of presynaptic cells and adaptive postsynaptic cells; the concurrent postsynaptic activation must be high enough to exceed a threshold for effective ATF-DTF interaction. I have hypothesized that this is accomplished by auxiliary excitatory priming of adaptive neurons during heightened arousal (Trehub 1975a, 1977) and, for episodic learning, by additional priming from the autaptic cells of a clock ring (Trehub 1983).

Short-Term Phasic Representation

The ability to capture arrayed patterns of excitation or single neuronal events in short-term memory is necessary for a variety of cognitive processes. This capability is assumed to be mediated by autaptic neurons. Cells of this kind have one or more of their axon collaterals in feedback synapse with their own dendrites or cell body. If there is sufficient sustained excitatory bias on such cells from an auxiliary source, a transient stimulus will cause autaptic cells to continue firing even after input from the initiating stimulus has stopped. If the auxiliary bias is removed, however, excitation from its own recurrent axon collateral is insufficient to sustain spike discharge, and the autaptic cell stops firing. Autaptic neurons are key elements in a number of cognitive modules, such as the retinoid system, clock circuits, latching circuits, and mechanisms for mapping stimulus magnitude to labeled lines.

Visual Cognition

The cognitive brain has a remarkable capacity to learn the ecologically significant properties of the visual world and to model these properties within its neuronal structures. Humans are not only able to learn, represent, and analyze environments that they have directly experienced but also are able to construct and analyze internal models of imaginary and novel environments. In my theoretical model of the cognitive brain, this ability is instantiated by the normal operation of a subsystem of explicated neuronal mechanisms, chief among which are the synaptic matrices and the retinoids.

Synaptic Matrix

The synaptic matrix is the basic neuronal mechanism for learning, memory, and imagery. Its adaptive elements are called filter cells and mosaic cells; synaptic modification in these neurons occurs according to the constraints of the learning formula. The synaptic matrix at the first level of visual learning receives its input in the form of a parsed excitation pattern from the retinoid system and maps the pattern as an exemplar of its kind onto a discrete output cell called a class cell, which constitutes a physical symbol or token of the exemplar it has learned. Recurrent axon collaterals of class cells synapse on dendrites of the mosaic cell array in the synaptic matrix. When a class cell is discharged, it evokes an analog image of the exemplar with which it was associated during the course of learning. Thus the brain is able to recall a visual image of a learned object or scene simply by the firing of its class cell token.

Input patterns to the synaptic matrix can be transformed in size and angular orientation by the action of two integrated neuronal circuits, a size transformer and rotation transformer. This enables the system to learn a single exemplar in a variety of sizes and orientations or to transform a given stimulus to test its match against patterns that have been learned.

Higher-level synaptic matrices organize hierarchical conceptual representations by adaptively forming selective synaptic links among neuronal tokens that signal levels of increasing abstraction. For example, class cell tokens of a particular cat and a particular dog may be mapped to a single token that signifies *pet;* tokens of a car and a television set may be mapped to a token that signifies *artifact;* and tokens of both *pet* and *artifact* may be mapped to a yet higher-level token signifying *property.* The normal operating characteristics of the model provide automatic backward chaining among hierarchically organized neuronal tokens down to the first level of sensory image evocation on the mosaic cell array. This means that when a class cell token of a high-level concept is discharged, a neuronal representation (image) of its semantic content is also evoked.

In addition to the ability to learn and recall static semantic representations, the synaptic matrix is capable of learning sequences of tokened experience that are related and rendered meaningful by their temporal contiguity within particular time frames (episodic representations). Episodic learning and recall in which temporal excursions of remembrance can be brought under motivational guidance is achieved by sequential priming of filter cells and class cells. Clock rings and recall rings are the auxiliary mechanisms that provide the priming sequences for episodic representation.

Retinoid System

A retinoid is a reticulated sheet of autaptic cells each joined to its neighbors by excitatory and inhibitory interneurons. It receives retinotopic input from visual afferents and from images on the mosaic cell array of the synaptic matrix. It serves as a visual scratch pad with spatially organized information (patterns of autaptic cell activity) stored as short-term memory. The retinoid also has an important dynamic property in that selective excitatory biasing of its interneurons by shift control cells can move a "captured" pattern of autaptic discharge to any position on a retinoid surface. The complete retinoid system consists of many interconnected retinoid layers with specialized functions. Within subsystems, patterns of autaptic activity on one layer can be projected to other layers and combined with previously captured patterns to compose extended and complex retinoid displays. Output from the central region of the retinoid system is projected to the mosaic cell array of the level-1 synaptic matrix for learning, recognition, or analysis.

Retinoids are spatially organized around a central point of reference, the normal foveal axis. This is the key axis of egocentric reference and corresponds to the line of sight when the eyes and head point straight ahead and the shoulders are square with the upright body. I hypothesize the existence of a specialized retinoid layer, which I call a self-locus retinoid. Within this layer, a spatially compact region of sustained autaptic cell discharge is centered on the normal foveal axis and defines the origin or home position of the self-locus. Selective activation of shift control cells can cause heuristic excursions of self-locus excitation from its home position to other regions of retinoid space. Since spatially focused excitation from the self-locus retinoid can be projected to corresponding coordinates on other retinoid layers, local excitatory priming of the corresponding regions will be induced. This process provides one of the neuronal means for selective attention.

Excursions of the self-locus also provide another way for mediating selective spatial attention. Shifting the heuristic self-locus to a particular region of retinoid space entails a set of shift commands on horizontal and vertical shift control cells. If the self-locus has already settled in a retinoid region, then any subsequent visual target in that area can, by a simple reversal of the shift commands already specified for the self-locus excursion, be immediately translated to the normal foveal axis, where it will be projected to the synaptic matrix for recognition.

The retinoid surface is quadrantally organized so that autaptic cell activity on right and left hemifields and top and bottom hemifields can be independently summed. This property, together with the auxiliary mechanisms of the afferent field constrictor and the hemifield disparity detector, enable the system to parse complex stimulus patterns and to position the centroids of their parsed retinoid representations on the normal foveal axis. As a result of this intrinsic normalizing capability, the number of exemplars of an object that must be learned and stored in the memory of the synaptic matrix for effective recognition is greatly reduced.

The complete retinoid system can be roughly divided into two major subsystems: a 2-D subsystem consisting of a separate monocular module for each of the eyes and the 3-D retinoid, which receives input from each of the 2-D retinoid modules. It is characterized by having multiple retinoid layers corresponding to the egocentric distances of visual targets in depth. The retinoid layers in this module are arrayed along the Z-axis and are called Z-planes. Thus the monocular subsystem represents objects on X,Y retinoid coordinates, and the binocular (3-D) subsystem represents objects on X,Y, and Z coordinates. In addition, heuristic excursions of the self-locus can be made along the three axes of the 3-D retinoid; its coordinates can be sensed, learned, and stored in a synaptic matrix where they can be adaptively associated with any object that it has targeted. This capability allows us to recall where an object was located as well as to know what the object was.

An important structural feature of the 3-D retinoid is the arrangement of its axonal projections to the mosaic cell array of the synaptic matrix. There are spatiotopic projections from each Z-plane to the mosaic array. But from the nearest Z-plane to the farthest, there is a corresponding progressive expansion of axonal projections to the target mosaic cells. The result is an increasing magnification of an object's represented size on the mosaic cell array as the distance of an object increases. This connectivity property can account for the phenomenon of size constancy.

Among the many visual-cognitive functions served by the retinoid system are the following:

1. Parsing objects in complex visual environments.
2. Constructing 3-D visual representations of objects and scenes.
3. Locating a representation of the self within a represented environment.
4. Representing the paths of moving objects and paths of self-excursion in complex environments.
5. Effecting selective shifts of focal attention.
6. Performing geometric and relational analysis of veridical and/or hypothetical objects and scenes.
7. Modeling situational schemas.

Although the retinoids are short-term memory mechanisms, information that is represented in their excitatory patterns can be selectively captured in a synaptic matrix and stored in long-term memory.

Semantic Processing

A simple neuronal elaboration of the basic synaptic matrix enables it to operate as a network for semantic processing. In this mechanism, a set of autaptic cells captures lexical tokens in short-term memory. When a sentential proposition is learned, the activity of these word cells is sustained during the temporal span of each sentence and provides input to the mosaic cells of the matrix so that subject and predicate are adaptively linked through synaptic modification. After learning has occurred, the semantic network can be queried by the discharge of a mosaic cell or a class cell. The discharge of any particular mosaic cell selects a token of a word or phrase taken as the subject of a sentence and evokes its associated predicate tokens. The discharge of any particular class cell selects a token of a word or phrase taken as the predicate of a sentence and evokes its associated subject tokens. A query of the first kind defines a selected subject in terms of its learned predicates; a query of the second kind infers a subject on the basis of selected predicates.

The putative neuronal mechanism for semantic processing is not only able to respond appropriately (logically, sensibly) to queries related to single sentences, it can also make sense out of combinations of logically related sentences. Moreover, it can deduce chains of logical implications that are only implicit over a body of lexically based knowledge. The semantic network is capable of narrative comprehension, including appropriate pronominal reference, and can deal effectively with negation.

Self-query can be generated by endogenously evoked discharge of lexical tokens within the semantic network. In this way, the neuronal mechanism can monitor the semantic and logical implications of lexical communications in an on-line fashion without mediation or prompting from an outside source. Communications subject to semantic processing can be self-generated sentences (inner speech) as well as the lexical productions of others. By means of backward chaining of class cell tokens, lexical events can be bound to neuronal representations (images) of events in the real world. Inferences drawn by the semantic network can provide information on which to base reasonable plans of action. These plans, in turn, can be expressed and learned as new tokened representations (lexical productions) of action schemes that are subject to elaboration and interpretation within the semantic network.

Planning and Composing Behavior

A subsystem within the executive processes of the cognitive brain consists of a semantic network, neuronal mechanisms for encoding physical magnitudes, synaptic matrices for binding consequences to actions, and adaptive neuronal registers for learning, storing, and selectively executing action sequences. These interrelated mechanisms provide the biological substrate for composing plans and controlling the particular sequences of behavior called for by each plan. Their neuronal properties and component circuits entail the same basic operating principles employed in the other modules of the cognitive brain.

Self-query is an essential operation in the process of composing a plan. Having the ability to recognize particular situations and to recall the specific behavioral affordances bound to each situation, the system is able to learn elementary tokened propositions of the form *A gets B* where A represents a situation and B represents a different situation or goal that can be achieved by the affordances inherent in A. Starting with a desired goal (say G), the self-query "What gets G?" evokes the necessary situation-action (say H) that obtains G. Iteration of this operation back to a desired starting situation completes a chain of neuronally tokened situation-contingent actions that constitute a plan. When plans are composed, they are stored as long-term resources in the synaptic weight distributions of neuronal registers, where they can serve the efficient pursuit of goals and the solution of diverse ecological problems. Given appropriate motivation, a plan is selectively initiated when a current situation is recognized as similar to an earlier situation in which the particular plan achieved the desired goal (either in fact or in imagination).

Motivation

Motivation, the core function among the executive processes, is biologically instantiated and developed by a complex of specialized interoceptive sensors and neuronal circuits that I have called the central hedonic system. Within this system, I assume two principal kinds of homeostatic subsystems, designated as HS-I and HS-II. In HS-I, the loop of events serving to hold a physiological state near an optimal set point does not require the activation of a neuronal token of an external referent. An example of HS-I is modulation of cardiac output to hold blood pressure within a normal range. HS-II, which I call cognitive homeostasis, is exhibited by all of the processes that depend on the discharge of one or more referential tokens to complete a homeostatic loop that can correct a deviation from an internal set point. Processes of this type may be entirely covert or may require instrumental behavior to close the homeostatic loop. An example is obtaining a glass of water to satisfy thirst.

The affective brain states of pleasure and displeasure are intimately related to individual motivation and are assumed to be modulated by homeostatic events. Experimental findings indicate that a necessary condition for the experience of pleasure (activation of its cellular substrate) is a deviation from a homeostatic set point in the brain. This, together with some action or event that tends to restore equilibrium to the perturbed system, seems sufficient to evoke pleasure. When homeostasis is achieved, the experience of pleasure dissipates.

Secular set points are distinguished from those that directly serve vegetative and appetitive homeostasis. A secular set point is an enduring brain state that represents an imagined and desired worldly situation—a personal goal. As long as the imagined neuronal representation of a goal is not effectively matched by the perception of its corresponding events in the real world, the homeostatic system of which it is a part remains in disequilibrium. This is the neuronal mechanism that initiates goal-directed behavior. Plans and actions that lead to a situation that matches the goal are selectively activated and are said to be motivated by the goal.

A specialized set of autaptic cells within the central hedonic system contains the discrete neuronal tokens of secular goals. In order for one of these cells to be instantiated as an active goal in the networks of the brain, it must be stimulated by the token of an imagined goal situation and receive a priming margin of excitatory input from the sum of associated adiant events sufficient to overbalance the inhibitory input from the sum of associated abiant events. Under these conditions, an autaptic token of a secular goal will fire and sustain its activity as long as the margin of input from adiant sources over input from abiant sources is great enough. The continued discharge of a goal token represents the departure from the set point (disequilibrium) of a specific secular goal and signals the need to construct an appropriate plan of action for achieving the goal. Recognition of a realized goal sends an inhibitory input to the goal token, squelching its autaptic activity and restoring equilibrium.

An enormous number of objects and events stimulate our senses, but only a relatively few elicit significant responses. We exhibit a selective sensitivity to those that must be discriminated in order to reach a goal and ignore the rest. This kind of selective perceptual sensitivity is automatically induced through associative excitatory priming of discrete filter cells (in detection matrices) by the activated tokens of autaptic set points (goals) that happen to be in a current state of disequilibrium.

The motivational system must resolve the problem of multiple current goals. One of the putative brain mechanisms in the system resolves competition among many different energetic goals on the joint basis of the current relative strength (demand) of each goal and the presence or absence of affordances needed to continue on a path to each goal. In this model, control of behavior is captured by the strongest tokened motive having the supporting bias of perceived available affordances.

Neuronal Capacity

If we accept the hypothesized neuronal system as a strong candidate model of the cognitive brain on the grounds of neurophysiological plausibility and functional competency, can it pass the test of accommodation within the capacity limitations of the brain? As it learns more about the world during normal ontological development, will performance be prematurely impaired because the necessary long-term store of world knowledge too quickly exhausts the available neuronal resources of the brain? No definitive answer can be given, but some reasonable estimates suggest that the putative mechanisms are viable over a human lifetime.

Let us assume an average life span of 80 years. As a rough estimate, let us say that because of the ubiquitous novelty of new-found experience and a generally high level of arousal, the young child learns several new things from external and internal sources every minute of a 16-hour waking day. (Of course, the child's waking day is usually less than 16 hours, but for the sake of simplicity, let us posit 16 hours per day for every day of one's life as the period in which learning occurs.) Assume that there is a general decline in the number of things learned as one ages so that, on average, during an 80-year span, something is learned every 2 minutes (0.5 events per minute) when one is awake. I think it would be fair to characterize this as very active learning—perhaps unnaturally active, but in the context of the analysis it can only strengthen the conclusion. We can now calculate 80 (years) $\times$ 365 (days/year) $\times$ 16 (hours/day) $\times$ 60 (minutes/hour) $\times$ 0.5 (things learned/minute) $=$ 14,016,000 as the estimated number of things learned over an 80-year lifetime. (Landauer 1986 provides a different approach to the estimation of lifetime memory.) If each learned event were represented by a discrete filter cell–class cell (token) couplet in lifelong memory, then 28,032,000 neurons would be needed to store the accumulated information.

I have proposed an essentially deterministic cognitive model, but there is considerable evidence that underlying random events and stochastic processes can influence some aspects of brain activity (Gersuni 1971, Trehub 1971a, 1971b, 1973, 1975b). Suppose that when a thing is learned, random perturbations affecting the thresholds of unmodified filter cells often result in the redundant storage of a single learned event. If this occurs, then the number of available (unmodified) adaptive cells in the brain will be "used up" more rapidly. On this account and in the interest of making a more conservative estimate, let us increase by a factor of 10 the number of neurons needed to store accumulated information (memory). Now the cognitive brain will require approximately 280,320,000 cells to store the information acquired over a lifetime. But even if we accept this increase, a much larger part of the brain's neuronal resources will still be available for other functions. On the basis of cell counts, the estimated number of neurons in just the cortical mantle of the human brain ranges from 10 billion to somewhat more than 16 billion. If we assume that, on average, there are approximately 13 billion cortical neurons, the number dedicated to accumulated memory over a full lifetime represents only 2 percent of the total number of neurons in the cortex of the human brain. This means that even under a conservative estimate that allows for random redundancy of memory storage but does not allow for cellular forgetting and reuse, over 12.5 billion cortical neurons are still available for other processes after all memory requirements are met. Chief among the other neuronal structures are the sensory afferents, retinoids and mosaic arrays, accessory mechanisms, simple feed-forward and feedback lines, the central hedonic system, and adaptive interfaces between major processing modules in the various sensory modalities as well as the action-command system. I believe that these structures can be effectively accommodated without straining the resources of more than 12 billion cortical neurons.

Synaptic Capacity

Cytological evidence suggests that there are more than enough synaptic connections in the neocortex to satisfy the structural requirements of the proposed model of the cognitive brain. It is estimated that the number of synapses on individual cortical neurons ranges from fewer than a few hundred to over 100,000 for the larger pyramidal cells. An estimate of 2000 if often given as the average number of synapses per cell. On this basis, we can say that there are about 2.6 trillion synaptic junctions in the human cortex.

In the case of adaptive cells that accept relatively few axonal inputs, there is clearly no problem about the number of synaptic sites that must be accommodated on the dendrites of each cell. However, hypothesized mechanisms that are characterized by very large numbers of parallel axonal inputs on single neurons require a closer look. For example, each filter cell in the level-1 synaptic matrix receives from the mosaic cell array a large number of visual afferents from retinoid representations of retinal images. Retinotopic excitation is carried in parallel to the higher centers of the brain through a bundle of ~1 million optic nerve fibers (Kuffler, Nicholls, and Martin 1984).

If effective performance of the proposed model were to require a correspondingly large array of axo-dendritic synapses on each filter cell in the synaptic matrix, it would not be a physiologically credible model; however, only a small region around the normal foveal axis (10 degrees or less of visual angle) needs to be projected to the synaptic matrix for effective object recognition. Even this limited number of visual projections can be markedly reduced without causing significant stimulus degradation if the afferent neurons sample retinal activity at an inceasing interval as a function of retinal eccentricity. In addition, should the need for a great abundance of synaptic sites require a dendritic surface larger than that provided by a single cell, two or more cross-coupled filter cells converging on a common class cell would serve the purpose.

Combinatorial Explosion?

The fact that a distinct rigid object can undergo a vast number of fortuitous transformations in 3-D space poses one of the seemingly insurmountable challenges to an understanding of human visual pattern recognition. Each object can project to any one of a great many retinal locations; at each location, it may be represented in any one of a great many different sizes; at each size, it may be represented at any one of a great many angular orientations on the 2-D frontal plane; at each angular orientation on the frontal plane, it may be represented at any one of a great many angular orientations on the 3-D depth plane. Any effort to capture (learn) each representation of an object over all its possible transformations is thwarted by what has been dubbed a combinatorial explosion—a demand for storage beyond any conceivable brain capacity. If the brain cannot store all the diverse representations of discrete objects, how can it recognize them given their transformational vicissitudes in the natural world?

The visual-cognitive system that I have hypothesized solves the problem of combinatorial explosion in three principal ways. First, the range of proximal neuronal representations of any discrete object that the detection matrices might have to discriminate is greatly reduced by the action of specialized mechanisms and structures (size transformer, size constancy projections from Z-planes, rotation transformer). These can perform transformations of the size and angular orientation of any given visual representation so that its shape can be tested for a match against the shapes of previously learned patterns having different sizes and orientations. Second, before an object is tested for recognition or is learned, its retinoid representation for of these putative brain structures is the inventive synthesis of specialized retinoid patterns of autaptic cell activity that can be transferred to long-term memory in the detection matrix for use as perceptual tools. These gaugelike tools (templates) can be used for quick and rough assessment of significant geometric properties in the visual environment. Within a more general perspective, the synthesis of novel and useful neuronal patterns that would be committed to long-term memory in the individual and shared cumulatively in the larger society would represent the evolutionary development of biological, intraorganismic cognitive tools in the same sense as the evolutionary development of material extraorganismic artifacts (Trehub 1977).

The Brain's "I" and States of Belief

I strongly suspect that the pragmatics of the cognitive brain model can help resolve current philosophical disputes about intentionality (Churchland 1984, 1986; Putnam 1988; Pylyshyn 1986), but I will not pursue this line directly because I have no clear sense of the norms of engagement on the issue. Rather, I will argue that certain properties of the theoretical model that I have already delineated provide sufficient biological grounds for generating and supporting a distinct internal token that warrants the lexical designation "I." This special token (the I-token), when joined in an internal stimulus complex with other active tokens, establishes a distinct internal state that warrants the lexical designation "belief."

I-tokens are a special subset of neurons characterized by having an excitatory input from the autaptic cells that constitute the self-locus—the source of constant excitation in the center of the self-locus retinoid. The discharge of an I-token can be thought of as a neuronal signal of oneself taken as an object. Because it is a labeled line, the I-token can be linked to the character "I" in the lexical assignment matrix and can serve as the subject in all kinds of subject-predicate propositions within the semantic network. Any recognized internal state or perceived event involving oneself can contribute to a store of learned predicates uniquely induced by activation of the I-token—for example, *I am sad* or *I travel a lot.* I-activated predicate tokens, in turn, can evoke sensory images by their chain of backward links to the imaging matrix in a level-1 synaptic matrix. The extended set of such neuronal associations can be taken as the biological substrate for one's sense of self.

In addition to signifying the center of the self-nexus, the I-token can mark a subset of neuronal propositions that have a very special status in the cognitive brain—those that have passed a test of personal validity. Consider the proposition "Kumquats are smaller than oranges." Now imagine two different individuals, each well acquainted with oranges, who read the sentence. One has never before seen, read, or heard of a kumquat; the other has seen the fruit and has learned that it is called a kumquat. The first person knows an assertion has been made that something called a "kumquat" is smaller than an orange, but there is no test that he or she can perform to establish that the predicate "smaller than an orange" is a true (sensory-world) property of the subject "kumquat." The second person can recall an image of a kumquat and actually compare its size with an imaged exemplar of an orange. When the outcome of this personal test establishes that a kumquat is indeed smaller than an orange, the proposition assumes the status of a truth within the cognitive system of the individual making the test.

I suggest that propositions of this kind are gated to a privileged semantic network that contains what can be appropriately called the system of personal belief. I also suggest that every proposition evoked from the network of belief is neuronally marked by the joint discharge of an I-token (I!). Thus:

(⟨Birds⟩ ⟨fly⟩)I!

⟨People⟩ ⟨fly⟩

(⟨People⟩ ⟨walk⟩)I!

⟨I⟩ ⟨can read Sanskrit⟩

(⟨I⟩ ⟨can read English⟩)I!

⟨Dan⟩ ⟨needs a new jacket⟩

(⟨Dan⟩ ⟨needs a new jacket⟩)I!

(⟨I⟩ ⟨think Dan needs a new jacket⟩)I!

⟨I⟩ ⟨think Dan needs a new jacket⟩

⟨Dan⟩ ⟨says he needs a new jacket⟩

(⟨Dan⟩ ⟨says he needs a new jacket⟩)I!

Neuronal propositions accompanied by the parallel discharge of an I-token are expressions or states of belief; those that are not accompanied by an activated I-token are subjunctive expressions or states. Notice that identical sentential propositions can differ in intentional stance, expressing a state of belief in one instance and a subjunctive state in another. Detailed consideration of this aspect of the cognitive brain would take us well beyond the intended scope of this book. It is worth emphasizing, however, that our ongoing interpretation of the world and our formulations of plans of action are critically dependent on our prior beliefs. And these, in turn, depend on individually learned routines (not necessarily rational) as well as innate mechanisms for signaling the ostensive validity of propositions.

Conclusion

My proposed theoretical model of the cognitive brain consists of a number of putative neuronal mechanisms that together constitute the biophysical and structural basis for certain essential cognitive properties of the human brain. An interesting aspect of the component mechanisms, and a fact that supports their evolutionary likelihood, is that most of them are replications or thematic variations of either one of only two principal neuronal designs: the synaptic matrix or the retinoid. Current neurophysiological and neuroanatomical knowledge tends to confirm the biological plausibility of the hypothesized mechanisms. Computer simulation tests of the mechanisms demonstrate that they are competent in basic visual-cognitive and lexical-semantic domains. The extended integrated model of the cognitive brain is responsive to all of the ecologically relevant tasks listed in chapter 1 as reasonable tests of a human cognitive system. In addition, the model accurately predicts many classical illusions and perceptual anomalies as epiphenomena of its normal operation. Finally, a large body of diverse experimental and clinical findings can be explained within a coherent framework by the biophysical and structural properties of the model.

On these grounds, I believe that the neuronal mechanisms and systems that I have proposed represent a credible biophysical explanation of human cognition in the domains assayed. Although a number of important processes have been covered, many more remain to be explicated, although I expect that the mechanisms that have proved competent for the tasks considered in this book will, with some minor changes and elaborations, be equally effective for other modalities and tasks.

We are on the verge of a biological understanding of human cognition, but we have only a dim appreciation of the opportunities and challenges that such an understanding entails. As competing theories of cognition appear, we face the scientifically exciting task of deciding among them on the basis of competence, biological plausibility, and parsimony. This effort can illuminate and help clarify the daunting complexity of cognition and sharpen our sense of what it means to be human. Reasonable models of the human brain can provide a physical account of the mechanisms and processes of cognition. Interactions among such models in simulated social and physical contexts can provide an account of the evolution of the various contents of cognition. It is the total specific content of cognition, the current physical state of specialized mechanisms in an individual brain shaped by encounters in a world both real and imagined, that constitutes a mind.

Bibliography

Akers, R. F., Lovinger, D. M., Colley, P. A., Linden, D. J., and Routtenberg, A. (1986). Translocation of protein kinase C activity may mediate hippocampal long-term potentiation. *Science* 231: 587–589.

Albert, M. L., Reches, A., and Silverberg, R. (1975). Associative visual agnosia without alexia. *Neurology* 25: 322–326.

Algom, D., and Cohen-Raz, L. (1987). Sensory and cognitive factors in the processing of visual velocity. *Journal of Experimental Psychology: Human Perception and Performance* 13: 3–13.

Alkon, D. L., Chen, C., and Galant, P. E. (1987). C-kinase activation mediates protease regulation of voltage-dependent K+ currents. Society for Neuroscience 17th Annual Meeting, New Orleans.

Ambron, R. T., Schacher, S., and Rayport, S. G. (1985). Proteins rapidly transported to the synapses of a single identified neuron of Aplysia Californica. *Journal of Neuroscience* 5: 2866–2873.

Andersen, R. A., Essick, G. K., and Siegel, R. M. (1985). Encoding of spatial location by posterior parietal neurons. *Science* 230: 456–458.

Andersen, R. A., and Mountcastle, V. B. (1983). The influence of angle of gaze upon the excitability of the light-sensitive neurons of the posterior parietal cortex. *Journal of Neuroscience* 3: 532–548.

Anderson, J. A., Silverstein, J. W., Ritz, S. A., and Jones, R. S. (1977). Distinctive features, categorical perception, and probability learning: Some applications of a neural model. *Psychological Review* 84: 413–451.

Anderson, J. R., and Bower, G. H. (1973). *Human Associative Memory*. Washington, D.C.: Winston.

Anderson, S. W., Damasio, H., Damasio, A. R., Bellugi, U., Tranel, A. F., Brandt, J. P., and O'Grady, L. (1989). Acquisition of sign language following left hemisphere damage and aphasia. Society for Neuroscience 19th Annual Meeting, Phoenix.

Arbib, M. A., and Hanson, A. R., eds. (1987). *Vision, Brain, and Cooperative Computation*. Cambridge, Mass.: Bradford/MIT Press.

Attneave, F. (1974). How do you know? *American Psychologist* 29: 493–499.

Bank, B., LoTurco, J. J., and Alkon, D. L. (1987). Long-term translocation of protein kinase C by in vivo and in vitro conditioning. Society for Neuroscience 17th Annual Meeting, New Orleans.

Banks, W. P., and Flora, J. (1977). Semantic and perceptual processes in symbolic comparisons. *Journal of Experimental Psychology: Human Perception and Performance* 3: 278–290.

Barash, S., Anderson, R., Bracewell, M., Gnadt, J., and Fogassi, L. (1988). Saccade-related activity in area LIP. Society for Neuroscience 18th Annual Meeting, Toronto.

Barlow, H. B. (1985). The Twelfth Bartlett Memorial Lecture: The role of single neurons in the psychology of perception. *Quarterly Journal of Experimental Psychology* 37A: 121–145.

Barlow, H. B., Hill, R. M., and Levick, W. R. (1964). Retinal ganglion cells responding selectively to direction and speed of image motion in the rabbit. *Journal of Physiology* 173: 377–407.

Baylis, G. C., Rolls, E. T., and Leonard, C. M. (1985). Selectivity between faces in the responses of a population of neurons in the cortex in the superior temporal sulcus of the monkey. *Brain Research* 342: 91–102.

Becklen, R., Wallach, H., and Nitzberg, D. (1984). A limitation of position constancy. *Journal of Experimental Psychology: Human Perception and Performance* 10: 713–723.

Ben-Shakhar, G., and Gati, I. (1987). Common and distinctive features of verbal and pictorial stimuli as determinants of psychophysiological responsivity. *Journal of Experimental Psychology: General* 116: 91–105.

Bender, M. B., Feldman, M., and Sobin, A. J. (1968). Palinopsia. *Brain* 91: 321–338.

Benevento, L. A., and Miller, J. (1981). Visual responses in the caudal lateral pulvinar of the macaque monkey. *Journal of Neuroscience* 1: 1268–1278.

Benson, D. F. (1989). Disorders of visual gnosis. In *Neuropsychology of Visual Perception,* J. W. Brown, ed. Hillsdale, N.J.: Lawrence Erlbaum Associates.

Biederman, I. (1987). Recognition by components: A theory of human image understanding. *Psychological Review* 94: 115–147.

Biederman, I., Blickle, T. W., Teitelbaum, R. C., and Klatsky, G. J. (1988). Object search in nonscene displays. *Journal of Experimental Psychology: Learning, Memory, and Cognition* 14: 456–467.

Biederman, I., Glass, A. L., and Stacy, E. W. (1973). Searching for objects in real-world scenes. *Journal of Experimental Psychology* 97: 22–27.

Biederman, I., and Ju, G. (1988). Surface versus edge-based determinants of visual recognition. *Cognitive Psychology* 20: 38–64.

Biederman, I., Rabinowitz, J. C., Glass, A. L., and Stacy, E. W. (1974). On the information extracted from a glance at a scene. *Journal of Experimental Psychology* 103: 597–600.

Bisiach, E., and Berti, A. (1989). Unilateral misrepresentation of distributed information: Paradoxes and puzzles. In *Neuropsychology of Visual Perception,* J. W. Brown, ed. Hillsdale, N.J.: Lawrence Erlbaum Associates.

Bisiach, E., Capitani, E., and Porta, E. (1985). Two basic properties of space representation in the brain: Evidence from unilateral neglect. *Journal of Neurology, Neurosurgery, and Psychiatry* 48: 141–144.

Bisiach, E., and Luzzatti, C. (1978). Unilateral neglect of representational space. *Cortex* 14: 129–133.

Bisiach, E., Luzzatti, C., and Perani, D. (1979). Unilateral neglect, representational schema and consciousness. *Brain* 102: 609–618.

Blasdel, G. G., Lund, J., and Fitzpatrick, D. (1985). Intrinsic connections of macaque striate cortex: Axonal projections of cells outside lamina 4C. *Journal of Neuroscience* 5: 3350–3369.

Blinkov, S. M., and Glezer, I. I., eds. (1968). *The Human Brain in Figures and Tables.* New York: Basic Books.

Bliss, T. V. P., and Gardner-Medwin, A. R. (1973). Long-lasting potentiation of synaptic transmission in the dentate area of the unanesthetized rabbit following stimulation of the preforant pathway. *Journal of Physiology* 232: 357–374.

Bliss, T. V. P., and Lømo, T. (1973). Long-lasting potentiation of synaptic transmission in the dentate area of the anesthetized rabbit following stimulation of the preforant pathway. *Journal of Physiology* 232: 331–356.

Bonhoeffer, T., Staiger, V., and Aertsen, A. M. H. J. (1989). Unexpected properties of "Hebb synapses" in rat hippocampal slice cultures. Society for Neuroscience 19th Annual Meeting, Phoenix.

Boring, E. G. (1929). *A History of Experimental Psychology.* New York: Appleton-Century.

Boring, E. G. (1940). Size constancy and Emmert's law. *American Journal of Psychology* 53: 293–295.

Boring, E. G. (1943). The moon illusion. *American Journal of Physics* 11: 55–60.

Boring, E. G. (1962). On the moon illusion. *Science* 137: 902–906.

Brain, R. (1941). Visual disorientation with special reference to lesions of the right hemisphere. *Brain* 64: 244–272.

Broadbent, D. (1985). A question of levels: Comment on McClelland and Rumelhart. *Journal of Experimental Psychology: General* 114: 189–192.

Brooks, L. R. (1968). Spatial and verbal components of the act of recall. *Canadian Journal of Psychology* 22: 349–368.

Brown, J. W., ed. (1989). *Neuropsychology of Visual Perception.* Hillsdale, N.J.: Lawrence Erlbaum Associates.

Brown, T. H., Chapman, P. F., Kairiss, E. W., and Kennan, C. L. (1988). Long-term synaptic potentiation. *Science* 242: 724–728.

Browning, M., Dunwiddie, T., Bennett, W., Gispen, W., and Lynch, G. (1979). Synaptic phosphoproteins: Specific changes after repetitive stimulation of the hippocampal slice. *Science* 203: 60–62.

Bundesen, C., and Larsen, A. (1975). Visual transformation of size. *Journal of Experimental Psychology: Human Perception and Performance* 1: 214–220.

Burr, D., and Ross, J. (1986). Visual processing of motion. *Trends in Neurosciences* 9: 304–307.

Buschke, H. (1974). Spontaneous remembering after recall failure. *Science* 184: 579–581.

Caplan, D. (1981). On the cerebral localization of linguistic functions: Logical and empirical issues surrounding deficit analysis and functional localization. *Brain and Language* 14: 120–137.

Carey, S., and Diamond, R. (1977). From piecemeal to configurational representation of faces. *Science* 195: 312–314.

Carpenter, G. A., and Grossberg, S. (1990). Neural dynamics of category learning and recognition: Structural invariants, reinforcements, and evoked potentials. In *Computational and Clinical Approaches to Pattern Recognition and Concept Formation,* M. J. Commons, R. J. Herrnstein, S. M. Kosslyn, and D. B. Mumford, eds. Hillsdale, N.J.: Lawrence Erlbaum Associates.

Casco, C., and Morgan, M. (1984). The relationship between space and time in the perception of stimuli moving behind a slit. *Perception* 13: 429–441.

Cave, K. R., and Kosslyn, S. M. (1989). Varieties of size-specific visual selection. *Journal of Experimental Psychology: General* 118: 148–164.

Chambers, D., and Reisberg, D. (1985). Can mental images be ambiguous? *Journal of Experimental Psychology: Human Perception and Performance* 11: 317–328.

Churchland, P. M. (1984). *Matter and Consciousness.* Cambridge, Mass.: Bradford/MIT Press.

Churchland, P. S. (1986). *Neurophilosophy.* Cambridge, Mass.: Bradford/MIT Press.

Clifton, C., and Ferreira, F. (1987). Modularity in sentence comprehension. In *Modularity in Knowledge Representation and Natural-Language Understanding,* J. L. Garfield, ed. Cambridge, Mass.: Bradford/MIT Press.

Cohen, N. J., and Squire, L. R. (1980). Preserved learning and pattern-analyzing skill in amnesia: Dissociation of knowing how and knowing that. *Science* 210: 207–210.

Corballis, M. C. (1986). Is mental rotation controlled or automatic? *Memory and Cognition* 14: 124–128.

Coren, S. (1986). An efferent component in the visual perception of direction and extent. *Psychological Review* 93: 391–410.

Cotman, C. W., and McGaugh, J. L. (1980). *Behavioral Neuroscience*. New York: Academic Press.

Damasio, A. R., and Tranel, D. (1989). Knowing that "Colorado" goes with "Denver" does not imply knowledge that "Denver" is in "Colorado." Society for Neuroscience 19th Annual Meeting, Phoenix.

DeLoache, J. S. (1987). Rapid change in the symbolic functioning of very young children. *Science* 238: 1556–1557.

Derthick, M., and Plaut, D. C. (1986). Is distributed connectionism compatible with the physical symbol system hypothesis? *Proceedings of the Eighth Annual Conference of the Cognitive Science Society, Amherst, Mass.*

Desimone, R., Albright, T. D., Gross, C. G., and Bruce, C. (1984). Stimulus-selective properties of inferior temporal neurons in the macaque. *Journal of Neuroscience* 4: 2051–2062.

Duncan, J. (1984). Selective attention and the organization of visual information. *Journal of Experimental Psychology: General* 113: 501–517.

Estes, W. K. (1986). Memory storage and retrieval processes in category learning. *Journal of Experimental Psychology: General* 115: 155–174.

Fahlman, S. E. (1979). *NETL: A System for Representing and Using Real-World Knowledge.* Cambridge, Mass.: MIT Press.

Fahlman, S. E. (1981). Representing Implicit Knowledge. In *Parallel Models of Associative Memory*. G. E. Hinton and J. A. Anderson, eds. Hillsdale, N.J.: Lawrence Erlbaum Associates.

Farah, M. J. (1988). Is visual imagery really visual? Overlooked evidence from neuropsychology. *Psychological Review* 95: 307–317.

Farah, M. J. (1989). Neuropsychology of mental imagery. In *Neuropsychology of Visual Perception,* J. W. Brown, ed. Hillsdale, N.J.: Lawrence Erlbaum Associates.

Farah, M. J., Peronnet, F., Gonon, M. A., and Giard, M. H. (1988). Electrophysiological evidence for a shared representational medium for visual images and visual percepts. *Journal of Experimental Psychology: General* 117: 248–257.

Feldman, J. A. (1981). A connectionist model of visual memory. In *Parallel Models of Associative Memory,* G. E. Hinton and J. A. Anderson, eds. Hillsdale, N.J.: Lawrence Erlbaum Associates.

Feldman, J. A. (1985). Four frames suffice: A provisional model of vision and space. *Behavioral and Brain Sciences* 8: 265–289.

Feldman, J. A., and Ballard, D. H. (1982). Connectionist models and their properties. *Cognitive Science* 6: 205–254.

Ferguson, E. S. (1977). The mind's eye: Nonverbal thought in technology. *Science* 197: 827–836.

Finke, R. A., and Kosslyn, S. M. (1980). Mental imagery acuity in the peripheral visual field. *Journal of Experimental Psychology: Human Perception and Performance* 6: 126–139.

Finke, R. A., and Pinker, S. (1983). Directional scanning of remembered visual patterns. *Journal of Experimental Psychology: Learning, Memory, and Cognition* 9: 398–410.

Finke, R. A., Pinker, S., and Farah, M. J. (1989). Reinterpreting visual patterns in mental imagery. *Cognitive Science* 13: 51–78.

Fite, K. V., ed. (1976). *The Amphibian Visual System.* New York: Academic Press.

Fodor, J. A. (1981). *Representations: Philosophical Essays on the Foundations of Cognitive Science.* Cambridge, Mass.: MIT Press.

Fodor, J. A. (1984). *The Modularity of Mind.* Cambridge, Mass.: Bradford/MIT Press.

Fodor, J. A., and Pylyshyn, Z. W. (1988). Connectionism and cognitive architecture:

A critical analysis. In *Connections and Symbols,* S. Pinker and J. Mehler, eds. Cambridge, Mass.: Bradford/MIT Press.

Frederickson, R. E., and Bartlett, J. C. (1987). Cognitive impenetrability of memory for orientation. *Journal of Experimental Psychology: Learning, Memory, and Cognition* 13: 269–277.

Funahashi, S., Bruce, C. J., and Goldman-Rakic, P. S. (1989). Visual and mnemonic coding in the primate prefrontal cortex during oculomotor delayed-response performance. Society for Neuroscience 19th Annual Meeting, Phoenix.

Gainotti, G., D'Erme, P., and DeBonis, C. (1989). Visual attention disrupted in unilateral neglect. In *Neuropsychology of Visual Perception,* J. W. Brown, ed. Hillsdale, N.J.: Lawrence Erlbaum Associates.

Georgeopolous, A. P., Lurito, J. T., Petrides, M., Schwartz, A. B., and Massey, J. T. (1989). Mental rotation of the neuronal population vector. *Science* 243: 234–236.

Gerren, R. A., and Weinberger, N. M. (1983). Long-term potentiation in the magnocellular medial geniculate nucleus of the anesthetized cat. *Brain Research* 265: 138–142.

Gersuni, G. V. (1971). *Sensory Processes at the Neuronal and Behavioral Levels.* New York: Academic Press.

Geschwind, N. (1980). Neurological knowledge and complex behaviors. *Cognitive Science* 4: 185–193.

Gilchrist, A. L. (1977). Perceived lightness depends on perceived spatial arrangement. *Science* 195: 185–187.

Gnadt, J. W., and Mays, L. E. (1989). Posterior parietal cortex, the oculomotor near response and spatial coding in 3-D space. Society for Neuroscience 19th Annual Meeting, Phoenix.

Gould, J. L. (1985). How bees remember flower shapes. *Science* 227: 1492–1494.

Graham, C. H. (1951). Visual perception. In *Handbook of Experimental Psychology,* S. S. Stevens, ed. New York: Wiley.

Gray, C. R., and Gummerman, K. (1975). The enigmatic eidetic image: A critical examination of methods, data, and theories. *Psychological Bulletin* 82: 383–407.

Grossberg, S., ed. (1988). *Neural Networks and Natural Intelligence.* Cambridge, Mass.: Bradford/MIT Press.

Guenther, R. K., and Klatsky, R. L. (1977). Semantic classification of pictures and words. *Journal of Experimental Psychology: Human Learning and Memory* 3: 498–514.

Gustafsson, B., and Wigstrom, H. (1986). Hippocampal long-lasting potentiation produced by pairing single volleys and brief conditioning tetani evoked in separate afferents. *Journal of Neuroscience* 6: 1575–1582.

Gustaffson, B., Wigstrom, H., Abraham, W. C., and Huang, Y.-Y. (1987). Long-term potentiation in the hippocampus using depolarizing current pulses as the conditioning stimulus to single volley synaptic potentials. *Journal of Neuroscience* 7: 774–780.

Haith, M. M., Bergman, T., and Moore, M. J. (1977). Eye contact and face scanning in early infancy. *Science* 198: 853–855.

Harnad, S., ed. (1987). *Categorical Perception.* Cambridge: Cambridge University Press.

Heath, R. G. (1964). Pleasure response of human subjects to direct stimulation of the brain: Physiologic and psychodynamic considerations. In *The Role of Pleasure in Behavior,* R. G. Heath, ed. New York: Hoeber.

Hebb, D. O. (1949). *The Organization of Behavior.* New York: Wiley.

Helmholtz, H. (1867). *Handbook of Physiological Optics.* 3d ed. translation, 1962. New York: Dover.

Henderson, J. M., Pollatsek, A., and Rayner, K. (1989). Covert visual attention and extrafoveal information use during object identification. *Perception and Psychophysics* 45: 196–208.

Hillman, D. E., and Chen, S. (1979). Determination of postsynaptic membrane structure is intrinsic to the Purkinje cell. Society for Neuroscience 9th Annual Meeting, Atlanta.

Hinton, G. E. (1981). Implementing semantic networks in parallel hardware. In *Parallel Models of Associative Memory,* G. E. Hinton and J. A. Anderson, eds. Hillsdale, N.J.: Lawrence Erlbaum Associates.

Hinton, G. E., and Anderson, J. A., eds. (1981). *Parallel Models of Associative Memory.* Hillsdale, N.J.: Lawrence Erlbaum Associates.

Hoffman, D. D., and Richards, W. A. (1984). Parts of recognition. *Cognition* 18: 65–96.

Holland, J. H., Holyoak, K. J., Nisbett, R. E., and Thagard, P. R., eds. (1986). *Induction: Processes of Inference, Learning, and Discovery.* Cambridge, Mass.: Bradford/MIT Press.

Holway, A. H., and Boring, E. G. (1940). The apparent size of the moon as a function of the angle of regard: Further experiments. *American Journal of Psychology* 53: 537–553.

Hopfield, J. J. (1982). Neural networks and physical systems with emergent collective computational abilities. *Proceedings of the National Academy of Sciences, USA* 79: 2554–2558.

Hopfield, J. J. (1984). Neurons with graded response have collective computational properties like those of two-state neurons. *Proceedings of the National Academy of Sciences, USA* 81: 3088–3092.

Hopfield, J. J., and Tank, D. W. (1986). Computing with neural circuits: A model. *Science* 233: 625–633.

Horridge, G. A. (1968). *Interneurons.* London: Freeman.

Hubel, D. H., and Wiesel, T. N. (1959). Receptive fields of single neurons in the cat's striate cortex. *Journal of Physiology* 148: 574–591.

Hubel, D. H., and Wiesel, T. N. (1962). Receptive fields, binocular interaction and functional architecture in the cat's visual cortex. *Journal of Physiology* 160: 106–154.

Hubel, D. H., and Wiesel, T. N. (1963). Shape and arrangement of columns in cat's striate cortex. *Journal of Physiology* 165: 559–568.

Hyson, M. T., Julesz, B., and Fender, D. H. (1983). Eye movements and neural remapping during fusion of misaligned random-dot stereograms. *Journal of the Optical Society of America* 73: 1665–1673.

Ingle, D. (1968). Visual releasers of prey-catching behavior in frogs and toads. *Brain, Behavior, and Evolution* 1: 500–518.

Inhoff, A. W., and Rayner, K. (1980). Parafoveal word perception: A case against semantic preprocessing. *Perception and Psychophysics* 27: 457–464.

Irwin, D. E., Brown, S. J., and Sun, J. (1988). Visual masking and visual integration across saccadic eye movements. *Journal of Experimental Psychology: General* 117: 276–287.

Ito, M. (1983). Evidence for synaptic plasticity in the cerebellar cortex. *Acta Morphilogica, Academy of Sciences, Hungary* 31: 213–218.

Jackendoff, R. (1985). *Semantics and Cognition.* Cambridge, Mass.: Bradford/MIT Press.

Jackendoff, R. (1987a). *Consciousness and the Computational Mind.* Cambridge, Mass.: Bradford/MIT Press.

Jackendoff, R. (1987b). On beyond zebra: The relation of visual and linguistic information. *Cognition* 26: 89–114.

Jacobs, L. (1989). Comments on some positive visual phenomena caused by diseases of the brain. In *Neuropsychology of Visual Perception,* J. W. Brown, ed. Hillsdale, N.J.: Lawrence Erlbaum Associates.

Johnson-Laird, P. N. (1983). *Mental Models: Toward a Cognitive Science of Language, Inference and Consciousness.* Cambridge, Mass.: Harvard University Press.

Johnson-Laird, P. N., Herrmann, D. J., and Chaffin, R. (1984). Only connections: A critique of semantic networks. *Psychological Bulletin* 96: 292–315.

Jolicoeur, P. (1985). The time to name disoriented natural objects. *Memory and Cognition* 13: 289–303.

Jolicoeur, P., Ullman, S., and MacKay, M. (1986). Curve tracing: A possible basic operation in the perception of spatial relations. *Memory and Cognition* 14: 129–140.

Julesz, B. (1971). *Foundations of Cyclopean Perception.* Chicago: University of Chicago Press.

Kaas, J. H. (1987). The organization of neocortex in mammals: Implications for theories of brain function. *Annual Review of Psychology* 38: 129–151.

Kandel, E. R. (1976). *Cellular Basis of Behavior.* San Francisco: W. H. Freeman.

Karluk, D., and Ebner, T. J. (1989). Spatial representation of movement distance and direction in the premotor cortex. Society for Neuroscience 19th Annual Meeting, Phoenix.

Kase, M., Noda, H., Suzuki, D. A., and Miller, D. C. (1979). Target velocity signals of visual tracking in vermal Purkinje cells of the monkey. *Science* 205: 717–720.

Kauer, J. A., Malenka, R. C., and Nicoll, R. A. (1988). A persistent postsynaptic modification mediates long-term potentiation in the hippocampus. *Neuron* 1: 911–917.

Kaufman, L., and Richards, W. (1969). Spontaneous fixation tendencies for visual forms. *Perception and Psychophysics* 5: 85–88.

Klopfer, D. S. (1985). Constructing mental representations of objects from successive views. *Journal of Experimental Psychology: Human Perception and Performance* 11: 566–582.

Knapp, A. G., and Anderson, J. A. (1984). Theory of categorization based on distributed memory storage. *Journal of Experimental Psychology: Learning, Memory, and Cognition* 10: 616–637.

Kohonen, T. (1977). *Associative Memory: A System Theoretical Approach.* New York: Springer-Verlag.

Kolers, P. A., Duchnicky, R. L., and Sundstroem, G. (1985). Size in the visual processing of faces and words. *Journal of Experimental Psychology: Human Perception and Performance* 11: 726–751.

Komatsu, Y., Toyama, K., Maeda, J., and Sakaguchi, H. (1981). Long-term potentiation investigated in a slice preparation of striate cortex of young kittens. *Neuroscience Letters* 26: 269–274.

Koriat, A., and Norman, J. (1988). Frames and images: Sequential effects in mental rotation. *Journal of Experimental Psychology: Learning, Memory, and Cognition* 14: 93–111.

Kosslyn, S. M. (1975). Information representation in visual images. *Cognitive Psychology* 7: 341–370.

Kosslyn, S. M. (1978). Measuring the visual angle of the mind's eye. *Cognitive Psychology* 10: 356–389.

Kosslyn, S. M. (1980). *Image and Mind.* Cambridge, Mass.: Harvard University Press.

Kosslyn, S. M. (1987). Seeing and imaging in the cerebral hemispheres: A computational approach. *Psychological Review* 94: 148–175.

Kosslyn, S. M. (1988). Aspects of a cognitive neuroscience of mental imagery. *Science* 240: 1621–1626.

Kosslyn, S. M., Ball, T. M., and Reiser, B. J. (1978). Visual images preserve metric spatial information: Evidence from studies of image scanning. *Journal of Experimental Psychology: Human Perception and Performance* 4: 47–60.

Kosslyn, S. M., Flynn, R. A., Amsterdam, J. B., and Wang, G. (1990). Components of high-level vision: A cognitive neuroscience analysis and accounts of neurological syndromes. *Cognition* 34: 203–277.

Kosslyn, S. M., Holtzman, J. D., Farah, M. J., and Gazzaniga, M. S. (1985). A computational analysis of mental image generation: Evidence from functional dissociations in split-brain patients. *Journal of Experimental Psychology: General* 114: 311–341.

Kosslyn, S. M., Reiser, B. J., Farah, M. J., and Fliegel, S. L. (1983). Generating visual images: Units and relations. *Journal of Experimental Psychology: General* 112: 278–303.

Kroll, J. F., and Corrigan, A. (1981). Strategies in sentence-picture verification: The effect of an unexpected picture. *Journal of Verbal Learning and Verbal Behavior* 20: 515–531.

Kroll, J. F., and Potter, M. C. (1984). Recognizing words, pictures, and concepts: A comparison of lexical, object, and reality decisions. *Journal of Verbal Learning and Verbal Behavior* 23: 39–66.

Kuffler, S. W. (1953). Discharge patterns and functional organization of mammalian retina. *Journal of Neurophysiology* 16: 37–68.

Kuffler, S. W., Nicholls, J. D., and Martin, A. R. (1984). *From Neuron to Brain.* Sunderland, Mass.: Sinauer Associates.

Lal, R., and Friedlander, M. J. (1989). Gating of retinal transmission by afferent eye position and movement signals. *Science* 243: 93–96.

Landau, B., Gleitman, H., and Spelke, E. (1981). Spatial knowledge and geometric representation in a child blind from birth. *Science* 213: 1275–1277.

Landauer, T. K. (1986). How much do people remember? Some estimates of the quantity of learned information in long-term memory. *Cognitive Science* 10: 477–493.

Landis, T., Cummings, J. L., Benson, D. F., and Palmer, E. P. (1986). Loss of topographic familiarity: An environmental agnosia. *Archives of Neurology* 43: 132–136.

Laroche, S., Jay, T. M., and Thierry, A. M. (1989). Long-term potentiation in the prefrontal cortex following stimulation of the hippocampal CA1/subicular region. Society for Neuroscience 19th Annual Meeting, Phoenix.

Larsen, A., and Bundesen, C. (1978). Size scaling in visual pattern recognition. *Journal of Experimental Psychology: Human Perception and Performance* 4: 1–20.

Larson, L., and Lynch, G. (1987). The NMDA antagonist AP5 blocks a component of the postsynaptic response to theta burst stimulation and prevents LTP induction. Society for Neuroscience 17th Annual Meeting, New Orleans.

Lee, K. S. (1982). Sustained enhancement of evoked potentials following brief, high frequency stimulation of the cerebral cortex in vitro. *Brain Research* 239: 617–623.

Leehey, S. C., Moskowitz-Cook, A., Brill, S., and Held, R. (1975). Orientational anisotropy in infant vision. *Science* 190: 900–901.

Levick, W. R., Cleland, B. G., and Dubin, M. W. (1972). Lateral geniculate neurons of cat: Retinal inputs and physiology. *Investigative Ophthalmology* 11: 302–311.

Levinson, J. Z., and Frome, F. S. (1979). Perception of size of one object among many. *Science* 206: 1425–1426.

Levy, W. B., Anderson, J. A., and Lehmkuhle, S., eds. (1985). *Synaptic Modification, Neuron Selectivity, and Nervous System Organization.* Hillsdale, N.J.: Lawrence Erlbaum Associates.

Lewis, D. J. (1979). Psychobiology of active and inactive memory. *Psychological Bulletin* 86: 1054–1083.

Linden, D. J., Sheu, F. S., and Routtenberg, A. (1987). DL-aminophosphonovalerate (APV) blockade of hippocampal long-term potentiation (LTP) prevents an LTP-associated increase in protein F1 phosphorylation. Society for Neuroscience 17th Annual Meeting, New Orleans.

Livingstone, M., and Hubel, D. (1988). Segregation of form, color, movement, and depth: Anatomy, physiology, and perception. *Science* 240: 740–749.

Loftus, G. R., Johnson, C. A., and Shimamura, A. P. (1985). How much is an icon worth? *Journal of Experimental Psychology: Human Perception and Performance* 11: 1–13.

LoTurco, J. J., Coulter, D. A., Bank, B., and Alkon, D. L. (1987). Enhanced summation of synaptic potentials: A correlate of associative learning in rabbit hippocampal CA1 neurons mimicked by kinase-C activation. Society for Neuroscience 17th Annual Meeting, New Orleans.

Lynch, G., and Baudry, M. (1984). The biochemistry of memory: A new and specific hypothesis. *Science* 224: 1057–1063.

Lynch, G., McGaugh, J. L., and Weinberger, N. M., eds. (1984). *Neurobiology of Learning and Memory.* New York: Guilford Press.

Lynch, J. C., Mountcastle, V. B., Talbot, W. H., and Yin, T. C. T. (1977). Parietal lobe mechanisms for directed visual attention. *Journal of Neurophysiology* 40: 362–389.

McClelland, J. L., and Rumelhart, D. E. (1985). Distributed memory and the representation of general and specific information. *Journal of Experimental Psychology: General* 114: 159–188.

McClelland, J. L., and Rumelhart, D. E., eds. (1986). *Parallel Distributed Processing,* vol. 2. Cambridge, Mass.: Bradford/MIT Press.

McClelland, J. L., Rumelhart, D. E., and Hinton, G. E. (1986). The appeal of parallel distributed processing. In *Parallel Distributed Processing,* vol. 2. J. L. McClelland and D. E. Rumelhart, eds. Cambridge, Mass.: Bradford/MIT Press.

McCloskey, M., and Watkins, J. W. (1978). The seeing-more-than-is-there phenomenon: Implications for the locus of iconic storage. *Journal of Experimental Psychology: Human Perception and Performance* 4: 553–564.

McGeoch, J. A. (1942). *The Psychology of Human Learning.* New York: Longmans, Green.

McNamara, T. P., Ratcliff, R., and McKoon, G. (1984). The mental representation of knowledge acquired from maps. *Journal of Experimental Psychology: Learning, Memory, and Cognition* 10: 723–732.

NcNaughton, B. L., Barnes, C. A., Rao, G., Baldwin, J., and Rasmussen, M. (1986). Long-term enhancement of hippocampal synaptic transmission and the acquisition of spatial information. *Journal of Neuroscience* 6: 563–571.

Maffei, L., and Campbell, F. W. (1970). Neurophysiological localization of the vertical and horizontal visual coordinates in man. *Science* 167: 386–387.

Margolis, H. (1987). *Patterns, Thinking, and Cognition.* Chicago: University of Chicago Press.

Mark, V. H., Ervin, F. R., and Sweet, W. H. (1972). Deep temporal lobe stimulation in man. In *The Neurobiology of the Amygdala,* B. E. Elephtheriou, ed. New York: Plenum Press.

Marr, D. (1982). *Vision.* San Francisco: W. H. Freeman.

Mays, L. E., and Sparks, D. L. (1980). Saccades are spatially, not retinocentrically, coded. *Science* 208: 1163–1165.

Meyer, D. E. (1970). On the representation and retrieval of stored semantic information. *Cognitive Psychology* 1: 242–300.

Michel, E. M., and Troost, B. T. (1980). Palinopsia: Cerebral localization with computed tomography. *Neurology* 30: 887–889.

Miles, F. A., and Fuller, J. H. (1975). Visual tracking and the primate flocculus. *Science* 189: 1000–1002.

Miller, G. A., Galanter, E., and Pribram, K. H. (1960). *Plans and the Structure of Behavior.* New York: Henry Holt and Company.

Miller, G. A., and Johnson-Laird, P. N. (1976). *Language and Perception.* Cambridge, Mass.: Belknap/Harvard University Press.

Minsky, M. L., and Papert, S. A. (1988). *Perceptrons.* Exp. ed. Cambridge, Mass.: MIT Press.

Mishkin, M., Ungerleider, L. G., and Macko, K. A. (1983). Object vision and spatial vision: Two cortical pathways. *Trends in Neuroscience* 6: 414–417.

Miyashita, Y., Rolls, E. T., Cahusac, P. M. B., Niki, H., and Feigenbaum, J. D. (1989). Activity of hippocampal formation neurons in the monkey related to a conditional spatial response task. *Journal of Neurophysiology* 61: 669–678.

Møllgaard, K., Bennett, E. L., Rosenzweig, M. R., and Lindner, B. (1971). Quantitative synaptic changes with differential experience in rat brain. *International Journal of Neuroscience* 2: 113–127.

Moran, J., and Desimone, R. (1985). Selective attention gates visual processing in the extrastriate cortex. *Science* 229: 782–784.

Morrison, R. E., and Rayner, K. (1981). Saccade size in reading depends upon character spaces and not visual angle. *Perception and Psychophysics* 30: 395–396.

Motter, B. C. (1989). Reactivation responses in striate and extrastriate visual cortex during a peripheral attention task. Society for Neuroscience 19th Annual Meeting, Phoenix.

Motter, B. C., and Mountcastle, V. B. (1981). The functional properties of the light-sensitive neurons of the posterior parietal cortex studied in waking monkeys: Foveal sparing and opponent vector organization. *Journal of Neuroscience* 1: 3–26.

Mueller-Leyer, F. C. (1889). Optische Urteilstauschungen. *Dubois-Reymonds Archive fur Anatomie und Physiologie.* Supplement volume: 263–270.

Murakami, K., Whitely, M. K., and Routtenberg, A. (1987). Cooperative action of Zn (II) and Ca (II) in the regulation of protein kinase C activity from rat brain. Society for Neuroscience 17th Annual Meeting, New Orleans.

Myers, N. A., Clifton, R. K., and Clarkson, M. G. (1987). When they were very young: Almost-threes remember two years ago. *Infant Behavior and Development* 10: 123–132.

Necker, L. A. (1832). Observations of some remarkable phaenomena seen in Switzerland; and an optical phaenomenon which occurs on viewing of a crystal or geometrical solid. *Philosophical Magazine (Ser. 1)* 3: 329–337.

Newell, A. (1973). You can't play 20 questions with nature and win. In *Visual Information Processing,* W. G. Chase, ed. New York: Academic Press.

Newell, A. (1980). Physical symbol systems. *Cognitive Science* 4: 135–183.

Nissen, H. W. (1951). Phylogenetic comparison. In *Handbook of Experimental Psychology,* S. S. Stevens, ed. New York: Wiley.

Nosofsky, R. M. (1988). Exemplar-based accounts of relations between classification, recognition, and typicality. *Journal of Experimental Psychology: Learning, Memory, and Cognition* 14: 700–708.

Olds, J. (1958). Satiation effects in self-stimulation of the brain. *Journal of Comparative and Physiological Psychology* 51: 675–678.

Olds, J. (1962). Hypothalamic substrates of reward. *Physiological Reviews* 42: 554–604.

Oomura, Y. (1976). Significance of glucose, insulin, and free fatty acid on the hypothalamic feeding and satiety neúrons. In *Hunger: Basic Mechanisms and Clinical Implications,* D. Novin, W. Wyrwicka, and G. Bray, eds. New York: Raven.

Paivio, A. (1971). *Imagery and Verbal Processes.* New York: Holt, Rinehart, and Winston.

Parks, T. (1965). Pøst-retinal visual storage. *American Journal of Psychology* 78: 145–147.

Parks, T. (1970). A control for ocular tracking in the demonstration of post-retinal visual storage. *American Journal of Psychology* 83: 442–444.

Parks, T. E. (1984). Illusory figures: A (mostly) atheoretical review. *Psychological Bulletin* 95: 282–300.

Perris, E. E., Myers, N. A., and Clifton, R. K. (1988). Long-term memory for infant experience: Once is enough. International Conference on Infant Studies, Washington, D.C.

Phillips, W. A. (1974). On the distinction between sensory storage and short-term visual memory. *Perception and Psychophysics* 16: 283–290.
Pinker, S. (1980). Mental imagery and the third dimension. *Journal of Experimental Psychology: General* 109: 354–371.
Pinker, S. (1984). Visual cognition: An introduction. *Cognition* 18: 1–63.
Pinker, S., Choate, P. A., and Finke, R. A. (1984). Mental extrapolation in patterns constructed from memory. *Memory and Cognition* 12: 207–218.
Pinker, S., and Finke, R. A. (1980). Emergent two-dimensional patterns in images rotated in depth. *Journal of Experimental Psychology: Human Perception and Performance* 6: 244–264.
Pinker, S., and Kosslyn, S. M. (1983). Theories of mental imagery. In *Imagery: Current Theory, Research, and Application,* A. A. Sheikh, ed. New York: Wiley.
Pinker, S., and Mehler, J., eds. (1988). *Connections and Symbols.* Cambridge, Mass.: Bradford/MIT Press.
Pinker, S., and Prince, A. (1988). On language and connectionism: Analysis of a parallel distributed processing model of language acquisition. In *Connections and Symbols,* S. Pinker and J. Mehler, eds. Cambridge, Mass.: Bradford/MIT Press.
Pitts, W., and McCulloch, W. S. (1947). How we know universals: The perception of auditory and visual forms. *Bulletin of Mathematical Biophysics* 9: 127–147.
Podgorny, P., and Shepard, R. N. (1978). Functional representations common to visual perception and imagination. *Journal of Experimental Psychology: Human Perception and Performance* 4: 21–35.
Podgorny, P., and Shepard, R. N. (1983). Distribution of visual attention over space. *Journal of Experimental Psychology: Human Perception and Performance* 9: 380–393.
Pollatsek, A., Rayner, K., and Collins, W. E. (1984). Integrating pictorial information across eye movements. *Journal of Experimental Psychology: General* 113: 426–442.
Pollatsek, A., Rayner, K., and Henderson, J. M. (1990). Role of spatial location in integration of pictorial information across saccades. *Journal of Experimental Psychology: Human Perception and Performance* 16: 199–210.
Posner, M. I. (1980). Orienting of attention. *Quarterly Journal of Experimental Psychology* 32: 3–25.
Posner, M. I. (1982). Cumulative development of attentional theory. *American Psychologist* 37: 168–179.
Posner, M. I., Peterson, S. E., Fox, P. T., and Raichle, M. E. (1988). Localization of cognitive operations in the human brain. *Science* 240: 1627–1631.
Posner, M. I., Snyder, C. R. R., and Davidson, B. J. (1980). Attention and the detection of signals. *Journal of Experimental Psychology: General* 109: 160–174.
Potter, M. C. (1975). Meaning in visual search. *Science* 187: 965–966.
Potter, M. C. (1983). Representational buffers: The eye-mind hypothesis in picture perception, reading, and visual search. In *Eye Movements in Reading, Perception, and Language Processes,* K. Rayner, ed. New York: Academic Press.
Potter, M. C., and Faulconer, B. A. (1975). Time to understand pictures and words. *Nature* 253: 437–438.
Potter, M. C., Kroll, J. F., and Harris, C. (1980). Comprehension and memory in rapid sequential reading. In *Attention and Performance VIII,* R. S. Nickerson, ed. Hillsdale, N.J.: Lawrence Erlbaum Associates.
Potter, M. C., Kroll, J. F., Yachzel, B., Carpenter, E., and Sherman, J. (1986). Pictures in sentences: Understanding without words. *Journal of Experimental Psychology: General* 115: 281–294.
Putnam, H. (1988). *Representation and Reality.* Cambridge, Mass.: Bradford/MIT Press.
Pylyshyn, Z. W. (1973). What the mind's eye tells the mind's brain: A critique of mental imagery. *Psychological Bulletin* 80: 1–24.

Pylyshyn, Z. W. (1986). *Computation and Cognition*. Cambridge, Mass.: Bradford/MIT Press.

Quillian, M. R. (1968). Semantic memory. In *Semantic Information Processing*, M. Minsky, ed. Cambridge, Mass.: MIT Press.

Quintana, J., Yajeya, J., and Fuster, J. M. (1988). Prefrontal representation of stimulus attributes during delay tasks. I. Unit activity in cross-temporal integration of sensory and sensory-motor information. *Brain Research* 474: 211–221.

Racine, R. J., Milgram, N. W., and Hafner, S. (1983). Long-term potentiation phenomena in the rat limbic forebrain. *Brain Research* 260: 217–231.

Racine, R. J., Wilson, D. A., Gingell, R., and Sunderland, D. (1986). Long-term potentiation in the interpositus and vestibular nuclei in the rat. *Experimental Brain Research* 63: 158–162.

Ratcliff, R. (1990). Connectionist models of recognition memory: Constraints imposed by learning and forgetting functions. *Psychological Review* 97: 285–308.

Ratliff, F., and Riggs, L. A. (1950). Involuntary motions of the eye during monocular fixation. *Journal of Experimental Psychology* 40: 687–701.

Rayner, K., and Bertera, J. H. (1979). Reading without a fovea. *Science* 206: 468–469.

Rayner, K., McConkie, G. W., and Ehrlich, S. (1978). Eye movements and integrating information across fixations. *Journal of Experimental Psychology: Human Perception and Performance* 4: 529–544.

Rayner, K., McConkie, G. W., and Zola, D. (1980). Integrating information across eye movements. *Cognitive Psychology* 12: 206–226.

Reed, C. F. (1984). Terrestrial passage theory of the moon illusion. *Journal of Experimental Psychology: General* 113: 489–498.

Reimann, E. (1902). Die scheinbare Vergrosserung der Sonne und des Mondes am Horizont. *Zeitschrift fur Psychologie* 30: 1–38, 161–195.

Richards, W., and Kaufman, L. (1969). "Center-of-gravity" tendencies for fixations and flow patterns. *Perception and Psychophysics* 5: 81–84.

Riddoch, M. J., and Humphreys, G. W. (1989). Finding the way around topographical impairments. In *Neuropsychology of Visual Perception*, J. W. Brown, ed. Hillsdale, N.J.: Lawrence Erlbaum Associates.

Riggs, L. A., and Day, R. H. (1980). Visual aftereffects derived from inspection of orthogonally moving patterns. *Science* 208: 416–418.

Riggs, L. A., Armington, E. C., and Ratliff, F. (1954). Motions of the retinal image during fixation. *Journal of the Optical Society of America* 44: 315–321.

Roberts, L. (1989). Are neural nets like the human brain? *Science* 243: 481–482.

Rock, I., and Ebenholtz, S. (1962). Stroboscopic movement based on change of phenomenal location rather than retinal location. *American Journal of Psychology* 75: 193–207.

Rock, I., and Kaufman, L. (1962). The moon illusion, II. *Science* 136: 1023–1031.

Rock, I., Halper, F., DiVita, J., and Wheeler, D. (1987). Eye movement as a cue to figure motion in anorthoscopic perception. *Journal of Experimental Psychology: Human Perception and Performance* 13: 344–352.

Rolls, E. T. (1975). *The Brain and Reward*. Oxford: Pergamon Press.

Rosch, E., and Mervis, C. (1975). Family resemblances: Studies in the internal structure of categories. *Cognitive Psychology* 7: 573–605.

Rosenbaum, D. A. (1977). Selective adaptation of "command neurons" in the human motor system. *Neuropsychologia* 15: 81–91.

Rosenbaum, D. A., Kenny, S., and Derr, M. A. (1983). Hierarchical control of rapid movement sequences. *Journal of Experimental Psychology: Human Perception and Performance* 9: 86–102.

Rosenblatt, F. (1962). *Principles of Neurodynamics.* New York: Spartan.

Routtenberg, A. (1984). Brain phosphoproteins kinase C and protein F1: Protagonists of plasticity in particular pathways. In *Neurobiology of Learning and Memory,* G. Lynch, J. L. McGaugh, and N. M. Weinberger, eds. New York: Guilford Press.

Rumelhart, D. E., Hinton, G. E., and McClelland, J. L. (1986). A general framework for parallel distributed processing. In *Parallel Distributed Processing,* vol. 1, D. E. Rumelhart and J. L. McClelland, eds. Cambridge, Mass.: Bradford/MIT Press.

Rumelhart, D. E., and McClelland, J. L. (1985). Levels indeed! A response to Broadbent. *Journal of Experimental Psychology: General* 114: 193–197.

Rumelhart, D. E., and McClelland, J. L., eds. (1986). *Parallel Distributed Processing,* vol. 1. Cambridge, Mass.: Bradford/MIT Press.

Sagi, D., and Julesz, B. (1985). "Where" and "what" in vision. *Science* 228: 1217–1219.

Saito, H., Yukie, M., Tanaka, K., Hikosaka, K., Fukada, Y., and Iwai, E. (1986). Integration of direction signals of image motion in the temporal sulcus of the macaque monkey. *Journal of Neuroscience* 6: 145–157.

Schur, E. (1925). Mondtauschung und Sehgrosskonstanz. *Psychologische Forschung* 7: 44–80.

Segal, S. J., and Fusella, V. (1970). Influence of imaged pictures and sounds on detection of visual and auditory signals. *Journal of Experimental Psychology* 83: 458–464.

Sheikh, A. A., ed. (1983). *Imagery: Current Theory, Research, and Application.* New York: Wiley.

Shepard, R. N. (1978). Externalization of mental images and the act of creation. In *Visual Learning, Thinking, and Communication,* B. S. Randhawa and W. E. Coffman, eds. New York: Academic Press.

Shepard, R. N., and Cooper, L. A. (1982). *Mental Images and Their Transformations.* Cambridge, Mass.: Bradford/MIT Press.

Shepard, R. N., and Judd, S. A. (1976). Perceptual illusion of rotation of three-dimensional objects. *Science* 191: 952–954.

Shepard, R. N., and Metzler, J. (1971). Mental rotation of three-dimensional objects. *Science* 171: 701–703.

Shepard, R. N., and Zare, S. L. (1983). Path-guided apparent motion. *Science* 220: 632–634.

Shepherd, G. M. (1979). *The Synaptic Organization of the Brain.* New York: Oxford University Press.

Shepherd, G. M. (1983). *Neurobiology.* New York: Oxford University Press.

Shimojo, S., and Richards, W. (1986). "Seeing" shapes that are almost totally occluded: A new look at Park's camel. *Perception and Psychophysics* 39: 418–426.

Shulman, G. L., Remington, R. W., and McClean, J. P. (1979). Moving attention through visual space. *Journal of Experimental Psychology: Human Perception and Performance* 5: 522–526.

Smith, R. (1738). *A Compleat System of Opticks,* vol. 1. Cambridge, England.

Smolensky, P. (1988). On the proper treatment of connectionism. *Behavioral and Brain Sciences* 11: 1–74.

Sparks, D. L., and Jay, M. (1987). The role of the primate superior colliculus in sensorimotor integration. In *Vision, Brain, and Cooperative Computation,* M. A. Arbib and A. R. Hanson, eds. Cambridge, Mass.: Bradford/MIT Press.

Sparks, D. L., and Mays, L. E. (1983). The spatial localization of saccade targets. I. Compensation for stimulation-induced perturbations in eye position. *Journal of Neurophysiology* 49: 45–63.

Sperling, G., and Melchner, M. J. (1978). The attention operating characteristic: Examples from visual search. *Science* 202: 315–318.

Spinelli, D. N. (1987). A trace of memory: An evolutionary perspective on the visual system. In *Vision, Brain, and Cooperative Computation,* M. A. Arbib and A. R. Hanson, eds. Cambridge, Mass.: Bradford/MIT Press.

Spitzer, H., Desimone, R., and Moran, J. (1988). Increased attention enhances both behavioral and neuronal performance. *Science* 240: 338–340.

Squire, L. R., and Cohen, N. (1979). Memory and amnesia: Resistance to disruption develops for years after learning. *Behavioral and Neural Biology* 25: 115–125.

Stein, B. E., Magalhaes-Castro, B., and Kruger, L. (1975). Superior colliculus: Visuotopic-somatotopic overlap. *Science* 189: 224–226.

Stiles-Davis, J., Kritchevsky, M., and Bellugi, U., eds. (1988). *Spatial Cognition.* Hillsdale, N.J.: Lawrence Erlbaum Associates.

Stillings, N. A., Feinstein, M. H., Garfield, J. A., Rissland, E. L., Rosenbaum, D. A., Weisler, S. E., and Baker-Ward, L., eds. (1987). *Cognitive Science: An Introduction.* Cambridge, Mass.: Bradford/MIT Press.

Thompson, J. A. (1983). Is continuous visual monitoring necessary in visually guided locomotion? *Journal of Experimental Psychology: Human Perception and Performance* 9: 427–443.

Tieger, T., and Ganz, L. (1979). Recognition of faces in the presence of two-dimensional sinusoidal masks. *Perception and Psychophysics* 26: 163–167.

Trehub, A. (1967). Learning Machines and Methods. Patent 3,331,054. Washington, D.C.: U.S. Patent Office.

Trehub, A. (1969). A Markov model for modulation periods in brain output. *Biophysical Journal* 9: 965–969.

Trehub, A. (1970). The synaptic matrix: Pattern processing in the brain. Technical Report TR-9A-70. Psychology Research Laboratory, VA Hospital, Northampton, Mass.

Trehub, A. (1971a). The brain as a parallel coherent detector. *Science* 174: 722–723.

Trehub, A. (1971b). Signal characteristics of visual cortex and lateral geniculate during contralateral and ipsilateral photic stimulation. *Electroencephalography and Clinical Neurophysiology* 30: 113–122.

Trehub, A. (1973). Stimulus intensity and modulation of brain output. *Biophysical Journal* 13: 705–710.

Trehub, A. (1975a). Adaptive pattern processing in the visual system. *International Journal of Man-Machine Studies* 7: 439–446.

Trehub, A. (1975b). First-occupancy model for signal transfer in the brain. *Journal of Theoretical Biology* 50: 387–395.

Trehub, A. (1977). Neuronal models for cognitive processes: Networks for learning, perception and imagination. *Journal of Theoretical Biology* 65: 141–169.

Trehub, A. (1978). Neuronal model for stereoscopic vision. *Journal of Theoretical Biology* 71: 479–486.

Trehub, A. (1979). Associative sequential recall in a synaptic matrix. *Journal of Theoretical Biology* 81: 569–576.

Trehub, A. (1983). Neuronal model for episodic learning and temporal routing of memory. *Cognition and Brain Theory* 6: 483–497.

Trehub, A. (1985). A pendulum illusion in anorthoscopic perception. Unpublished manuscript.

Trehub, A. (1986). A model for parsing, learning, and recognizing objects in a complex environment. *Proceedings of the Eighth Annual Conference of the Cognitive Science Society, Amherst, Mass.*

Trehub, A. (1987). Visual-cognitive neuronal networks. In *Vision, Brain, and Cooperative Computation,* M. A. Arbib and A. R. Hanson, eds. Cambridge, Mass.: Bradford/MIT Press.

Trehub, A. (1990). A confusion matrix for hand-printed alphabetic characters: Testing a neuronal model. In *Computational and Clinical Approaches to Pattern Recognition and Concept Formation,* M. L. Commons, R. J. Herrnstein, S. M. Kosslyn, and D. B. Mumford, eds. Hillsdale, N.J.: Lawrence Erlbaum Associates.

Trehub, A., and Pollatsek, A. (1986). Seeing-more-than-is-there: A probe of retinoid networks. *Proceedings of the Eighth Annual Conference of the Cognitive Science Society, Amherst, Mass.*

Ts'o, D. Y., Gilbert, C. D., and Wiesel, T. N. (1986). Relationships between horizontal interactions and functional architecture in cat striate cortex as revealed by cross-correlation analysis. *Journal of Neuroscience* 6: 1160–1170.

Tsal, Y. (1983). Movements of attention across the visual field. *Journal of Experimental Psychology: Human Perception and Performance* 4: 523–530.

Tulving, E. (1972). Episodic and semantic memory. In *Organization of Memory,* E. Tulving and W. Donaldson, eds. New York: Academic Press.

Tulving, E. (1989). Remembering and knowing the past. *American Scientist* 77: 361–367.

Turing, A. M. (1950). Computing machinery and intelligence. *Mind* 59: 433–460.

van der Loos, H., and Glaser, E. M. (1972). Autapses in neocortex cerebri: Synapses between a pyramidal cell's axon and its own dendrites. *Brain Research* 48: 355–360.

Van Essen, D. C. (1985). Functional organization of primate visual cortex. In *Cerebral Cortex,* vol. 3, A. Peters and E. G. Jones, eds. New York and London: Plenum.

Voronin, L. L. (1985). Synaptic plasticity at archicortical and neocortical levels. *Neirofiziologiya* 16: 651–665.

Wallace, B. (1984). Apparent equivalence between perception and imagery in the production of various visual illusions. *Memory and Cognition* 12: 156–162.

Wallach, H. (1962). On the moon illusion. *Science* 137: 900–902.

Wallach, H. (1987). Perceiving a stable environment when one moves. *Annual Review of Psychology* 38: 1–27.

Weber, R. J., and Malmstrom, F. V. (1979). Measuring the size of mental images. *Journal of Experimental Psychology: Human Perception and Performance* 5: 1–12.

Weisstein, N., and Harris, C. S. (1974). Visual detection of line segments: An object-superiority effect. *Science* 186: 752–755.

Weisstein, N., Maguire, W., and Williams, M. C. (1982). The effect of perceived depth on phantoms and the phantom motion aftereffect. In *Organization and Representation in Perception,* J. Beck, ed. Hillsdale, N.J.: Lawrence Erlbaum Associates.

Wheeler, J. A. (1956). A septet of sibyls: Aids in the search for truth. *American Scientist* 44: 360–377.

Wickelgren, W. A. (1974). Single-trace fragility theory of memory dynamics. *Memory and Cognition* 2: 775–780.

Yajeya, J., Quintana, J., and Fuster, J. M. (1988). Prefrontal representation of stimulus attributes during delay tasks. II. The role of behavioral significance. *Brain Research* 474: 222–230.

Yamamoto, N., Kurotani, T., and Toyama, K. (1989). Neural connections between the lateral geniculate nucleus and visual cortex in vitro. *Science* 245: 192–194.

Yantis, S., and Johnston, J. C. (1990). On the locus of visual selection: Evidence from focused attention tasks. *Journal of Experimental Psychology: Human Perception and Performance* 16: 135–149.

Yonas, A., Cleaves, W. T., and Pettersen, L. (1978). Development of sensitivity to pictorial depth. *Science* 200: 77–79.

Zöllner, F. (1862). Uber einer neue Art anorthoscopischer Zerrbilder. *Annalen der Physik und Chemie* 27: 477–484.

Index